THE FINANCIAL TIMES

GUIDE TO

INVESTING

THE FINANCIAL TIMES

GUIDE TO

INVESTING

THE DEFINITIVE COMPANION TO INVESTMENT AND THE FINANCIAL MARKETS

GLEN ARNOLD

An imprint of Pearson Education

London • New York • Toronto • Sydney • Tokyo • Singapore
Hong Kong • Cape Town • Madrid • Paris • Amsterdam • Munich • Milan

PEARSON EDUCATION LIMITED

Edinburgh Gate
Harlow CM20 2JE
Tel: +44 (0)1279 623623
Fax: +44 (0)1279 431059

First published in Great Britain in 2004

ISBN: 978 0 273 66309 6

British Library Cataloguing in Publication Data
A CIP catalogue record for this book can be obtained from the British Library

Library of Congress Cataloging-in-Publication Data
Arnold, Glen
The Financial Times guide to investing: a definitive introduction to investment and the financial markets / Glen Arnold.
p. cm.
Includes bibliographical references and index.
ISBN 0–273–66309–7 (alk. paper)
1. Investments. I. Title: Guide to investing. II. Financial Times Limited. III. Title.

HG4515.A76 2004
332.6—dc22

2004043239

10 9 8
08 07

Typeset by 70
Printed and bound in the UK by Ashford Colour Press Ltd., Gosport, Hants.

The publishers' policy is to use paper manufactured from sustainable forests.

To two inspiring teachers of what is really valuable,
Chris and Brenda Arnold, my parents

About the author

Glen Arnold is an investor, author of many investment and corporate finance publications and professor of finance (part-time) at the University of Salford. He heads a research team focused on stock market mispricing. He is also engaged in consulting activities and a lecturer on finance and investment. He can be reached at *g.c.arnold@salford.ac.uk.*

Acknowledgements

This book draws on the talents, knowledge and contributions of a great many people. I would especially like to thank the following.

Warren Buffett who kindly assisted the illustration of key points by allowing the use of his elegant, insightful and witty prose.

Dr Mike Staunton and Professors Elroy Dimson and Paul Marsh of the London Business School who granted permission to present some important data from *Triumph of the Optimists: 101 Years of Global Returns* (Princeton University Press, 2002).

Tim Bond, Mark Capleton, Fred Cleary and Sreekala Kochugovindan at Barclays Capital who granted permission to reproduce key stock market return figures.

Gill Hart at the Financial Times for her energetic support for the project.

The team at Pearson Education (FT Prentice Hall) who, at various stages, contributed to the production of the book: Jonathan Agbenyega, Laurie Donaldson, Julie Knight, Richard Leigh, Lisa Reading, Kate Salkilld, Richard Stagg, Amanda Thompson, Stephen York, Elizabeth Wilson, Geoff Chatterton, Annette Musker.

Sarah Mitchell, Liz Royle, and my wife Lesley, who bravely faced my handwriting to type much of the manuscript.

Huw Morgan and Alison Kennedy of the University of Salford who devoted time to reading chapters 11, 12 and 13, and suggested valuable improvements.

The publishers are grateful to the following companies for their permission to reproduce copyright material:

The Financial Times Ltd for extracts and financial data published in the *Financial Times*

The London Stock Exchange for Table 3.1, Exhibit 3.4, Exhibit 4.2 and Exhibit 4.4.

Exhibit 14.1 reprinted with permission of the Free press, a division of Simon and Schuster Adult Publishing Group from COMPETITIVE STRATEGY: Techniques for Analyzing Industries & Competitors by Michael E. Porter.

Contents

Foreword

For the writers and editors of the *Financial Times*, clarity is second only to accuracy. For that reason, we have made increasingly determined efforts in recent years to make the content of the FT newspaper and of FT.com, its internet companion, as accessible as possible to a broad range of readers.

In spite of our efforts, of course, many people continue to find the terms, concepts and presentation of detailed financial news difficult – especially if they are relatively new to the worlds of business and finance. This book is intended to help put that right by offering a comprehensive guide to how to interpret and act upon the vast amount of information you will find in our pages.

The capital markets are more important now than they have ever been. The growing interdependence of the countries of the world – for which the shorthand term is globalisation – has limited the ability of individual governments to act independently. If you doubt this, think of the UK's exit from the exchange rate mechanism of the European Monetary System in 1992 in the face of persistent attacks on sterling, or the reversal of President Mitterrand's economic strategy in the early 1980s after the financial markets decided that French economic policy was imprudent.

Now, as then, much of what is happening in the global economy can be inferred from reports on activity in the markets. Trends in business activity, which underlie the prosperity of nations, can be tracked by watching the prices of shares, bonds and commodities. The foreign exchange markets can signal early concerns about the direction of national economic policies, or the impact of structural change. And economic statistics can tell you not only what has been happening in this and other countries, but a great deal about what is going to happen in the future.

In spite of this global influence, the markets can seem remote from the lives of ordinary people. But most of us are deeply involved in the financial markets in a personal sense, as well. Many people think of saving as a matter of depositing cash in an interest bearing account at a bank or building society. Yet millions of us now save for the long-term in the form of investments in stocks and shares, often through workplace schemes operated by our employers. And everyone who has a pension, an endowment mortgage or a with-profits policy is exposed to the markets through the investment activities of pension funds and life assurance companies.

Against this background, we are also living through a period of big changes in the way our society funds retirement for its citizens. For much of the last century, most people could rely on a combination of the state and their employer to provide a long-term financial safety net through their state and occupational pensions. But rising longevity (women can now expect to live to 80, men to 75) combined with a decline in state pension funding and the closure of many defined benefit pension schemes means that we must all take more responsibility for our own financial health.

To do that properly, we need to understand what is going on in the markets. Fortunately, that is easier than it used to be. The pages of the *Financial Times* are no longer full of impenetrable slabs of jargon, accompanied by visually off-putting tables of figures that can be fully understood only by experts. Much of the information we bring you can be understood even by readers who have only a casual acquaintance with the markets. Some of it, of course, remains unavoidably complex and detailed, but all of it can be mastered with the help of this book. It will deepen your understanding of the concepts underlying our reporting, give you easily followed guidance on interpreting even the most complex information, and – most of all – show you why understanding the markets can be fun, as well as profitable.

Many of our own experts have learnt new things from this guide. They keep it close by when they read the FT, and you may find it useful to do the same. For understanding what is going on, and where to find information, there are few better sources than this.

Andrew Gower
Editor, *Financial Times*

Introduction

There are some myths about investment, many of which are perpetuated by finance industry insiders. Myth one is that financial assets and markets are hideously complicated and confusing. Myth two is that you have to pay large sums to 'experts' who will then make far greater returns on your money than you could achieve on your own.

In truth the most important things you need to know about investing are simple. They are based on common sense and can be understood by anyone with a modicum of intelligence. It is just that the jargon and the detail obscure the view of outsiders peering through trying to see what it is all about. This book, in a step-by-step way, first explains the simple essence of investment and the functioning of the financial markets. It allows you to focus on what is really valuable, discarding grand-sounding but unimportant layers of mumbo-jumbo. It then goes on to explain the practicalities of investing, such as where to find a broker and how to go about buying shares. It explains the variety of financial securities you can place money into, from bonds and unit trusts to traded options and exchange traded funds. It also has a key section providing tools allowing you to analyse companies.

As for the argument that you *need* to employ an 'expert' to run your investments – well, this is complete nonsense. For a start, the majority of professional fund managers underperform the stock market. This has been observed year after year. You haven't heard about this? Well, of course you haven't. It is not the sort of thing that fund managers publicise. Some researchers even asked various fund managers to pit their wits against an ape in the selection of share portfolios. The subsequent portfolio performance was noted most carefully. You guessed who won! Even on a random basis we should find that 50 per cent of professional fund managers beat the market and 50 per cent do worse, but they don't even manage that.

Don't misunderstand me: some professionals, in some circumstances, have their uses. But to imagine that the private investor is generally at a disadvantage to the professional and should always defer to their superior insight is just plain wrong. Sure, you need some basic knowledge (which this book will help with), and you need some dedication to the task, but please don't be browbeaten into believing that the pinstriped suits have a competitive advantage over you, with your down-to-earth focus on what really matters and some sound investment tools. Share investment is about businesses – when you buy a share you buy a portion of the ownership of a business. Let me emphasise that: a share is not a gambling counter in a short-term random game of chance, it represents ownership of something that will probably outlive you, and its value depends on what will happen to that company years from now. It is not too difficult for you to become more knowledgeable about that business than a fund manager stuck in London who has a portfolio of shares in 200 different companies.

Once you have a grounding in the principles of investment you will free yourself from the assumption that the professionals know best and that you could not achieve a good return without them. You will be aware of a range of alternatives to simply handing your money to, say, an ISA manager. Sometimes the financial service house can do things better and cheaper than you could on your own. But quite often you end up paying huge fees for atrocious performance. This book will help you decide when to manage your money yourself and when to employ others.

A third myth is that only wealthy people can afford shares and other financial assets. In reality people of relatively modest means invest in the stock market. It is possible to start with only £20 per month. In Chapter 2 there is an example of a woman who stretched herself to put £100 per month into shares over a 20-year period. The sacrifice was worth it: by the time she retired the fund had grown to be worth many millions of pounds – all for £100 per month. And this was achieved by gaining the same annual returns as the UK stock market as a whole – it wasn't that she bought all the best shares on the market and with perfect foresight ignored what turned out to be the worst ones.

Read on: investing can be profitable and fun!

PART 1

Investment basics

1

What is investment?

To appreciate fully what it means to be an investor, I ask you to imagine that you do not live in the twenty-first century, with its vast range of financial instruments. You live in a simpler time. You are a member of the Victorian middle class, and life has been good to you. A substantial nest-egg has been built up over the years, but you are dissatisfied with the 2 per cent annual return you are getting on it in the local bank.

A couple of acquaintances, Mr Stephenson and Mr Brunel, are enthusiasts for a revolutionary technology that will improve the lives of the British people tremendously: the railways. Although the social benefits are wonderful, and it gives Stephenson and Brunel a warm feeling to think that they might contribute to people's well-being, this is not their primary motivation. No, they like the idea of becoming very wealthy. The way in which they expect to become rich is to build and operate a railway.

There is one thing stopping them from building their railway: it costs £2 million to build the line and pay for carriages, provide working capital, etc. They have only £100,000 between them. What a frustrating situation. They know that the railway will generate profits that dwarf the £2 million initial cost, and yet they can't persuade a bank to put up the £1.9 million needed.

Partnerships

An alternative approach of funding has been tried – indeed they suggested it to you as well as a couple of dozen other investors. This is to form a **partnership**. Each partner puts in, say, £50,000 and the rest is borrowed from a bank. Then, when the profits start to roll in (after paying the bank interest) the partners get an equal share. Of course, in addition Stephenson and Brunel would take a salary to compensate them for giving up time to manage the railway. You and most of the other investors who were approached rejected this offer for two very simple reasons. First, under partnership law each partner is **liable** for all the debts of the business. So if the business failed to produce a profit and the assets became worthless, and yet there are large bank debts, the bank would first of all try to get its money back from the business. Its next move would be to claim the money it is owed from each of the partners. Business partners have been known to lose their houses, furniture, everything, in order to pay off a business's creditors. You have seen too many landed gentry made homeless to want to invest in a business under a partnership, thus you decided to keep your money safe and would not risk it in industry of any kind.

The second problem with partnership arises if one of the partners wishes to leave (or dies). The leaving partner is generally entitled to a fair share of the value of the partnership. This can be terribly disruptive to a business, as assets may have to be sold to pay the partner off. Indeed, partnerships tend to be dissolved if one member wishes to leave and then a new partnership is created to carry on the business thereafter. It is certainly no way to run a railway.

So the two issues Stephenson and Brunel have to deal with are: the **unlimited liability** of the investors; and the **continuity** of business in the case of investors wishing (or forced) to disinvest.

Limited liability

Fortunately there is a form of business structure that addresses these two difficulties that lead to a restricted flow of funds from the **savers** in society to **productive investment** in real business assets: a **company** or **corporation** is set up as a '**separate person**' under the law. It is the company that enters legal agreements such as bank loan contracts, not the owners of the company shares. The company can have a **perpetual life**. So, if an investor wishes to cash in his chips he does not have the right to insist that the company liquidate its assets and pay him his share. The company continues but the investor sells his share in the company to another investor. This is great – it gives managers the opportunity to plan ahead, knowing the resources of the business will not be withdrawn; it gives other shareholders the reassurance that the company can achieve its goals without disruption.

One of the most important breakthroughs in the development of UK capitalism and economic progress was the introduction of **limited liability** in 1855. There were strong voices heard against the change in the law. It was argued that it was only fair that **creditors** to a business could call on the shareholders in that business to bear the responsibility of failure. However, a stronger argument triumphed. This is that it is better for society as a whole if we encourage individuals to place their savings at the disposal of entrepreneurial managers for use in a business enterprise. Thus factories, ships, shops, houses and even railways will be built and society will have more goods and services.

Insisting on *un*limited liability for investors made them hesitant to invest and thus reduced overall wealth. Limited liability companies are what (for the most part) we have today, and we should be very grateful for it. Creditors quickly adjusted to the new reality of lending without a guarantee other than from the company. They became more expert and thorough in assessing the risk of the loan going bad (**credit risk**) and they called for more information; legislators helped by insisting that companies publish key information.

So, back to your nineteenth-century dilemma over whether to invest in Stephenson and Brunel's brilliant idea. What they intend to do is to create a company with limited liability for the shareholders. The company will issue 1.5 million shares. Each share will have a **par value** of £1. Sometimes companies sell shares at the par value and sometimes they sell them at greater than the par value. The par value (also called the nominal or face value) is merely a nominal figure, useful for record keeping, but unrelated to the market value of a share. In the case of Stephenson and Brunel Ltd, the shares are to be offered to investors at par. The company also borrows £500,000 from a bank.

Ordinary shares and extraordinary returns

The vast majority of shares issued by companies are **ordinary shares**. When you buy one of these you are buying a set of legal rights. Significantly, one of the rights you do not receive is a guarantee of any return on the money you hand over to buy the ordinary shares. The company, run by its managers, has no obligation either to give you a **dividend** (a payout of profit) or to hand your **capital** back. The managers may promise to do their best with the financial resources entrusted to them, but they cannot be legally forced to give a return. This contrasts sharply with the deal the company agrees to with **bank lenders**. Here the company is legally responsible to provide regular **interest** payments and pay off the capital at the end of the loan term.

It does not sound like such a good deal for the ordinary shareholders. They put money in, they cannot take it out again (the best they can hope for is to sell the holding to another investor), and the company has no obligation to pay them anything. It gets worse. If the company is **wound up**, then the assets are sold and the shareholders will be entitled to receive a share of the money raised from the sale. Ah yes, but not until all other interested parties have had their guaranteed amounts first. So if taxes are owed the **Inland Revenue** gets its money, and then it's the turn of the various lenders and **trade creditors** (suppliers of goods and services not yet paid). If the company issued **preference shares** (see Chapter 7) then these holders are entitled to receive a payment. It is only in the (unlikely) event that there is any money left after so many snouts in the trough that the ordinary shareholders get anything.

Given these disadvantages of shares, there must be something attractive to entice investors. There is. Shareholders own all the value that is created by a business after lenders and others have received the amounts they are owed. If the business does well then it is perfectly possible for a £1,000 investment in ordinary shares to become worth over £1 million. It has happened time and again. There are millionaires today who put relatively small amounts into companies destined to become market leaders – Racal Vodafone, Glaxo, Microsoft, Intel, and Berkshire Hathaway are just a few examples.

Shareholder rights

Shareholders own the business and have ultimate control over any surplus it generates now and into the future. To try and protect their wealth, **ordinary shareholders have rights** under the law. For example, they each have **votes** in exact proportion to their shareholding. They can vote on important matters such as the composition of the team of **directors**. If the directors appear to be steering the company in the wrong direction or merely feathering their own nest, then they can be voted off the board in an **annual general meeting (AGM)** or an **extraordinary general meeting (EGM)** called by the shareholders. Shareholders vote on whether **more shares** should be issued, and whether the company should **merge** with another company. Shareholders are also entitled to receive regular **financial information**. Every year the company must produce **accounts** which must be sent to all shareholders. Shareholders must also have **notice** of important events affecting the business, such as a major downturn in business, loss of a key contract, or the sale of a division.

Let us imagine that Stephenson Brunel Ltd has sold all 1.5 million ordinary shares at £1 each. You have agreed to buy 50,000 of these shares. You are legally committed to deliver £50,000 to the company. That is the maximum amount that can be claimed from you. In transferring this money from your bank account you accept that you are taking on significantly more risk than if it was steadily accumulating at 2 per cent per year. **Risk** merely means that there is a range of possible outcomes rather than certainty over what will happen. While there wasn't complete certainty over the bank account investment (the bank might have gone bankrupt), the dispersion of possible outcomes was likely to be in a narrow range with the probability of complete loss very low. The return on the Stephenson Brunel Ltd shares, however, has a very wide dispersion of possible outcomes with fairly high probabilities of an extremely good outcome or of an extremely poor outcome (loss of all money).

You hold 50,000 of the 1,500,000 shares and therefore your votes account for 3.33 per cent of the total – the vast majority of ordinary shares have the right to one vote each. (This is not always the case. Companies can issue shares that have, say, 10 votes while issuing other shares with only one vote each. Alternatively, they can issue some shares with **no votes** at all, alongside others with votes.) You use your votes at the EGM to help select directors. So, the company is up and running, ready to lay track.

A money-making machine

Over the next 2 years the line is constructed, trains are bought, stations built and the first paying passengers are delighted. The company now has total assets of £2.3 million. It also has unpaid bills (trade creditors) of £400,000 and bank debt of £500,000. The £1.4 million of **net assets** (i.e., after deduction of liabilities, £2,300,000–£400,000–£500,000) are owned by the ordinary shareholders. This will be shown in the year-end **balance sheet** as **shareholders' funds**. Because Stephenson Brunel Ltd has 1.5 million ordinary shares outstanding, each share has a claim of 93.33 pence of net assets (£1,400,000 divided by 1,500,000 shares). A holder of 50,000 shares would be entitled to £46,667 if the company were liquidated (assuming the assets could be sold at balance sheet values). A holder of 100,000 shares would be entitled to £93,333, and so on. So you can see why ordinary shares are often referred to as **equities** – each share represents an equal stake in the business, not just for dividends but also for assets.

You might now be thinking you've made a big mistake in buying these shares: you put in £50,000 and the assets of the firm have declined by 6.67 pence per share. But you must not be hasty in reaching a judgement. Very few shares are valued on the basis of their **asset backing**. In buying a share you are entitled to receive the *future* value generated by the business, and a business is a lot more than the assets shown on the balance sheet. **What creates value** is the physical assets *combined with* a number of **intangible** elements such as the strong strategic position of the firm, the reservoir of experience of the managerial team, or the special relationship the company forms with customers, government, suppliers, etc.

Stephenson Brunel Ltd didn't just build a railway, it created an **economic franchise** (see the discussion in Chapter 15). That is, it put itself in a position that gives it **pricing power**, whereby it can charge customers a price far above the cost of providing the service. It has an almost impregnable **monopoly** in providing rail transport in the part of the country where it operates. Would-be competitors simply can't challenge the company for its customers (termed '**strong barriers to entry**'). As a result of its economic franchise it is able to generate exceptional long-run rates of return on the capital put into the business.

Dividends and retained earnings

The power of that franchise starts to become apparent in the third year. The company makes a **profit (earnings)**, after paying interest and taxes, of £750,000. The directors now have a choice to present to the equity holders (ordinary shareholders). The company could retain all of its earnings to invest in extending the network (**retained earnings**) or it could pay out some (or all) of it to shareholders in the form of dividends. Note that, whichever course of action is taken, the money belongs to shareholders – earnings retained in a business are there because shareholders consent to their money being left there.

Suppose that the directors (with the agreement of the shareholders) decide on a 50 per cent **payout ratio**, that is, half of the earnings after tax are paid out in dividends. The shareholders will receive a dividend of 25p per share (£375,000 divided by 1,500,000 shares).

The retained earnings of £375,000 increases shareholders' funds from £1,400,000 to £1,775,000. So, shareholders have not only received a 25p dividend for each share they hold, but the retained earnings have increased the asset value of each share in the company from 93.33 pence to 118.33 pence (£1,775,000 divided by 1,500,000 shares).

It is crucial to note that 118.33p does not represent the value of one share should you wish to sell. There will be plenty of people willing to pay a lot more than this to buy the right to receive all the future dividends from a company with such a strong market position. There is every reason to believe that the earnings and dividends per share will rise by large percentages over the next decade or two. Perhaps someone will pay £10 per share, or maybe even £100, for a fast-growing company of this kind. Not bad, considering that you paid only £1.

What if I want to sell?

This leads us neatly on to another piece of the jigsaw that is the **modern financial system**. If you did want to sell your shares, where would you go? And how do you know you are getting a reasonable amount for your shares?

Well, you could advertise in the local newspaper, but you are unlikely to attract a great deal of interest. Or, perhaps, you could ask friends if they want to buy from you – but this could be a social gaffe.

Fortunately, long before the Victorian era, systems had been set up to assist investors wanting to sell (and buy) company shares. Way back, in the sixteenth and seventeenth centuries, companies had been formed for sea voyages and trading with distant places around the world. If an investor wanted to sell his share of the future profits he could do so by going through the market in shares in the coffee houses around Threadneedle Street in the City of London. In 1773 the New Jonathan's coffee house had become known as Britain's leading '**stock exchange**'. In 1802, the London Stock Exchange was formally constituted. By the 1840s there were hundreds of companies' shares **listed**. Investors could buy or sell shares through **members** of the stock exchange.

Primary and secondary markets

The London Stock Exchange performs two vital roles to encourage investors to invest in industry. The first is the operation of a **primary market**. This is where companies sell shares to investors and then use the proceeds in their businesses. Stock markets also provide a **secondary market** where shares are traded between investors. An efficient and trustworthy secondary market is needed to encourage investors to buy shares in the primary market. Investors like to know that there is a place they can go to sell shares quickly, cheaply and without having to reduce the price, that is, to sell at the going rate. In other words, investors need a **liquid** market. A liquid market is one where there are numerous competing buyers and sellers allowing the outcomes of many buy and sell orders to set the market price. It is one where there is so much activity that the sale of 50,000 shares in a day would not cause the price to fall: the market would quickly absorb the shares.

The market also needs to be a **fair game** (or a level playing field) and not a place where some investors, brokers, fund raisers or financiers are in a position to profit unfairly at the expense of other participants. This means, for instance, that **insider dealing** is prohibited, that is, company officers or others with private knowledge do not use that knowledge to trade in the company's shares. **Brokers** who act for shareholders are well regulated so that they act in the interest of investors. **Market makers**, who stand ready to buy and sell shares from investors on their own behalf in the stock exchange, follow strict codes of behaviour. It is a market that is **well regulated** to avoid abuses, negligence and fraud in order to reassure investors who put their savings at risk. Furthermore, investors need information on companies and share price activity so stock exchanges insist on minimum standards of information flow from companies and help **disseminate company announcements**. They also **publish prices** at which trading occurred and other **share trading data** (e.g. volume of trades).

A good secondary market allows the separation of long-term investment in **real assets** by firms and short-term investment by shareholders in **financial assets** called ordinary shares. The English language is often inadequate, and here is a case in point. The word 'investment' is used for two purposes. Companies invest in real assets that range from buildings and machinery to intangibles such as patents, brands and copyrights. This is productive investment that adds to the output of an economy. However, investment in the form of buying shares in the secondary market, from another investor, is not necessarily going to put more money into wealth-creating assets. It is simply the transfer of cash from one investor, and the ownership of the shares from the other. Then again, without a good secondary market, people will invest less in the primary market and **less productive real investment** will take place.

Bonds

If you wish to invest in a business but are unable to bring yourself to take the risk associated with shares, a good alternative is to purchase a **corporate bond**. A bond is a long-term contract in which bondholders lend money to a company. In return the company (usually) promises to pay the bond owners a series of interest payments known as **coupons**, until the bond matures. At **maturity** the bondholder receives a specified **principal sum** called the **par**, **face** or **nominal** value of the bond. This is usually £100 in the UK. The time to maturity is generally between 7 and 30 years. Bonds are a form of debt finance and are not ownership capital. The holders are not entitled to vote at the company meetings (AGMs or EGMs). A lower **rate of return** is offered on bonds than on shares because bond investors have a number of **safeguards** that equity investors do not. The interest on bonds is paid out before ordinary share dividends are paid, so there is a greater certainty of receiving a return than there is for equity holders. Also, if the firm goes into liquidation, the bondholders are paid back before shareholders receive anything. Furthermore, bondholders often insist on taking **collateral** for the loan, and may restrict managerial action so they don't make the firm too risky. Offsetting these plus points for bonds is the fact that lenders do not, generally, share in the value created by an extraordinarily successful business. They receive only the contracted amount of interest.

Bonds are often traded in the secondary market of the stock exchange. So despite companies obtaining long-term finance for years ahead, the investor who provides that money can sell the bond to another investor to **liquidate** his holding.

Capital structure

The shareholders in a company such as Stephenson Brunel Ltd may be more than happy for the company to borrow some funds either from a bank or a bond issue due to the **leverage (or gearing)** effect. To understand this, imagine that the firm is now 5 years old and has long since paid off all its bank borrowings. It has proposed a major new investment in branch lines that will require £5 million of new investment. It could go to its shareholders, selling them additional shares through a **rights issue** (more about this later) to obtain all the extra £5 million from them. But consider this: the investment is expected to produce a return of 20 per cent per year on the money invested: £1 million per year on the £5 million raised from the shareholders. This is good, but the shareholders could be made even better off by an alternative **capital structure**.[1] If the company obtained £1 million from equity holders and £4 million from bondholders it could generate much higher returns for its shareholders. If we assume that bondholders require a return of 6 per cent per year, then the benefit of financial leverage to shareholders can be seen. The company creates £1 million of extra pre-interest income per year. Of that £240,000 (6 per cent of £4 million) has to go to pay the interest on bonds. That leaves £760,000 per year for the equity holders, who only put up an extra £1 million – a 76 per cent return per year!

Not bad. But there is a downside to financial leverage. A company can have too much debt, too many **regular interest payment commitments**, so that it cannot survive a decline in its underlying business. By borrowing more it adds to its **fixed costs** (the extra interest each year), and a couple of years of losses can wipe out the net assets and force liquidation. However, in the case of Stephenson Brunel Ltd there is little need to worry. Balance sheet net assets after 5 years of operating now stand at £10 million and revenues are still growing. Debt of £4 million and annual interest of £240,000 should not be too much of a problem.

Stocks and shares

The terms '**stocks**' and '**shares**' are used interchangeably and confusingly in the financial press, particularly when referring to the US markets. In the UK we define shares as equity in companies. Stocks are financial instruments that pay interest, such as bonds. However, in the USA shares are also called '**common stocks**' and the shareholders are sometimes referred to as '**stockholders**'. So when some people use the term 'stocks' they could be referring to either bonds or shares.

[1] Capital structure: the proportion of debt to equity making up the total finance supplied to the company.

Rights issues

Now imagine that the railway company has been operating for 10 years. It has paid out large dividends over the decade and still has shareholders' funds of £12 million on its balance sheet. Unfortunately, borrowings are also quite large at £15 million, and interest rates in the economy generally are high and on an upward trend. The directors, still led by Mr Stephenson and Mr Brunel, would like to spend £10 million building an extension to the current lines. This plan makes good economic sense and should be funded, but the company would be taking on too much risk if it borrowed the additional £10 million – the annual fixed cost of the interest bill could cripple the company. So it decides to sell more shares, which have the advantage over debt capital of not carrying the right to receive an annual payout. Equity capital has the benefit that it acts as a '**shock absorber**' to business crises because a company can choose not to pay a dividend when times are bad.

Under UK law it is generally not possible for the company to sell the new shares to raise the £10 million to outside investors without first offering them to existing shareholders (called **a pre-emption right)**. The owners of the company are entitled to subscribe for the new shares in proportion to their existing holding. This will enable them to maintain their **existing percentage ownership** – so, if a shareholder currently owns 10 per cent of the shares he/she is entitled to purchase 10 per cent of any new shares issued. While those shareholders who take up their rights will have the same proportion of the company cake as they had before, each slice of the cake becomes bigger because the company has more financial resources under its control. Rights issues are a popular method of raising new funds – they are relatively easy and cheap for companies. (There is a lot more on rights issues in Chapter 16.)

Financial institutions

So we have now covered the absolute core issues in investment. It is about buying legal rights (shares, bonds, etc.) from a company. The company then uses the money raised from investors to create wealth (hopefully!), which is then shared between the investors. If a company's shares and bonds are traded on a stock exchange they can easily be sold on to other investors in the secondary market.

Having dealt with the basics we need to explain the role of **financial intermediaries** in assisting the working of the system.

Investment banks

The directors and managers of a railway company, or a manufacturing or service firm, are not generally expert in the workings of the financial markets. They tend to buy such expertise from the **investment banks** (also called **merchant** or **wholesale banks**). These organisations will, for a fee, advise a company considering **floating** its shares on the stock exchange. Companies coming to the market for the first time to raise fresh equity capital (or merely to allow a secondary market in the company's shares) have to go through a number of procedures to reassure the market regulators, and, through them, the investing public, that they are sound companies run by trustworthy people. The merchant bank can act as a **sponsor** to a company. It will investigate the company thoroughly before attaching its good name to the stock market newcomer. Agreeing to be a sponsor sends a signal to investors that the company is well run and has good prospects. If the sponsor suspects that the senior managerial team is too dependent on one individual or is lacking in vital expertise and balance it will suggest (insist on) the appointment of some new directors before flotation can take place. If the company is judged to be worthy of joining the stock market then the sponsor will coordinate the activities of all the other organisations involved: **brokers** assist with pricing and selling the shares; **underwriters** agree to buy any shares not bought by the investing public; **accountants** draw up detailed figures on performance; **solicitors** deal with all the legal contracts. The sponsor also helps to create the **prospectus**, which provides vital information on the company needed for potential investors to make a buy decision. (New issues are covered in Chapter 16.)

Other areas in which investment bankers help companies include the process, tactics and regulatory issues of **merger** with other companies (mergers are discussed in Chapter 18). They might also assist with raising new funds for the firm after its shares have been quoted on the stock exchange for a while. This could be by selling new equity (e.g. rights issue), or by selling bonds, or selling some other financial instrument (e.g. convertibles).

Initial public offerings (companies floating on the stock market), **seasoned equity offerings** (e.g. rights issues) and mergers can be big money-spinners for the investment banks. The fees earned can run into tens of millions of pounds and an individual banker with a good reputation can earn millions of pounds a year in bonuses from completing these deals.

Investment banks also act as brokers for the buying and selling of securities on the financial markets. Some may have market-making arms that assist the operation of secondary markets. Another branch of the bank may assist companies with **export finance**.

A major field for many investment banks is assisting investors rather than companies. They offer **portfolio management services** to rich individuals who lack the time or expertise to devise their own investment strategies. They also manage collective investment vehicles such as unit trusts (see Chapter 5) as well as the portfolios of some pension funds and insurance companies.

The asset transformers

So, investment banks are completely different from retail high street banks (although many are owned by **financial service companies** or **universal** banks that have both investment banking and retail banking branches). The primary role of the retail banks is to take in numerous small deposits lent to the banks for short periods of time (i.e. you can get at the money in your current account instantly) by offering low-risk investment to millions of savers (not many of us have to worry about the risk of failure of banks to pay out what we have in our bank accounts). They then lend this money to companies needing large sums for long periods of time, and that money is put at considerable risk. The retail banks act as asset **transformers**. They **transform small deposits** into large loans for firms by aggregating the savers' money. They **transform risk**, offering depositors (investors in bank accounts) low risk but lending the money out at high risk. And they **transform maturity**: taking in short-term money and lending it long-term. They can do this very valuable trick because of the economies of scale they enjoy: efficiencies in gathering information on the risk of lending to a particular firm; the ability to spread risk by lending to a large number of companies; the systems they have developed to reduce transaction costs associated with setting up a lending agreement or monitoring a loan.

The investment banks have virtually abandoned the activity of taking in deposits and lending to borrowers; although some activity of this kind does go on, it tends to be for large sums, at least £250,000. They much prefer to charge fees to companies and investors for carrying out specialist tasks and to trade on their own account in various markets, such as foreign exchange, derivatives and equity markets, to try and make a profit – this is called **proprietary trading**.

Pension funds

Most of us pay into **pension funds** during our working lives to build up a pot of money that we can draw from on retirement. The pension fund **trustees** have to decide what to do with this money over the decades between payment in and withdrawal in the form of a pension. They place some or all of the money with specialist **investment managers**. Large sums have built up in pension funds over the last 50 years – over £800,000 million. Something like half to two-thirds of pension fund money is used to buy UK shares, amounting to about 30 per cent of all the shares listed on the London Stock Exchange. Thus, when selling shares, companies regard the pension fund managers as gatekeepers to a key source of funds. It is also interesting to note that even though only 12 million or so UK individuals are capitalist owners of industry by owning shares directly, almost all the rest of the adult population has a substantial proportion of their wealth tied up in equities via their pension schemes. So almost all of us have an interest in the stock market and the performance of company shares.

Insurance companies

Insurance companies also own a large proportion of UK shares (over 20 per cent). As well as general insurance against contingencies such as fire, theft and accident, insurance companies build up large funds by persuading savers to buy products such as life assurance, endowment policies and personal pensions (more on this in Chapter 5). This money is invested mostly in UK shares but also in bonds, property and overseas shares. Over £900,000 million is invested in this way.

The risk spreaders

Investors with only a few thousand pounds to invest know that they should diversify, but if they buy 10 different companies' shares the transaction costs would swallow a large proportion of the fund. Also investors often wish to invest in specialist areas, say Japanese shares or US hi-tech shares, but are wary of doing so because they lack the expertise. This is where the **pooled funds** (also known as collective funds) come in. They assist the flow of money from savers to productive investment by gathering together lots of small amounts that are then invested in dozens or hundreds of company shares, bonds or other securities.

Unit trusts, investment trusts and open-ended investment companies (OEICs) offer investors a way of spreading risks. They even present the possibility of the investor putting just a few dozen pounds a month into the markets. There are over 1,600 different unit trusts, investment trusts and OEICs, with over £350,000 million invested.

Be proud to be a capitalist!

We have seen that the modern financial system encourages savers to plough their money into real assets to produce wealth. It is this wealth that all the social services (health care, education, etc.) rely on for resources. There simply would not be this wealth without the revolution in **social technology** over the last two hundred years. We need to mobilise the savings of millions of people. We do that by permitting limited liability, by developing well-regulated primary and secondary markets, by having strong **property rights** defendable in the courts, and by having financial institutions that assist firms or investors to find one another, to form contracts, to provide specialist knowledge and to monitor the progress of companies. In this way the financial system is the vital lubricant of the industrial revolution. Investors, even though they act in their own self-interest – they want to become rich – in doing so bring about the creation of vast quantities of real assets, leading to greater social well-being. This is not an original thought. Even before the formal creation of the Stock Exchange, Adam Smith in 1776 pointed out the value to society of individuals acting for profit.

> The businessman by directing . . . industry in such a manner as its produce may be of the greatest value, intends only his own gain, and he is in this, as in many other cases, led by an invisible hand to promote an end which was no part of his intention. Nor is it always the worse for the society that it was no part of it. By pursuing his own interest he frequently promotes that of the society more effectually than when he really intends to promote it.
>
> (*The Wealth of Nations*, 1776)

So, be proud to be a capitalist. Your saving results in wealth creation. Hold the banner high: I invest to make myself rich, but I also **allocate resources** to firms that I think can use them best to produce goods and services people need and/or want. In a world without equity and bond investors looking purely for profit the railways would not have been built, the drugs industry would be a lot smaller and Silicon Valley would still be producing fruit.

A note of warning – investment and speculation

Benjamin Graham is regarded as the greatest thinker on investment who has ever lived. He was a young man working on **Wall Street** in the 1920s and got caught up in the euphoria of the time. It was described as a '**new era**' because of all the new technology driving industry forward. Share prices rose, and experienced market participants and newcomers bought vast quantities of shares without investigating the companies underlying the shares. They would buy on a rumour, or a tip, or because the share price had risen a lot the week before. They had seen other people succeed by buying anything fashionable, so they figured they could also join the bandwagon. (Similar buying attitudes prevailed towards companies with '-tech' at the end of their names in the 1960s or with '.com' in the 1990s.)

Benjamin Graham lost a fortune in the Crash. He gave a lot of thought in the Great Depression to differences between investment and mere **speculation**. The conclusion of his ruminations led him to reject the common idea that the difference lies in the *type* of investment purchased. He also dismissed the *length of time a security* is held. He saw that the distinction lies in the *mind* of the person making the buying and selling decisions. It is the attitude of the individual that is key. The speculator's primary concern is with anticipating and profiting from market fluctuations. In contrast, 'an investment operation is one which, upon thorough analysis, promises safety of principal and a satisfactory return. Operations not meeting these requirements are speculative.'[2]

We return to the railway-building story. If you were an investor rather than a speculator you would have thoroughly considered the business plan of Stephenson and Brunel and satisfied yourself that your capital was not being exposed to unreasonable risk. You would have judged the competence and integrity of the managerial team and you would not have expected to make short-term profits by quickly trading the shares. You would also have ensured that the shares were not being offered to you at a high price.

Many of the early investors in the nineteenth-century railway companies achieved terrific returns, rather like the returns that early buyers of Internet and telecom shares achieved in the late 1990s. Then speculative fever took over. People just threw money at

[2] B. Graham and D. Dodd, *Security Analysis* (McGraw-Hill, 1934), p.54.

anyone who proposed the setting up of a railway. Share prices skyrocketed and eventually the bubble burst, leaving many with massive losses and a lifelong aversion to the stock market. This book will hopefully help you to be an informed investor and not a speculator in shares. You will not develop an aversion to shares, but rather respect shares as portions of a business, and enjoy the thrill of finding good companies to invest in at reasonable prices.

2

The rewards of investment

Becoming a millionaire

At the age of 20, Sally Kelk decided to put £100 per month into an investment fund that invested in a broad range of shares on the London Stock Exchange. She did this for the last 20 years of the twentieth century. The return that she achieved during this period amounted to 19 per cent per annum (the actual average annual return for UK shares between 1980 and 1999). At the age of 40, in the first week of the new millennium, she sold all of her shares. She banked £215,245. Not bad for the sacrifice of £100 per month, or a total of £24,000. She feels the sacrifice was not too onerous as she spread the pain of saving over 20 years.

It gets even better. Sally has a chance of being a millionaire! She concluded in 2000 that she does not need to use any of the £215,245 and decided to invest it in the stock market again and leave it there for the next 25 years when she expects to retire. Will she retire comfortably? You bet she will. If average annual returns over the first 25 years of the twenty-first century are the same as those over the last 20 years of the twentieth century, so that the fund grows by 19 per cent per year, Sally will have over £16.6 million by her 65th birthday. That is the power of compounding the return! **Compounding** is ploughing back the income received and then getting a return on the accumulated ploughed-back money as well as the original capital.

Of course, we have made some crude assumptions in this analysis. First, the annual rate of return of 19 per cent is what is called a **nominal** return. That is, it does not take into account the fact that much of the return is compensation for inflation, which was high in the 1980s. If we remove the inflation element and concentrate on the returns in constant purchasing power terms (that is, the **real** rate of return) the annual rate of return falls to 13.1 per cent. This is still good, but does not lead to such an impressive sum at the end of Sally's 25-year investment, in 2025: she would have to scrape by in her retirement with a mere £4.7 million.

Second, the last two decades of the twentieth century produced unusually high returns on shares. The second half of this chapter contains some more precise returns figures, but suffice to say that over the twentieth century as a whole equities gave a real return (after taking off inflation) of 5.7 per cent per year on average, not the 13.1 per cent for the last two decades. If we were to project forward from the year 2000 to Sally's retirement date the growth of £215,245 at a rate of 5.7 per cent the total amounts to £860,613. This is less impressive, perhaps, but it is expressed in year 2000 purchasing power. In other words, Sally can buy four times as many goods and services at the end as at the beginning.

If we allow for a little inflation, then we can make an estimate of the size of the pot of money in nominal terms (in year 2025 money): £215,245 compounded at a rate of return of 9 per cent for 25 years amounts to £1.86 million. So, Sally has every chance of being a millionaire in 2025 regardless of other incomes, assets, etc. Good luck to her. She had the foresight and the discipline to leave her money in shares, and it has paid off handsomely.[1]

[1] There is a third factor we have ignored – taxation. Sally might (probably will) have to pay income tax on dividends and capital gains tax on the sale of shares – we consider this in Chapter 17.

Simple and compound interest

Exhibit 2.1 demonstrates the power of compounding. It shows the difference in the size of a pot of money at various points in the future when the pot is allowed to grow at simple interest (i.e. interest on the initial capital only) and compound interest (each year interest is added to the pot and future interest is paid on both the initial capital and the interest that has accumulated from previous years). The figures are based on an initial investment of £100 with annual interest of 10 per cent. At simple interest a £100 fund becomes worth only £600 after 50 years. However, if interest is received on accumulated interest (compound interest) the £100 is turned into £11,739.[2]

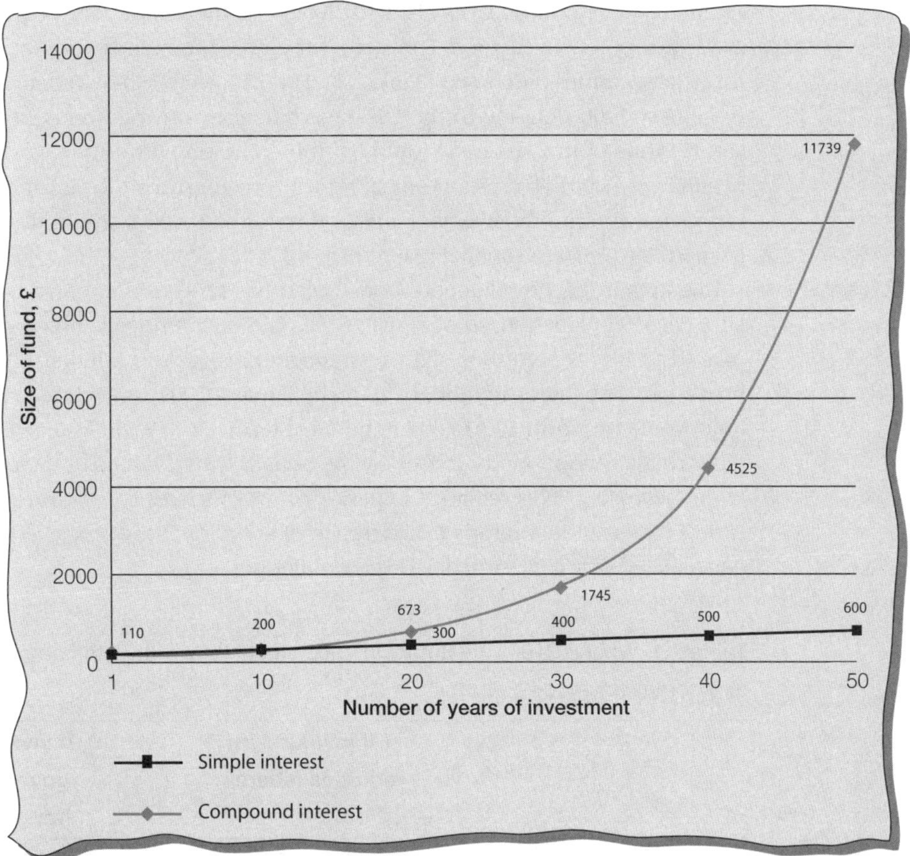

Exhibit 2.1 The magic of compounding

Long-term investment is like planting trees. At first you can only find enough money to buy a few saplings. They look small and pathetic. Then you add to your collection month by month. For the first few years your wood looks unimpressive and hardly worth

[2] Compounding calculations are explained in the appendix to Chapter 2 of G. Arnold, *Corporate Financial Management* (Financial Times Prentice Hall, 2002).

the effort. Still, you nurture and keep adding to it. Perhaps later you stop buying more saplings and decide to devote merely the minimal effort. Perhaps you turn away to other interests for a few years. Then, when you do look again, you are amazed to find that what was scrubland has been transformed into a magnificent arboretum with fine strong specimens. Time has worked its magic. What seem like small annual rates of growth can, with compounding, produce a great mass from small beginnings.

How well have investors fared in the past?

An interesting question to ask is: what would be the value today of an investment made at various points in history? The size of the return depends very much on the type of financial securities purchased (Table 2.1). For instance, £100 placed in government bonds in January 1900 (lending to the UK government by buying bonds from it is one of the safest forms of investment) would, with income reinvested, be worth £20,300 by the beginning of 2001. This is a nominal return (no adjustment for inflation) of 5.4 per cent per year. Even with the effects of inflation removed the real size of the investment grows from £100 to £370 (an annual real return of 1.3 per cent).

Investing in UK government bonds (gilts) has produced a return that has more than kept pace with inflation, so perhaps you should be impressed. However, when you compare this with the return on shares you might change your mind. If £100 was placed in a broad range of shares in January 1900, by January 2001, with dividends reinvested, the fund would be worth £1,616,000 in nominal terms or £29,150 in real terms – that is, 291 times as many goods and services can be bought with the fund at the end of 101 years as at the beginning. This remarkable performance of shares comes from a seemingly small extra average annual return (a difference of 4.7 per cent: whereas equities earned 10.1 per cent per year gilts earned 5.4 per cent per year).

Table 2.1 What a £100 investment in 1900 would be worth at the beginning of 2001, with all income reinvested

	If invested in equities (shares)	**If invested in government bonds (gilts)**
Money (nominal) return	£1,616,000	£20,300
Real return	£29,150	£370

Source: Elroy Dimson, Paul Marsh and Mike Staunton, *Triumph of the Optimists: 101 Years of Global Investment Returns* (Princeton University Press, 2002).

Perhaps 101 years is a little too long as a time frame for even the most dedicated long-term investor, so let's look at the returns over shorter periods. Table 2.2 shows equities producing superior returns over all the periods shown here, except for the first few years of the twenty-first century. Placing money in a building society account is the preferred choice of many savers. The table shows that this generally produces very poor returns compared with equities, or even gilts.

Table 2.2 Real returns on UK financial securities (per cent per annum) and the value of an initial investment of £100 at the end of the period

	101 years (1900–1.1.2001)[a]	**51 years (1950–1.1.2001)[a]**	**25 years (1976–1.1.2001)[a]**	**10 years (1993–1.1.2003)[b]**	**3 years (2000–1.1.2003)[b]**
Equities	5.8%	8.6%	10.9%	3.9%	−15.9%
	£29,150	£6719	£1328	£147	£60
Gilts	1.3%	1.6%	7.1%	7.2%	4.4%
	£370	£225	£556	£200	£114
Building society accounts[b]		(41 years 1960–2001) 1.5%	2.2%	1.9%	2.9%
		£181	£173	£121	£109
Inflation[b]	4%	6.1%	6.3%	2.5%	2.2%

[a] Source: Dimson *et al.*, *Triumph of the Optimists*. (for equities and gilts only)
[b] Source: Barclays Capital, *Equity-Gilt Study* (2003), 48th edition.

The end of the twentieth century was an unusually good period for equity investors. It was the best two consecutive decades for as far back as records go – Table 2.3 breaks the returns down by decade.

Table 2.3 Real rates of return (% p.a.)

	Equities	**Gilts**
1900–1909	1.8	−0.2
1910–1919	−1.3	−9.2
1920–1929	9.3	8.3
1930–1939	2.6	5.9
1940–1949	3.1	0.7
1950–1959	13.7	−2.3
1960–1969	6.5	−1.5
1970–1979	−1.4	−4.4
1980–1989	15.4	7.5
1990–2000	9.3	8.9

Source: Dimson *et al.*, *Triumph of the Optimists*.

The importance of income

The total return that an equity investor receives consists of two elements:

- **Dividends.** These are generally paid every six months from the after-tax profits of the company. Directors decide the proportion of earnings to be paid to shareholders, subject to shareholder approval. Note, however, that a company may not pay dividends. The reason for this may be that the company is currently unprofitable, or that it is fast-growing and needs to use all cash generated to invest in productive assets.
- **Capital gain.** The share price rises over time due to an increase in the underlying value of the business (or to temporary enthusiasm for the shares by investors, which may or may not be rational).

So, where do the terrific returns on shares come from: is it predominantly from dividends or capital gains? Well, over a single year the returns on equities are largely due to share price movement; dividend income contributes a relatively small amount. However, long-term returns are overwhelmingly due to dividends. For example, if an investor had chosen to spend dividends received on a £100 investment made in 1900 as each year passed, rather than reinvest, by January 2001 capital gains alone take the fund to only £14,916[3] (nominal return). On the other hand, another investor who reinvested dividends over the 101 years would have had a fund worth £1,616,200 (nominal return).

International comparison

To test if the returns on UK equities and gilts are unusual, Table 2.4 shows the real returns on shares and government bonds for 15 other countries for 101 years. Clearly there is a great similarity in the returns across countries and in the size of the gap between equity returns and government bond returns. However, it is important to note that the small differences in annual percentage returns shown can compound to large differences in the wealth available to investors at the end of a long period. For example, over 101 years the investment of one unit of local currency in the Belgian market in 1900 would have grown by a factor of 12.1 in real terms, whereas a corresponding investment in Sweden would have grown 1,633-fold.

[3] Dimson *et al.*, *Triumph of the Optimists*.

Table 2.4 Real returns on equities and government bonds: an international comparison, 1900–2000 (% p.a.)

	Equities	Bonds
Sweden	7.6	2.4
Australia	7.5	1.1
South Africa	6.8	1.4
USA	6.7	1.6
Canada	6.4	1.8
The Netherlands	5.8	1.1
UK	5.8	1.3
Switzerland	5.0[a]	2.8
Ireland	4.8	1.5
Denmark	4.6	2.5
Japan	4.5	−1.6
France	3.8	−1.0
Spain	3.6	1.2
Germany	3.6	−2.2[b]
Italy	2.7	−2.2
Belgium	2.5	−0.4

[a] From 1911.
[b] Excluding 1922–23.

Source: Dimson *et al.*, *Triumph of the Optimists*.

Equities versus gilts

Another interesting question: how many times over a five-year period has equity provided a real return greater than gilts? The answer is provided in Table 2.5, which shows that of the 99 (overlapping) five-year periods between 1900 and 2002 in 77 cases equities have performed better than gilts. Similar results are obtained from periods of 2, 3, 4 and 10 years. Shares generally perform best, but there can be quite long periods where equities perform badly – equities underperformed gilts for a decade or more on 14 occasions.

Table 2.5 Performance of equities relative to gilts 1900–2002

	Length of holding period in years				
	2	**3**	**4**	**5**	**10**
Equities outperform gilts, number of periods	71	78	80	77	80
Equities underperform gilts, number of periods	31	23	20	22	14
Total number of periods	102	101	100	99	94
Equity outperformance proportion of periods	70%	77%	80%	78%	85%

Source: Barclays Capital, *Equity-Gilt Study* (2003), 48th edition.

What about risk?

So shares have generally been a fantastic form of investment, but there is a downside. We have already seen that shares can produce negative real returns for periods as long as a decade (e.g. 1910–19 and 1970–79). More recently the first three years of the twenty-first century have reminded us that shares 'can go down as well as up'. In 2000 UK share investors lost 8.6 per cent, even after receiving dividend income of around 2–3 per cent. This was much worse than the positive return of 6.1 per cent on gilts. Those investors expecting shares to bounce back in 2001 and 2002 were sorely disappointed. The total real return on shares in 2001 was –13.8 per cent; whereas gilts returned +0.6 per cent. In 2002 shares again lost investors money, this time 24.5 per cent (gilts produced a real return of +6.7 per cent). That's an overall loss of over 40 per cent over 3 years. And it was much worse for those investors who concentrated their holdings in technology, dot-com and telecom shares – many of these lost 90 per cent or more of their value.

There have been some terrible periods for equity investors. For example, in just one month, October 1987, investors lost over a quarter of their money. In June 1940 and March 1974 over a fifth was wiped out.

It does not take long when looking at statistics like these to form the impression that shares are risky. This is confirmed by Exhibit 2.2, which shows the real annual returns on shares for each year going back to 1900. Over the 103-year period shares produced

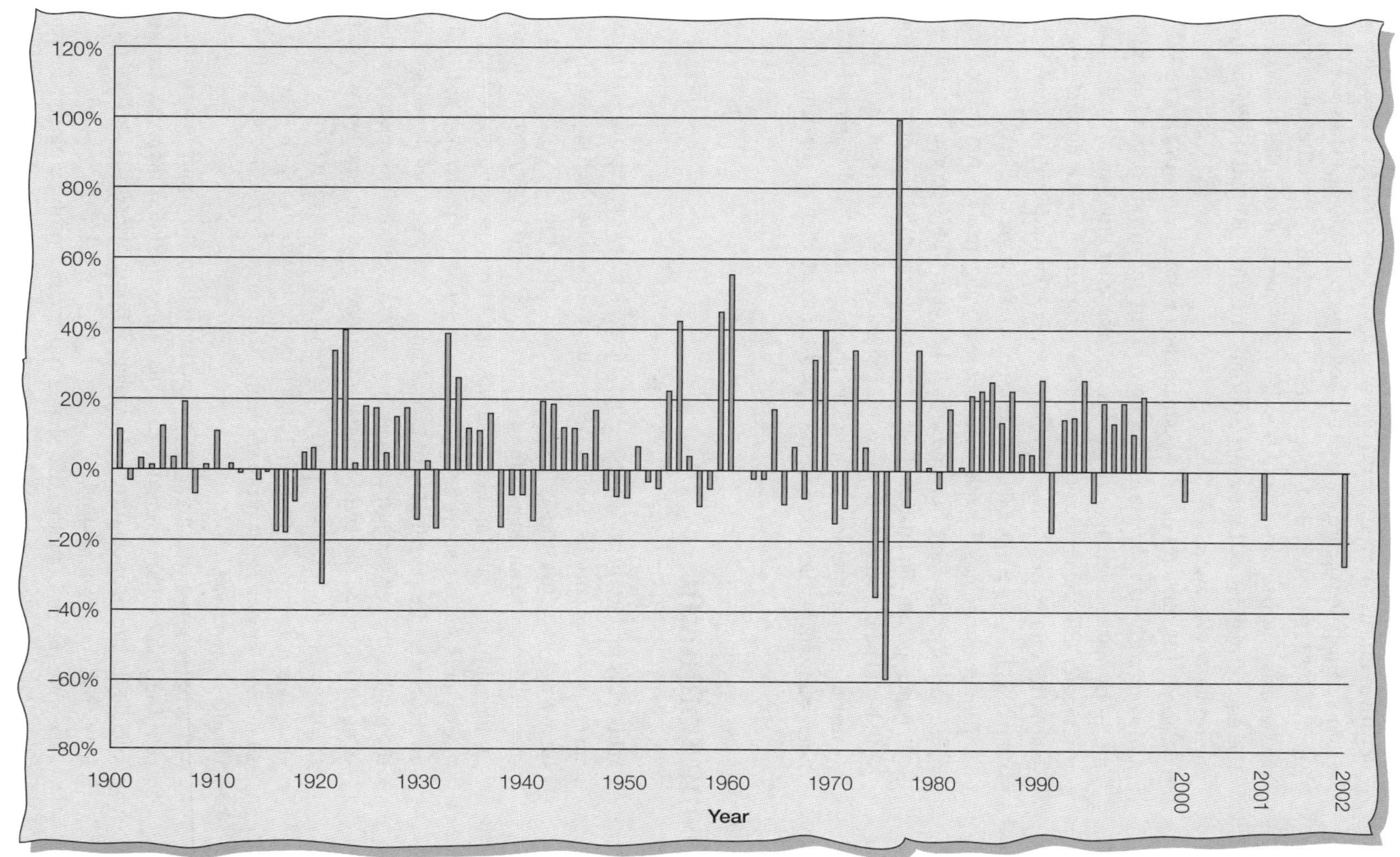

Exhibit 2.2 Annual real equity returns, 1900–2002 (%)

Source: Barclays Capital, *Equity-Gilt Study* (2002, 2003)

negative returns in over a third of the years. Some of these losses are very large. For example, imagine you are an investor holding a portfolio of shares worth £100,000 at the start of 1973. By the end of that year your portfolio would be valued at only £65,000. Perhaps at that point you would swallow the line that equities always bounce back (as the equity analysts and press are so fond of telling us) and decide to hold on to your shares for another year.

Calamity! By the end of 1974 your holding would be worth a mere £27,235. Now you are, along with many investors, feeling very fed up with shares and everything to do with the stock market. Perhaps you decide to take what little you have left and put it somewhere safer. But the capricious and restless market tricks you again. If you held on to the shares the value would have risen by 99.6 per cent during 1975. However, it would take until 1983 for your £100,000 to be restored to you (in real terms).

Share investors must be able to accept that equity markets can fall by very large percentages during a day and that individual holdings can become worthless overnight as companies go into liquidation. If you are unable to accept this degree of volatility perhaps you should be investing somewhere else. Building society and bank accounts beckon.

Year to year real returns on gilts can also be volatile. As Exhibit 2.3 shows, there have been many years when gilt investors have lost more than 10 per cent of their investment.

■ Closing comment

While it is important to acknowledge the possibility of negative share return performance, even over periods as long as 10 years, we must not become too pessimistic. Shares on average gave investors very good returns during the last century. I am convinced that they will do so again, just as long as investors avoid buying when the market is being 'irrationally exuberant' and blowing up a bubble. Shares should be viewed as long-term investments and not short-term gambling counters. Good returns are available for equity investors who are prepared to bide their time. Note that even if you had bought shares at the peak of the market at the beginning of 1973 and you had experienced a fall in market value to a mere 27 per cent of initial investment over the first two years, if you had held these shares for a further 28 years your average annual real return would have been 7 per cent. Your initial investment of £100,000 would be worth £664,884 in 1973 money or over £5 million in year 2000 money. Clearly patience and resilience in the face of market volatility can pay off.

There are good reasons for the superior returns to equity investment. Shares represent the risk capital of businesses. This money is put at high risk. Companies go into liquidation and markets turn down violently. Bond investors settle for a trade-off between lower risk and lower returns.

Despite the risk of individual shares and the risk of the entire share market at certain times, broadly based portfolios held for substantial periods have given handsome returns.

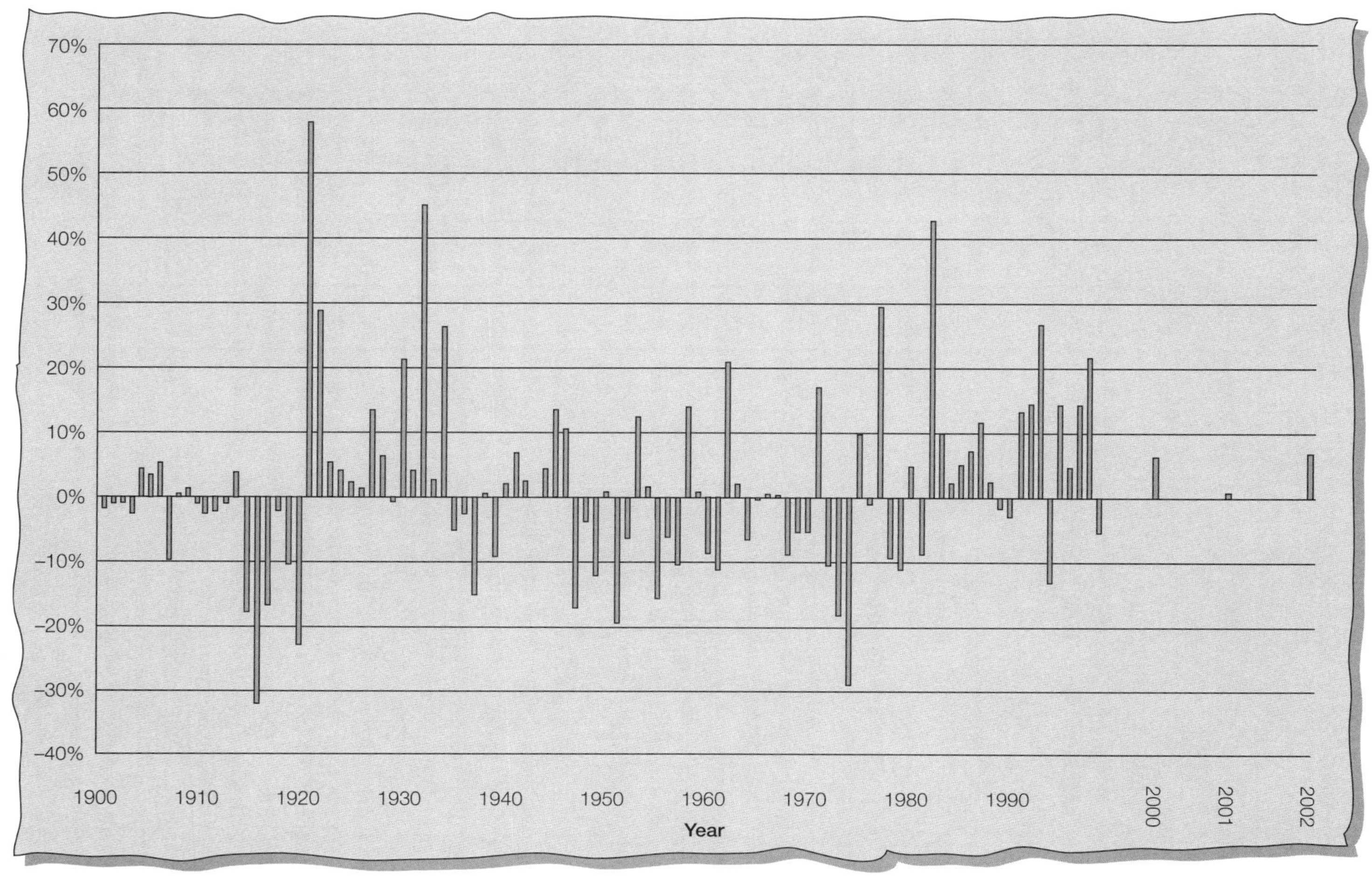

Exhibit 2.3 Annual real gilt returns, 1900–2002 (%)

Source: Barclays Capital, *Equity-Gilt Study* (2002, 2003)

3

Stock markets

The World has changed dramatically in the last 20 years. The strong ideological opposition to capitalism has been replaced with stock markets in Moscow, Warsaw and Ho Chi Minh City. China, of all places, has two thriving stock exchanges, in Shanghai and Shenzhen, with over 1,000 companies listed. There are more than 20 million Chinese investors – more than in the UK – who can only be properly described as 'capitalists' given that they put at risk their savings on the expectations of a reward on their capital.

Over 100 countries now have stock markets. There must be something of great value offered by stock markets to pull so many societies towards them. Jiang Zemin, China's president, spoke with the fervour of a recent convert in declaring that robust stock markets are a vital component of a modern economy – they can bring great benefits to investors, companies and society, according to this new enthusiast. This chapter will concentrate on describing UK markets, but the principal features tend to be found in all stock exchanges.[1]

■ What is a stock market?

Stock markets are where government and industry can raise long-term capital and investors can buy and sell securities. Markets, whether they are for shares, bonds, cattle or fruit and vegetables, are simply mechanisms to allow the possibility of trade between individuals or organisations. Some markets (e.g. for sheep) are physical: there is a place at which the buyers and sellers meet. Other markets (e.g. for foreign currency), are merely a network, based on communication via telephone and computer, with no physical meeting place.

A few stock exchanges around the world still have a place where buyers and sellers (or at least their representatives) meet to trade. For example, the **New York Stock Exchange (NYSE)** continues to make use of a large **trading floor** with thousands of face-to-face deals taking place every working day (**open outcry trading**). This is the traditional image of a stock market, and if a television reporter has a story about what is going on in the world's security markets, they often show an image of traders rushing around, talking quickly amid a flurry of small slips of paper on the NYSE trading floor.

Such a television reporter in London has more difficulty finding an image to represent security dealing. The London Stock Exchange (LSE), like many in the world today, has no trading floor. In the 1980s it decided to switch to a computer system to link the buyers and sellers. This allows for a more efficient market than the old system and allows traders to be located anywhere; so long as they can link up to the LSE central computer, they can trade. Television journalists usually resort to reporting from one of the many dealing rooms owned by the financial groups. There they find rows of desks with hundreds of computer screens. The people in front of the screens may be **brokers** acting on behalf of

[1] Stock exchange and stock market will be used interchangeably. *Bourse* is an alternative word used particularly in Continental Europe.

investors buying or selling shares into the market. One of the screens on a desk will display the information on the LSE central computer, showing latest trading prices, for example. Other screens may show information about companies, news, or perhaps provide analytical tools. Even though these **agents** of the buyers and sellers of shares don't physically meet their counterparts in other security house dealing rooms to complete a deal, there are times good TV camera shots of frazzled and exhausted brokers can be obtained to show on the evening news – usually when the market has fallen a lot in one day.

Brokers and market makers

It is perfectly legal for investors to deal directly with each other **off the exchange**. (There are special forms that record the transfer of shares from one name to another – see Chapter 4.) However, the majority of share deals are conducted through brokers who act as agents for buyers and sellers. One broker will not contact another broker to complete the deal but will instead (usually) go to a **market maker**. These middlemen stand ready to buy or sell shares on their own account. They quote two prices: the price at which they are willing to buy and the price they offer shares for sale (called '**making a book**'). During the day they anticipate that they will make numerous deals buying shares and a roughly equal number selling shares in a company. The small **margin** between the buying and selling prices delivers a profit to the market maker. There are usually many market makers trading in a particular company's shares. A high degree of competition between them ensures that the market makers' spread between the **bid** (buying) and **offer** (selling) prices does not get too wide, putting investors at a disadvantage.[2]

Pricing: good old supply and demand

How are the prices of shares and other securities set? They are determined in much the same way as the prices for other goods and assets bought and sold in market places: by the forces of supply and demand.

Imagine a share is currently priced by market makers at 149p–150p. This means that the (say) 10 different market makers trading in this share stand ready to buy at 149p and sell at 150p. (It is unusual that all the market makers offer exactly the same prices, but please bear with the simplification for now.) Let us further assume that the current market price is in **equilibrium** – that is, the forces of supply and demand are evenly balanced. The market makers will experience this equilibrium by a steady flow of buy and

[2] For more details on share trading, see Chapter 4. Note that there is an alternative system also operated by the LSE which does not require market makers, but it operates only for the largest company shares.

sell orders roughly matched in terms of volume. So we start with stability and the market makers feel no pressure to alter the price.

Now suppose that a negative item of news is released about the company. Investors become more pessimistic about the prospects for the firm's future profits. Many of those who would have been buyers at 150p now decide not to pick up the telephone to ask their brokers to buy, thus demand falls. At the same time an increased number of sellers contact their brokers with instructions to sell. The price of 149p seems excellent to them given the poorer prospects.

The market makers stand in the middle receiving an unbalanced set of orders: there are now many more sell orders than buy orders. At 149p–150p the shares are no longer in equilibrium. Market makers need to **balance their books**, that is, they need to find a roughly equal number of buyers and sellers. In the situation described they are faced with a deluge of sell orders and a **buyers' strike**. Something has to give. Most of the market makers are quick to change the prices they offer. In fact many changed prices when they saw the news about the company on one of their computer screens. That is, they **marked down** the bid–offer spread. Some tried 148p–149p, but found that this was still not low enough to balance supply and demand. Certainly some investors were attracted to buy at 149p but nothing like enough to create equilibrium. At prices of 145p–146p the number of sell orders (at 145p) slows dramatically, while the number of buy orders (at 146p) increases. Finally the market reaches a new equilibrium at 144p–145p. At least it does until the next piece of news or sentiment hits shares generally, or this company specifically.

What about those market makers who kept their price at 149p–150p? They would have found a massive number of investors offering to sell shares at 149p. The rule is that market makers are obliged to buy at the price they advertise on the LSE computer system. They do not hold high levels of inventory in the shares in which they deal because they don't have the enormous sums of money this would require (they deal in hundreds of different companies' shares). They must quickly sell the shares they purchase. Unfortunately they find that the highest price available from other market makers has fallen to 144p. They lose 5p on every share they purchase. It is clear that all market makers have to respond to shifting market forces and cannot stand still.

A short history of the London Stock Exchange

Businesses need capital to begin and to grow. '**Capital**' simply means stored wealth and resources. Stock markets assist the flow of capital from savers to businesses seeking funds. They do this through two main types of capital markets: the equity markets for trading of company shares; and the bond markets for trading the debt of companies and governments.

Capital markets go back a long time. In the late Middle Ages in the Italian city states securities very much like modern shares were issued and traded, as were government bonds. The demand from investors in British companies to be able to buy and sell shares led to the creation of a market in London. At first this was very informal; holders of financial securities (e.g. shares) would meet at known places, especially **coffee-houses** in the ancient part of London: **the City** (the '**Square Mile**' that the Romans built a wall around, just to the north-west of the Tower of London). Early in the nineteenth century the Stock Exchange developed a set of rules and procedures designed to enable investors to buy and sell shares with ease and to minimise the risk of fraud or unfairness.

The rapid economic expansion of the nineteenth century fuelled the demand for share issuance and the trading of shares between investors. Eventually there were 20 stock exchanges in cities up and down the UK. These have now been amalgamated with London.

'Big Bang'

Because of the LSE's origin it tended to be a very clubby place. Members of the club (brokers, etc.) ran things with a bias toward their own interests. There was little competition and commission rates were kept high. It became clear in the 1970s and 1980s that the LSE was losing trade to overseas stock markets. The large financial institutions, such as pension funds and insurance companies, were naturally in favour of a shift from fixed commission rates being paid to brokers to negotiated commissions. Further pressure was applied by the Office of Fair Trading to break up the cosy cartel.

The gentlemanly way of doing business ended in 1986 with the '**Big Bang**'. This is the term used for a collection of reforms implemented at the same time: fixed broker commissions disappeared; foreign competitors were allowed to own member firms (market makers or brokers); and the screen-based computer system of trading replaced floor-based trading.

The market makers and brokers quickly passed into the hands of large **financial conglomerates**. Commission fell sharply for large orders (from 0.4 per cent to around 0.2 per cent of the value traded). However, **private clients** (investors buying small quantities of shares on their own account) saw an initial slight rise in commission because it had previously been subsidised by the fees charged to the institutions. Brokers started to specialise. Some would offer the traditional service of advice and dealing, whereas others would offer a no-frills dealing-only service. (This **execution-only** service is now very cheap – see Chapter 4.)

The new financial conglomerates offering a wide range of services, such as, retail banking, market making, broking, investment management and insurance, were now able to compete with the big players in New York, Tokyo, Frankfurt and Geneva. To prevent conflicts of interest within the financial service firms damaging the position of clients, '**Chinese walls**' were established. These were designed as barriers to prevent sensitive information being passed on to another branch of the organisation. For example, if an investor holding 10 per cent of the shares of a company asks the broker department to sell his shares, he does not want, say, the fund (asset) management department to hear about it before he has off-loaded his shares at a good price – the fund managers may sell first, depressing the price. Likewise, the **corporate finance** department assisting a company trying to acquire a competitor should be prevented from passing on this information to other members of the financial conglomerate as they may be tempted to buy shares in the target company prior to the bid, in the expectation of making a large return on the announcement (a form of **insider dealing**).

Chinese walls have worked reasonably well, but as you can see from Exhibit 3.1 they are not as strong as the public relations department of these financial organisations would have you believe.

Analysts face curbs over stock pick bias

By Lina Saigol, Investment Banking Correspondent

City analysts were last night facing potential draconian new regulations after the Financial Services Authority said it had found evidence that they had misled investors with biased stock picks.

The City watchdog said it could introduce a range of measures, including US-style disclosure requirements or forcing analysts to label reports as being either advice or promotional material.

Sir Howard Davies, FSA chairman, said that, although the UK market was different from the US with no specific examples of bias or corrupt advice here, it was dominated by the same firms who operated in the US.

'There is some evidence both that analysts' recommendations have been systematically more positive than market performance would justify and, more seriously, that analysts' recommendations in relation to companies with which their parent house has a relationship are systematically more positive than the average,' Sir Howard said.

Angela Knight, chief executive of the Association of Private Client Investment Managers and Stockbrokers, agreed that the UK had not had the same problems as the US.

'We have got Chinese Walls which are policed in the UK, but the FSA is right to ask whether there is more that can be done.'

Exhibit 3.1 Chinese walls could be thicker, higher and more soundproof

Source: *Financial Times* 1 August 2002

Recent moves

For the majority of shares traded in London the 'quote-driven' system, with market makers at its centre, supported by the LSE's **Stock Exchange Automated Quotation (SEAQ)** service, remains the main way of trading shares. However, in 1997 the LSE introduced an '**order-driven**' service called **the Stock Exchange Trading Service (SETS)**. This cuts out the need for a market maker as it links buyers and sellers through a computerised matching system (see Chapter 4 for more details).

After centuries of being an organisation owned and run by its members, in 2001 the LSE became a public limited company with its shares traded on a secondary market – the shares are quoted on its own Official List and anyone is now free to purchase these shares. It has come a long way from its clubby days. It is now the leading stock exchange in the world for trading shares in overseas companies and is the third largest in the trading of domestic company shares (after New York and the other major US market, the NASDAQ – see Exhibit 3.2). In 2004 the Stock Exchange will move from its historic site in Old Broad Street to Paternoster Square near St Paul's Cathedral. The exchange toyed with the idea of moving out of the City but decided that its identity is tied too closely to the Square Mile to move outside.

The international scene

More change is in the air. Stock exchanges all over Europe are merging. Already the French, Dutch, Belgian and Portuguese *bourses* have merged to form **Euronext**. The **Deutsche Börse** has ambitions to become the most significant market in Europe. It has been prowling around looking for likely partners. It even came close to agreeing a merger with the LSE in 2000. More mergers and alliances are bound to follow, not least because the major financial institutions that operate across the globe desire a seamless, less costly way of trading shares across borders.

Variety of securities traded

The LSE creates a market place for many other types of financial securities besides shares – see Exhibit 3.3.

There are four types of **fixed-interest securities** traded in London: government bonds, local authority bonds, corporate bonds and eurobonds. The **UK government bond** (or **gilt**) market (lending to the UK government) is big. In 2002, for example, £22,190 million of gilts were sold to add to the £200,000 million already in issue. In addition, foreign governments sold £1,613 million of bonds through the LSE. **Sterling bonds** issued by companies (**corporate bonds** where the interest and the final redemption payment are in pounds sterling) comprise a much smaller market than government bonds (the total value outstanding is less than one-tenth that of gilts). During 2002 UK companies sold 817 new **eurobonds** in London worth a total of £86,657 million, making this the biggest fixed-income market (bonds are described in Chapter 6).

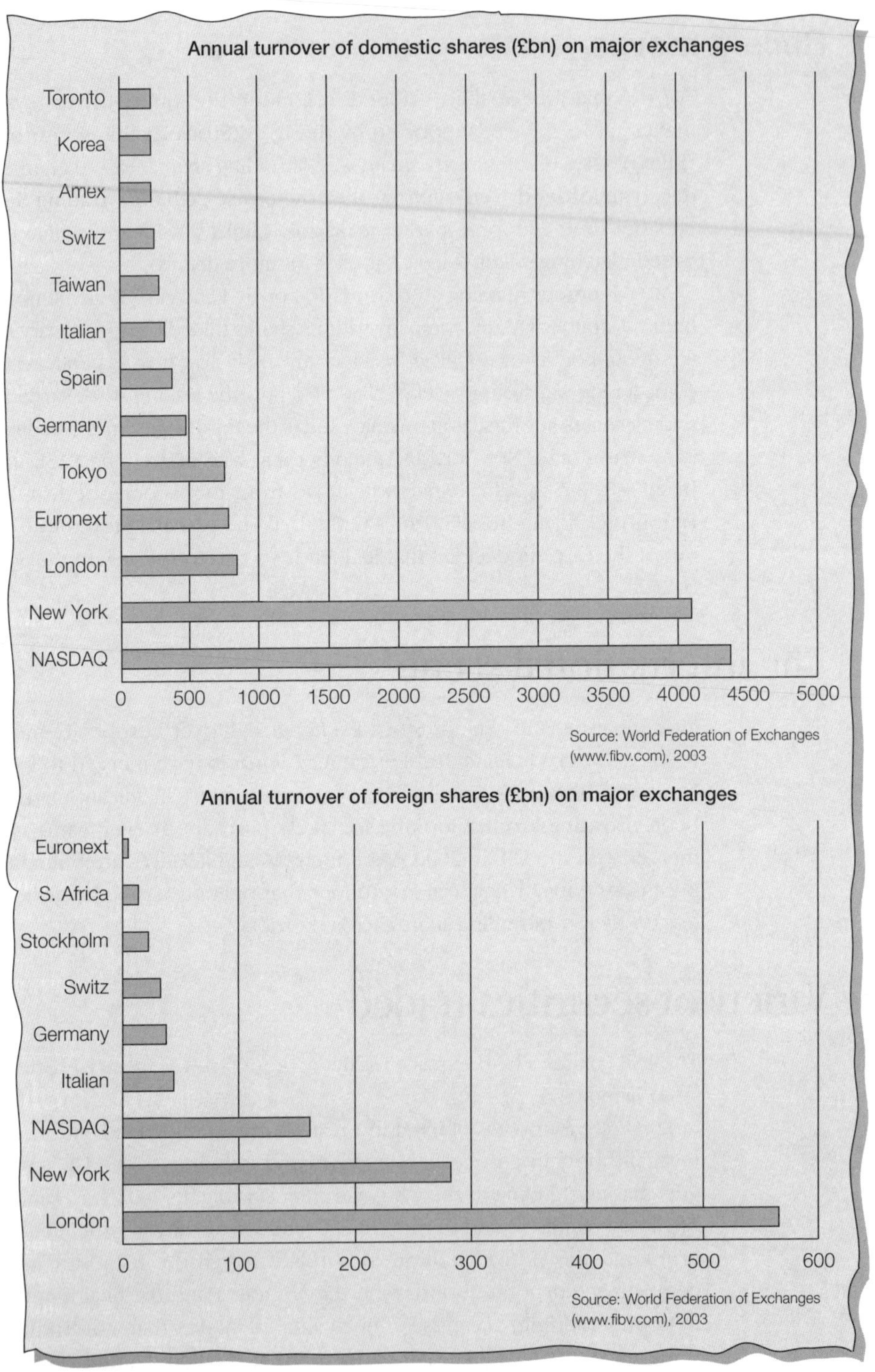

Exhibit 3.2 Domestic and foreign equity turnover on major exchanges

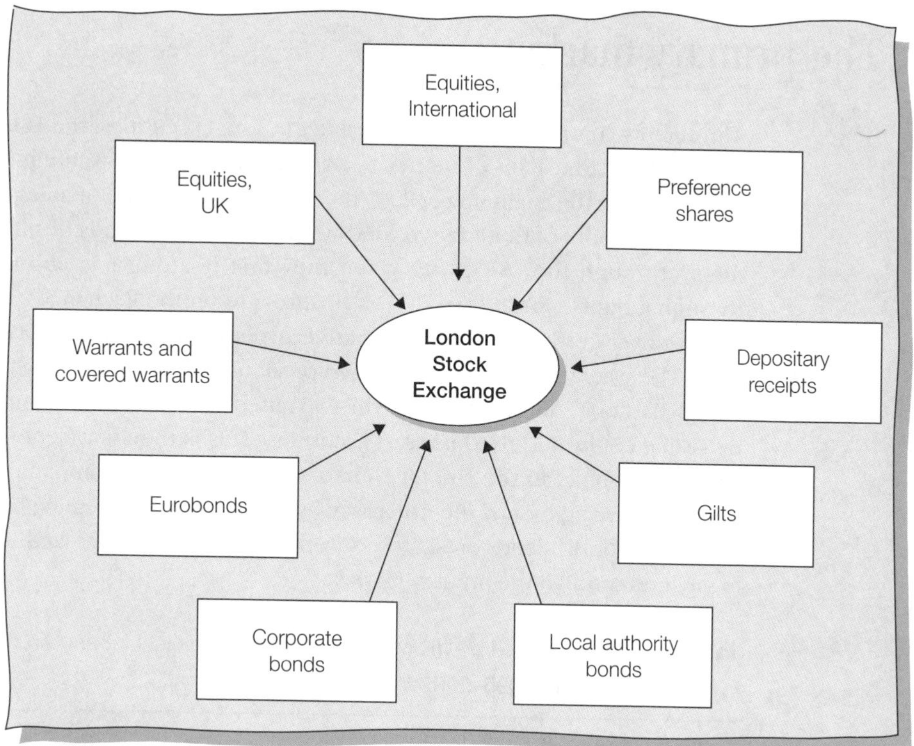

Exhibit 3.3 Types of financial security sold on the London Stock Exchange

Specialist securities, such as **warrants** and **covered warrants**, are normally bought and traded by a few investors who are particularly knowledgeable in investment matters (warrants are a type of derivative security and are discussed in Chapter 10).

In addition to trading shares of overseas companies (**international equities**), there has been the rapid development of a market in **depositary receipts** since 1994. These are certificates that can be bought and sold, and represent evidence of ownership of a company's shares held by a depository. Thus, an Indian company's shares could be packaged in, say, groups of five by a depository (usually a bank) which then sells a certificate representing a bundle of shares. The depositary receipt can be denominated in a currency other than the corporation's domestic currency and dividends can be received in the currency of the depositary receipt (say, pounds) rather than the currency of the original shares (say, rupees). These are attractive securities for sophisticated international investors because they may be more liquid and more easily traded than the underlying shares.

The LSE is both a *primary market* and a *secondary market*. The primary market is where firms and another organisations can raise finance by selling financial securities to investors. The secondary market is where existing securities are sold by one investor to another.

The primary market

Through its control of the primary market in listed securities, the LSE has succeeded in encouraging large sums of money to flow annually to firms wanting to invest and grow (Table 3.1). By the beginning of 2003 there were over 2000 companies on the Official List. The vast majority of these raised funds by selling shares, bonds or other financial instruments through the LSE either when they first floated or in subsequent years (e.g. through a rights issue). Over 700 companies are on the Exchange's market for smaller and younger companies, the **Alternative Investment Market (AIM)**, which started in 1995. These companies, too, have raised precious funds to allow growth.

In 2002 alone UK-listed firms on the LSE raised new capital amounting to £103.4 billion by selling equity and fixed interest securities. This is the equivalent of £1,753 per man, woman and child in the UK. Of course, in the same year companies would also have been transferring money the other way by, for example, redeeming bonds, paying interest on debt or dividends on shares. Nevertheless, it is clear that large sums are raised for companies through the primary market.

Table 3.1 Money raised by UK companies on the Official List and on the Alternative Investment Market, 1995–2002

Year	Total raised for listed companies (£bn)	New companies		Other issues[a]		Eurobonds		AIM	
		Number of companies	Money raised (£bn)	Number of Issues	Money raised (£bn)	Number of Issues	Money raised (£bn)	Number of Issues	Money raised (£bn)
1995	37.6	190	3.0	1,710	9.9	903	24.8	162	0.09
1996	55.2	230	10.6	1,773	8.9	1,026	35.7	388	0.82
1997	57.2	135	7.1	1,486	6.5	1,167	43.6	454	0.69
1998	66.8	124	4.2	851	6.8	926	55.8	432	0.56
1999	100.8	106	5.4	895	9.9	1,022	85.5	562	0.93
2000	125.9	172	11.4	897	14.0	1,012	100.6	1,038	3.07
2001	105.1	113	6.9	869	14.8	935	83.3	787	1.13
2002	103.4	59	5.1	764	11.7	817	86.6	707	0.98

[a] 'Other issues' are for companies that have been on the Stock Exchange for many years raising more funds through, say, a rights issue or bond sale.

Source: London Stock Exchange (www.londonstockexchange.com).

Each year there is great interest and excitement inside dozens of companies as they prepare for flotation. The year 2002 was a watershed year for 59 UK and 9 foreign companies that joined the Official List, and 160 that joined the AIM.

Given the high costs associated with gaining a place on the Official List in the first place (£400,000 or more) it may be a surprise to find that the **market capitalisation** (share price × number of shares in issue) of the majority of quoted companies is less than £100 million – see Exhibit 3.4.

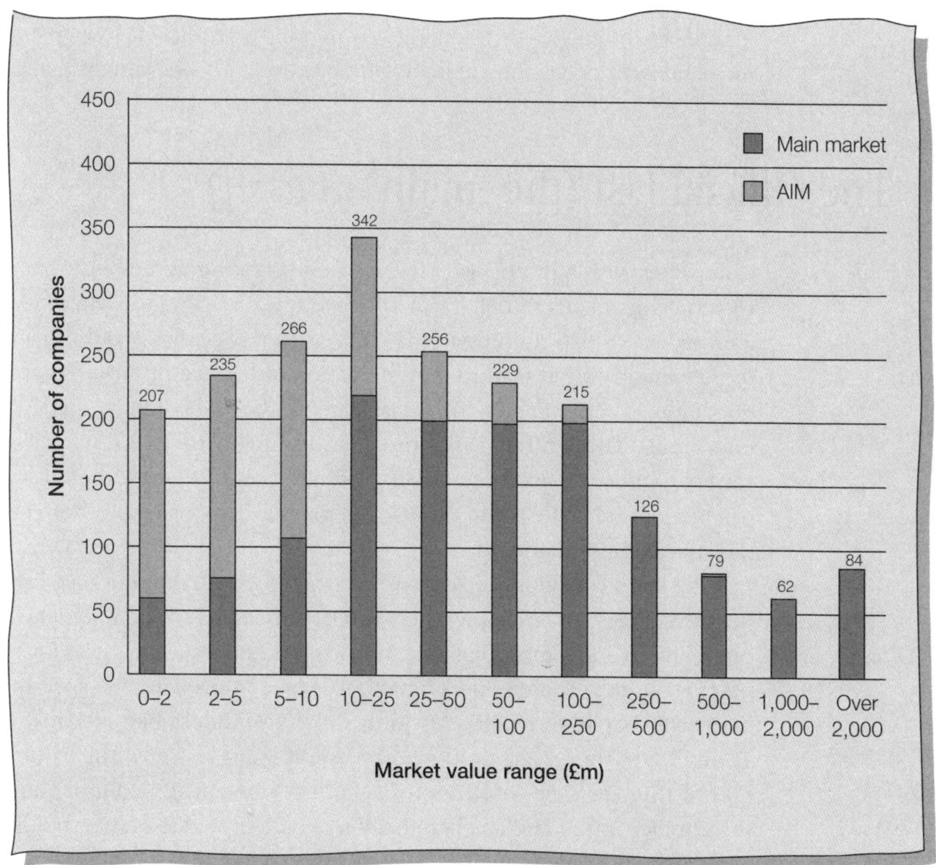

Exhibit 3.4 Distribution of UK companies by equity market value, 30 June 2003

Source: London Stock Exchange website (www.londonstockexchange.com/cmsattach/2152.pdf)

The secondary market

The amount of shareholder-to-shareholder trade is very large. On a typical day over 100,000 bargains (trades between buyers and sellers) are struck between investors in UK shares, worth over £7 billion. The size of bargains varies enormously, from £500 trades by private investors to hundreds of millions by the major funds, but the average is around £60,000. In addition to these domestic equities, a further 60,000 bargains in foreign shares, worth over £10 billion are struck on an average day. This is a market for the bigger players, with average bargain values of over £180,000.

The secondary market turnover exceeds the primary market sales. Indeed, the amount raised in the primary equity market in a *year* is about the same as the value of shares that trade hands *daily* in the secondary market. This high level of activity ensures a liquid market enabling shares to change ownership speedily, at low cost and without large movements in price – one of the main objectives of a well-run exchange.

The Official List (the 'main' market)

Companies wishing to be listed have to sign a **listing agreement** that commits directors to certain standards of behaviour and levels of reporting to shareholders. To '**go public**' and become a **listed company** is a major step for a firm, and the substantial sums of money involved can lead to a new, accelerated phase of business growth. Obtaining a quotation as a listed company is not a step to be taken lightly; the legal implications are enormous. The **United Kingdom Listing Authority (UKLA)**, part of *the Financial Services Authority (FSA)* rigorously enforces a set of demanding rules, and the directors will be put under the strain of new and greater responsibilities both at the time of flotation and in subsequent years.

Many firms consider the stresses and the costs worth it because listing brings numerous advantages. For example, there are large benefits to shareholders. The Official List is one of the world's most dynamic, transparent and liquid markets for trading shares and other securities. Shareholders benefit from the availability of a speedy, cheap secondary market if they wish to sell. Not only do shareholders like to know that they can sell shares when they want to, they may simply want to know the value of their holdings even if they have no intention of selling at present. By contrast, an unquoted firm's shareholders often find it very difficult to assess the value of their holding.

Also, the floated companies gain access to a large pool of investment capital allowing firms to grow. Because investors in financial securities with a stock market quotation are assured that they are generally able to sell their shares quickly, cheaply and with a reasonable degree of certainty about the price, they are willing to pay a higher price than they would if selling was slow, or expensive, or the sale price was subject to much uncertainty caused by illiquidity.

The status and visibility of a company can be enhanced by being included on the prestigious Official List. Banks and other financial institutions generally have more confidence in a quoted firm and therefore are more likely to provide funds at lower cost. Their confidence is raised because the company's activities are now subject to detailed scrutiny. The publicity surrounding the process of gaining a quotation may have a positive impact on the image of the firm in the eyes of customers, suppliers and employees, and so may lead to a beneficial effect on day-to-day business.

In order to create a stable market and encourage investors to place their money with companies, the UKLA tries to minimise the risk of investing by ensuring that the firms obtaining a quotation abide by high standards and conform to strict rules. For example, the directors are required to prepare a detailed **prospectus ('listing particulars')** to inform potential investors about the company. (More on this in Chapter 16.)

All companies obtaining a full listing must ensure that at least **25% of their share capital is in public hands**, to ensure that the shares are capable of being traded actively on the market. 'Public' means people or organisations not associated with the directors or major shareholders. If a reasonably active secondary market is not established, trading may become stultified and the shares may become illiquid.

The UKLA tries to ensure that the **'quality' of the company** is sufficiently high to appeal to the investment community. The management team must have the necessary range and depth, and there must be a high degree of continuity and stability of management over recent years. Investors do not like to be over-reliant on the talents of one individual and so will expect a team of able directors, including some non-executives, and an appropriately qualified finance director. The UKLA usually insists that a company has a **track record** (in the form of accounting figures) stretching back at least **three years**.

The company floating on the Official List hires a **sponsor** (**issuing house**) to advise on the process and provide reassurance to the UKLA and the investment community about the quality of the company. The sponsor (approved by the UKLA) may be a merchant bank, stockbroker or other professional adviser. Even though the sponsor's fee is paid by the company floating, the sponsor is an organisation with a high reputation to preserve and will not hesitate to drop a bad company or suggest changes to a mediocre one.

Company directors have to jump through hoops to obtain a listing in the first place. But even after flotation they are unable to relax. The UKLA insists on '**continuing obligations**' designed to protect or enlighten shareholders. All **price-sensitive information** has to be given to the market as soon as possible and there must be '**full and accurate disclosure**'. Information is price-sensitive if it might influence the share price or the trading in the shares. Investors need to be sure that they are not disadvantaged by market distortions caused by some participants having the benefit of superior information. Public announcements will be required in a number of instances, for example: the development of major new products; the signing of significant contracts; details of acquisitions; a sale of large assets; a change in directors; or a decision to pay a dividend.

There are strict rules concerning the **buying and selling of the company's shares by its own directors** once it is on the stock exchange. Directors are prevented from dealing for a minimum period (normally two months) prior to an announcement of regularly recurring information such as annual results. They are also forbidden to deal before the announcement of matter of an exceptional nature involving unpublished information that is potentially price-sensitive. These rules apply to any employee in possession of such information. All dealings in the company's shares by directors have to be reported to the market

The Alternative Investment Market

There is a long-recognised need for small young companies to be able to raise equity capital. However, many of these are excluded from the Official List because of the cost of obtaining and maintaining a listing. London, like many developed stock exchanges, has an alternative equity market that sets less stringent rules and regulations for joining or remaining quoted.

Lightly regulated or unregulated markets have a continuing dilemma. If the regulation is too lax, scandals of fraud or incompetence will arise, damaging the image and credibility of the market, and thus reducing the flow of investor funds to companies. The German small companies market, Neuer Markt, was forced to close down in 2002 because of the loss of confidence amongst investors: there were some blatant frauds as well as over-hyped expectations, and share prices fell an average of 95 per cent. On the other hand, if the market is too tightly regulated, with more company investigations, more information disclosure and a requirement for longer trading track records prior to flotation, the associated costs and inconvenience will deter many companies from seeking a quotation.

The driving philosophy behind the AIM is to offer young and developing companies access to new sources of finance, while providing investors with the opportunity to buy and sell shares in a trading environment run, regulated and marketed by the LSE. Efforts were made to keep the costs down and make the rules as simple as possible. In contrast to the Official List, there is no requirement for AIM companies to have been in business for a minimum three-year period or for a set proportion of their shares to be in public hands – if they wish to sell only 1 per cent or 5 per cent of the shares to outsiders then that is OK. However, investors have some degree of reassurance about the quality of companies coming to the market. These firms have to appoint, and retain at all times, a **nominated adviser** and **nominated broker**. The nominated adviser ('**nomad**') is selected by the corporation from a Stock Exchange approved register. These advisers have demonstrated to the Exchange that they have sufficient experience and qualifications to act as a 'quality controller', confirming to the LSE that the company has complied with the rules. Nominated brokers have an important role to play in bringing buyers and sellers of shares together. Investors in the company are reassured that at least one broker is ready to help shareholders to trade. The adviser and broker are to be retained throughout the company's life on the AIM. They have high reputations and it is regarded as a very bad sign if either of them abruptly refuses further association with a firm.

AIM companies are also expected to comply with strict rules regarding the publication of price-sensitive information and the quality of annual and interim reports (there is more on accounts in Chapter 11). Upon flotation, a prospectus is required. This even goes so far as to state the directors' unspent convictions and all bankruptcies of companies where they were directors. The LSE charges companies a few thousand pounds per year to maintain a quotation on AIM. If to this is added the cost of financial advisers and of management time spent communicating with institutions and investors, the annual cost of being quoted on AIM runs into tens of thousands of pounds. This can be a deterrent for many companies. AIM companies are not bound by the Listing Rules administered by the UKLA but instead are subject to the AIM rules, written and administered by the LSE.

However, there are cost savings compared with the Official List. The flotation prospectus is less detailed and therefore cheaper. The annual expense of managing a quotation is less. For example, AIM companies do not have to disclose as much information as companies on the Official List. Price-sensitive information will have to be published, but normally this will require only an electronic message from the adviser to the Exchange rather than a circular to shareholders.

AIM is not just a stepping-stone for companies planning to graduate to the Official List. It has many attractive features in its own right – see Exhibit 3.5.

Taking Aim to fire smaller ambitions

More companies are retreating from the main exchange, writes **David Blackwell**

The number of companies moving from the official list to Aim is growing, while the number graduating from Aim to the full list is shrinking.

So far this year, more than 20 companies have moved to Aim – and most of them have tiny market capitalisations.

Four years ago the flow was overwhelmingly towards the official list, with 25 companies moving from Aim while just five went in the other direction. But in 2000, for the first time, fewer companies graduated to the official list than moved to Aim. Last year, 36 companies switched to Aim, with only seven moving to the official list.

Aim was set up to provide a less costly route to market for young and growing companies than the official list.

But the trend now is for small companies, possibly with a recent history of restructuring to move to Aim, sometimes after a lengthy sojourn on the official list.

They want to cut costs and they are also hoping to put themselves back on the radar screens of the growing number of institutions interested in investing in Aim.

Ensor Holdings, a building materials group, said in April: 'A transfer to Aim would result in the simplification of administration and reporting requirements, with a consequential reduction in the costs associated with being a public company, and should help to keep down the costs associated with making further capital transactions.'

Cradley Group, a lithographic printer, said: 'The lower costs of maintaning a quotation on Aim and the less onerous requirements will lead to cost savings.'

Exhibit 3.5 The growing strength of the AIM

Source: *Financial Times* 26 July 2002

techMARK and the other MARKs

In 1999, at the height of the high technology fever, the LSE launched a 'market within a market' called techMARK. This is part of the Official List and is therefore not really a separate market. It is a grouping of technology companies on the Official List. One of the reasons for its creation was that many companies failing to fulfil the requirement of a three-year account history necessary to join the Official list had relatively high market values and desired the advantages of being on a prestigious market. The LSE relaxed its rule and permitted a listing if only **one year's accounts** are available for techMARK companies. This allowed investors to invest through a well-regulated exchange in companies at an early stage of development, such as Freeserve and lastminute.com. The LSE does insist that all companies joining techMARK have a **market capitalisation of at least £50 million** and they must **sell at least £20 million** of new or existing shares when floating. Also at least **25 per cent of their shares must have a free float** (in public hands) and they must publish **quarterly reports** on the company's activities, including financial and non-financial (e.g. number of website hits) operating data.

Another reason for creating techMARK as a separate segment of the Official List is to give technology companies a higher profile and visibility, resulting in more attention from investors and research analysts, and enticing more technology-led companies to seek a public quote. Most of the companies on techMARK are firms that were previously on the general part of the Official List, such as Vodafone and AstraZeneca, but it has managed to attract a few dozen young, fast-growing companies as well.

Critics say it is less like a market than an index (merely a measure of how high-tech shares are performing), and it has done little to address the issue of stimulating investment in technology. It was also seen as a competitor to AIM, which is the home of some exciting technological companies.

The LSE recently launched some more 'markets within markets'. These are called **'attribute' markets**. **techMARK mediscience** is focused on healthcare companies. **landMARK** is a market for quoted regional companies. To create landMARK the LSE allocated the 2,200+ quoted companies to regional categories (e.g. East Anglia has 122 companies) this ensures that they 'stand apart . . . attracting the interest of both local investors and the media' (LSE website). **extraMARK** is an attribute market for investment companies and products – the first products are **exchange traded funds** – for more details see Chapter 5).

OFEX

Companies that do not want to pay the costs of a flotation on one of the markets run by the LSE (this can range from £100,000 to £1 million just for getting on the market in the first place) and the ongoing annual costs could go for a '**secondary market trading facil-**

ity' on **OFEX**. By having their shares quoted on OFEX companies provide a service to their shareholders: allowing them to buy and sell shares at reasonable cost. It also allows the company to gain access to capital, for example, by selling more shares in a rights issue, without submitting to the rigour and expense of a quotation on LSE.

OFEX was set up by the broker, J.P. Jenkins in 1995. It is a dealing facility with few of the rules that apply to the Official List or AIM. However, there is an annual fee of a few thousand pounds. OFEX companies are generally very small and often brand new, but there are also some long-established and well-known firms, such as Thwaites and Arsenal Football Club.

OFEX uses its electronic small company news service, **Newstrack**, as the basis for 'trading'. This runs on four of the City's main financial news services and acts as a noticeboard for company news. Jenkins makes a market in a company's shares by giving two prices to brokers who enquire about a share: the price at which it is willing to buy and a price at which it is willing to sell. The spread between these prices is normally a maximum of around 5 per cent. Winterflood and Hoodless Brennan are to become the second and third market makers in 2004. Having competing market makers should improve the position for investors considerably, leading (hopefully) to greater liquidity and tighter bid–offer spreads.

OFEX is not a **recognised investment exchange (RIE)** under the law, therefore securities traded on OFEX are defined as **unlisted** and **unquoted** and are not traded **on-exchange**. OFEX has now been formally separated from J.P. Jenkins so it can be regulated by the FSA. While it is termed 'a regulated exchange', market investors must note that the companies on OFEX are not subject to the same rigorous rules as the Official List or AIM. OFEX is described as a **'prescribed' market**, which means that companies have to adhere to its code of conduct: insider trading by directors is prohibited; companies raising fresh capital on OFEX must have a sponsor (e.g. a stockbroker, accountant or lawyer); OFEX insists on seeing a prospectus produced to raise funds for companies, and expects this to comply with certain minimum standards as laid down in law. There are over 160 companies with a combined market capitalisation of around £1,500 million paying for an OFEX dealing facility. Note that: the criteria for companies gaining admission do not include compliance with the UKLA rules, so investors have far fewer quality assurances about these companies. Also, the secondary market can be relatively illiquid, with the total number of transactions in a typical month for *all* companies at around 1,000–2,000. So shareholders need to be wary, but it is better than no secondary market at all.

Exhibit 3.6 describes some recent challenges to OFEX, including another market from J.P. Jenkins.

New front in battle for small companies

David Blackwell, Small Talk

Aim and Ofex are well established as the second and third tiers of the London market – but a fourth tier is emerging, sometimes poaching their clients.

ShareMark, an internet-based facility for dealing in shares through regular auctions, is starting to attract some companies from Aim.

The lesser known 535x, a bulletin board that posts trades between brokers, has just four companies signed up – one already listed on Ofex and another also listed on ShareMark. A fortnight ago, JP Jenkins, the firm that founded Ofex, entered the fray with a web-based trading facility for companies unquoted elsewhere.

Barry Hocken, head of Jenkins' www.jpjl.co.uk, believes the facility is deepening rather than fragmenting the market. 'It is an alternative platform for companies not trading on any other exchange.'

It is still early days – but the first trade on jpjl has already been completed, in Dart Valley Railway shares. Only a single trade has been done on www.535x.com, in Trixter, a maker of exercise bikes.

Richard Poulden is chairman of Eyebright, which listed its shares on ShareMark after raising £2.2m independently in order to roll out a chain of eye clinics, the first of which is due to open in Hull in November. He has also posted the shares on 535x 'partly because I am a missionary who wants to see smallcap shares traded on an easy facility'.

The estimated cost of belonging to both is about £3,000 a year – far lower than listing on Aim or Ofex. 'I am trying to provide a facility for my shareholders – but if no-one is using it I probably should not be spending the company's money,' said Mr Poulden, whose ambition is to take the company to Aim.

Exhibit 3.6 Recent challenges to OFEX

Source: *Financial Times* 8 September 2003

Who owns UK shares?

There was a transformation in the pattern of share ownership in Britain over the last four decades of the twentieth century. The tax-favoured status of pension funds made them a very attractive vehicle for savings, resulting in billions of pounds being put into them each year. Most of this money was invested in equities, making pension funds the most influential investing group on the stock market.

Insurance companies similarly rose in significance, doubling their share of quoted equities from 10 per cent to about 20 per cent by the early 1990s (see Table 3.2). The group that decreased in importance was ordinary individuals holding shares directly.

They used to dominate the market, with 54 per cent of quoted shares in 1963. By the late 1980s this had declined to about 20 per cent. Investors tended to switch from direct investment to pooled (collective) investment vehicles. Another factor was the increasing share of equities held by overseas investors: only 7 per cent in 1963, but 32 per cent by 2001. In 1980 only 3 million individuals held shares. After the privatisation programme of the 1980s and the flotations of Abbey National, the water companies and regional electricity companies the numbers rose to 11 million. The stampede of building societies to market in 1997 produced a record 16 million individual shareholders. This has now fallen back to under 12 million (27 per cent of the adult population), and many of these own only one or two stocks.

Although the mode of investment has changed from direct to indirect, Britain remains a society with a deep interest in the stock market. Very few people are immune from the performance of the Exchange. The vast majority have a pension plan or endowment savings scheme, an individual savings account (ISA) or a unit trust investment. Some have all four. The **equity culture**, or trend toward '**equitisation**', is even stronger in some other countries. In the USA, for instance, almost one-half of all households now own shares (either directly or through mutual funds and self-select pension funds).

Table 3.2 Ownership of quoted shares in Britain, distribution by sector (%)

Sector	1963	1975	1989	1997
Individuals	54.0	37.5	17.7	20.5
Pension funds	6.4	16.8	34.2	27.9
Insurance cos.	10.0	15.9	17.3	23.1
Others (banks, public sector, unit trusts, overseas, etc.)	29.6	29.6	30.8	28.5

Source: Office for National Statistics. Crown Copyright 1997. Reproduced by permission of the Controller of HMSO and the Office for National Statistics.

The role of stock exchanges

The following is a summary of what exchanges do:

- Supervision of trading to ensure fairness and efficiency.
- The authorisation and regulation of market participants such as brokers and market makers.
- Creation of an environment in which prices are formed efficiently and without distortion (**price discovery**). This requires not only regulation of a high order and low

transaction costs but also a liquid market in which there are many buyers and sellers, permitting investors to enter or exit quickly without moving the price.

- Organisation of the **settlement** of transactions (after the deal has been struck the buyer must pay for the shares and the shares must be transferred to the new owners – see Chapter 4).
- The regulation of the admission of companies to the exchange and the regulation of companies on the exchange.
- The dissemination of information (trading data, prices and company announcements). Investors are more willing to trade if prompt and complete information about trades and prices is available.

In recent years there has been a questioning of the need for stock exchanges to carry out all these activities. In the case of the LSE the settlement of transactions was long ago handed over to an organisation called **CREST** (discussed in Chapter 4). In 2001 the responsibility for authorising the listing of companies was transferred to the UKLA arm of the FSA. In 2002 the LSE's **Regulatory News Service** (which distributes important company announcements and other price-sensitive financial news) was told that it will have to compete with other distribution platforms outside the LSE's control. This gives listed companies a choice of route for publicising crucial information. Despite all this upheaval, the LSE still retains an important role in the supervision of trading and the distribution of trading and pricing information.

Useful websites

www.londonstockexchange.com	London Stock Exchange
www.fsa.gov.uk/ukla	The United Kingdom Listing Authority
www.fsa.gov.uk	The Financial Services Authority
www.ofex.com	OFEX
www.ft.com	The *Financial Times*
www.fibv.com	World Federation of Exchanges

4

Buying and selling shares

There is absolutely no reason to be in awe of stockbrokers, nor of the process of buying or selling shares. Stockbrokers need you more than you need them. It is a highly competitive business, with dozens of brokers offering to help you make a transaction – so much so that you can now deal for less than £10. These people are very keen on offering you a service. So regard yourself as being in charge and shop around.

This chapter will allow you to find the service that suits you best. You will, after reading it, be more informed about the different levels of service that you can ask for. For example, do you want to choose shares yourself without advice? In which case you will be looking for a cheap and efficient '**execution-only**' service. On the other hand, you may welcome **advice** from a broker. This service will cost more, but not as much as when you ask a broker to **manage your portfolio at their discretion**.

This chapter also considers what to look for when choosing a broker, and describes what happens behind the scenes after you have instructed your broker to act. Stockbroking has moved so far away from the days of long lunches and high charges that a high proportion of dealing is now done without the need to speak to a broker – via the Internet. Again online dealing is a highly competitive market and you just need a modicum of knowledge to get the most appropriate service for you.

Stockbroker services

If you wish to buy or sell shares on the London Stock Exchange you have to do it through a stockbroker. There are two types of broker: **retail** (also called **private-client**) **brokers** act for investors; **corporate brokers** act on behalf of companies (e.g. providing advice on market conditions or representing the company to the market).

Before being able to deal you will have to **register** with a private-client broker – this simply involves providing a few details about yourself. The broker will check your creditworthiness (e.g. banker's reference). Many brokers then set up **an account** so that you can deposit money into it. This will reassure the broker that you will have money to pay for a trade in a timely fashion (rather than having to wait for a cheque in the post). There are three main types of service provided by retail brokers (hereafter referred to simply as 'brokers'): execution-only, advisory and discretionary. Which of these is most suitable for you depends on your circumstances.

Execution-only (or dealing-only) service

Here the broker carries out your purchase or sale order as instructed without offering any investment advice. It is the cheapest way to buy and sell shares. A typical minimum **commission** is around £15–£20, but can be as little as £7.50. These figures would apply if you were buying, say, £1,000 of shares. Charges normally rise as the size of order increases. So for a £5,000 bargain £20–£30 is more typical. However, brokers have become so keen to gain business that it is possible to deal for £15 or so, even for orders of £25,000. Some brokers charge even when you are not dealing through a 'quarterly inactivity charge'. This is usually around £10 for each quarter you do not trade. The justification is that the fee covers the cost of distributing dividends and issuing statements. Shop around! There are over 50 dealing-only brokers in the UK to choose from. This type of service is very popular, with over 90% of investors now in the habit of using an execution-only broker. Around 10 million orders are completed this way each year. The instruction to buy or sell can be communicated through a variety of channels including the telephone, the Internet, by post or in person (e.g. walking into a high street bank with a brokerage arm). Execution-only dealing is particularly appropriate if you have the time and inclination to make investment decisions on your own. If you have greater confidence in your own research and judgement than the broker's, then execution-only is the service for you. The downside is that you will not be able to discuss your ideas with a broker. It is also said that you will miss out on hot tips – but then, selecting on the basis of hot tips is not investing but speculating, and is generally unprofitable (according to the academic evidence).

Advisory dealing service

Under this arrangement the broker will give you investment advice, but the decision on whether to buy or sell rests with you. The broker will not take any investment decisions without your authority. Roughly one-quarter of UK investors have opened these 'dealing with advice' accounts. This is the more traditional stockbroking service in which the broker knows the client sufficiently well for meaningful discussion of ideas and strategies. It allows the investor to test ideas with someone who is in touch with the market full-time. Also, broker reports on companies or sectors, newsletters or market reviews may be sent to clients. Tax advice and portfolio valuation may also be forthcoming. The advisory service costs more than execution-only. The broker earns money through charging commission on each deal rather than by charging for advice directly. A typical minimum transaction charge would be between £20 and £50. This rises to £40–£100 for £5,000 deals and £200–£300 for £25,000 transactions. The cost varies tremendously from broker to broker, as does the quality of the service. Some advisory brokers go further for their clients than others. While many will wait for a call from an investor before offering advice, others are more willing to initiate the contact. Taking the initiative one stage further, some brokers now differentiate between their advisory dealing service and their **advisory portfolio management service**. The advisory dealing service is taken to be a reactive one in which the broker gives advice after being asked for it, whereas under the advisory portfolio management service the client is contacted once or twice per month with advice on their portfolio. With the advisory portfolio management approach the broker is knowledgeable about the client's overall financial profile and can advise appropriately. One drawback with this type of arrangement is that the investor might be encouraged to deal frequently – good for brokers but, more often than not, very bad for the wealth of investors. You can ask some brokers to accept a fee based on the size of the investment fund they handle for you, that is, an asset-based fee system. This removes some of the incentive for the stockbroker to **churn** your portfolio (make unnecessary trades to generate fees). It also gives an incentive to increase the size of the pot. Thus the broker may choose to go into cash rather than sticking with shares at times of market exuberance, so that total asset size is preserved.

Discretionary service

Under this type of service the broker is paid to manage the investor's portfolio at the broker's discretion. Thus the broker takes decisions on which shares to buy and sell without consulting the investor on each deal. The client is informed after the event. Giving the broker authorisation to act before getting the investor's approval allows the snatching of good opportunities as they arise in fast-moving markets (one of the common complaints of advisory brokers is that their clients are not always near a telephone – oddly enough, they like to live a life beyond their portfolio – and so fleeting chances are missed as permission to buy is not given quickly). Furthermore, many clients simply do not want to spend time managing their portfolios. They don't want to devote effort to developing investment skills. They therefore place their money in the hands of professionals. Prior to running your portfolio the broker will meet you to gain an understanding of your particular circumstances, your investment aims and any restrictions you would like to place on the portfolio (e.g. no investment in tobacco or arms).

Only 5 per cent of UK investors have discretionary portfolio management accounts with brokers. One of the reasons for the low take-up is that brokers generally insist on a minimum portfolio size of £50,000 (although a few go as low as £25,000). Some set the minimum at £100,000 or even higher. The average discretionary portfolio is £270,000. Another reason is the cost of the service. Not only are investors charged commission (at about the same level as advisory clients) on each transaction but they are also charged an **annual fee** related to the total value of the portfolio. This is generally between 0.5 and 1 per cent. Some brokers have high dealing charges and low annual fees, whereas others charge a mere £20 or so for each transaction but load the costs on to the annual fee. Naturally the amount you pay depends on the frequency of trading – the discretion which you have granted to the broker. Be on your guard against churning. It is disturbing that very few brokers offer to charge on the basis of the returns they achieve. Exhibit 4.1 demonstrates the importance of having a clear and agreed framework for the management of your portfolio.

This week: decisions to be regretted

Isabel Berwick Your Money

I have a portfolio of shares managed on a discretionary basis by a well-known stockbroker. The management instruction for the portfolio is that it should be managed for 'growth: an overall balance of low, medium and high-risk stocks'.

However, the shares bought by my broker seem to be entirely higher-risk and my £87,800 investment is now worth £18,000. Do I have any claim against my broker for compensation for some of my losses on the grounds that my portfolio has been mismanaged?

Investment performance complaints are a notoriously difficult area because clients can't claim compensation just because an investment performs badly (otherwise we'd all be doing it). Most complaints about investment performance hinge on the original contract and/or the suitability of the advice. The first step is to contact the broker and ask how to make a complaint.

Once you have been through the firm's internal complaints process you may reach a settlement with the company. If you don't, you can take the dispute to the Financial Ombudsman Service.

For those with similar problems, there's an interesting discussion about performance complaints on the Financial Ombudsman's website or in its November 2001 newsletter.

Exhibit 4.1 Complaining about discretionary service

Source: *Financial Times* 29/30 June 2002

Choosing a stockbroker

There are many ways of finding a stockbroker. The London Stock Exchange (*www.londonstockexchange.com*) publishes a complete list of its members. The Association of Private Client Investment Managers and Stockbrokers (APCIMS) provides lots of information on their website *www.apcims.co.uk* (or telephone 020 7247 7080), including stockbrokers' contact names, addresses, telephone numbers and an outline of the kinds of services offered. Investors are regularly surveyed for their opinions on broker performance and costs in investment magazines such as *Investors Chronicle*. Investors also find brokers through personal recommendation.

Choosing a broker means selecting the right combination of cost and services. The following selection criteria may help you draw up a shortlist of brokers and make a final selection:

- **Charges.** Of course, the lower the commissions for trading the better, but you should allow for the possibility of improved service at extra cost. The charging structure will make a big difference to your choice of broker. For example, an investor who does not want to pay for advice and trades many times each month with bargain sizes of around £5,000 will prefer a broker who charges a low fixed rate regardless of bargain size, say £20 each time. Another trader, who buys and sells £1,000 of shares, may prefer a broker who charges a percentage of the amount of the trade, say, 1.5 per cent. If you are a '**buy-and-hold**' investor, with few transactions, commission costs will not be a great concern. But if you are very active the charges mount up dramatically. Then you may opt for the cheapest mode of transacting – usually online, though some telephone brokers can also be very cheap.
- **Location.** The possibility of being able to talk to a broker face-to-face may lead investors to favour a local broker. This can be particularly valuable for discretionary and advisory portfolio management, where the broker needs to know the investor's circumstances and investing objectives. Local brokers may also be knowledgeable about companies in the region.
- **Contact.** In surveys investors usually place the ability to contact brokers at the top of their worry list. There are many complaints about telephone lines being busy when a client wishes to deal. People can be put on hold for 20 minutes or more. This can seem like an eternity when you are trying to sell and the market is falling like a stone. Brokers are also criticised for not calling back when they promised to do so. Online orders are often executed very slowly at busy times, as the IT systems suffer from overload. Unfortunately, this is one of those factors that you do not really find out about until you experience it. However, it might be worth asking other clients of your shortlisted brokers if they have any complaints.
- **Administration.** The second factor most complained about is the quality of the administration. Record keeping is sometimes poor, as is the administration of dividends and taxation matters. Often the paperwork reaches the investor weeks after the event. You do not have to put up with this: other brokers are highly praised for the speed and efficiency of their administration.
- **Expertise.** You need a broker who is well resourced, has access to high-quality external data and attracts talented managers. This is especially important if you are asking for portfolio management services. You do not want your nest-egg managed by a graduate trainee trying to learn on the job. Ask what experience the firm has in managing portfolios of the type and size you have in mind.
- **Performance.** Unfortunately independently constructed league tables of portfolio managers' performance are not available and so comparison is all but impossible. Brokers do provide statistics, but you must view them with a sceptical eye.

Recommendation may be your main hope.

- **Interest.** Brokers hold money in cash accounts on behalf of investors. Some of these accounts offer miserly rates of interest of around 1%. If you are likely to deposit substantial sums with a broker you need to ask what rate of interest you will receive prior to the purchase of shares. Also, if you need temporary **credit**, what limit will the broker allow you to go up to?

Here are some other questions you might ask:

- Is the firm authorised by the Financial Services Authority? Your assets may have little protection if it is not. Try *www.fsa.gov.uk/register*, or telephone the FSA help line (0845 606 1234).
- What insurance does the brokerage have in place against fraud or negligence?
- What can you expect in terms of newsletters, company analysis, sector analysis, or regular portfolio valuation?
- Does the broker offer a dealing service for securities other than UK listed shares, such as AIM shares, overseas shares, traded options and bonds?
- If you are trading online, what Internet security features are in place?

About half of UK investors open accounts with more than one broker. One reason for this is to avoid the frustration of not being able to contact a broker – if one is not picking up the phone another might. Investors may also require specific services that their main broker either does not provide or supplies at a higher price.

Finding prices

So, you've chosen your broker and you're ready to invest, but where can you find share prices? Well, one source is the newspapers. The only problem with this is that the information is quite old – at least 12 hours. In the days before the information revolution the only alternative was to telephone your broker and ask for the latest prices. Things have moved on since then.

Some television programmes, such as Bloomberg and CNBC, display prices on the screen in a continuous stream. The problem is that you can wait a long time for the share you are interested in to appear. The Ceefax service on BBC2 and Teletext on Channel 4 display prices for about 400 shares updated every 15 minutes. Channel 4 Teletext also shows prices for over 2,000 shares updated every 60–90 minutes. (BBC1 Ceefax has a similar service for 2,000+ shares, but the updates are less frequent.)

At the height of the Internet and telecommunications bubble around the turn of the millennium, financial websites were falling over each other to offer free real-time prices to investors. Now many of these providers are interested in profits, and not purely in increasing user numbers, and so have started charging for up-to-the-second prices while offering 20-minute delayed prices free. Who is offering what changes from week to week in the fast-moving Internet world so it would be silly to list those currently offering free real-time and those offering 20-minute delay services. Here are some of the players in the business – consult their websites for current services:

www.advfn.com	ADVFN
www.citycomment.co.uk	City Comment
www.teletext.co.uk	Teletext
www.londonmoneymarket.com	London Money Market
www.iii.co.uk	Ample
www.mytrack.co.uk	MyTrack
www.proquote.net	ProQuote
www.wsj.com	WSJ
www.hemscot.net	Hemscott

These websites will offer much more than just share prices, including price histories in the form of charts, trading volume data, and company accounting information.

When you are about to trade shares through a broker it is now possible to have one window open to your online broker displaying current prices, with second and third browser windows open showing real-time prices from other brokers. In this way you can monitor the real-time prices on several websites and satisfy yourself that your broker has achieved a good price. If your broker is consistently poor then switch to another. Some websites (e.g. *www.hemscot.net* and *www.mytrack.co.uk*) show the last 50 or so trades for a company's shares, so it is even possible to see your own trade go through the system.

Increasingly, brokers are offering free **level II prices**. Level II pricing allows you to see on your computer the market makers' orders to buy or sell stocks. You can see both the prices and the size of the orders, which permits a better feel for current supply and demand conditions.

Finally, in the Monday edition of the *Financial Times* telephone numbers are assigned to each company. Calling these **Cityline** numbers will give you up-to-the-second share prices (Cityline also has a general information number, 020 7873 4378, and website, *www.ftcityline.com*). This is not a cheap service, at 60p per minute, but might be useful now and again.

What happens when I buy or sell shares?

Now you've reached the exciting moment of actually buying (or selling) a share. There are many ways you can do this, the most common being via the telephone or the Internet. When you telephone your broker you will be asked your name and account number. Then you will tell the broker that you want to trade in the shares of a particular company and ask for the current price. The broker will give you not one price, but two. The first is the price at which you can buy the shares, the other is the price you can sell at.

What happens is this: when you mention the company name the broker immediately punches into his computer the company code. The computer is linked to the **London Stock Exchange Automated Quotations (SEAQ**™, pronounced 'see-ack') system. This is a computerised system for distributing the prices offered by market makers. So within milliseconds of your mentioning your interest in the company the broker has on his/her screen all the prices that different market makers are willing to pay as well as all the prices they are willing to sell the shares for.[1] A typical SEAQ screen is shown for the company ABC Holdings in Exhibit 4.2. There are about 40 market makers but not all of them choose to make a market in ABC holdings. This screen shows that 11 market makers are offering prices in ABC. The fact that there are a relatively large number of competing organisations willing to quote prices indicates that ABC is a large company with a liquid secondary market in its shares. Small companies may have only three or four market makers willing to display prices on SEAQ. The '**bid**' price is the price at which the market maker is willing to buy. So, in the case of the market maker HSBC the bid price is 105p (bottom left of Exhibit 4.2). The '**offer**' price is the price at which the market makers are willing to sell – HSBC offers these shares at 110p. The spread between the two prices represents a hoped-for return to the market maker.

It can be confusing and time-consuming for the broker to look at all the prices to find the best current rates. Fortunately he does not have to do this as SEAQ displays a '**yellow**

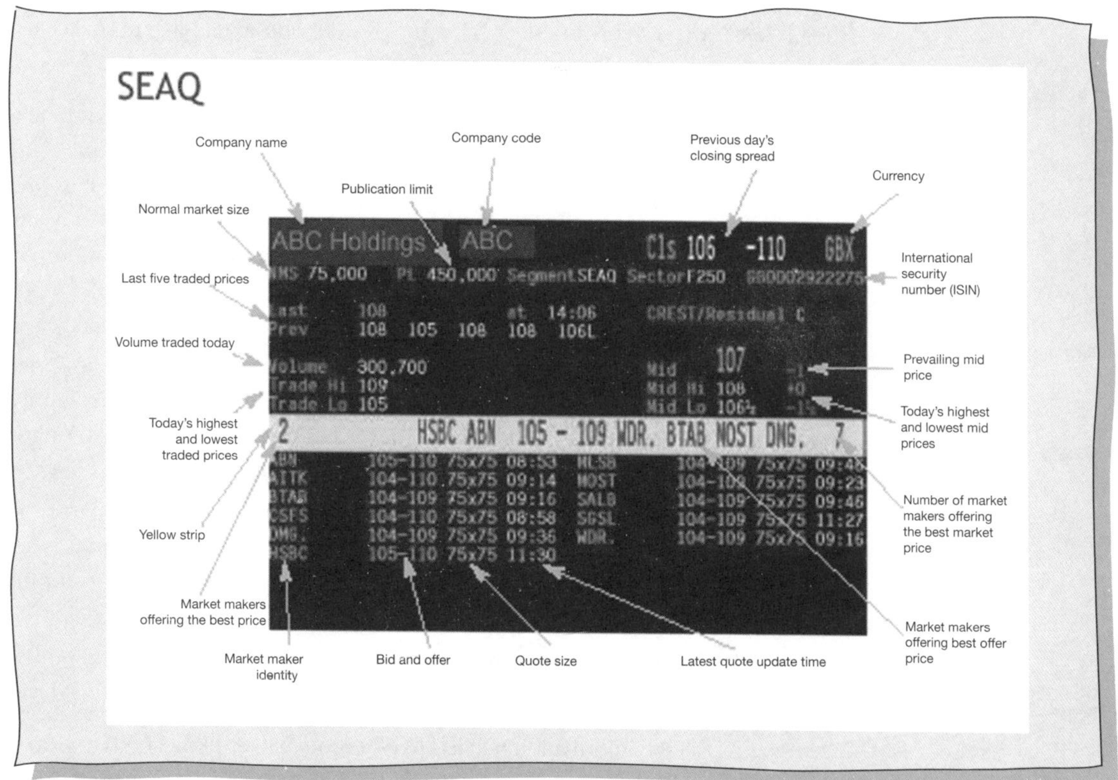

Exhibit 4.2 Typical SEAQ screen

Source: www.londonstockexchange.com/international/pdfs/trading_systems.pdf

[1] If you are dealing online instead of speaking to a broker, you will call up the broker's website using your user ID and password. You will then input the name of the company or its code and view the prices.

strip' above the market makers' prices, which provides the identity of the market makers offering the best bid and offer prices (these are called '**touch prices**'). It is the price in the yellow strip that the broker will immediately report to you over the telephone. In the case of ABC you will be told 105–109. So, if you were happy with 109p you would then instruct your broker to buy, say, 1,000 shares.

The market makers prices are quoted as '**firm**' prices. That is, the LSE insists that the market maker trade at these prices if a broker (investor) has been attracted to do a deal based on the posted prices. They cannot change them when they are contacted by the broker if the transaction is below **the normal market size or NMS**. (This is set at approximately 2.5 per cent of the average daily customer turnover.) It is displayed in the top left of the screen. For deals larger than the NMS the market maker is allowed to change prices and will give the broker a price when he calls. Of course prices can be changed at any time on the SEAQ system so the market maker can adjust in response to the weight of buying and selling pressure, and in response to what other market makers are offering. In the case of ABC the NMS is 75,000, so your 1,000 share order does not require a special price quote and you will be able to trade at the prices shown.

Next, the broker (or the website) asks what type of order you would like to make. You have several options:

- You could ask your broker to execute your order **at best**. This means that the trade is completed immediately at the best price available. If the broker is unable to obtain the shares at the price he quoted to you (because, say the SEAQ market makers' quotes change in the few seconds or minutes between you saying you would like to buy and the market makers' being contacted), you may end up paying more than you thought (or less).
- If the uncertainty of dealing at best is too much, you can place a **limit order**. Here you specify the maximum price at which you are willing to buy at or the minimum price you are willing to sell at. The order can stay on the system until it is fulfilled or until a fixed expiry date is reached regardless of whether it has been completed. An online limit order is usually only good for the day (you have to re-enter it for the next day).
- An **execute and eliminate** order means that the transaction is completed in part or in full immediately, rather like an at best order. The difference is that a price limit is set by the investor. If not completed immediately the order expires on the spot. If only some of an order is fulfilled the remainder expires.
- With a **fill or kill order** a maximum (minimum) price is stated. If the deal cannot be executed in its entirety at this price or better, the entire order expires.

Now the broker has all the information needed to enter the market place and buy shares. A good broker will read back your order to you: 'Buy 1,000 shares in ABC on a fill or kill basis with a maximum price of 109p.' He will then ask you to confirm that you would like him to go ahead (telephone calls are recorded). At this point you are making a legal commitment to enter the transaction with the broker. This is your last chance to back out.

When your broker hears that you wish to go ahead you can either stay on the line to await confirmation that the order has been completed or ask the broker to call you back.

Next, the broker telephones the market maker offering the keenest price and a deal is struck verbally.[2] All trades are reported to the central computer at the heart of SEAQ and disseminated to market participants within 3 minutes.[3] This gives a great deal of transparency to the system, allowing everyone to see a range of recent prices – see Exhibit 4.3.

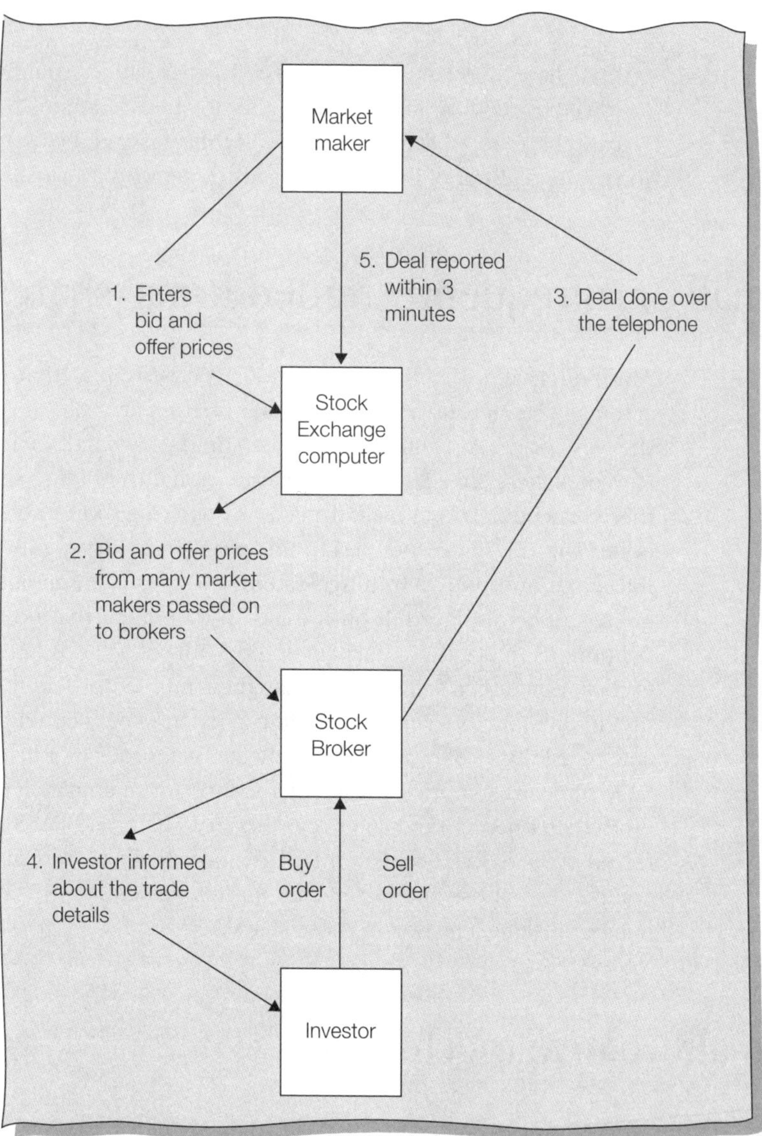

Exhibit 4.3 The SEAQ quote-driven system for trading shares

[2] The stockbroker is allowed to complete the deal 'in-house' by taking on the deal himself if he can match the best prices offered by the market makers.

[3] Market makers are permitted to delay reporting very large orders for a few hours, or even days, to allow them to unwind very large positions.

The next day you should receive a **contract note** in the post (or by email). This will state the price, the time of the deal, the number of shares, the broker's commission and the charge of 0.5 per cent of the value of your purchase in **stamp duty** (this is a form of taxation that applies to purchase only). Check the details to make sure they match your expectations and file the note so you have a record (it will be useful when it comes to filling out tax returns).

If you have a broking account linked to your bank account, then the broker will debit (credit) the account 3 business days after the transaction.

If you have opted to receive **share certificates** (see below) then these will be sent to you by the registrar of the firm in which you now hold shares.

Small or infrequently traded firms' shares

The underlying logic of the quote-driven system is that through the competitive actions of numerous market makers, investors are able to buy and sell at any time at the best price. A problem arises for some very small or infrequently traded firms. Market makers are reluctant to commit capital to holding shares in such firms and so there may be only one market maker's quote for some, while for others there may be none. The LSE has responded to this problem by developing **SEATS plus™ (the Stock Exchange Alternative Trading System)** on which an appointed single market maker's quote can be displayed. If business is so infrequent that no market maker will make a continuous quote the computer screen will act as a '**bulletin board**' on which stock exchange member firms can display their unfilled orders for shares (price and quantity) in the hope of eventually finding a match (which could take weeks). An investor is able to ask his broker to place a buy and sell order in a little-traded company on the bulletin board at a price chosen by the investor (a limit order) for as long as he likes. If more than one market maker registers in a share on SEATS plus, the security is transferred to SEAQ. However, this does not apply to Alternative Investment Market companies, whose market maker quotes remain on SEATS plus regardless of the number making a market in those shares.

An alternative mechanism

There has been some criticism of trading systems based on market makers quoting bid and offer prices – the so-called '**quote-driven** systems'. Investors comment that the middle man's (the market maker's) cut comes from them. Wouldn't it save them money if buyers could trade with sellers at a single price so as to eliminate the loss of the bid–offer spread? Well, many stock exchanges in the world do operate this type of '**order-driven**' system. These markets allow buy and sell orders to be entered on a central computer, and investors are automatically matched (they are sometimes called **matched-bargain systems** or **order book** trading). In 1997 the LSE introduced an order-driven service known as **SETS (Stock Exchange Electronic Trading System)**. This now operates for about 200 of the largest companies.

SETS is a computerised system in which dealers (via brokers) enter the prices at which they are willing to buy or sell. They can then wait for the market to move to the price they set as their limit. Alternatively, they can instruct brokers to transact immediately at the best price currently available on the order book system. The LSE SETS computer does not simply act as a price-information system – as the SEAQ does – it **executes the trades**.

SETS derives market prices as follows: Buyers and sellers enter a price limit at which they are willing to deal as well as the quantity of shares they want to trade. These prices are displayed anonymously to the entire market. An example of prices and quantities is shown in the lower half of Exhibit 4.4 – a reproduced SETS screen as seen by brokers. The buy orders are shown on the left and the sell orders on the right. So, we can observe for the company ABC's shares someone (or more than one person) has entered that they are willing to buy 400 shares at a maximum price of 519p (bottom line on screen). Someone else (via a broker) has entered that they would like to sell 50,000 shares at a minimum price of 529p. Clearly the computer cannot match these two orders and neither of these two investors will be able to trade. They will either have to adjust their limit prices or wait until the market moves in their favour.

As we travel up the screen we observe a closing of the gap between the prices buyers are willing to pay and the offering price of sellers. On the fifth line from the bottom we see that buyers want 20,000 shares at 524p, whereas sellers are prepared to accept 525p for 10,000 shares. Now we are getting much closer to a match. Indeed, if we look above the yellow strip we can see the price where buyers and sellers were last matched – the 'last traded price' is 524½p. These screens are available to market participants at all times and so they are able to judge where to pitch their price limits. For example, if I was a buyer of 5,000 shares entering the market I would not be inclined to offer more than 525p given the current state of supply and demand. On the other hand, if I was a seller of 5,000 shares I would recognise that the price offered would not have to fall below 524p to attract buyers. If, however, I was a buyer of 80,000 shares rather than just 5,000 I would have two options: I could set a maximum price of 525p in which case I would transact for 10,000 immediately but would leave the other 70,000 unfilled order in the market, hoping for a general market price decline; alternatively, I could set my limit at 526p in which case I could transact with those investors prepared to sell at 525p, 525½p and 526p. The unfilled orders of the sellers (81,900–80,000 = 1,900 shares at 526p) are carried forward on SETS.

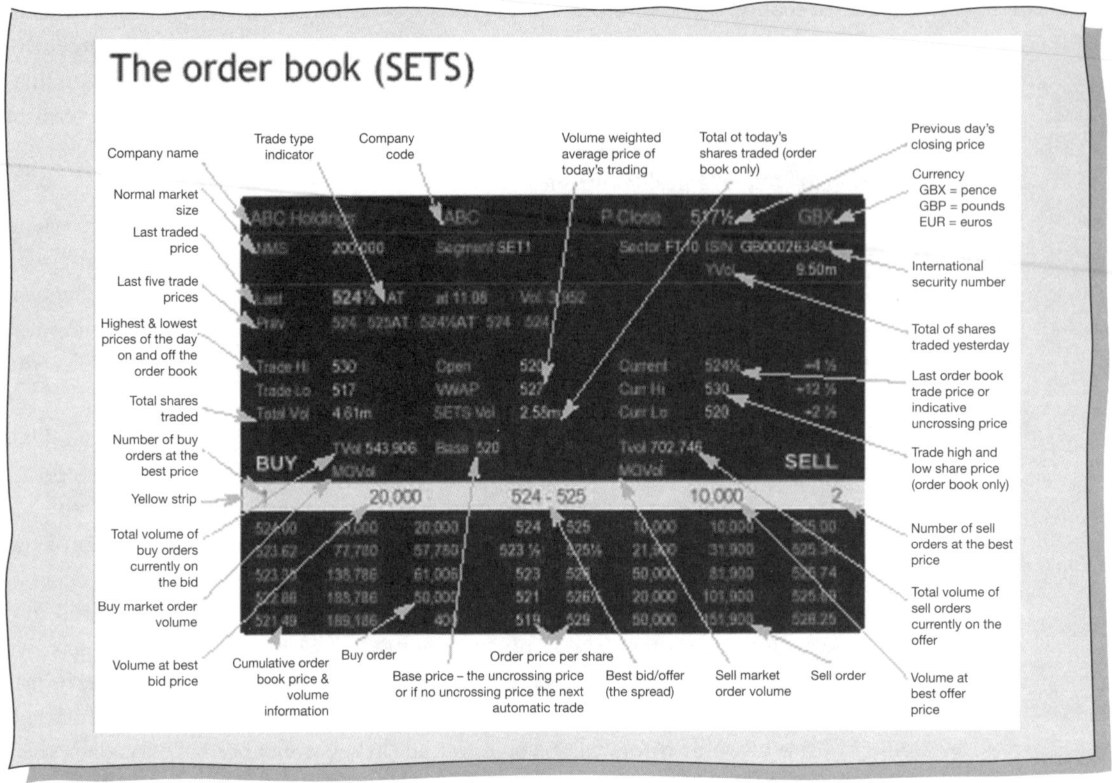

Exhibit 4.4 Typical SETS screen

Source: www.londonstockexchange.com/international/pdfs/trading_systems.pdf

Supporters of the quote-driven system say that a major problem with the order-driven system is that there may be few or no shares offered at prices close to a market clearing rate – so little trade can take place. In other words, the market can be very illiquid. There may be times when no sellers are posting sensible prices and other times when buyers are scarce. The quote-driven system is more liquid because market makers who make a book in a company's shares continuously offer prices and are obliged to trade at the price shown on SEAQ. By way of counter-criticism, it is alleged there have been times when it is difficult to contact market makers on the telephone to trade at the prices they show on SEAQ – they don't pick up the telephone! So this system is not always as liquid as the market makers like to claim. The situation today is that the market maker system is used for the relatively small and medium-sized companies, which would be too illiquid for trading on the SETS system. The SETS system is only used for those shares traded frequently.

What happens after dealing?

When a trade has been completed and reported to the exchange it is necessary to **clear** the trade. That is, the exchange ensures that all reports of the trade are reconciled to make sure all parties are in agreement as to the number of shares traded and the price. The exchange also checks that the buyer and seller have the cash and securities to do the deal. Also the company registrar is notified of the change in ownership. Later the transfer of ownership from seller to buyer has to take place; this is called **settlement**.

In 2001 the exchange moved to **'three-day rolling settlement' (Trading day +3, or T+3)**, which means that investors normally pay for shares 3 working days after the transaction date. Before 1996 the transfer of shares involved a tedious paperchase between investors, brokers, company registrars, market makers and the Exchange. The new system, called **CREST**, provides an electronic means of settlement and registration. This 'paperless' system is cheaper and quicker – ownership is transferred with a few strokes of a keyboard.

Under the Crest system (*www.crestco.co.uk*) shares are often held in the name of a **nominee company** rather than in the name of the **beneficial owner** (i.e. the individual or organisation that actually bought them). Brokers and investment managers run these nominee accounts. So your broker would hold your shares electronically in his nominee account and would arrange settlement through his membership of the Crest system. There might be dozens of investors with shares held by a particular nominee company. The nominee company appears as the **registered owner** of the shares as far as the company (say, BA or BT) is concerned. Despite this, the beneficial owners will receive all dividends and the proceeds from the sale of the shares via the nominee company. One reason for this extra layer of complexity in the ownership and dealing of shares is that the nominee holdings are **recorded in electronic form** rather than in the form of a piece of paper (the inelegant word used for the move to electronic records is '**dematerialisation**'). Thus, if a purchase or sale takes place a quick and cheap adjustment to the electronic record is all that is needed. Investors have no need to bother with share certificates.[4] It is hoped that eventually one-day settlement can be achieved.

Placing shares in a nominee account can remove a lot of administrative work for investors. For example, if you wish to sell shares held in **certificated form** (i.e. a piece of paper) it is necessary to sign a stock transfer form and send it with the share certificate to your broker, who will then check the form and pass it on to the company registrar. Postal dealing and settlement is clearly impossible within the T+3 settlement time, as well as being more fiddly for brokers. Many brokers allow you to delay settling a deal beyond 3 days. They may permit T+5, T+10, or even T+25. This is subject to special arrangement, and there will be additional administrative costs to pay. So those clients

[4] The nominee company is ring-fenced, so that if the broker goes bust the shares in the nominee are unaffected. In the event of fraud investors are guaranteed compensation of up to £48,000 under the Investor Compensation Scheme if they are dealing through an authorised broker (see Chapter 19).

who use the nominee system will be settled at T+3 while for the majority of private investors, who prefer to receive certificates, settlement is more likely to be T+10.

Many investors oppose the advance of CREST nominee accounts because under such a system they do not automatically receive annual reports and other documentation, such as an invitation to the AGM.[5] They also lose the potential to vote (after all, the company does not know who the beneficial owners are). Shareholders can also miss out on **perks**, such as vouchers to spend in Boots The Chemists if you are a shareholder in Boots plc. Those investors who take their ownership of a part of a company seriously can insist on remaining **outside CREST**. In this way they receive share certificates and are treated as the real owners of the business. This is more expensive when share dealing, but that is not a great concern for investors who trade infrequently. Another advantage of being outside the nominee system is that you are not tied to a single broker for all your deals. The cost of transferring 20 shares in a nominee account to another broker can be over £400. Of the 12 million UK shareholders, 8 million still hold their shares in certificated form.

There is a compromise position: **personal membership of CREST** (also called **sponsored membership**). The investor is then both the legal owner via CREST and the beneficial owner of the shares, and also benefits from rapid (and cheap) electronic share settlement. The owner will be sent all company communications and retain voting rights. However, this can be more expensive than the nominee CREST accounts run by brokers. Personal CREST account costs vary from broker to broker. Some do not charge, while others ask for up to £100 per year. Some brokers make an extra charge for each trade through a personal CREST account.

If you are thinking of opting for a nominee service you might like to ask the following:

- What charges will be levied for what services?
- How will the investments be protected while in the nominee account?
- Will I receive annual reports and accounts, the right to vote, invitations to AGMs and EGMs, and perks?

Ways of paying for your shares

- Send a cheque in the post. Your broker may not be willing to buy for you until the cheque is cleared, especially if you have a three-day deadline for settlement.
- Visit a high street broker and pay there and then, for example by credit card.
- Pay by debit card over the telephone.
- Open a deposit account with the broker or bank. Your broker is able to draw money from the account on your behalf at any time to settle deals.

[5] With the standard nominee service offered by brokers, investors can request that reports and accounts, perks and invitations to company meetings be passed on. They may be charged extra for this.

Internet dealing

One third of execution-only share trades are conducted online. Internet dealing has many advantages: it can be very cheap and quick to deal; and you can trade wherever you like, without having to communicate with a broker in normal office hours. Furthermore, your PC can be used to download vast amounts of information, including real time price quotes, market news and commentary, charts of share prices and volume of trades, detailed company information, brokers reports and forecasts. You can even test out portfolio ideas, compiling and tracking a **virtual portfolio** over time.

There are two types of online dealing. The first is largely an **email system (order-placing service)**. Your broker receives the email and then trades with market makers in the normal way. Details of the transaction will be emailed to you a little while afterwards. The second system, **real-time dealing** (or '**fully automated**') is far more interesting. This allows you to connect directly to the market maker system. The market makers who offer **automated connections** are likely to be providing the service as a **retail service provider (RSP)**. The automated service is over and above their market-making activities. The RSPs can choose for themselves whether they will trade a share automatically. The broker connects to a number of RSPs to gain a broad coverage of shares and to allow the investor to benefit from competing prices.

In a typical Internet-based transaction, when you have viewed the prices on screen and placed an order you are given 15 seconds to accept or reject the deal. If you click 'accept' the transaction is completed immediately and a contract note is emailed.

While online trading is low-cost, there are still some problems:

- When markets are busy online orders are sometimes executed very slowly. Many of the IT systems seem unable to cope at present, but over time improvements are being made.
- Some systems are crash-prone. Computer failure can be very frustrating, so always have back-up method of trading.
- If you are thinking of buying a computer principally in order to trade, then the set up costs (£500–£1,000) need to be considered.
- The security of information in cyberspace is a worry for many people, although encryption technology is helping the situation.
- Internet dealing almost invariably requires the use of a nominee account to allow for speedy and cheap settlement.
- The simplicity and speed of trading may lead investors to trade too frequently or to make reckless trades – most day traders in the late 1990s bubble lost a fortune in transaction costs.
- Watch out for silly mistakes resulting in purchase of the wrong number of shares by punching on the wrong key.

Transferring shares without brokers

It is possible to complete an **off-market transfer** without the use of a broker if the transfer is between people you know, such as friends or spouses. You need to complete a **stock transfer form**, which is available free from the company registrar, or from brokers (legal stationers will charge you for the form). The transfer form on the back of share certificates is for use when you are trading in the stock market, so is not suitable for DIY share selling or gifting. You need to have a share certificate to complete a transaction without a broker. If the shares are held in a broker's CREST nominee account the broker will charge for the transfer. Stamp duty does not apply to transfers between spouses or gift transfers. For other transfers the completed form is sent to the **Inland Revenue Stamp Office** with a cheque for stamp duty of 0.5 per cent. The stamp office will return the form (after stamping it) for you to send to the registrar of the company who will issue a new certificate.

PART 2

The investment spectrum

5

Pooled investments

Instead of buying shares individually, investors can pool their money and buy shares (and other assets) collectively. There are some significant advantages of **pooled (collective)** investment. First, a more diversified portfolio can be created. Investors with a relatively small sum to invest, say £3,000, would find it difficult to obtain a broad spread of investments without incurring high transaction costs. If, however, 10,000 people each put £3,000 into a fund there would be £30 million available to invest in a wide range of securities. A large fund like this can buy in large quantities, say £100,000 at a time, reducing dealing and administrative costs per pound invested. Thus risk is reduced by diversification and costs are reduced by economies of scale in share dealing and administration (e.g. time spent managing the portfolio).

Second, even very small investors can take part in the stock market. If you have only £30 a month to invest it is possible to gain exposure to the equity market by investing through pooled funds. Unit trusts, for example, are often willing to sign you up for a drip feed approach to investing in the markets.

Third, you can take advantage of professional management. You can avoid the demanding tasks of analysing and selecting shares, going into the market place to buy, collecting dividends, etc., by handing the whole process over to professional fund managers. Finally, you can enter exotic markets that would otherwise be beyond your reach. Perhaps you wish to invest in South American companies, US hi-tech or some other category of far-flung financial securities, but consider the risk and the complexities of buying shares direct too great. Collective funds run by managers familiar with the relevant country or sector can be a good alternative to going it alone.

These advantages are considerable but they can often be outweighed by the disadvantages of pooled funds, including high costs of fund management and underperformance compared with the market index. And you lose the fun of selecting your own shares with its emotional highs and lows, triumphs and lessons in humility.

Unit trusts

With unit trusts the securities purchased by the investor are called '**units**'. The value of these units is determined by the market valuation of the securities owned by the fund. So, if, for example, the fund collected together £1 million from hundreds of small investors and issued 1 million units in return, each unit would be worth £1. If the fund managers over the next year invest the pooled fund in shares which rise in value to £1.5 million the value of each unit rises to £1.50.

Unit trusts are '**open-ended**' funds, which means that the size of the fund and the number of units depend on the amount investors wish to put into the fund. If a fund of 1 million units suddenly doubled in size because of an inflow of investor funds (not because the underlying investments rise in value), it would become a fund of 2 million units through the creation and sale of more units. So, if the example trust with 1 million units attracts a lot of interest because of its great first year performance it might sell an additional million units at £1.50 each to become a fund with total assets of £3 million.

Unit holders sell units back to the managers of the unit trust if they want to liquidate their holding (turn it into cash). The manager would then either sell the units to other investors or, if that is not possible because of low demand, sell some of the underlying investments to raise cash to redeem the units. Thus the number of units can change daily, or at least every few days.

Pricing

The pricing of unit trusts is not quite as simple as described above. In fact, the units generally have two prices. The total value of the investments underlying the fund is usually calculated once a day using a method prescribed by the Financial Services Authority. From this value the price a new investor has to pay to buy – the **offer price** – is calculated.[1] The **bid price** (the price you can get if you want to sell) is usually set 5–6 per cent below the offer price (for funds invested in shares). The **spread** between the bid and offer prices pays for two things: firstly, fund administration, management, marketing, as well as commission paid to incentivise intermediaries selling the units; secondly, the market makers' spreads and brokers' commissions payable by the fund when it buys and sells shares.

Most unit trusts are now priced on a **forward basis**, which means that the price paid by a buyer of units will be fixed at a particular time of the day (often 12.00 noon) that is yet to come – so when you make out an order to buy you do not know what price you will pay. Some funds still charge the **historic** price, taking the value from the last valuation.[2]

Quite a high proportion of the initial charge in the bid–offer spread (maybe 4–5 per cent) could be commission payable to financial advisers selling the units to investors. Frequently your financial adviser (or discount broker) will waive some of this commission – it is certainly worth asking. Fund supermarkets (see later in this chapter) frequently give a discount on the initial charge. Thus we have the slightly odd situation where going directly to the fund manager to buy units will result in being charged the full initial fee, whereas buying through an agent may cost 4–5 per cent less.

When judging the performance of a unit trust you must bear in mind the influence of the spread. For example, if the quoted prices for a unit moves up from 200p–210p to 250p–262.5p the return (the difference between buying and selling price) is 250p–210p, which is merely 19 per cent, not 25 per cent. Clearly the bid–offer spread means that your fund has to work hard to produce good returns in the short term. One way of looking at this is: if you sign a cheque for £10,000 and the initial fee is 5 per cent, only £9,500 is left in the fund for you to draw out after one day.

1 The offer price is the price the trust would have to pay to purchase the investments currently held. To this are added dealing costs, management expenses and other charges. The total sum divided by the number of units in issue is the maximum offer price that the trust can charge.

2 Some use a mix of historic and forward pricing.

Charging

There are three charges:

- Initial charge ('sales' or 'front-end' charge). This is included in the spread between the bid and offer prices. So if the fund has a spread of 6 per cent it might allocate 5 per cent as an initial charge. Some unit trusts have dropped initial charges to zero – particularly those investing in interest-bearing securities (bonds, etc.) and tracker funds.
- Annual charges. The annual management fee is typically 0.75–1.5 per cent. A further charge of about 0.2 per cent covers legal, audit and other administration costs. Over time the annual fees have a larger effect in reducing the value of your investment than the initial charge. Typically, about one-third of the annual fee is paid to the financial adviser who recommended the fund. You may be able to get some or all of this reimbursed – discount brokers may be willing to cut this charge.
- Exit charges. Some funds make an exit charge instead of an initial charge if you cash in within, say, the first five years.

Reading the *Financial Times*

The *Financial Times* publishes unit trust bid and offer prices every day. An example is shown in Exhibit 5.1. Concentrate for now on the bottom half of the table headed 'Unit Trusts'.

How do you buy or sell units?

You can buy direct from the unit trust management company. You would normally contact them by telephone or write a letter asking for an application form. Addresses are given daily in the *Financial Times*, and the Investment Management Association (*www.investmentfunds.org.uk*) will provide contact details. Alternatively, you could buy through a financial adviser, discount broker or fund supermarket.

If you are worried by prices being set on a forward basis, you can set a **limit** on the price you are prepared to pay. When it comes to selling, you can sell units back to the management company, which is obliged to purchase. You should receive payment within 5 days. You don't have to sell all your holding – you can dispose of as much or as little as you want.

Who looks after the unit holders' interests?

There are four levels of protection for the unit holder:

- *The trustee*. These organisations, usually banks or insurance companies, keep an eye on the fund managers to make sure they abide by the terms of the **trust deed** – for example, sticking to the stated investment objectives. Importantly, the trustee holds all the assets of the fund in their name on the unit holder's behalf, so if anything untoward happens to the fund manager the funds are safeguarded. The trustee also oversees the unit price calculation and ensures the FSA regulations are abided by.

- *The Financial Services Authority*. Only funds authorised by the FSA are allowed to advertise in the UK. Unauthorised unit trusts, most of which are established offshore (outside the jurisdiction of the FSA) are available, but you should be aware that they carry more risk by virtue of their unregulated status.
- *The Ombudsman*. Complaints that have not been satisfactorily settled by the management company can be referred to the Financial Ombudsman – see Chapter 19.
- *The Financial Services Compensation Scheme*. Up to £48,000 is available for a valid claim – for example, when an FSA *authorised* fund becomes insolvent or suffers from poor investment management – see Chapter 19.

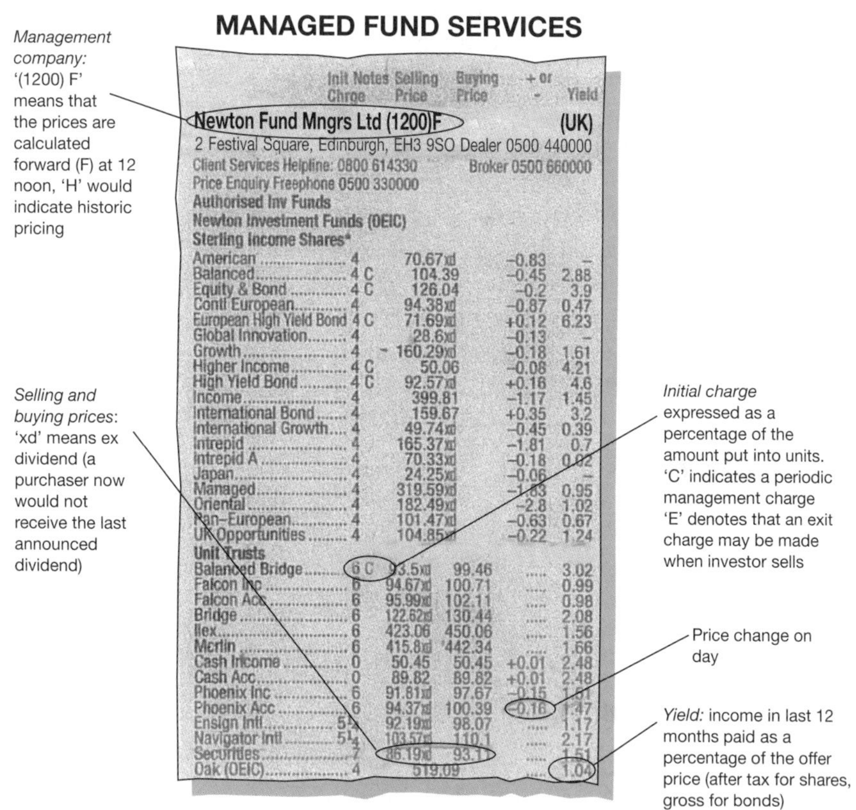

MANAGED FUND SERVICES

	Init Chrge	Notes	Selling Price	Buying Price	+ or -	Yield
Newton Fund Mngrs Ltd (1200)F						**(UK)**
2 Festival Square, Edinburgh, EH3 9SO Dealer 0500 440000						
Client Services Helpline: 0800 614330 Broker 0500 660000						
Price Enquiry Freephone 0500 330000						
Authorised Inv Funds						
Newton Investment Funds (OEIC)						
Sterling Income Shares*						
American	4		70.67xd		–0.83	–
Balanced	4	C	104.39		–0.45	2.88
Equity & Bond	4	C	126.04		–0.2	3.9
Contl European	4		94.38xd		–0.87	0.47
European High Yield Bond	4	C	71.69xd		+0.12	6.23
Global Innovation	4		28.6xd		–0.13	–
Growth	4		160.29xd		–0.18	1.61
Higher Income	4	C	50.06		–0.08	4.21
High Yield Bond	4	C	92.57xd		+0.16	4.6
Income	4		399.81		–1.17	1.45
International Bond	4		159.67		+0.35	3.2
International Growth	4		49.74xd		–0.45	0.39
Intrepid	4		165.37xd		–1.81	0.7
Intrepid A	4		70.33xd		–0.18	0.02
Japan	4		24.25xd		–0.06	–
Managed	4		319.59xd		–1.83	0.95
Oriental	4		182.49xd		–2.8	1.02
Pan–European	4		101.47xd		–0.63	0.67
UK Opportunities	4		104.85xd		–0.22	1.24
Unit Trusts						
Balanced Bridge	6	C	93.5xd	99.46	.....	3.02
Falcon Inc	6		94.67xd	100.71	.....	0.99
Falcon Acc	6		95.99xd	102.11	.....	0.98
Bridge	6		122.62xd	130.44	.....	2.08
Ilex	6		423.06	450.06	.....	1.56
Merlin	6		415.8xd	442.34	.....	1.66
Cash Income	0		50.45	50.45	+0.01	2.48
Cash Acc	0		89.82	89.82	+0.01	2.48
Phoenix Inc	6		91.81xd	97.67	–0.15	1.61
Phoenix Acc	6		94.37xd	100.39	–0.16	1.47
Ensign Intl	5¼		92.19xd	98.07	.....	1.17
Navigator Intl	5¼		103.57xd	110.1	.....	2.17
Securities	7		86.19xd	93.11	.....	1.51
Oak (OEIC)	4		519.09		.....	1.04

Exhibit 5.1 Unit trust prices in the *Financial Times*

Source: *Financial Times* Friday 19 September 2003

Types of trust available

There are around 150 fund management groups offering over 1,600 unit trusts (or their cousins, the OEICs – see below). **UK All Companies** funds invest at least 80 per cent of their assets in UK shares. To this classic type of unit trust have been added a very wide range of trusts with amazingly diverse objectives. Some funds focus investment in shares paying high dividends (**UK Equity Income**), others split the funds between equity and bonds (**UK Equity and Bond Income**), while some invest mostly in **gilts** or **corporate bonds**. Some place the bulk of their money in **smaller companies**, some in **Far East** shares. A few trusts invest in **property**. The possibilities are endless – see *www.investmentfunds.org.uk* for a definition of dozens of classes of funds.

Returns

The return on a unit trust consists of two elements. First, income is gained on the underlying investments in the form of interest or dividends. Second, the prices of the securities held could rise over time. Some unit trusts pay out all income, after deducting management charges etc., on set dates (usually twice a year)[3] in cash. On the other hand, **accumulation units** reinvest the income on behalf of the unit holders in units, and as a result the price of accumulation units tend to rise more rapidly than income units. The *Financial Times* shows listings for prices of **income** ('Inc') units (also called **distribution units**) and accumulation ('Acc') units. With accumulation units the income is reinvested net of basic rate tax. Income units pay income to investors after deduction of basic rate tax. Accumulation units offer the benefit of avoiding reinvestment costs and the hassle to the unit holder of purchasing new units. Any capital gains made within the fund are not taxed. However gains made by the *unit holder* on selling units are taxed in the normal way (see Chapter 17).

Minimum investment

Some trusts ask for an initial minimum investment of only £250 or so, whereas others insist on at least £1,500. Thereafter you are often entitled, under a **savings plan**, to put in as little as £25. It is often possible to use shares instead of cash as payment for units through a **share exchange scheme**.

Following your units' progress

A **manager's report** will be sent to you every 6 months detailing the performance of the fund over the half year and the events in the market(s) in which the fund invests, and explaining the manager's investment strategy. It will also comment on future prospects, list the securities held by the fund and display the fund's financial accounts.

[3] Some trusts pay out quarterly or monthly.

At least once a year you will receive a **statement** showing the number of units you hold and latest prices. The statement will also give a run-down of any additional investment, reinvestment or encashments you have made since the last statement.

Between receiving reports and statements you can contact the management company over the telephone. The staff *may* be prepared to discuss the investment performance of the fund and current outlook. They will certainly be willing to deal with general administration queries and, of course, give information on other products they might sell you.

The most obvious place to track your units is in **newspapers** such as the *Financial Times*. *Money Management* magazine tracks fund performance over periods of 1, 2, 3, and 5 years. Many websites, such as fund supermarket websites, carry details of units. You could visit the fund managers website, or go to a general site such as:

www.funds-sp.com	Standard and Poor's funds
www.morningstar.co.uk	Morningstar UK
www.lipperweb.com	Lipper (Reuters)
www.trustnet.com	Trustnet
www.moneyextra.com	MX Moneyextra
www.iii.co.uk	Ample
www.moneyweb.co.uk	Moneyweb
www.citywire.co.uk	Citywire

Switching funds

Many fund management companies allow you to switch from one trust within its stable to another for a charge much lower than the usual initial charge. So, if you think US hi-tech has reached its peak you might ask the manager to transfer your holding to, say, a UK smaller company fund.

Points to bear in mind when choosing a unit trust

- It costs more to run a fund in which the manager is spending time and effort carefully selecting shares (an '**actively managed**' fund) than one where the manager simply buys and holds a broad range of shares matching a market index (e.g. FTSE 100), called a **tracker** (or **passive** or **indexed**) fund. A government-commissioned study concluded that investors should be encouraged to opt for trackers because actively managed funds fail to outperform the market (on average) – see Exhibit 5.2. (The average British unit trust underperformed the equity market by 2.5 per cent a year because of high charges and poor performances by active managers.)

Key report casts doubts on active fund management

Government-commissioned study encourages investors to place savings in less risky stock market tracker funds

By Deborah Hargreaves, Personal Finance Editor

Long-term investors should think twice about paying fees to have their stock market savings actively managed, a government-commissioned report has concluded.

Investors should instead weigh the virtues of putting their savings into so-called tracker funds, which attempt to mirror a stock market index and are therefore cheaper to run and may be less risky.

Ron Sandler's long awaited report – to be published on Tuesday – will cast doubt on whether star fund managers can deliver long-term returns for private investors.

According to research by the Consumers' Association, only one third of active funds managed to beat the FTSE 100 index during the past 10 years.

'Active funds really do have to earn their money. They're charging you a lot more and if they're not beating the index, what's the point?' said Teresa Fritz, researcher at the Consumers' Assocation.

The consumer body found that average charges varied widely – for index tracking funds the initial fee was 1.5 per cent and annual management charge 0.8 per cent compared with 4.3 per cent and 1.2 per cent for active funds

Exhibit 5.2 Doubts over actively managed funds

Source: *Financial Times* 6/7 July 2002

- Investors who don't need advice can go to online fund supermarkets or discount-broking independent financial advisers to have some or all the commission returned. (These intermediaries make an income from a share of the annual management charge – called **trail commission**.) The saving on a £100,000 fund could be as much as £5,000.
- Unit trusts should be viewed as medium- to long-term investments, given that the upfront charges are so high. It is no good flitting in and out.
- To compare the cost of investing in funds use **total expense ratios (TERs)** which incorporate all annual operating costs (e.g. administration, custody, legal, audit) and not just the management charges revealed in promotional material. The difference is usually around 15 per cent, but can be 40 per cent. The TER can vary tremendously between managers – see Exhibit 5.3. Total expense ratios can be obtained from *www.funds.ft.com* and *www.bestinvest.co.uk*

Fund charges raise eyebrows

New figures from Fitzrovia, the specialist research firm, show a continuing rise in average annual charges for actively managed mutual funds offered in the UK.

'In these market conditions, charges can make all the difference to what investors earn,' said Ed Moisson, associate director of Fitzrovia. 'The important thing is to look at the total expense ratio [TER].'

'We have argued for the use of TER in marketing literature, but that hasn't happened,' said the Investment Management Association, the UK trade body.

Jupiter International said fund charges needed to be viewed against performance.

'It's important to deliver value for money and we have the performance record to prove that,' it said.

League table: fund management charges

Highest charges:	TER*	Lowest charges:	TER*
Premier Asset Management	2.35%	Halifax	0.76%
City Financial Managers	2.03%	Coutts & Co	0.82%
Jupiter International	1.98%	TU Fund Managers	0.97%
Global Asset Management	1.86%	Royal London	1.03%
Govett Asset Management	1.81%	Scottish Life	1.05%

Source: Fitzrovia

*Ranked according to Total Expense Ratio

Mr Moisson said his firm might try to take the discussion forward by linking its expense data with performance statistics.

'Investors are prepared to pay higher charges in the hope that these will be offset by significantly better performance. But the link between charges and performance is not quite clear,' he said.

Exhibit 5.3 Actively managed funds can be expensive

Source: *Financial Times* 17 June 2002

- Advertisements showing fund manager's performance should be taken with a large pinch of salt. They will be very selective about the starting date (choosing a low point) in order to impress you. Furthermore, there is a mass of evidence to show that past performance is a very poor guide to how well a fund will perform in the future. It is very unusual for a fund to outperform consistently over the medium and longer term. Frequently top performing funds over one- or five-year periods end up falling to the bottom of the league tables in the next period. Even if you find a fund that has shown a sustained high performance you may then discover that what made the fund work well in one economic period serves less well in the next – see Exhibit 5.4 for one of the commonest tricks.

'Fund managers do a lot of window dressing'

Alexander Jolliffe meets an academic who is deeply unimpressed by the past performance of many high-profile fund managers

David Blake has no time for fund managers. A professor of financial economics at Birkbeck College, London, he believes fund management groups mislead investors, urging them to invest without giving them the full picture.

Prof Blake compares fund advertisements with a dubious practice in the US in which people mislead investors into paying for share tips.

This US practice has several stages. First, the organisers write to 10,000 people, telling half of them that a particular share price will rise in the next week, and the other half that it will fall.

If the share price rises, the organisers write to the 5,000 people who were told that it would go up. They tell half that the stock will rise again, and the other half that it will fall. They repeat this process numerous times, and after a month have a small group of investors who have repeatedly been given the right forecast.

At this stage, the organisers write to this small group, offering to sell them share tips for $100. Prof Blake explains: 'The people say: "They got it right four times in a row, so I'll pay." But it's a pure scam.'

Blake says this is analogous with fund management groups, because they set up, say, 20 funds but only promote the ones that succeed. Just as the US operators did not tell their ultimate target investors that many others had been given inaccurate forecasts, so fund management groups rarely tell customers about mediocre or bad funds. 'It's not providing consumers with the full range of information.' comments Prof Blake.

Exhibit 5.4 Fund managers may sometimes mislead investors

Source: *Financial Times* 2/3 August 2003

- A dilemma arises for investors when a fund manager leaves a management company. Should you stick with the trust or move with the manager? This is a serious issue given that less than two-thirds of managers have run their funds for as long as 3 years. Following a 'star' fund manager to a new company is not always possible, and besides the costs of doing so can be high. Some funds have one star player, while others have a talented team. Going for a team may leave you less vulnerable to the departure of particular managers. Citywire (*www.citywire.co.uk*) tracks the performances of individual fund managers rather than funds.

Open-ended investment companies (OEICs)

OEICs (pronounced 'oiks') have been around since the late 1990s, and many unit trusts have turned themselves into OEICs. An OEIC is a company that issues shares rather than a trust that issues units. It is similar to a unit trust, in that it is diversified collective investment vehicle, but it differs in some important respects. One similarity is that it is 'open-ended' in that it can expand or contract the number of shares in issue in response to demand. Also OEICs are regulated by the FSA in a similar way to unit trusts, so investor protection is much the same.

OEICs have **directors** managing the fund and a **depository** supervising activities to safeguard its assets. OEICs have a simpler pricing system because there is one price for both buyers and sellers. Charges and dealing commissions are shown separately (which makes them more transparent than unit trusts). When OEICs are bought or sold the price is directly related to the value of the underlying assets and not based on the supply and demand for its shares (as with investment trusts). The price is calculated daily.

The OEIC may be a stand-alone fund or created under an '**umbrella**' structure, which means that there are a number of sub-funds each with a different investment objective (one sub-fund may focus on US shares, another on UK shares, etc.) Each sub-fund could have different investors and asset pools.

Exchange traded funds (ETFs)

Exchange traded funds (ETFs) take the idea of tracking a stock market index or sector a stage further. ETFs are set up as companies issuing shares. The ETF shares are used to buy a range of shares in a particular stock market index or sector, such as the FTSE 100 or pharmaceutical shares. They are open-ended funds – the ETF shares are created and cancelled as demand rises or falls. However, they differ from unit trusts and OEICs in that the pricing of ETF shares is left up to the market place. ETFs are quoted companies and you can buy and sell their shares at prices subject to change throughout the day (unlike unit trusts and OEICs, where prices are set by formula once a day).

Despite an ETF's price being set by trading in the stock market they tend to trade at, or near to, the underlying net asset value (NAV) – the value of the shares in the FTSE 100, for instance. This is different from investment trusts, which frequently trade significantly below net asset value.

Newly created ETF shares are delivered to market makers in exchange for an entire portfolio of shares matching the index (not for cash). The underlying shares are held by the fund manager, while the new ETF shares are traded by the market maker in the secondary market. To redeem ETF shares the ETF manager delivers underlying shares to the market maker in exchange for ETF shares. ETF managers only create new ETF shares for market makers with at least £1 million to invest, so private investors are excluded at this level. However, private investors can trade in existing ETF shares in the secondary market.

If the price of an ETF share rises above the value of the underlying shares, there will be an **arbitrage** opportunity for the market maker. Arbitrage means the possibility of simultaneously buying and selling the same or similar securities in two markets and making a risk-free gain, for example buying bananas for £1 in one market and selling them for £1.05 in another. In this case the ETF share representing, say, the top 100 UK shares is trading above the price of the 100 shares when sold separately. Market makers, spotting this opportunity, will swap the underlying basket of shares for a creation unit of ETF shares, thus realising a profit by then selling the ETF shares into the market. Then the new supply of ETF shares will satisfy the excess demand and ETF prices should fall until they are in line with the underlying NAV.

If the ETF share price falls below the underlying shares' value the market maker will exploit this by having the ETF share redeemed by the ETF manager. The market maker ends up with the more valuable underlying shares and the supply of ETFs in the market place has fallen, bringing the price back up to the NAV.

The advantage arising from market makers and ETF managers not handing over cash, but instead swapping ETF shares and underlying shares, is that there are no brokerage costs for buying and selling shares. This makes transactions cheap.

Spreads – the difference between market maker's buying and selling prices of ETFs – are generally around 0.1–0.3 per cent (although spreads can widen to 10 per cent or more at times of extreme volatility, for example, after 11 September 2001). There is no initial charge with ETFs but annual management charges range between 0.2 and 0.75 per cent (these are deducted from dividends). All in all, ETFs are a cheaper way of benefiting from a rising market than unit or investment trusts.

Private investors can purchase ETFs from brokers. Their minimum charge is between £10 and £40 per trade, and no stamp duty is payable on purchase. Prices are shown with other share prices in the *Financial Times* – see Exhibit 5.5. The *Financial Times* shows ETFs that track the US market (e.g. S&P 500 index), European shares (e.g. EuroStoxx 50) or the UK market (e.g. FTSE 100). ETFs pay dividends in line with the underlying constituent shares. This is reflected in the yield column.

Useful websites for ETF investors are iShares (*www.ishares.net*) and Trustnet (*www.trustnet.com/etf*).

EXCHANGE TRADED FUNDS

Notes	Price	Chng	52 week high	52 week low	Yld	P/E	Vol '000s
EuroStoxx50 .	1856	+1	1886	1285	1.9	–	–
Stoxx 50.......	1807	....	1821	1313	2.0	–	–
iShs iFTSE100†	433½xd	+1¾	454	317½	2.8	97.1	1,899
Euro100	552	+1	560	385	1.8	–	9
Eurotop100	1423	....	1791	1034	2.0	–	–
S & P 500.....	641½xd	–1½	659½	485	1.0	–	59

Exhibit 5.5 Exchange traded fund prices in the *Financial Times*

Source: *Financial Times* Friday 19 September 2003

Pros and cons of ETFs

Among the advantages of ETFs are the following:

- ETFs are listed companies on the London Stock Exchange with an active secondary market. Being open-ended, there is no danger of over-supply of shares as ETF managers always stand ready to buy.
- They trade at, or very near to, net asset value and track the index very closely.
- They can be traded at real-time prices throughout the day.
- They incur low management and other costs (which are transparent).
- They can be held in an ISA to save tax.
- They can be bought to gain exposure to foreign markets cheaply.

There are, however, disadvantages:

- Stockbrokers' fees can eat into profits of frequent traders.
- No sales commissions are paid to commission-based independent financial advisers for recommending ETFs so they don't push them – despite ETFs being ideal for many investors.

Investment trusts (investment companies)

Investment trusts (companies) place the money they raise in assets such as shares, gilts, corporate bonds and property. Unlike unit trusts, they are set up as companies (they are not trusts at all!) and are subject to company law. If you wish to place your money with an investment trust you do so by buying its shares. Investment trusts are floated on the London Stock Exchange where there is an active secondary market. They are described as **closed-end funds** because they do not create or redeem their shares on a daily basis in response to increases or decreases in demand (in contrast to unit trust and OEICs). The number of shares is fixed for a long period of time, as with any other company that issues shares.

The trust will have a **constitution**[4] that specifies that its purpose is to invest in specific types of assets. It cannot deviate from this. So it may have been set up to invest in Japanese large company shares, US biotechnology shares, or whatever, and it is forbidden from switching to a different category of investment. This reassures the investor that money placed with a particular trust to invest in, say, UK large companies won't end up in, say, Russian oil shares. Of course, if you want to take the risk (and possible reward) of investing in Russian oil shares you can probably find an investment trust that specialises in these – there are, after all, over 350 investment trusts quoted in London, with total assets of over £60 billion, to choose from.

[4] Comprising its memorandum, articles of association and the prospectus on flotation.

As a company an investment trust will have a **board of directors** answerable to shareholders for the trust's actions and performance. With investment trusts being closed-end funds the amount of money under the directors' control is fixed, which enables them to plan ahead with confidence unconcerned, that tomorrow investors may want to withdraw money from the fund. Investors cannot oblige the trust to buy the shares should they want to sell (in contrast to unit trusts and OEICs). They have to sell to another investor at a price determined by the forces of supply and demand in the secondary market. Purchases and sales are made through stockbrokers in the same way as for any other company share.

The selection of investments for the trust and the general management of the fund may be undertaken by an in-house team of investment managers who are employees of the trust (a '**self-managed**' trust) or the investment management task may be handed over to **external managers**. Most are externally managed.

Discounts and premiums

There are two factors that influence the share price of an investment trust. Firstly, the value of the underlying assets owned by the trust. This is expressed as a **net asset value per share**. In theory the trust's share price should be pretty close to the value of the assets held. But in practice they frequently sell at large a **discount** to NAV – only a few sell at a **premium** to NAV. Discounts of 10–20 per cent are not uncommon; they have even reached 45 per cent. The main factor that drags the price below NAV is the lack of demand for the shares. Here is a typical scenario.

In year X there is great interest in, say, eastern European smaller companies so an investment trust is set up and offers its shares (say, 50 million) for sale at £1 each. With the money raised £50 million of eastern European company shares are bought by the trust. For the next year the underlying assets (all those shares in Polish companies, etc.) do no more than maintain their value of £1 per investment trust share, and so NAV is constant. Nothing in the fundamentals has changed. However, the enthusiasm for investing in these up-and-coming nations grows amongst the UK investing public. The investment trust shareholders who want to sell find that they can do so in the LSE secondary market at above NAV. New buyers are willing to pay £1.08 per share – an 8 per cent premium to the NAV.

However, in the following year a worldwide recession strikes and investors head for safe havens; they pile into bonds and familiar shares at home. The NAV of the trust's shares falls to 60p as prices plummet on the eastern European stock exchanges. What is worse for the investment trust shareholders is that sentiment has become so pessimistic about eastern European companies that they can only sell their shares for 50p. They trade at a discount of 16.67 per cent to NAV (10p/60p).

Discounts may seem to present an excellent opportunity: you can buy assets worth 60p for 50p. However, they can be bad for the investor if the discount increases during the time you hold the shares. As you can see from the last column in Exhibit 5.6, the discounts can be much larger than the example above. The *Financial Times* publishes the share prices and NAVs of investment trusts (companies) daily.

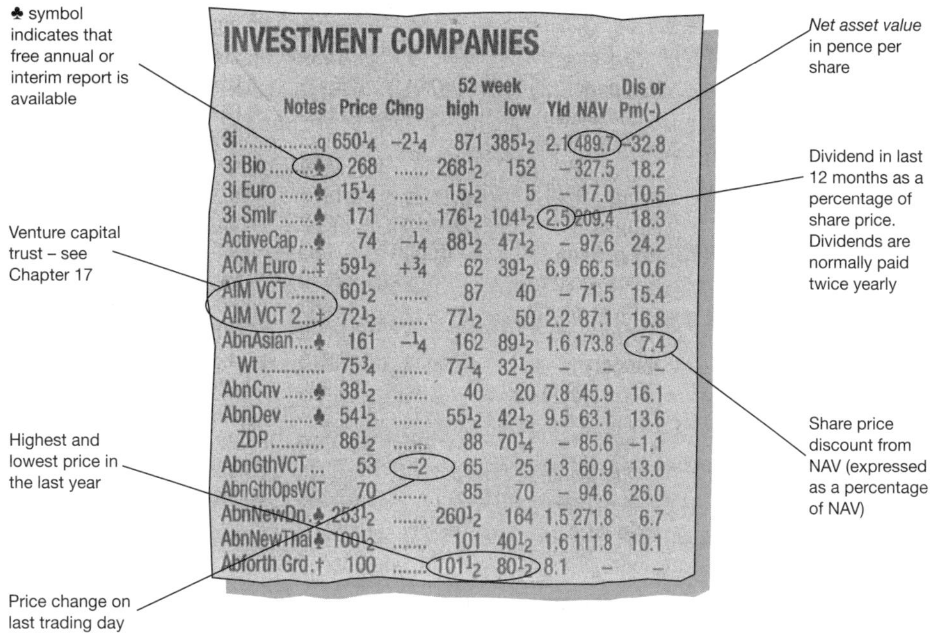

INVESTMENT COMPANIES

	Notes	Price	Chng	52 week high	low	Yld	NAV	Dis or Pm(-)
3i	q	650¼	−2¼	871	385½	2.1	489.7	−32.8
3i Bio	♣	268	....	268½	152	–	327.5	18.2
3i Euro	♣	15¼	....	15½	5	–	17.0	10.5
3i Smlr	♣	171	....	176½	104½	2.5	209.4	18.3
ActiveCap	♣	74	−¼	88½	47½	–	97.6	24.2
ACM Euro	‡	59½	+¾	62	39½	6.9	66.5	10.6
AIM VCT		60½	....	87	40	–	71.5	15.4
AIM VCT 2	‡	72½	....	77½	50	2.2	87.1	16.8
AbnAsian	♣	161	−¼	162	89½	1.6	173.8	7.4
Wt		75¾	....	77¼	32½	–	–	–
AbnCnv	♣	38½	....	40	20	7.8	45.9	16.1
AbnDev	♣	54½	....	55½	42½	9.5	63.1	13.6
ZDP		86½	....	88	70¼	–	85.6	−1.1
AbnGthVCT		53	−2	65	25	1.3	60.9	13.0
AbnGthOpsVCT		70	....	85	70	–	94.6	26.0
AbnNewDn	♣	253½	....	260½	164	1.5	271.8	6.7
AbnNewThai	♣	100½	....	101	40½	1.6	111.8	10.1
Abforth Grd	†	100	....	101½	80½	8.1	–	–

Exhibit 5.6 Investment trust prices in the *Financial Times*

Source: *Financial Times* Friday 19 September 2003

Note: The Monday edition of the *Financial Times* displays the change in price over the week, the actual dividend in pence per share, when dividends are paid and market capitalisation.

While much of the discount on a typical investment trust is due to negative sentiment there are some rational reasons for shares selling below NAV:

- Investors may think trust managers are incompetent and likely to lose more value in the future.
- NAV is calculated after deducting the nominal (stated book) value of the debt and preference shares. In reality, the trust may have to pay back more on the debt and preference shares than this.
- Liquidating the fund incurs costs (e.g. contract cancellations, advisers' fees, stockbrokers' fees) so NAV is not achieved.

Costs for the investor

When buying (or selling) investment trust shares commission will be payable to the stockbroker[5] as usual when buying shares (see Chapter 4). There will also be market

[5] Investment trusts are also sold through financial advisers.

marker's spread between the buying and selling price. This is generally 1–2 per cent, but for less frequently traded trusts it can be 5–10 per cent.

The trust managers' costs for managing the investments and for administration are charged to the fund, either against annual income or against capital. An average TER, including the costs of investment management and administration, directors' fees, audit fees and share registration expenses, is 1 per cent (but this excludes performance fees that managers sometimes take).

Borrowing

Investment trusts have the freedom to borrow (unlike unit trusts or OEICs). Borrowing to buy assets is fine if the value of those assets is rising by more than the interest charge. However, it is a two-edged sword. The risk associated with gearing up returns becomes all too apparent when asset values fall. Take the case of our trust investing in eastern Europe. If it had sold 50 million shares at £1 each and also borrowed £50 million to buy £100 million of eastern European shares the NAV would still start at £1 per share (£100 million of assets minus £50 million debt owed, for 50 million shares). If underlying asset values fall by 40 per cent because of the fall in the Warsaw Stock Exchange, the *net* asset value per share falls dramatically from £1 to 20p – an 80 per cent fall – because the assets fall to £60 million, but the debt remains at £50 million:

Value of eastern European shares			£60m
Less debt			£50m
			£10m
Net asset value per share: £10m/50m	=	20p	

You can see why trusts that borrow a lot can be very volatile.

Tax

Capital gains tax is not payable by a trust on gains made within the trust. The income received by the trust is taxed, but then shareholders receive a tax credit to reflect the fact that tax has already been paid. Shareholders pay capital gains tax on the sale of trust shares in the normal way – see Chapter 17. ISAs can be used to hold trust shares. Stamp duty of 0.5 per cent is payable when buying investment trust shares.

Split-capital investment trusts ('dual capital' trusts)

Around the turn of the millennium many perplexed trust shareholders lost a lot of money on split-capital investment trusts largely as a result of not understanding the nature of the financial instruments they had bought. In the late 1990s they were often told that 'split' shares were some of the safest you could buy. The reality was that many of these shares were highly risk-loaded.

Split-capital trusts simultaneously issue different types of shares – the shares are 'split' into different forms. Generally they offer **income shares** that entitle the holder to receive all (or most) of the income from the investment portfolio (e.g. dividends from underlying shares), and **capital shares** that entitle the owner to receive all (or most) of the rise in the capital value of the portfolio over the life of the company, but not to receive dividends. Splits have a specified number of years (usually less than 10) of existence so that the capital shareholder knows when these shares will pay out (and the income shareholder knows when payments will cease).

Income shares offer a relatively high income to compensate for the low predetermined sum that will be paid at the end of the trust's life when the shares are redeemed (some pay the initial amount back, some may only pay 1p at the end). The high yields on these shares seem very attractive to some people (e.g. the retired); but these investors must also weigh up the potential loss on capital value of the shares. For example, a £1 share that offers an income of 15 pence per year may seem good value, but not if the capital value is declining at 12 per cent per year. Also the income is not guaranteed and is likely to fluctuate from year to year.

Capital shares attract investors wanting high exposure to rises in stock markets. The drawback is they are last in the queue for payouts after all the other classes of shareholders have received their entitlements. So if the trust goes into liquidation they are unlikely to get anything back.

While splits started with these two categories of shares it wasn't long before other types appeared. For example, some trusts issued income, capital shares and a third type of share called **zero dividend preference shares**. **'Zeros'** pay no income during the life of the trust but they do offer a **predetermined return** at the end. They are therefore less risky than income or capital shares.

The problem that arose in the period 2000–2002 was that many split-capital investment trusts borrowed significant sums of money. Debt interest and the capital repayment on debt take precedence over the payout to zero or to capital and income shares on an annual basis or in liquidation. When the stock market declined the effect of this gearing was to exaggerate the fall in trusts' underlying share values. What really messed things up for shareholders of splits was that many trusts surreptitiously invested large proportions of their funds in other highly borrowed splits (over 70 per cent of the fund was invested in other splits in some cases). They were later accused of artificially keeping other splits alive as a form of mutual back-scratching between trust managers. Panic ensued as investors realised the danger to which they were exposed, especially for those in the technology sector. Some lost 90 per cent or more of value on their shares. Zeros were supposed to be very safe because of the guaranteed payout at the end and the superiority over other shares for any payout. However, the gearing and the cross-shareholding in a declining market meant that in many cases they failed to pay out the promised amounts – some became worthless.

There are two lessons from this story: keep an eye on the borrowing; and keep an eye on cross-shareholdings in other trusts.

Websites for investment trusts

www.aitc.co.uk	Association of Investment Trust Companies (general)
www.funds-sp.com	Standard and Poors (performance statistics)
www.trustnet.com	Trustnet (general)
www.citywire.com	Citywire (breaking news and performance)
www.hemscot.net	Hemscott (company accounts, news and backgrounds)
www.splitsonline.co.uk	Splits Online (split capital trusts)
www.iii.co.uk	Ample (general)

With-profits policies

Over 10 million UK citizens have around £380 billion saved in with-profits funds. These could be in the form of an **endowment** policy (often linked to a mortgage), a **personal pension** or a long-term investment in **with-profits bonds**. Many company pension schemes also invest in with-profits funds.

Technically and contractually, a with-profits policy is a form of life insurance (i.e. there is a payment on death). In reality, the majority of policies are essentially savings products with a nominal insurance content. With-profits policies generally work as follows: Life insurance companies set up a fund and invite people to place their savings in the fund either as a lump sum or through a regular savings plan (say, £20 per month). The fund then invests in a range of international and UK shares, bonds and property. The life insurer guarantees a minimum return to be paid out at the end of the policy life, which can be 5, 10 or even 25 years away. This is called the **basic sum assured**. Suppose, for the sake of argument, that this is £10,000 in 10 years' time.

When the underlying investments in the fund produce returns the policyholders are given '**bonuses**' – a share of the profits the insurance company has achieved on the invested money. Policyholders receive a **reversionary** bonus (also called a **regular** bonus) annually. This is added to the policy's guaranteed sum.

However, if the year's returns have been particularly good – say, the stock market rocketed – the policyholders will not receive a reversionary bonus of the same magnitude, because insurance companies attempt to smooth reversionary bonus rates over time, avoiding sharp changes from one year to the next. They hold back profits in good years so that they can maintain a reasonably good reversionary bonus in years of poor investment performance (this is called **smoothing**).

Once the reversionary bonus is added to the fund it cannot be taken away. So, if the basic sum assured starts at £10,000 and at the end of the first year the insurance company announces a reversionary bonus of 4 per cent the new guaranteed sum becomes £10,400. If in the second year the reversionary bonus is 5 per cent then the guaranteed sum due 8 years later becomes £10,400 × 1.05 = £10,920.[6] The guaranteed amount is payable on death or at maturity of the policy.

The attraction of such instruments to risk-averse investors is clear. As profits are made on underlying investments the insurance company locks in a return for the policyholder that cannot be taken away. So even if, in future years, shares, bond and property markets crumble, the investor is guaranteed a minimum amount (this is assuming the life assurance company manages to avoid liquidation in such dire circumstances – as we shall see later, this is not always a safe assumption).

As well as the reversionary bonuses the insurer pays a **terminal** bonus at the end of the policy (or on death if this is earlier). The terminal bonus is frequently more valuable than all the reversionary bonuses put together. The insurers are naturally cautious in adding reversionary bonuses because of the danger of a market decline later in the life of the policy. So they hold back on the level of the guarantee, but then boost the policy's value dramatically via the terminal bonus once they know the returns on the fund can no longer be lost in future years.

A variation on the theme is **unitised with-profits funds**. Here the premiums paid by individuals buy units of a fund in a similar way to investing in unit trusts. Unlike the conventional with-profits funds there is no basic sum assured but the bonuses are smoothed. Another alternative is a **whole life policy**, which is open-ended, having no defined maturity date at which benefits can be taken other than at death.

Taxation

The insurance company pays basic rate income tax and capital gains tax on the fund's returns before the investor receives a return. If you are a basic rate taxpayer there is no further tax to pay. Higher rate taxpayers may have to pay additional tax.

The controversy over with-profits funds

Criticism has been heaped on with-profits policies. The first problem is that the insurance companies have far too much discretion over bonuses. This combined with the fact that directors' duties are to maximise the returns to their shareholders rather than policyholders, means that with-profits policyholders cannot be entirely sure that they are getting the full benefit from the returns generated using their money.[7]

The opacity surrounding the granting of returns to policyholders has been described by the head of Financial Services Authority, Sir Howard Davies, as too much of a 'black box'. Martin Dickson, a writer for the *Financial Times*, has been even more scathing – see Exhibit 5.7.

[6] An alternative way of operating is for the life insurer to add, say, a 5 per cent reversionary bonus to the original guaranteed sum and, say, a 6 per cent bonus to the reversionary bonuses previously announced.

[7] Many insurance organisations are not companies but mutually owned organisations nominally run in the interests of policyholders. However, they too have received much the same criticisms.

Putting the pig in a more transparent poke

Martin Dickson, Lombard

It is not generally wise to buy a pig in a poke, unless you have total trust in the farmer who is supposed to have been fattening it up. Still less is it wise to buy when it will be years before you can open the sack and discover whether you own a nice fat porker or a miserable little runt.

Yet that, crudely speaking, is what consumers have been doing for decades when buying a with-profits policy, the flagship product of the British insurance industry. It is supposed to protect investors from market volatility by smoothing returns. But the manner in which this is achieved is utterly opaque.

For a long time consumers bought the pig because they valued the smoothing process and trusted the farmer. But that faith has been undermined by a decade-long succession of scandals involving with-profits, ranging from pensions mis-selling to the Equitable affair.

Exhibit 5.7 Lack of transparency in with-profits policyholders' returns

Source: *Financial Times* 29 May 2002

There is a lack of transparency in four areas:

- the underlying investment return;
- the smoothing of the return;
- the charging of costs;
- the connection between the with-profits fund and the insurance firm's other businesses.

The wide discretion of insurance companies has been used to build up **orphan assets**. These are reserves that an insurance company holds back from policyholders to act as a buffer should the market decline. There were many years when returns on funds were much greater than the bonuses granted on policies. It would seem that the insurance companies have been far too cautious: these orphan assets amounted to between £30 and £45 billion in 2001 (over £500 per man, woman and child in the UK!).

In other words, policyholders have been underpaid. If these assets were now simply attributed to policyholders, then all would be well. Government policy on this is that policyholders should get 90 per cent of orphan assets, with the remainder going to insurance company shareholders. Judging by their recent actions it would seem that few insurance companies have any intention of being so 'generous' to policyholders – for example, Axa paid 30 per cent. Naturally, the size of the orphan assets declined with the market falls of 2000–03, but this problem is likely to recur.

An even bigger problem with these policies is the massive penalty imposed on holders if they cash in early. This affects millions of people. Only about one-third of 25-year policies are held to maturity. Even with 10-year policies only one-half of savers maintain payments for the full term. In many cases holders receive less than the money they put in (and less than the guaranteed value) especially if they surrender the policy within the first 3–5 years. One of the reasons for the negative returns in the first few years of a policy is that the insurance companies pay large commissions to financial advisers to sell these policies (moral: weigh careful the words of financial advisers being offered large monetary inducements to push with-profits policies).

If there are adverse market conditions the policy providers are allowed to impose another penalty called a **market value adjuster (MVA)** – an '**exit penalty**' – when holders withdraw from their policies. In 2003 these were running at up to 27 per cent of the value of the policy. The justification for this is that the guaranteed payout has been boosted by a series of large annual bonuses when stock markets bounded ahead. If the markets then fall by a large amount it would be unfair to the continuing members of the fund to pay the full amount previously guaranteed to members who leave early, just after a market peak.

An alternative to **surrendering the policy** (i.e. cease paying into it and asking for cash back) is to sell it in the **second-hand endowment market** (**traded endowment policy** market). The buyers of your policy will then generally hold on to it until maturity. The price paid can be as much as 15 per cent higher then the surrender value.

Ned Cazalet, an independent analyst of the life assurance sector, claimed in November 2003 that the sector's spending on administration and on gaining new business (sale, teams etc.) was 'a staggering £12 billion in 2002, equivalent to an absurd £570 for every household in the land'. Apparently £7 billion was expenditure (including commission) relating to acquisition of new business, or about £300 per UK household. 'An industry that is spending more than £300 per household per annum on seeking new business is clearly operationally dysfunctional', Mr Cazalet was quoted in the *Financial Times* (15–16 November 2003) as saying.

With-profits policies are marketed as a low-risk product, but this is not always true. For example, Equitable Life was forced to severely cut the bonuses to some policyholders because it had promised high returns to other savers, and was forced by the courts to pay out on the guaranteed annuities, leaving a shrunken pot of money for everyone else. The lack of transparency at Equitable Life meant that policyholders were unable to discern the risk to their savings until it was too late.

Insurance companies have also been accused of being too optimistic at times. For example, many people were sold endowment policies related to house mortgages. The monthly payments into the policies were set at a level thought to be enough to pay off the mortgage in, say, 25 years. When markets turned sour many shocked policyholders received a letter stating that they were unlikely to have enough saved in the policy to be able to pay off the mortgage at the end of the term – unless, of course, they handed over more money to the insurance company to increase the size of the pot.

There appears to be no correlation between the levels of charges and the performance of the funds. Dame Sheila McKechnie of the Consumers' Association does not mince words when she talks about the behaviour of the insurance industry – see Exhibit 5.8.

'If this industry can rip off consumers, it will'

Veteran campaigner Dame Sheila McKechnie believes the financial services industry treats its customers with contempt. She tells **Alexander Jolliffe** how it needs to be reformed.

Dame Sheila McKechnie is angry. In fact, the director of the Consumers' Association is incensed that Prudential, the insurer, has taken £650,000 from private investors' funds to pay a fine for mis-selling pensions instead of using shareholders' money. 'That is one of the biggest financial institutions in the country – what does this say about the culture of the industry?'

This is typical of an industry that despises its customers but still makes profits, she says. 'The culture of the life assurance industry is: "give us your money, we'll decide how to invest it and what share of the returns you get, and you can't leave until we've got what we want from you".' Dame Sheila echoes other observers, who criticise life assurers' with-profits investment funds for levying high charges and being opaque.

The industry treats consumers with contempt because it can do so without losing business, she says. 'There's no evidence that the worst-behaving companies suffer detriment. If this industry can rip off consumers, it will do so.'

Companies do not compete for investors' business, but to win distribution of their products by offering high commissions to financial advisers. The result is an industry less responsive to the public than any other.

The financial services industry's indifference to consumers makes her mad. When she talks to life assurance executives, she gets the impression they are on different planets.

'Just because people are stupid about their finances doesn't mean we can let them be ripped off, because of the social and political consequences.'

The government must act because the industry will not solve problems alone, she says.

Exhibit 5.8 A bad deal for consumers at the hands of the insurance industry

Source: *Financial Times* 6/7 July 2002

The government is also worried about these products and commissioned a report under the chairmanship of Ron Sandler. It reported in 2002 (*www.hm-treasury.gov.uk*), proposing the following changes to with-profits policies:

- No creaming off profits for shareholders.
- Insurance companies to make a single, explicit management charge as a proportion of assets.

- Investors to be given information on smoothing – vitally, it should be neutral in the long run (in other words, not biased to give low bonuses).
- Customers to be given four figures annually: the current redemption value of the policy; the proceeds available on death; a projection of the payout on maturity; and the value of the underlying assets (unsmoothed).
- Customers to be given an annual report on the financial condition of the fund, investment performance, its asset allocation (what it invests in), and its costs.
- The terms terminal and reversionary bonuses should go as they are unnecessary jargon. Even the term 'with-profits' should go as it 'conveys no useful meaning'.

We'll have to wait to see if matters improve.

Unit-linked policies

Unit-linked insurance policies incorporate both life insurance and a collective investment. The insurance company creates a fund that is divided into units. The investor buys units in a similar way to the purchase of units in unit trusts. Alternatively, the funds may be invested through the insurance company in actual unit trusts.

With unit-linked insurance there is usually a guaranteed sum assured. But returns beyond that are determined by ups and downs in the value of the units. The death benefit is the higher of the sum assured and the value of the units at time of death.

There is a wide range of underlying assets. Some funds invest in UK or overseas shares, while others invest by lending short-term in the money markets. Others just buy property, and some buy a range of different asset types.

Return are determined by the performance of the underlying market and by the manager's performance. Unit-linked policies are riskier than with-profits policies because there are no unwithdrawable reversionary bonuses. It is possible for the unit value to plummet if the underlying assets do badly. However, they are not as risky as investing directly in unit trusts or shares because of the sum assured.

The units are quoted at two prices in the Managed Fund Service section of the *Financial Times*: the price you pay to buy (the offer price) and the price at which you can sell (the bid price). These usually differ by 5–6 per cent. There is also a management charge (0.5–1.5 per cent per year). In addition, in the first few years of a policy you are likely to find that large deductions are made for administration and life insurance: you might only get a 60 per cent unit allocation in the first year or two.

Insurance companies usually have a wide variety of types of units and will probably allow you to switch without paying an initial charge again. So you could switch from, say, Asia Pacific share units to gilt income units. Policies can be started with as little as £10 per month.

Insurance company bonds

With insurance company bonds you invest a lump sum (£1,000 or more) with an insurance company for a fixed period, say 5 years, in return for a fixed rate of interest. **Guaranteed income bonds** (**GIBs**) pay a regular income net of basic rate income tax once a year (or monthly). With **growth bonds** the interest accumulates until the maturity date. Insurance company bonds are relatively safe investments if held to maturity, but returns are low – of the order of 2–4 per cent in 2004. If you don't hold to maturity and choose to cash in early (if the insurance company allows this) you will probably suffer a penalty.

Distribution bonds (also sold by insurance companies) tend to invest in a mixture of equity and fixed income securities (e.g. gilts, corporate bonds) but will be biased toward interest paying instruments. Unlike with-profits funds they do not smooth out income from one year to the next or offer the protection of reversionary bonuses, so the payout fluctuates. Exit penalties for cashing in during the first 5 years can be high. They are more straightforward than with-profits policies because returns are not clouded by smoothing.

Money Management magazine provides a list of insurance bonds, allowing you to examine the rates of return on offer.

Stock market-linked bonds

Offered by insurance companies, banks, building societies and other investment firms, stock market-linked bonds provide a return that goes up with a stock market index. Products with similar characteristics are called by a variety of names, for example: **defined-return bonds, guaranteed equity bonds, protected bonds and structured products**. As an investor you commit a lump sum for, say, 5 years. Typically, the provider offers your capital back at the end, plus all of the increase in, say, the FTSE 100 index over the 5 years up to a maximum of, say, 65 per cent – if the index doubles you will not benefit beyond the 65 per cent limit. The provider does not actually buy shares but instead uses the money to buy a mixture of interest-bearing securities and derivatives, which rise in value if the FTSE 100 rises.

With the guarantee that you will at least get back your original lump sum these instruments provide a relatively safe way of benefiting should the stock market index rise significantly. However, bear in mind that your return is only *linked* to the stock market index. This is not the same as receiving the returns by holding, say, the top 100 shares. First, you are missing out on an important element of return, the dividend income. Second, you usually only receive a proportion of the capital gain over the 5 years, not the full gain. Furthermore, there are stock market-linked bonds that don't provide complete protection on the downside. If the index falls by more than a stated percentage the guaranteed amount will fall below the initial capital. Some providers offer the investor choices, such as a 100 per cent money-back guarantee plus 55 per cent of the rise in the in FTSE 100 index, or a 95 per cent guarantee and 110 per cent of the rise in the FTSE 100.

Many financial product providers are under attack for misselling what became known as **precipice bonds** to investors who thought they were buying a safe investment. Precipice bonds offer the return of the original capital, but only in specific circumstances. If the market index falls below a predetermined level the guarantee no longer applies. So, a typical precipice bond may offer 7 per cent annual income over the next 3 years. It also offers a return of the initial capital at the end of 3 years if the market index does not fall by more than, say, 20 per cent from its start level. However – and this is where the danger lies – after the 20 per cent barrier has been breached, for every 1 per cent fall in the FTSE 100 the investor loses 2 per cent of the capital value. Hence the nickname precipice bonds – the value of your savings can fall steeply. Look out for names such as '**high income**' or '**extra income**' bonds or 'plans'. Only invest in these products if you understand and can withstand the downside risk.

Two final points on stock market-linked bonds:

- The complicated payout conditions on all these bonds mean that investors need to be disciplined enough to read the small print.
- Enquire into the payout if you cash in early – is this guaranteed or dependent on market values?

Hedge funds

Hedge funds are collective investment vehicles that admit only a small number of wealthy individuals or institutions. They are free from most types of regulation designed to protect investors, being created either offshore or as private investment partnerships. To place your money with a hedge fund you are generally expected to have a net worth (excluding main residence) of at least £600,000 and to be prepared to commit hundreds of thousands of pounds to the fund.

Originally, the word 'hedge' made some sense when applied to these funds. They would, through a combination of investments, including derivatives, try to hedge risk while seeking a high absolute return (rather than a return relative to an index). Today the word 'hedge' is misapplied to these funds because they generally take aggressive bets on the movement of currencies, equities, stock markets, interest rates, bonds, etc. around the world. They frequently add to the risk by borrowing a multiple of the amount put in by the wealthy individuals or institutions.

The freedom from regulation is a major selling point for hedge funds as it means that they are not confined to investing in particular classes of security, or to particular investment methods. For example, they are free to go **short** (selling shares they don't own in the expectation of buying them back at a lower price later) which they wouldn't be able to do in many regulated environments. They can borrow 10 times the size of the fund to take a punt on small movements in currency rates. They can buy the bonds of distressed companies selling at bombed-out prices. Some are active in the share index futures market, the short-term interest rate future market and a range of other highly specialised markets that traditional domestic investment funds are much more cautious about entering.

Their freedom to jump in and out means that hedge funds often get the blame for destabilising markets by moving billions from one part of the globe to another, or from one instrument to another. For example, George Soros came under attack after reputedly making $1 billion by betting against sterling in 1992. Hedge funds were also an easy target for politicians in East Asia in 1997 as currencies collapsed and stock markets fell, leading to economic slow-downs. While it is true that hedge funds can move vast sums around the world – they have $650 billion under management and have access to hundreds of billions more by borrowing – more often than not financial crises are caused by poor economic policy. The hedge funds are on the lookout for governments trying to defy economic gravity and then take advantage of the situation.

Recently the popularity of hedge funds has boomed as stock markets have fallen. They have attracted new interest because of the drive to produce positive absolute returns. Onshore fund managers too often pat themselves on the back if they produce a negative return of 15 per cent while the market fell by 16 per cent. Hedge funds are seen as different in that they are not content with negative performance. Another attraction is that the investments and markets they enter frequently have a negative correlation[8] with domestic equities – an attractive proposition in a declining equity environment market. **Bear funds** take this idea a stage further. They are designed to do well when equities are falling. They can do this by going short on specific shares, by shorting a stock market index or by selling stock index future contracts (see Chapter 9).

If the hedge fund does well the managers receive exceptional rewards. A typical fee structure might be 1–2 per cent of the fund value regardless of performance; on top of this 10, 20 or 25 per cent of any generated profits are taken by the managers.

It is impossible to state where hedge funds as a whole sit in the risk–reward spectrum. Some are managed to be relatively safe, while others are dedicated to extreme actions in obscure corners of the financial world. Some have outperformed the FTSE 100 index while many have failed completely (only 60 per cent of those in business 5 years ago are still operating). Performance statistics are sketchy at best, and often downright misleading. One of the major risks investors have largely ignored is the lack of transparency about where their money is being used, which makes it difficult to assess how the fund would survive extreme and unpredictable markets. There is also a greater vulnerability to fraud due to the opacity of funds and absence of regulations. Moreover, there are now over 3,000 hedge funds to choose from and there is a fear that there simply aren't enough talented (and honest!) managers to go round.

[8] Negative correlation means that returns go the opposite way: when domestic equities are down the hedge fund instruments are up, and vice versa.

The Financial Services Authority has barred most hedge funds from being marketed and sold to UK retail investors. The only way into hedge funds for small investors[9] is via **funds of hedge funds**, which invest in a range of hedge funds. Some of these are listed on London Stock Exchange as closed-ended investment companies or OEICs.[10]

Critics point out that in buying fund of funds you end up paying two management charges and there is little evidence that managers of funds of hedge funds can consistently select the future best performers. Hedge funds are only for the seriously wealthy, and even then it does not make sense to devote more than 10 per cent of assets to this type of investment.

Websites for hedge funds

www.hedginfo.com	Allenbridge Hedge Fund Research
www.hedgefundsreview.com	HedgeFundsReview
www.hedgefund.net	Hedge Fund
www.hfr.com	HRF Asset Management and Hedge Fund Research Inc.

Fund supermarkets

Fund supermarkets, available online or offline, allow you to invest in a range of unit trusts, investment trusts and OEICs. You can pick one, two or a dozen funds from different management companies. Furthermore, you can get discounts on the initial charges[11] and can hold the funds tax-free within an ISA.

Additional services include statements that show the status and performance of all your different funds brought together, and the ability to switch funds within an ISA for a low (or no) charge. You can also make one-off lump-sum injections or regular (monthly) premium contributions.

Fund supermarkets on the internet have been hailed as the death-knell for independent financial advisers, (IFAs). Supermarkets try to replace IFAs by matching the funds to the investors' needs. Some do this through an online questionnaire, while others provide online advice.

Before bypassing IFAs you might like to consider the following:

- You may need more tailored advice, especially given the bewildering choice (there are at least 4,000 funds).
- Discount broking IFAs *may* provide a larger discount on the initial charge

[9] If you can satisfy the FSA that you are an 'expert' investor, then hedge funds are permitted to sell to you. However, you will not be entitled to compensation if the offshore fund goes bust.

[10] Many of these OEICs are listed on the Irish Stock Exchange.

[11] It can be cheaper to buy through a supermarket than direct from the fund management company because the supermarkets offer to discount the initial charge.

- Some are not true supermarkets permitting the holding of a consolidated ISA. They merely act as portals for selling specific funds, but do not allow you to mix-and-match those funds within an ISA.
- Additional fees for administration may be charged.
- No fund supermarket covers all funds.

Reports of the death of the IFA have been much exaggerated. Many investors seek advice from an IFA and then buy via an online supermarket. Others continue to let the IFA arrange buying.

Websites for fund supermarkets

www.iii.co.uk	Ample
www.egg.com	Egg
www.inter-alliance.com	Inter-Alliance
www.comdirect.co.uk	ComDirect
www.selftrade.co.uk	Self Trade Mutual Funds
www.fidelity.co.uk/fundsnetwork	FundsNetwork (Fidelity)
www.cofunds.com	Cofunds
www.tqonline.co.uk	Torquil Clark
www.bestinvest.co.uk	Bestinvest
www.h-l.co.uk	Hargreaves Lansdown

6

Bonds

Bonds can be good investments for private investors to hold. They offer a higher income than a building society deposit account, with the possibility of some capital growth. They offer lower risk than shares, but offsetting this is the fact that they generally offer a lower return.

A bond is a long-term contract in which the bondholder lends money to a company, government or some other organisation. In return the company or government promises to pay predetermined regular interest and a capital sum at the end of the bond's life. Basically, bonds may be regarded as merely IOUs with pages of legal clauses expressing the promises made. They are the most significant financial instruments in the world today, with over $37,000,000,000,000 ($37 trillion) in issue. They come in all shapes and sizes, from UK government bonds to Chinese company bonds.

The advantage of placing your money with an organisation via a bond is that you are *promised* a return. Bond investors are exposed to less risk than share investors because the promise is backed up with a series of legal rights, among them the right to receive the annual interest before the equity holders receive any dividend. So in a bad year (with, say, no profits) the bond investors are far more likely to receive a payout than the shareholders. This is usually bolstered with rights to seize company assets if the company reneges on its promise. There is a greater chance of saving some of your investment if things go very badly for the firm if you are holding its bonds rather than its shares, because on liquidation the proceeds raised by selling off the assets are used to pay the holders of debt-type financial securities first, before shareholders receive anything.

Offsetting these plus points are the facts that bondholders do not (usually) share in the value created by an extraordinarily successful business, and there is an absence of any voting power over the management of the company.

Confusingly, many investment products are described as 'bonds' but are not true bonds in the sense of being loans. For example, guaranteed equity bonds, with-profits bonds, distribution bonds and single-premium bonds issued by insurance companies, and 'bonds' issued by building societies. The only bonds we will deal with in this chapter are long-term *loan* contracts.

Bonds are often referred to collectively as **fixed-interest securities**. While this is an accurate description for many bonds, others do not offer *regular* interest payments that are *fixed* amounts. Nevertheless they are all lumped together as fixed-interest to contrast these types of loan instrument with equities that do not carry the promise of a return.

■ Gilts

In most years the British government does not raise enough in taxes to cover its expenditure. It makes up a large part of the difference by selling bonds. These are called 'gilts' because in the old days you would receive a very attractive certificate with gold-leaf edges (**gilt-edged securities**). Buying UK government bonds is among the safest form of lending in the world. The risk of the UK government failing to pay is infinitesimally small.

While the risk of non-receipt of interest and capital is minute if you buy and hold gilts to the maturity date, you can lose money buying and selling gilts from year to year (or month to month) in the secondary market before they mature. This was shown in Chapter 2 (Exhibit 2.3); there have been many occasions when, if you purchased at the start of the year and sold to another investor in the secondary market at the end of the year, even after receiving interest, you would have lost 5 per cent or more. On the other hand, there were many years when you would have made large gains.

The government issues gilts via the UK **Debt Management Office (DMO)** (*www.dmo.gov.uk*). The gilts are sold with a **nominal** (**face** or **par**) value of £100. This is not necessarily what you would pay. The nominal value signifies what the government will pay *you* at the end of, say, 5, 10 or 25 years. This is how much the gilt will be **redeemed** for on the **redemption date**. You might pay £100 or £99 or £100.50, or some other sum for it, depending on the coupon offered and the general level of interest rates in the markets.

The **coupon** is the stated annual rate of return on the nominal value of the bond. It is a percentage figure shown immediately after the name of each gilt. So, for example, a Treasury 6¼ pc '10 pays out £6.25 each year for every £100 nominal. Then in the year 2010 the nominal value of £100 is paid when the gilt is redeemed. The coupons are paid **twice yearly** in two equal instalments.

The names assigned to gilts (also called **stocks)**, such as Exchequer, Treasury or Funding, are useful for distinguishing one from another but have no particular significance beyond that. What is more important is whether they are dated, undated or conversion. **Dated** gilts have a fixed date(s) at which they are redeemed. Some have a range of dates, e.g. Treasury 7¾ pc, '12–'15. This gilt will not be redeemed before the first date, 2012, and it must be redeemed before the second, 2015. The government has the option of when to redeem between these dates. Until it is redeemed £7.75 will be paid each year in coupons.

A few **undated** gilts exist, such as War Loan 3½pc, which may never be redeemed. The government can go on paying £3.50 per year for ever. **Conversion** gilts allow the investor to choose whether to convert a gilt to another more attractive one.

Gilts are classified according to the current life left as from now (not from when they were first issued). **Shorts** are those that will be redeemed within 5 years. Those with 5–15 years to run are **medium-dated**. If maturity is at least 15 years away the gilt is **long-dated**. And, of course, there are undated gilts.

Prices and returns

The coupons showing on different gilts can have a wide range, from 2.5 per cent to 13.5 per cent. These were (roughly) the rates of interest that the government had to offer at the time of issue – some were issued 80 or more years ago. However, things have moved on since issue and these percentages are not the rates of return offered on the gilt to a buyer in the secondary market today.

So, if we take an undated gilt offering a coupon of 2.5 per cent on the nominal value we may find that investors are buying and selling a bond that offers £2.50 per year at a price of £50, not at its nominal value of £100. This gilt offers an investor today a yield of 5 per cent:

$$\frac{£2.50}{£50} \times 100 = 5\%$$

Thus we see some bonds trading above and, as in this case, below the nominal value of £100 in the secondary market. In this way investors can receive the current going rate of return for that type of investment.

Yield

There are, in fact, two types of yields on dated gilts. The case of a Treasury 10 pc with 5 years to maturity currently selling in the secondary market at £120 will serve to illustrate the two. From the name of the gilt we glean that it pays £10 per year (10 per cent of the nominal value of £100). For £120 investors can buy this gilt from other investors on the secondary market to receive an **interest yield** (also known as the **flat yield**, **income yield** and **running yield**) of 8.33 per cent:

$$\text{Interest yield} = \frac{\text{Gross (before tax) interest coupon}}{\text{Market price}} \times 100$$

$$= \frac{£10}{£120} \times 100 = 8.33\%$$

This is not the true rate of return available to the investor because we have failed to take into account the capital loss over the next 5 years. The investor pays £120 but receives only the nominal value of £100 at the end. If this £20 loss is apportioned over the five years it works out at £4 per year. The capital loss as a percentage of what the investor pays (£120) is £4/£120 × 100 = 3.33 per cent per year. This loss to redemption has to be subtracted from the annual interest yield to give an approximation to the **redemption yield** (also called **yield to maturity**): 8.33 per cent – 3.33 per cent = 5 per cent. While this example tries to convey the essence of redemption yield calculations, it oversimplifies in that a compound interest-type calculation is required to obtain a precise figure.[1]

The general rules are as follows:

- If a dated gilt is trading at less than £100 the purchaser will receive a capital gain between purchase and redemption and so the redemption yield is greater than the interest yield.
- If a dated gilt is selling at more than £100 a capital loss will be made if held to maturity and so the redemption yield is below the interest yield.

Of course, these capital gains and losses are based on the assumption that the investor buys the gilt and then holds to maturity. In reality many investors sell a few days or

[1] For more details, see Chapter 11 of G. Arnold, *Corporate Financial Management* (Financial Times Prentice Hall, 2002).

months after purchase, in which case they may make capital gains or losses dependent not on what the government pays on maturity but on what another investor is prepared to pay. This, in turn, depends on general economic conditions – in particular, projected general inflation over the life of the gilt: investors will not buy a gilt offering a 5 per cent redemption yield over 5 years if future inflation is expected to be 7% per year for that period. Interest rates (particularly for longer-term gilts) are thus strongly influenced by market perceptions of future inflation, which can shift significantly over a year or so, hence the high annual gains or losses in the secondary gilt market shown in Chapter 2.

Gilt prices and redemption yields move in opposite directions. Take the case of our five-year gilt offering a coupon of 10 per cent with a redemption yield of 5 per cent. If general interest rates rise to 6 per cent because of an increase in inflation expectations, investors will no longer be interested in buying this gilt for £120, because at this price it yields only 5 per cent. Demand will fall, resulting in a price reduction until the bond yields 6 per cent. A rise in yield goes hand in hand with a fall in price.

Quotes

The gilts market is focused around **gilt-edged market makers (GEMMs)** who are prepared to buy from or sell to investors. They quote two prices: the **bid** price is the price at which they will buy, and the **offer** price is their selling price. The UK gilts table shown daily in the *Financial Times* shows the middle price, half way between the bid and offer price – see Exhibit 6.1.

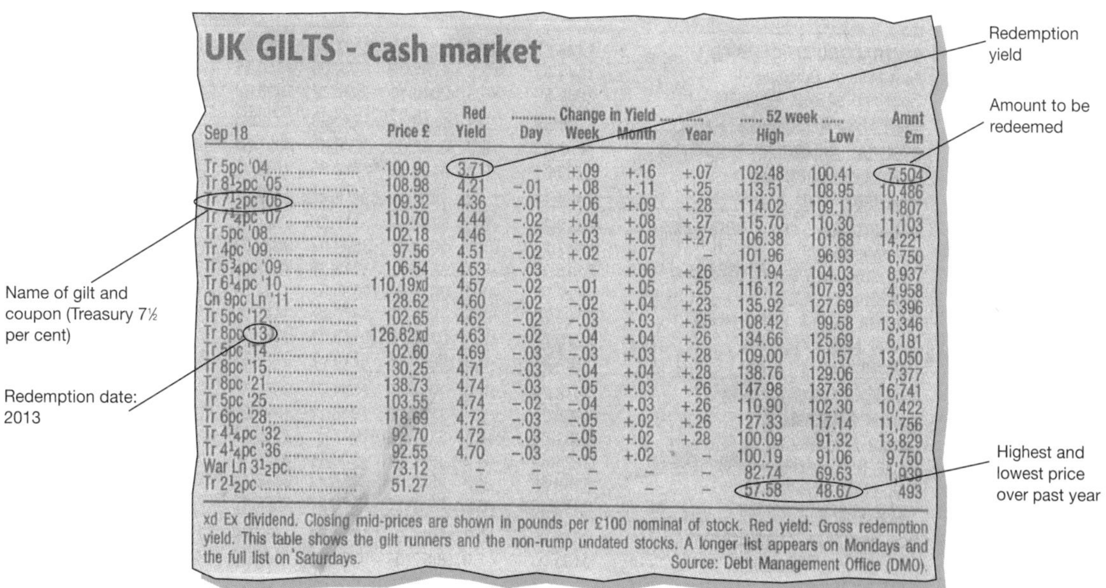

UK GILTS - cash market

Sep 18	Price £	Red Yield	Change in Yield Day	Week	Month	Year	52 week High	Low	Amnt £m
Tr 5pc '04	100.90	3.71	–	+.09	+.16	+.07	102.48	100.41	7,504
Tr 8½pc '05	108.98	4.21	–.01	+.08	+.11	+.25	113.51	108.95	10,486
Tr 7½pc '06	109.32	4.36	–.01	+.06	+.09	+.28	114.02	109.11	11,807
Tr 7¾pc '07	110.70	4.44	–.02	+.04	+.08	+.27	115.70	110.30	11,103
Tr 5pc '08	102.18	4.46	–.02	+.03	+.08	+.27	106.38	101.68	14,221
Tr 4pc '09	97.56	4.51	–.02	+.02	+.07	–	101.96	96.93	6,750
Tr 5¾pc '09	106.54	4.53	–.03	–	+.06	+.26	111.94	104.03	8,937
Tr 6¼pc '10	110.19xd	4.57	–.02	–.01	+.05	+.25	116.12	107.93	4,958
Cn 9pc Ln '11	128.62	4.60	–.02	–.02	+.04	+.23	135.92	127.69	5,396
Tr 5pc '12	102.65	4.62	–.02	–.03	+.03	+.25	108.42	99.58	13,346
Tr 8pc '13	126.82xd	4.63	–.02	–.04	+.04	+.26	134.66	125.69	6,181
Tr 5pc '14	102.60	4.69	–.03	–.03	+.03	+.28	109.00	101.57	13,050
Tr 8pc '15	130.25	4.71	–.03	–.04	+.04	+.28	138.76	129.06	7,377
Tr 8pc '21	138.73	4.74	–.03	–.05	+.03	+.26	147.98	137.36	16,741
Tr 5pc '25	103.55	4.74	–.02	–.04	+.03	+.26	110.90	102.30	10,422
Tr 6pc '28	118.69	4.72	–.03	–.05	+.02	+.26	127.33	117.14	11,756
Tr 4¼pc '32	92.70	4.72	–.03	–.05	+.02	+.28	100.09	91.32	13,829
Tr 4¼pc '36	92.55	4.70	–.03	–.05	+.02	–	100.19	91.06	9,750
War Ln 3½pc	73.12	–	–	–	–	–	82.74	69.63	1,939
Tr 2½pc	51.27	–	–	–	–	–	57.58	48.67	493

xd Ex dividend. Closing mid-prices are shown in pounds per £100 nominal of stock. Red yield: Gross redemption yield. This table shows the gilt runners and the non-rump undated stocks. A longer list appears on Mondays and the full list on Saturdays.

Source: Debt Management Office (DMO).

Exhibit 6.1 UK Gilts table from the *Financial Times*

Source: *Financial Times* Friday 19 September 2003

Note that the redemption yield shown in the *Financial Times* is relevant if you are an investor on that particular day paying the price shown. However, if you bought your gilt years ago and expect to hold to maturity you are likely to be receiving a different yield on the money you put in.

Other sources of information on prices, and on the gilts market generally, include the following:

www.bloomberg.co.uk	Bloomberg
www.gilt.co.uk	Kauders Portfolio Management
www.moody.com	Moody's
www.standardpoor.com	Standard and Poor's
www.fitch.com	Fitch
www.jpmorgan.com	J.P. Morgan
www.ft.com	Financial Times
www.bondscape.net	Bondscape

Buying and selling gilts

You can buy or sell gilts through brokers in the same fashion as with shares (see Chapter 4). Telephone or online dealing is offered by many brokers. You would state the nominal value of the gilts you want to deal and whether you want to trade 'at best' (the best price currently in the market) or with a limit on the price you are prepared to pay (or sell for).

High street banks, some building societies, independent financial advisers and even some solicitors and accountants will buy or sell gilts for you. The more liquid gilts can be sold through the **Bank of England Brokerage Service** (tel. 01452 398333) for a commission charge that compares favourably with brokers. The relevant forms are available at post offices or by writing to the Bank of England (*www.bankofengland.co.uk*).

You can buy gilts when they are first issued by bidding for them in the government auction (minimum £1,000). If selecting an appropriate bid price is too onerous, you could opt to pay the average price of the issue decided by other bidders. The advantages of buying direct are that no commission is payable and there is no market maker's spread.

Cum-dividend and ex-dividend

Gilts usually pay coupons twice a year. Between payments the interest **accrues** on a daily basis. If you buy a gilt you are entitled to the accrued interest since the last coupon. You will receive this when the next coupon is paid. That is, you buy the gilt **cum-dividend**.

Gilts are quoted at **clean prices** – that is, without taking account of the accrued interest. However, the buyer will pay the clean price plus the accrued interest value (called the **dirty price**) and receives all of the next coupon. So, if you buy a gilt 4 months before the next coupon due you would pay the clean price, say, £98 plus 60 days' accrued interest.

If you bought just before the coupon is to be paid the situation is different. There would not be enough time to change the register to make sure that the coupon goes to the new owner. To allow for this problem a gilt switches from being quoted cum-dividend to being **ex-dividend** 7 days before an interest payment. If you buy during the ex-dividend period the person you bought from would receive the accrued interest from the government – this would be reflected in the price you pay.

Index-linked gilts

There is a hidden danger with conventional gilts – **inflation risk**. Suppose that you, along with the rest of the gilt-buying community, figure that inflation over the next ten years will average 2.5 per cent. As a result you buy 10-year gilts that have a redemption yield of 4.8 per cent giving a comfortable real income over and above cost-of-living rises. However, 2 years later inflation starts to take off (oil prices quadruple, or the government goes on a spending spree). Now investors reckon that inflation will average 6 per cent over the following 8 years. As a result your gilt yield will fail to maintain your capital in real terms.

The government introduced a type of bond that ensures you receive a return above the inflation rate throughout the entire life of the bond. These are called **index-linked stocks (gilts)**. The gilt initially offers to pay £100 at the end of its term, say 10 years away. It also offers to pay a low coupon, say 2 per cent. The key thing about index-linked bonds is that neither the capital sum on maturity nor the coupon stays at these levels unless inflation is zero over the next 10 years.

Suppose inflation is 4 per cent over the first year of the bond's life. The payout on maturity rises to £104. This inflation-linked uplift happens every year. So, if over the 10 years the inflation measure has risen by 60 per cent, the payout on the bond is £160. This means that you can buy just as many goods and services at the end with the capital sum as at the beginning of the bond's life (if you paid £100). (The situation is slightly more complicated than this in that the inflation figures used are those for 8 months preceding the relevant coupon dates, but this example illustrates the principle.) Furthermore, the coupon rate also rises through the years if there is inflation. So, after the first year the coupons go up by 4%, that is, £2 × 1.04 = £2.08.

A final point on index linked gilts. Because most investors hold them to maturity secondary trading is thin and dealing spreads wider than for conventional gilts.

Corporate bonds

Corporate bonds offer a higher rate of return than gilts but, as you might expect, this comes with a greater degree of risk. It has been known for companies to be unable to pay interest and principal on the bonds they issue, and for bondholders to end up with nothing following liquidation. This downside should not be overemphasised because the vast majority of corporate bonds pay out the full promised amount. They are certainly much safer than investing in shares.

Corporate bonds are generally **negotiable** (that is, tradable in a secondary market). They come in a variety of forms. The most common is the type with regular (usually semi-annual) fixed coupons and a specified redemption date. These are known as **straight**, **plain vanilla** or **bullet** bonds. Other bonds are a variation on this. Some pay coupons every 3 months, some do not pay a fixed coupon but one which varies depending on the level of short-term interest rates (**floating-rate** or **variable-rate bonds**), some have interest rates linked to the rate of inflation. In fact, the potential for variety and innovation is almost infinite. Bonds issued in the last few years have linked the interest rates paid or the principal payments to a wide variety of economic events, such as a rise in the price of silver, exchange-rate movements, stock market indices, the price of oil, gold or copper – even to the occurrence of an earthquake. These bonds were generally designed to let companies adjust their interest payments to manageable levels in the event of the firm being adversely affected by some economic variable changing. For example, a copper miner pays lower interest on its finance if the copper price falls. In 1999 Sampdoria, the Italian football club, issued a €3.5 million bond that paid a higher rate of return if the club won promotion to the 'Serie A' division. If the club rose to the top four in Serie A the coupon would rise to 14 per cent.

Debentures and loan stocks

The most secure type of bond is called a **debenture**. They are usually secured by either a fixed or a floating charge against the firm's assets. **A fixed charge** means that specific assets are used as security, which, in the event of default, can be sold at the insistence of the debenture bondholders and the proceeds used to repay them. Debentures secured on property may be referred to as **mortgage debentures**. A **floating charge** means that the loan is secured by a general charge on all the assets of the corporation. In this case the company has a high degree of freedom to use its assets as it wishes, such as sell them or rent them out, until it commits a default which 'crystallises' the floating charge. If this happens a receiver will be appointed with powers to dispose of assets and to distribute the proceeds to the creditors. Even though floating-charge debenture holders can force a liquidation, fixed-charge debenture holders rank above floating-charge debenture holders in the payout after insolvency.

The terms 'bond', 'debenture' and '**loan stock**' are often used interchangeably and the dividing line between debentures and loan stock is a fuzzy one. As a general rule, debentures are secured (have the backing of collateral) and loan stock is unsecured, but there are examples that do not fit this classification. If liquidation occurs the unsecured loan stockholders rank beneath the debenture holders and some other categories of creditors such as the tax authorities.

Trust deeds and covenants

Bond investors are willing to lower the interest they demand if they can be reassured that their money will not be exposed to a high risk. This reassurance is conveyed by placing **risk-reducing restrictions on the firm**. A **trust deed** sets out the terms of the contract between bondholders and the company. The **trustees** ensure compliance with the contract throughout the life of the bond and have the power to appoint a receiver (to liquidate the firm's assets). The loan agreement will contain a number of **affirmative covenants**. These usually include the requirements to supply regular financial statements, interest and principal payments. The deed may also state the fees due to the lenders and details of what procedures are to be followed in the event of a technical default, such as non-payment of interest.

In addition to these basic covenants are the **negative covenants**. These restrict the actions and the rights of the borrower until the debt has been repaid in full. Some examples are:

- **Limits on further debt issuance.** If lenders provide finance to a firm they do so on certain assumptions concerning the riskiness of the capital structure. They will want to ensure that the loan does not become riskier due to the firm taking on a much greater debt burden relative to its equity base, so they limit the amount and type of further debt issues – particularly debt which is higher (**senior**) ranking for interest payments and for a liquidation payment. **Subordinated debt (junior debt)** – with low ranking on liquidation – is more likely to be acceptable.
- **Dividend level.** Lenders are opposed to money being taken into the firm by borrowing at one end, while being taken away by shareholders at the other. An excessive withdrawal of shareholders' funds may unbalance the financial structure and weaken future cash flows.
- **Limits on the disposal of assets.** The retention of certain assets, such as property and land, may be essential to reduce the lenders' risk.
- **Financial ratios.** A typical covenant here concerns the interest cover, for example: The annual profit will remain four times as great as the overall annual interest charge (see Chapter 12 for more on interest cover under 'income gearing'). Other restrictions might be placed on working capital ratio levels and the debt to net assets ratio.

While negative covenants cannot ensure completely risk-free lending, they can influence the behaviour of the managerial team so as to reduce the risk of default.

Repayments

The principal on many bonds is paid entirely at maturity. However, there are bonds which can be repaid before the final redemption date. A common approach is for the company to issue bonds with a range of dates for redemption; so a bond dated 2008–2012 would allow a company the flexibility to repay a part of the principal in each of four years. Another way of redeeming bonds is for the issuing firm to buy the outstanding bonds by offering the holder a sum higher than or equal to the amount originally paid. A firm is also able to purchase bonds on the open market.

Some bonds are described as '**irredeemable**' as they have no fixed redemption date.

From the investor's viewpoint they may be irredeemable, but the firm has the option of repurchase and can effectively redeem the bonds.

Bond variations

Bonds which are sold at well below the par value are called **deep discounted bonds**, the most extreme form of which is the zero coupon bond. These are sold at a large discount to the nominal value (e.g. sold for £60 when the nominal value is £100). The investor makes a capital gain by holding the bond instead of receiving coupons. These bonds are particularly useful for firms with low cash flows in the near term – for example, firms engaged in a major property development that will not mature for many years.

Floating rate notes (also called '**variable-rate notes**') are instruments that pay an interest that is linked to a benchmark rate – such as the **London Inter-Bank Offered Rate (LIBOR)**. LIBOR is the rate that banks charge each other for borrowed funds. The issuer will pay, say, 70 basis points (0.7 percentage points) over LIBOR. The coupon is set for, say, the first 6 months at the time of issue, after which it is adjusted every 6 months; so if LIBOR was 10 per cent, the floating rate note would pay 10.7 per cent for that particular period of 6 months.

Trading in the corporate bond market

The gilts secondary market is very liquid, with a government bond issue raising billions and with thousands of investors trading in the market. By contrast, corporate bond market activity can be very low. Companies may raise merely tens or hundreds of millions of pounds in an issue, and most investors buy and hold to maturity. Some corporate bonds are sufficiently liquid to trade on the London Stock Exchange, but the vast majority of trading occurs in the **over-the-counter (OTC) market** directly between an investor and a bond dealer. **Bond dealers** stand ready to quote a bid and an offer price depending on whether you want to buy or sell. Your broker will have to contact a number of these dealers by telephone to get quote prices.

Because most corporate bond market trading is a private matter between the dealer and its customer in the OTC market it is difficult to obtain prices of recent trades. They are not shown in the *Financial Times*, for example. The *Investors Chronicle*, in collaboration with Bondscape, publishes a corporate bond index and shows bond yields (see also *www.ic-community.co.uk/bonds*).

Credit rating

Firms often pay to have their bonds rated by specialist **credit-rating organisations**. Investors are advised to pay close attention to the outcome of these rating exercises. The **debt rating** depends on the likelihood of payments of interest and/or capital not being made (that is, **default**) and on the extent to which the lender is protected in the event of a default by the loan contract (the **recoverability of debt**). UK government gilts have an insignificant risk of default whereas unsecured subordinated corporate loan stock has a much higher risk. We would expect that firms in stable industries with conservative accounting and financing policies and a risk-averse business strategy would have a low risk of default and therefore a high credit rating. Companies with a high total debt burden, a poor cash flow position, in a worsening market environment causing lower and more volatile earnings, will have a high default risk and a low credit rating. The leading organisations providing credit ratings are Moody's, Standard and Poor's (S&P) and Fitch. The highest rating is AAA (S&P) or Aaa (Moody's), pronounced 'triple-A'. Such a rating indicates very high quality, with an extremely strong capacity to repay interest and principal. Single A, under both S&P and Moody's systems indicates a strong capacity to pay interest and capital, but some degree of susceptibility to impairment as economic events unfold. BBB indicates adequate debt service capacity but vulnerability to adverse economic conditions or changing circumstances. Debt rated B or C has predominantly speculative characteristics. The lowest is D, which indicates the firm is in default. Ratings of BBB– (S&P) or Baa3 (Moody's) or above are regarded as '**investment-grade**' – this is important because many institutional investors are permitted to invest in investment-grade bonds only (see Exhibit 6.2). Bonds rated below this are called **high-yield (or junk) bonds**.

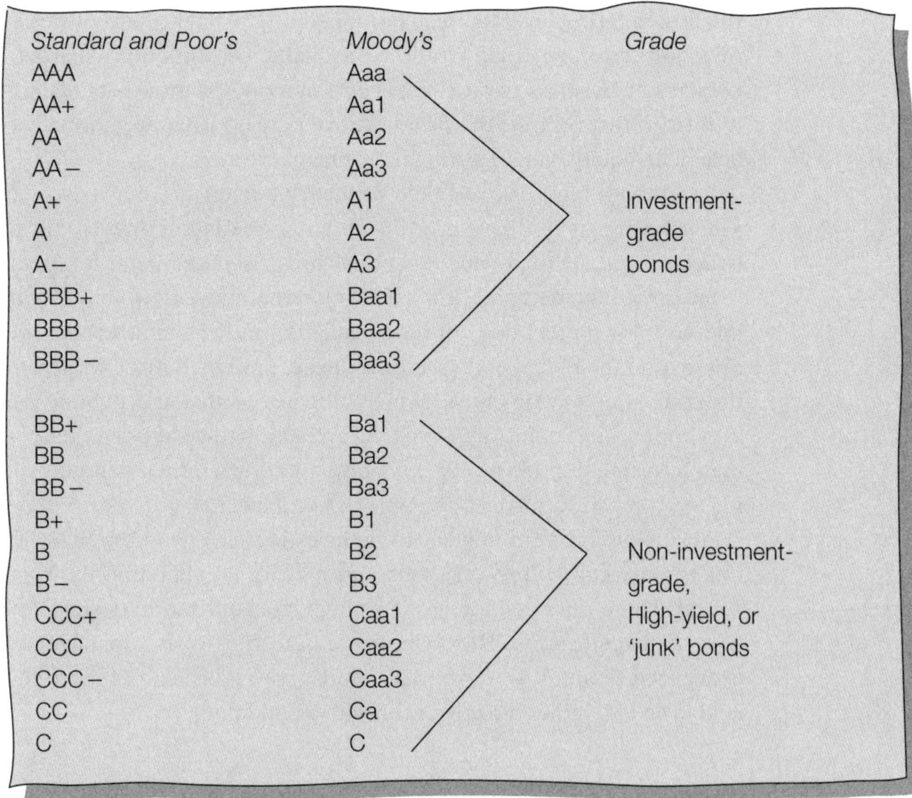

Standard and Poor's	*Moody's*	*Grade*
AAA	Aaa	
AA+	Aa1	
AA	Aa2	
AA–	Aa3	
A+	A1	Investment-grade bonds
A	A2	
A–	A3	
BBB+	Baa1	
BBB	Baa2	
BBB–	Baa3	
BB+	Ba1	
BB	Ba2	
BB–	Ba3	
B+	B1	
B	B2	Non-investment-grade, High-yield, or 'junk' bonds
B–	B3	
CCC+	Caa1	
CCC	Caa2	
CCC–	Caa3	
CC	Ca	
C	C	

Exhibit 6.2 Moody's and Standard and Poor's rating scales

Note that the specific loan is rated, rather than the borrower. If the loan does not have a rating it could be that the borrower has not paid for one, rather than implying anything sinister.

High-yield (junk) bonds

High-yield or junk bonds are debt instruments offering a high return with a high risk. They may be either unsecured, or secured but ranking behind senior loans. This type of debt generally offers interest rates 2–9 percentage points higher than that on senior debt and frequently gives the lenders some right to a share in equity values should the firm perform well. It is a kind of hybrid finance ranking for payment below straight debt but above equity – it is thus described alternatively as **subordinated, intermediate or low-grade**. One of the major attractions of this form of finance for the investor is that it often comes with equity warrants or share options attached (see Chapter 8 and 10) which can be used to obtain shares in the firm – this is known as an '**equity kicker**'. These may be triggered by an event taking place, such as the firm joining the stock market.

High-yield bond finance tends to be used when bank borrowing limits are reached and the firm cannot or will not issue more equity. The finance it provides is cheaper (in terms of required return) than would be available on the equity market, and it allows the owners of a business to raise large sums of money without sacrificing control. It is a form of finance that permits the firm to move beyond what are normally considered acceptable debt–equity ratios (gearing or leverage levels).

Bonds with high risk and high return characteristics may have started as apparently safe investments but have now become riskier ('**fallen angels**'), or they may be bonds issued specifically to provide higher-risk financial instruments for investors.

Investment-grade bond prices and returns tend to move in line with gilt interest rates influenced by perceptions of future inflation rather than the risk of default. Junk bond prices (and their yields), on the other hand, are much more related to the prospects for the company's fundamentals. Many of the factors that affect equity valuation (see Part 3) also impact junk bond valuations. As a result high-yield bonds tend to be more volatile than investment-grade bonds, going up and down depending on expectations concerning the company's survival, strength and profitability.

Private investors are unlikely to be investing directly in the high-yield bond market as this is a market for professionals, but may invest via corporate bond funds (e.g. unit trusts). These offer economies of scale in research and in dealing, as well as the advantage of diversification. However, there is a price to pay: management charges can be heavy (see Chapter 5). Corporate bonds (with a lifespan of more than 5 years) can be held in an ISA, either directly or through a bond fund.

Convertible bonds

Convertible bonds carry a rate of interest in the same way as ordinary bonds, but they also give the holder the **right to exchange** the bonds at some stage in the future into ordinary shares according to some prearranged formula. The owner of these bonds is not obliged to exercise this right of conversion, and so the bond may continue until redemption as an interest-bearing instrument. Usually the **conversion price** is 10–30 per cent greater than the existing share price. So, if a £100 bond offered the right to convert to 40 ordinary shares the conversion price would be £2.50 (that is, £100/40) which, given the market price of the shares of, say, £2.20, would be a **conversion premium** of:

$$\frac{2.50 - 2.20}{2.20} \times 100 = 13.6\%$$

In a rising stock market it is reasonable to suppose that most convertible bonds issued with a small conversion premium will be converted to shares. However, this is not always the case. Northern Foods issued convertible bonds in February 1993, raising £91.28 million. The bonds were to be redeemed in 15 years if they had not been converted before this and were priced at a par value of £100. The coupon was set at 6.75 per cent and the conversion price was 326p per share. From this information we can calculate the **conversion ratio**:

$$\text{Conversion ratio} = \frac{\text{Nominal (par) value of bond}}{\text{Conversion price}} = \frac{£100}{£3.26} = 30.67 \text{ shares}$$

The conversion price was set at a premium of 18.12 per cent over the ordinary share price at the time of pricing, which was 276p ((326 – 276)/276 = 18.12 per cent). At the time of the issue many investors may have looked at the low interest rate on the convertible (for 15-year bonds in 1993) and concluded that although this was greater than the dividend yield on shares (4–5 per cent) it was less than that on conventional bonds, but offsetting this was the prospect of capital gains made by converting the bonds into shares. If the shares rose to, say, £4, each £100 bond could be converted to 30.67 shares worth 30.67 × £4 = £122.68. Unfortunately the share price slid rather than rose and so the conversion right has not yet not gained any intrinsic value – perhaps by the year 2008 it will be worthwhile exchanging the bonds for shares. In the meantime the investors at least have the comfort of a £6.75 coupon every year.

The value of a convertible bond (also called an '**equity-linked bond**') rises as the value of ordinary shares increases, but at a lower percentage rate. If the share price rises above the conversion price the investor may choose to exercise the option to convert if he/she anticipates that the share price will at least be maintained and the dividend yield is higher than the convertible bond yield. If the share price rise is seen to be temporary the investor may wish to hold on to the bond. If the share price remains below the conversion price, the value of the convertible will be the same as a straight bond at maturity.

Convertibles with large conversion premiums trade much like ordinary bonds because the option to convert is not a strong feature in their pricing. They offer higher yields, and prices are not volatile. Those trading with a small conversion premium have lower yields and the prices are more volatile as they are more closely linked with the share price.

The advantages of convertible bonds to investors are:

- They are able to wait and see how the share price moves before investing in equity.
- In the near term there is greater security for their principal compared with equity investment, and the annual coupon is usually higher than the dividend yield.

The bonds sold may not give the right to conversion into shares of the issuing company, but shares of another company held by the issuer. The term '**exchangeable bond**' is probably more appropriate in these cases.

Foreign bonds

A foreign bond is a bond denominated in the currency of the country where it is issued when the issuer is a non-resident. For example, in Japan bonds issued by non-Japanese companies denominated in yen are foreign bonds. (The interest and capital payments will be in yen.) Foreign bonds in Tokyo are known as Samurai bonds; foreign bonds issued in New York and London are called Yankees and Bulldogs, respectively. In the Netherlands you will find Rembrandts and in Spain Matador bonds.

Foreign bonds are regulated by the authority where the bond is issued. These rules can be demanding and an encumbrance to companies needing to act quickly and at low cost. The regulatory authorities have also been criticised for stifling innovation in the financial markets. The growth of the less restricted eurobond market has put the once dominant foreign bond market in the shade.

Eurobonds

Let's get one misunderstanding out of the way: eurobonds are unconnected with the new currency! They were in existence decades before Europe thought of creating the euro. The term 'euro' in eurobond does not even mean European. So what are they, then?

Eurobonds are bonds sold outside the jurisdiction of the country of the currency in which the bond is denominated. So, for example, the UK financial regulators have little influence over the eurobonds denominated in sterling issued in Luxembourg, even though the transactions (e.g. interest and capital payments) are in pounds. Bonds issued in US dollars in Paris are outside the jurisdiction of the US authorities.

Eurobonds are medium- to long-term instruments (5 or more years) not subject to the rules and regulations which are imposed on foreign bonds, such as the requirement to issue a detailed prospectus. More importantly, they are not subject to an interest-withholding tax. In the UK most domestic bonds are subject to a **withholding tax** by which basic rate income tax is deducted before the investor receives interest. Interest on eurobonds is paid gross without any tax deducted – which has attractions to investors keen on delaying, avoiding or evading tax. Moreover, eurobonds are **bearer bonds**, which means that the holders do not have to disclose their identity – all that is required to receive interest and capital is for the holder to have possession of the bond. In contrast, UK domestic bonds are **registered**, which means that companies and governments are able to identify the owners. Bearer bonds have to be kept in a safe place as a thief could benefit greatly from possession of a bearer bond.

Despite the absence of official regulation, the International Securities Market Association (ISMA), a self-regulatory body founded in 1969 and based in Switzerland, imposes some restrictions, rules and standardised procedures on eurobond issue and trading.

The *Financial Times* publishes a table showing a selection of secondary-market prices of international and emerging market bonds. This gives the reader some idea of current market conditions and rates of return demanded for bonds of different maturities, currencies and riskiness – see Exhibit 6.3.

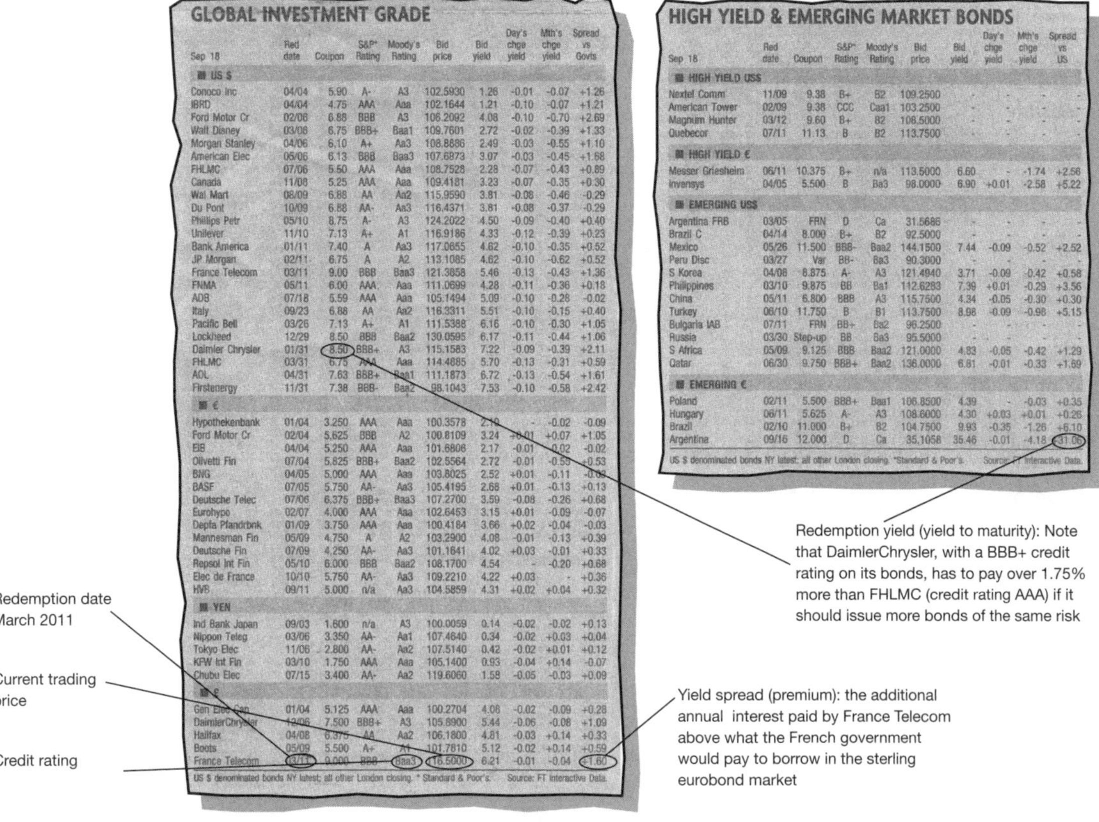

GLOBAL INVESTMENT GRADE

Sep 18	Red date	Coupon	S&P* Rating	Moody's Rating	Bid price	Bid yield	Day's chge yield	Mth's chge yield	Spread vs Govts
US $									
Conoco Inc	04/04	5.90	A-	A3	102.5930	1.26	-0.01	-0.07	+1.26
IBRD	04/04	4.75	AAA	Aaa	102.1644	1.21	-0.10	-0.07	+1.21
Ford Motor Cr	02/06	6.88	BBB	A3	106.2092	4.08	-0.10	-0.70	+2.69
Walt Disney	03/06	6.75	BBB+	Baa1	109.7601	2.72	-0.02	-0.39	+1.33
Morgan Stanley	04/06	6.10	A+	Aa3	108.8886	2.49	-0.03	-0.55	+1.10
American Elec	06/06	6.13	BBB	Baa3	107.6873	3.07	-0.03	-0.45	+1.68
FHLMC	07/06	5.50	AAA	Aaa	108.7528	2.28	-0.07	-0.43	+0.89
Canada	11/08	5.25	AAA	Aaa	109.4181	3.23	-0.07	-0.35	+0.30
Wal Mart	08/09	6.88	AA	Aa2	115.9590	3.81	-0.08	-0.46	-0.29
Du Pont	10/09	6.88	AA-	Aa3	116.4371	3.81	-0.08	-0.37	-0.29
Phillips Petr	05/10	8.75	A-	A3	124.2022	4.50	-0.09	-0.40	+0.40
Unilever	11/10	7.13	A+	A1	116.9186	4.33	-0.12	-0.39	+0.23
Bank America	01/11	7.40	A	Aa3	117.0655	4.62	-0.10	-0.35	+0.52
JP Morgan	02/11	6.75	A	A2	113.1085	4.62	-0.10	-0.62	+0.52
France Telecom	03/11	9.00	BBB	Baa3	121.3858	5.46	-0.13	-0.43	+1.36
FNMA	05/11	6.00	AAA	Aaa	111.0699	4.28	-0.11	-0.36	+0.18
ADB	07/18	5.59	AAA	Aaa	105.1494	5.09	-0.10	-0.28	-0.02
Italy	09/23	6.88	AA	Aa2	116.3311	5.51	-0.10	-0.15	+0.40
Pacific Bell	03/26	7.13	A+	A1	111.5388	6.16	-0.10	-0.30	+1.05
Lockheed	12/29	8.50	BBB	Baa2	130.0595	6.17	-0.11	-0.44	+1.06
Daimler Chrysler	01/31	8.50	BBB+	A3	115.1583	7.22	-0.09	-0.39	+2.11
FHLMC	03/31	6.75	AAA	Aaa	114.4885	5.70	-0.13	-0.31	+0.59
AOL	04/31	7.63	BBB+	Baa1	111.1873	6.72	-0.13	-0.54	+1.61
Firstenergy	11/31	7.38	BBB-	Baa2	98.1043	7.53	-0.10	-0.58	+2.42
€									
Hypothekenbank	01/04	3.250	AAA	Aaa	100.3578	2.10	-	-0.02	-0.09
Ford Motor Cr	02/04	5,625	BBB	A2	100.8109	3.24	+0.01	+0.07	+1.05
EIB	04/04	5.250	AAA	Aaa	101.6806	2.17	-0.01	-0.02	-0.02
Olivetti Fin	07/04	5.825	BBB+	Baa2	102.5564	2.72	-0.01	-0.55	+0.53
BNG	04/05	5.000	AAA	Aaa	103.8025	2.52	+0.01	-0.11	-0.08
BASF	07/05	5.750	AA-	Aa3	105.4195	2.68	+0.01	-0.13	+0.13
Deutsche Telec	07/06	6.375	BBB+	Baa3	107.2700	3.59	-0.08	-0.26	+0.68
Eurohypo	02/07	4.000	AAA	Aaa	102.6453	3.15	+0.01	-0.09	-0.07
Depfa Pfandrbnk	01/09	3.750	AAA	Aaa	100.4184	3.66	+0.02	-0.04	-0.03
Mannesman Fin	05/09	4.750	A	A2	103.2900	4.08	-0.01	-0.13	+0.39
Deutsche Fin	07/09	4,250	AA-	Aa3	101.1641	4.02	+0.03	-0.01	+0.33
Repsol Int Fin	05/10	6.000	BBB	Baa2	108.1700	4.54	-	-0.20	+0.68
Elec de France	10/10	5.750	AA-	Aa3	109.2210	4.22	+0.03	-	+0.36
HVB	09/11	5.000	n/a	Aa3	104.5859	4.31	+0.02	+0.04	+0.32
YEN									
Ind Bank Japan	09/03	1.600	n/a	A3	100.0059	0.14	-0.02	-0.02	+0.13
Nippon Teleg	03/06	3.350	AA-	Aa1	107.4640	0.34	-0.02	+0.03	+0.04
Tokyo Elec	11/06	2.800	AA-	Aa2	107.5140	0.42	-0.02	+0.01	+0.12
KFW Int Fin	03/10	1.750	AAA	Aaa	105.1400	0.93	-0.04	+0.14	-0.07
Chubu Elec	07/15	3.400	AA-	Aa2	119.6060	1.58	-0.05	-0.03	+0.09
£									
Gen Elec Cap	01/04	5.125	AAA	Aaa	100.2704	4.08	-0.02	-0.09	+0.28
DaimlerChrysler	12/06	7.500	BBB+	A3	105.8900	5.44	-0.06	-0.08	+1.09
Halifax	04/08	6.375	AA	Aa2	106.1800	4.81	-0.03	+0.14	+0.33
Boots	05/09	5.500	A+	A1	101.7810	5.12	-0.02	+0.14	+0.59
France Telecom	03/11	9.000	BBB	Baa3	116.5000	6.21	-0.01	-0.04	+1.60

US $ denominated bonds NY latest; all other London closing. * Standard & Poor's. Source: FT Interactive Data.

HIGH YIELD & EMERGING MARKET BONDS

Sep 18	Red date	Coupon	S&P* Rating	Moody's Rating	Bid price	Bid yield	Day's chge yield	Mth's chge yield	Spread vs US
HIGH YIELD US$									
Nextel Comm	11/09	9.38	B+	B2	109.2500	-	-	-	-
American Tower	02/09	9.38	CCC	Caa1	103.2500	-	-	-	-
Magnum Hunter	03/12	9.60	B+	B2	106.5000	-	-	-	-
Quebecor	07/11	11.13	B	B2	113.7500	-	-	-	-
HIGH YIELD €									
Messer Griesheim	06/11	10.375	B+	n/a	113.5000	6.60	-	-1.74	+2.56
Invensys	04/05	5.500	B	Ba3	98.0000	6.90	+0.01	-2.58	+5.22
EMERGING US$									
Argentina FRB	03/05	FRN	D	Ca	31.5686	-	-	-	-
Brazil C	04/14	8.000	B+	B2	92.5000	-	-	-	-
Mexico	05/26	11.500	BBB-	Baa2	144.1500	7.44	-0.09	-0.52	+2.52
Peru Disc	03/27	Var	BB-	Ba3	90.3000	-	-	-	-
S Korea	04/08	8.875	A-	A3	121.4940	3.71	-0.09	-0.42	+0.58
Philippines	03/10	9.875	BB	Ba1	112.6283	7.39	+0.01	-0.29	+3.56
China	05/11	6.800	BBB	A3	115.7500	4.34	-0.05	-0.30	+0.30
Turkey	06/10	11.750	B	B1	113.7500	8.98	-0.09	-0.98	+5.15
Bulgaria IAB	07/11	FRN	BB+	Ba2	96.2500	-	-	-	-
Russia	03/30	Step-up	BB	Ba3	95.5000	-	-	-	-
S Africa	05/09	9.125	BBB	Baa2	121.0000	4.83	-0.05	-0.42	+1.29
Qatar	06/30	9.750	BBB+	Baa2	136.0000	6.81	-0.01	-0.33	+1.69
EMERGING €									
Poland	02/11	5.500	BBB+	Baa1	106.8500	4.39	-	-0.03	+0.35
Hungary	06/11	5.625	A-	A3	108.6000	4.30	+0.03	+0.01	+0.26
Brazil	02/10	11.000	B+	B2	104.7500	9.93	-0.35	-1.26	+6.10
Argentina	09/16	12.000	D	Ca	35.1058	35.46	-0.01	-4.18	31.06

US $ denominated bonds NY latest; all other London closing. *Standard & Poor's. Source: FT Interactive Data.

Exhibit 6.3 International bond prices in the *Financial Times*

Source: *Financial Times* 19 September 2003

7

Unusual share investments

Buying shares in companies quoted on the London Stock Exchange's Official List, AIM or on OFEX remains the main investment route for most people. However, there are ways of spicing up your investment portfolio by stepping outside the conventional. You could, for example, invest in companies just starting up, or those that are young and looking for expansion capital. These companies will be years away from obtaining a secondary market quotation for their shares and so, in becoming a '**business angel**' investor, you are accepting that it may be difficult to dispose of your shares even if the company is progressing nicely. You are also accepting a relatively high degree of risk of complete failure. But the upside, if all goes well, can be tremendous. Investors putting just a few thousand pounds in a small company have become very wealthy following the firm's flotation, or when it is sold to another company. For example, Body Shop investor Mr Ian McGlinn was a garage owner who put £4,000 into Body Shop in 1976. He still owned 28 per cent of the shares in the late 1990s, worth millions.

Venture capital investing is usually on a larger scale than business angel investing and is generally conducted through venture capital funds, such as 3i or Candover, which are able to gather together money from numerous investors to channel it to unquoted companies needing millions of pounds to set up or grow. Investing in these funds has the advantage of diversified exposure to many fast-growing dynamic companies as well as benefiting from the experience of professional venture capital managers able to sort the wheat from the chaff.

A third possibility is investment in **overseas shares**. There is a certain logic to not having all your eggs in one economic basket (the UK economy) and spreading your portfolio across a number of countries. Many emerging economies offer the prospect of rapid development and high share returns. On the other hand, there are dangers of operating in poorly regulated and unfamiliar territory.

Finally, **preference shares** offer a route to investment with less risk than ordinary shares but with higher returns than on bonds.

Business angels

Business angels are wealthy individuals, generally with substantial business and entrepreneurial experience, who usually invest between £10,000 and £250,000 primarily in start-up, early stage or expanding firms. About three-quarters of business angel investments are for sums of less than £100,000, with the average investment around £25,000–£30,000. The majority of investments are in the form of equity finance but angels do purchase debt instruments and preference shares. They usually do not have a controlling shareholding and they are willing to invest at an earlier stage than most formal venture capitalists. (They often dislike the term 'business angel', preferring the title '**informal venture capitalist**'.)

Business angels are generally looking for entrepreneurial companies with high aspirations and potential for growth. A typical business angel makes one or two investments in a three-year period, often in an investment syndicate led by an '**archangel**'. They generally invest in companies within a reasonable travelling distance from their homes because most like to be '**hands-on investors**', playing a significant role in strategy and management – on average, angels allocate 10 hours a week to their investments. Most angels take a seat on the board.[1] Business angels are patient investors willing to hold their investment for at least 5 years.

The main way in which firms and angels find each other is through friends and business associates, although there are a number of formal networks. See British Venture Capital Association at *www.bvca.co.uk* for a list of networks. Other useful contacts include the following:

www.nban.com	National Business Angels Network
www.angelbourse.com	Angel Bourse
www.wave2.org	Wave2
www.vcr1978.com	Venture Capital Report
www.katalystventures.com	K@talyst Ventures
www.hotbed.uk.com	Hotbed
www.beerandpartners.com	Beer & Partners
www.entrust.co.uk	Entrust
www.dti.gov.uk	Department of Trade and Industry

There are hundreds of groups of business angels throughout Europe. Exhibit 7.1 highlights some of the activity around Cambridge.

Angel network events are organised where entrepreneurs can make a pitch to potential investors, who, if they like what they hear in response to their questions, may put in tens of thousands of pounds. Prior to the event the network organisers (or a member) will generally screen the business opportunities to avoid time wasting by the no-hopers. To be a member of a network investors are expected to either earn at least £100,000 per year or have a net worth of at least £250,000 (excluding main residence). If you have a specialist skill to offer (e.g. you are an experienced company director or chartered accountant), you may be permitted membership despite a lower income or net worth.

Many business angel deals are structured to take advantage of tax breaks such as those through enterprise investment schemes (EISs) which offer income tax relief and capital gains tax deferral. Even outside EISs the investments often qualify as business assets and for business property relief. This can reduce capital gains tax to 10 per cent after 2 years. A further relief for shares in unquoted companies is that the asset is removed from your estate for inheritance tax after 2 years of ownership. For more on tax, see Chapter 17.

[1] Having said this, many business angels (generally those with investments of £10,000–£20,000) have infrequent contact with the company.

Chance to save the most deserving

Phil Davis

A well-established group in Cambridge helps link investors and start-up companies in an unusual reversal of the usual process – by presenting young companies directly to investors through a kind of beauty contest.

The Great Eastern Investment Forum (GEIF), set up eight years ago by NW Brown, a Cambridge financial services firm, has a team of managers who sift through hundreds of business plans every year from start-ups seeking capital.

The best ones win the right to present their business to GEIF's 314-strong community, which comprises wealthy individuals, venture capitalists, corporate investors and professional advisers. The rapid-fire presentations, held four times a year, last 10 minutes, after which investors can talk at length with any company that has impressed them.

The process appeals to investors because of its transparency, but becoming a 'business angel' is only for the experienced, warns Nigel Brown, chairman of GEIF. 'The high-tech bubble made people think of quick, massive returns and that mentality remains.'

Derek Harris, a GEIF member with eight big investments to his name in a 20-year career as a business angel, takes his 'angel' responsibilities seriously.

Harris likes to be fully involved as a director or chairman of companies he invests in, and is chairman of Coffee Nation, a vending machine company that has raised £240,000 since it first made a presentation at the GEIF. His motivation is the buzz of seeing a business grow, rather than his 'very modest' salary as chairman.

'It is good fun working with youngsters and providing a steady hand on the wheel,' Harris says. 'I hated office politics and big organisations that don't focus on markets and customers, so I would never go back to being a salaried employee.'

Companies approaching the GEIF for funding range from biotechnology and IT to engineering projects and restaurant groups.

The Great Eastern Investment Forum at: www.geif.co.uk

Exhibit 7.1 Business angels in Cambridge

Source: *Financial Times* 13/14 September 2003

Venture capital

Venture capital (VC) funds provide finance for unquoted firms with high growth potential. VC is a medium- to long-term investment and can consist of a package of debt and equity finance. Venture capitalists take high risks by investing in the equity of young companies often with a limited (or no) track record. Often they invest in little more than a management team with a good idea – which may not have started selling a product or even developed a prototype. It is believed, as a rule of thumb in the VC industry, that out of ten investments two will fail completely, two will perform excellently and the remaining six will range from poor to very good.

High risk goes with high return. Venture capitalists expect to get a return of between five and ten times their initial equity investment in about 5–7 years. This means that the firms receiving equity finance are expected to produce annual returns for investors of at least 29 per cent. Alongside the usual drawbacks of equity capital from the investors' viewpoint (last in the queue for income and on liquidation, etc.), investors in small unquoted companies also suffer from a lack of liquidity because the shares are not quoted on a public exchange. There are a number of different types of VC:

- **Seedcorn.** This is financing to allow the development of a business concept. Development may also involve expenditure on the production of prototypes and additional research.
- **Start-up.** A product or idea is further developed, and/or initial marketing is carried out. These companies are very young and have not yet sold their product commercially.
- **Other early-stage.** Funds for initial commercial manufacturing and sales. Many companies at this stage will remain unprofitable.
- **Expansion (development).** Companies at this stage are on a fast-growth track and need capital to fund increased production capacity, working capital and further development of the product or market.
- **Management buy-outs (MBOs).** Here a team of managers make an offer to their employers to buy a whole business, a subsidiary or a section so that they own and run it for themselves. Large companies are often willing to sell to these teams, particularly if the business is underperforming and does not fit with the strategic core business. Usually the management team have limited funds of their own and so call on venture capitalists to provide the bulk of the finance. In 2002 dozens of managers at Homebase found themselves millionaires. They had bought Homebase from Sainsbury in an MBO with the backing of a VC fund. Later Homebase was sold to Great Universal Stores for a much greater sum.
- **Management buy-ins (MBIs).** A new team of managers from outside an existing business buy a stake, usually backed by a VC fund. A combination of an MBO and an MBI is called a 'BIMBO' – buy-in management buy-out – where a new group of managers join forces with an existing team to acquire a business.
- **Public-to-private.** The management of a company currently quoted on a stock exchange may return it to unquoted status with the assistance of VC finance being used to buy the shares.

The last three are sometimes classified separately – see the next section.

VC firms are less keen on financing seedcorn, start-ups and other early stage companies than expansions, MBOs, MBIs and public-to-private. This is largely due to the very high risk associated with early-stage ventures and the disproportionate time and costs of financing smaller deals. To make it worthwhile for a VC organisation to consider a company the investment must be at least £250,000 – the average investment is about £5 million.

Because of the greater risks associated with the youngest companies, the VC funds may require returns of the order of 50–80 per cent per annum. For well-established companies with a proven product and battle-hardened and respected management the returns required may drop to the high 20s. These returns may seem exorbitant, especially to the managers set the task of achieving them, but they have to be viewed in the light of the fact that many VC investments will turn out to be failures and so the overall performance of the VC funds is significantly less than these figures suggest. In fact the British Venture Capital Association reports that returns on funds are not excessively high. Taken as a whole, the return to investors net of costs and fees was 14.6 per cent per annum to the end of 2002 for funds raised between 1980 and 1998. This compares well with average annual returns of around 8.8 per cent on UK quoted shares in the 23 years to the end of 2002.

Exhibit 7.2 shows the thrills and spills of VC investing. In 11 months 3i turned £83.5 million into £231 million by investing in the airline Go, while also reporting massive losses on technology investments.

3i and funds gain £231m on Go stake

Katherine Campbell, Private Equity Correspondent

3i and its associated funds realised £231m on their stake in Go in less than a year, making it one of the best buy-out investments in the private equity group's history.

EasyJet is paying £374m for the discount airline 11 months after British Airways sold it for £110m.

3i's shares rallied 40p to close at 762p yesterday, despite the group unveiling losses of £960m for the year to March 31, alongside the deal. The losses came largely as a result of 3i's misadventures in technology.

3i's investment in Go from its own balance sheet, third party funds it manages and syndicate partners totalled £83.5m. The £231m proceeds from the sale represent a cash-to-cash multiple of about 2.7 times on the investment.

Losses on technology investments amounted to £937m, with another £73m in goodwill write-offs for technology investments – acquired during the dotcom bubble.

Buy-out and growth capital investments produced a small positive return of £50m.

3i saw 65 technology companies fail from its portfolio of 809, up from 25 last year. Another 80 non-technology businesses failed, the same number as 2001.

New investment levels for the year had halved to just over £1bn from £1.97bn.

Exhibit 7.2 Venture capital investing

Source: *Financial Times* May 2002

There are a number of different types of VC providers, although the boundaries are increasingly blurred as a number of funds now raise money from a variety of sources. The **independents** can be firms, funds or investment trusts, either quoted or private, which have raised their capital from more than one source. For example, 3i is a very large independent venture capital company with thousands of shareholders and its shares quoted on the stock exchange. The main sources are pension and insurance funds, but banks, corporate investors and private individuals also put money into these VC funds. **Captives** are funds managed on behalf of a parent institution, such as a bank or a pension fund. **Semi-captives** invest funds on behalf of a parent and also manage independently raised funds.

For the larger investments, particularly MBOs and MBIs, the venture capitalist may provide only a fraction of the total funds required. Thus, in a £50 million buyout the venture capitalist might supply (individually or in a syndicate with other VC funds), say, £15 million in the form of share capital (ordinary and preference shares). Another £20 million may come from a group of banks in the form of debt finance. The remainder may be supplied as **mezzanine debt** – high-return and high-risk debt which usually has some rights to share in the spoils should the company perform exceptionally well.

Venture capitalists generally like to have a clear target set as the eventual '**exit**' (or '**take-out**') date. This is the point at which the VC can recoup some or all of the investment. The majority of exits are achieved by the sale of the company to another firm, but a popular method is flotation on a stock market. Alternative exit routes are for the company to repurchase its shares or for the venture capitalist to sell the holding to an institution such as an investment trust.

VC funds are **rarely looking for a controlling shareholding** in a company and are often content with a 20–30 per cent share. They may also supply funds through the purchase of convertible preference shares which give them rights to convert to ordinary shares – which will boost their equity holding and increase the return if the firm performs well. They may also insist, in an initial investment agreement, on some **widespread powers**. For instance, the company may need to gain the venture capitalist's approval for the issue of further securities, and they may hold a veto over acquisition of other companies. Even though their equity holding is generally less than 50 per cent the VC funds frequently have special rights to **appoint a number of directors**. If specific negative events happen, such as a poor performance, they may have the right to appoint most of the board of directors and therefore take effective control. More than once the founding entrepreneur has been aggrieved to find him/herself removed from power. (Despite the loss of power, they often have a large shareholding in what has grown to be a multi-million-pound company.)

The venture capitalist can help a company with more than money. Venture capitalists usually have a wealth of experience and talented people able to assist the budding entrepreneur. Many of the UK's most noteworthy companies were helped by the VC industry – for example, Waterstone's bookshops, Derwent Valley Foods (Phileas Fogg Crisps), Oxford Instruments (and in America: Apple computers, Sun Microsystems, Netscape, Lotus, Compaq and most of Silicon Valley).

Private equity

As share investment outside of stock markets has grown it has become differentiated. The main categories are shown in Exhibit 7.3. The title overarching all these activities is **private equity**. Private equity is defined as medium- to long-term finance provided in return for an equity stake in potentially high-growth unquoted companies. In this more differentiated setting the term 'venture capital' is generally confined to describing the building of companies from the ground floor, or at least from a very low base. Management buy-outs and buy-ins of established businesses (already off the ground floor) have become a specialist task, with a number of dedicated funds. Many of these funds have been formed as private partnerships by wealthy individuals, a high proportion of which are American-owned. However, there are funds available to small investors, such as 3i, that still conduct traditional VC business and MBOs and MBIs. The small investor can buy shares in these stock market-listed funds. They are frequently classified as venture and development capital investment trusts (VDCITs). More details on these are available from *www.bvca.co.uk* and *www.aitc.co.uk*. The disadvantage of VDCITs is the absence of tax benefits. This is where the venture capital trusts and the Enterprise Investment Scheme come in. They both offer significant tax breaks to investors in small unquoted companies – see Chapter 17 for details.

Some have specialised in providing financial and professional support to quoted companies that wish to leave the stock market – public-to-private deals.

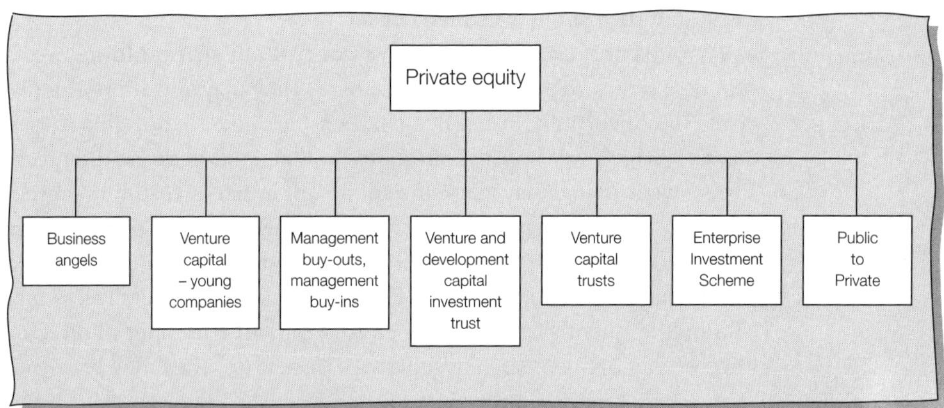

Exhibit 7.3 Private equity and its component parts

Points for investors concerning angels and venture capital

- The tax breaks for investors in this area are great.
- This is high risk investing. Because you have to be able to withstand the occasional disaster, you should not put a large proportion of your funds in investments of this type.

- Management charges can be high with VC. They could consist of an initial charge of 5 per cent, followed by annual charges of 2.5 per cent plus performance fees.
- These investments can be illiquid in the early years.
- Have you the time and experience to be a business angel in the 'hands-on' sense?

Overseas shares

UK shares account for about 7 per cent of the value of equities quoted on stock exchanges around the world. Why limit yourself to British companies when there are so many opportunities elsewhere? In the past the answer to this question from many investors was that trading foreign shares involved more cost, more risk and generally more hassle. Matters have improved dramatically in the last 5 years. The Internet has made the obtaining of information about overseas companies much easier, as well as allowing online trading. The intense competition between brokers invading each other's geographic territory has pushed down costs and increased the quality of services. The shift to electronic trading and settlement of share transactions in the majority of developed overseas markets has simplified administration processes enormously. Less paper passing through fewer hands and more electronic keyboard strokes has resulted in lower costs and fewer mistakes. Encouraged by this modernisation, over one-fifth of UK investors have taken the plunge and bought non-UK shares.

One route to buying overseas shares is to take advantage of a recently (2001) introduced service set up by the London Stock Exchange called the **International Retail Service (IRS)**. This allows UK private investors access to trading in over 380 major European and US companies. The neat thing about this is that the trades are all conducted in sterling.[2] Also it has been structured so that trading is as simple and as cheap as it is for UK shares. For example, settlement is through CREST (see Chapter 4), making the process quicker and more straightforward than investing through an overseas stock market. So, if you are thinking of buying into Microsoft or Nestlé, this is a good option. Dozens of brokers are now registered to trade in this market on your behalf. A further positive factor is that these IRS shares can be placed into an ISA or self-invested personal pension (see Chapter 17) to take advantage of tax concessions. More information on the IRS is available at *www.londonstockexchange.com/irs*.

The shares traded through IRS are just the tip of the iceberg. There are tens of thousands of other quoted overseas shares. There are over 3000 companies on the US NASDAQ market alone. So what are the options for investing outside of the world's mega-companies?

Firstly, many **UK brokers** offer access to international markets. Competition in this area is hotting up, particularly for online execution-only trading. In some cases commissions have fallen to the same level as for dealing in UK shares, but more typically you might pay 1.5–2 times as much. Charges for overseas broking are often raised because of

[2] Via a market maker-type system (they are actually called '**committed principals**').

the cost of paying **custodian fees**, that is, paying a broker in the other country to act as a nominee, holding the shares, handling dividends and other administrative activities. Orders placed with your broker are executed directly through the overseas exchange. You can set price limits or instruct your broker to trade **at best** (see Chapter 4).

Your broker is likely to ask you to sign an **International Risk Warning Notice** acknowledging that you are aware of additional risks of overseas investment. There is also a form (W-8) stating your non-US status so that US dividends can be paid with only 15 per cent tax withheld at source. In most developed markets settlement is 3 days after the trade, so brokers need access to your money quickly. Therefore they generally insist on the setting up of a **broker cash management account** and **nominee account** (see Chapter 4). It is usually wise to operate with semi-permanent **foreign currency accounts** in, say, dollars or euros as this will reduce the costs of regular currency conversions.

Secondly, it is possible to open a foreign currency account and trade through an **overseas broker**. The initial deposit is fairly high at around $10,000, but the Internet makes communicating cheap, quick and simple. Websites listing US stockbrokers include Gomez (*www.gomezadvisors.com*) and Smartmoney.com (*www.smartmoney.com/brokers*).

UK taxation is payable on income and capital gains from overseas equities in the normal way. However, if withholding tax has already been charged overseas the UK investor can claim a tax credit to avoid being charged twice. The Inland Revenue allows any share quoted on a recognised stock exchange to be held in an ISA. Most countries do not impose stamp duty on share purchases.

Points to consider about investing abroad

- Many brokers will only deal in the leading companies in the leading stock markets.
- Shareholder rights are not as well protected in many countries as in the UK. Even European countries have poor reputations for matters such as protecting small shareholders, openness to takeover, amount of information released and concentration of boardroom power in a clique (families often rule the roost from behind the scenes). Large international businesses tend to be better and follow best international practice.
- Keeping track of medium-sized and small companies can be difficult. Information may not be supplied in English, either by the company or brokers. Newspapers such as the *Financial Times* cover the large firms, but obviously cannot bring to your attention details about every foreign company. Try the websites *www.adr.com* from J.P. Morgan, *www.quicken.com* and national Yahoo Finance sites.
- You could be exposed to currency shifts. However, if you have investments in a number of currencies you can take a sanguine swings-and-roundabouts attitude to this.
- On the whole, it is still more expensive to buy abroad than at home.
- In the developing world trading systems may be inefficient: settlement systems often rely on paper, which can be carelessly handled, even lost. Share certificates have been known to arrive months after the transaction. Insider trading and corruption can mean that the outsider is at a considerable disadvantage. Political risks – meaning neg-

ative consequences as a result of government action, e.g. nationalisation without compensation – are a serious worry in some parts of the world, despite a general shift to international openness and respectability.

Alternatives to investing directly in overseas shares include the purchase of **depositary receipts** (see Chapter 3 for a description). Many foreign companies have depositary receipts traded on the London Stock Exchange. **American depositary receipts**, are available in the USA.

Also many UK companies (e.g. Cadbury Schweppes and Vodafone) derive a large part of their profits from overseas, and so you could gain international exposure by buying UK shares in a UK regulatory environment. A further possibility is to purchase unit trusts, OEICs or investment trusts specialising in particular parts of the world – a lot of the work selecting shares and managing the portfolio is passed on, but the management costs can be steep (see Chapter 5).

Some useful websites for investors in overseas shares

Stock exchanges such as the New York Stock Exchange (*www.nyse.com*), have very good websites providing information and links. As well as these you might like to try the following:

www.euroland.com	Euroland
www.bloomberg.com	Bloomberg
www.bridge.com	Reuters
www.hoovers.com	Hoovers Online
www.multexinvestor.com	MultexInvestor
www.ft.com	Financial Times
www.onvista.co.uk	OnVista
www.money.cnn.com	CNN Money
www.edgar-online.com	Edgar Online
www.corporateinformation.com	Corporate Information
www.comdirect.co.uk	comdirect
www.digitallook.com	Digital Look
www.tradingcentral.com	TRADING Central
www.wsrn.com	Wall Street Research Net
www.blueskyratings.com	BlueSky Ratings

Brokers' websites can provide you will details about their services and supply research tools. Try a search engine such as *www.google.com* to find brokers.

Preference shares

Preference shares appeal to investors seeking regular stable income as they offer their owners a fixed rate of dividend each year. However, if the firm has insufficient profits the amount paid will be reduced, sometimes to zero. Thus, there is no guarantee that an annual income will be received, unlike with debt capital. The dividend on preference shares is paid before anything is paid out to ordinary shareholders – indeed, after the preference dividend obligation has been met there may be nothing left for ordinary shareholders. Preference shares are attractive to some investors because they offer a regular income at a higher rate of return than that available on fixed-interest securities (e.g. bonds). However, this higher return also comes with higher risk, as the preference dividend ranks after bond interest, and upon liquidation preference holders are further back in the queue as recipients of the proceeds of asset sell-offs.

Preference shareholders are not usually able to benefit from any extraordinarily good performance of the firm – any profits above expectations go to the ordinary shareholders. Also preference shares usually carry no voting rights, unless the dividend is in arrears or in the case of a liquidation.

One of the reasons why companies issue preference shares is that the dividends can be omitted for one or more years. This can give the directors more flexibility and a greater chance of surviving a downturn in trading. Contrast this with debt capital, which carries an obligation to pay interest regardless of the firm's difficulties. Although there may be no legal obligation to pay a dividend every year the financial community is likely to take a dim view of a firm that missed a dividend – this may have a deleterious effect on the price of the ordinary shares as investors become nervous and sell. Also preference shares are an additional source of capital, which, because it does not (usually) confer voting rights, does not dilute the influence of the ordinary shareholders on the firm's direction.

While it is possible to make capital gains by trading in and out of preference shares they tend to be much less volatile than ordinary shares and generally behave more like bonds responding to interest rate changes.

There are a number of variations on the theme of preference share. Here are some features that can be added:

- **Cumulative.** If dividends are missed in any year the right to eventually receive a dividend is carried forward. These prior-year dividends have to be paid before any payout to ordinary shareholders.
- **Participating.** As well as the fixed payment, the dividend may be increased if the company has high profits.
- **Redeemable.** These have a finite life, at the end of which the initial capital investment will be repaid. Irredeemables have no fixed redemption date.
- **Convertibles.** These can be converted into ordinary shares at specific dates and on preset terms (e.g. one ordinary share for every two preference shares). These shares often carry a lower yield since there is the attraction of a potentially large capital gain.
- **Variable rate.** A variable dividend is paid. The rate may be linked to general interest rates or to some other variable factor.

The prices and dividend yields of preference shares are quoted in the *Financial Times*, alongside prices of ordinary shares.

8

Options

Derivatives – options, futures, warrants, etc. – are the subject of this chapter and the next two. Derivative instruments have become increasingly important for professional investors over the last 20 years. However, they are not just the province of professionals. Private investors can also exploit these powerful tools to either reduce risk or to go in search of high returns. Naturally, exceptionally high returns come with exceptionally high risk. So traders using derivatives for this purpose need to understand the risk they are exposed to. Many people (and giant companies) have lost fortunes by allowing themselves to be mesmerised by the potential for riches while failing to take the time to fully understand the instruments they were buying. They jumped in, unaware of or ignoring the potential for enormous loss.

These three chapters describe the main types of derivatives and show how they can be used for controlling risk (hedging) and for revving-up returns (speculation). They also try to convey the downside so that investors can go into these markets with their eyes open.

What is a derivative?

A derivative instrument is an asset whose performance is based on (derived from) the behaviour of the value of an **underlying** asset (usually referred to simply as the 'underlying'). The most common underlyings are commodities (e.g. tea or pork bellies), shares, bonds, share indices, currencies and interest rates. Derivatives are contracts which give the right, and sometimes the obligation, to buy or sell a quantity of the underlying, or benefit in another way from a rise or fall in the value of the underlying. It is the legal *right* that becomes an asset, with its own value, and it is the right that is purchased or sold.

Derivatives instruments have been employed for more than two thousand years. Olive growers in ancient Greece, unwilling to accept the risk of a low price for their crop when harvested months later, would enter into **forward agreements** whereby a price was agreed for delivery at a specific time. This reduced uncertainty for both the grower and the purchaser of the olives. In the Middle Ages forward contracts were traded in a kind of secondary market, particularly for wheat in Europe. A **futures market** was established in Osaka's rice market in Japan in the seventeenth century. Tulip bulb **options** were traded in seventeenth-century Amsterdam.

Commodity futures trading really began to take off in the nineteenth century with the Chicago Board of Trade regulating the trading of grains and other futures and options, and the London Metal Exchange dominating metal trading.

So derivatives are not new. What is different today is the size and importance of the derivatives markets. The last quarter of the twentieth century witnessed an explosive growth in volumes of trade, the variety of derivatives products, and the number and range of users and uses. In the twenty years to 2003 the face value of outstanding derivatives contracts rose dramatically to stand at about US$120 trillion. Compare that with the total production of all the goods and services in the UK in a year – around £1 trillion.

What is an option?

An option is a contract giving one party the right, but not the obligation, to buy or sell a financial instrument, commodity or some other underlying asset at a given price, at or before a specified date. The purchaser of the option can either exercise the right or let it lapse – the choice is theirs.

A very simple option would be where a firm pays the owner of a piece of land a non-returnable **premium** (say £10,000) for an option to buy the land at an agreed price (say, £1 million) because the firm is considering the development of a retail park within the next 5 years. The property developer may pay a number of option premiums to owners of land in different parts of the country. If planning permission is eventually granted on a particular plot the option to purchase may be **exercised**. In other words, the developer pays the price agreed at the time that the option contract was arranged, to purchase the land. Options on other plots will be allowed to lapse and will have no value. By using an option the property developer has 'kept the options open' with regard to which site to buy and develop and, indeed, whether to enter the retail park business at all.

Options can also be **traded**. Perhaps the *option* to buy could be sold to another company keener to develop a particular site than the original option purchaser. It may be sold for much more than the original £10,000 option premium, even before planning permission has been granted.

Once planning permission has been granted the site may be worth £1.5 million. If there is an option to buy at £1 million the option right has an **intrinsic value** of £500,000, representing a 4,900 per cent return on £10,000. From this we can see the gearing effect of options: very large sums can be gained in a short period of time for a small initial cash outlay.

Share options

Share options have been traded for centuries but their use expanded significantly with the creation of traded option markets in Chicago, Amsterdam and, in 1978, the London Traded Options Market. In 1992 this became part of the London International Financial Futures and Options Exchange (LIFFE – pronounced 'life'). Euronext bought LIFFE in 2002 and it is now officially Euronext.liffe.

A share **call option** gives the purchaser a right, but not the obligation, to *buy* a fixed number of shares at a specified price at some time in the future. In the case of traded options on LIFFE, one option contract generally relates to a quantity of 1,000 shares. The seller of the option, who receives the **premium**, is referred to as the **writer**. The writer of a call option is obliged to sell the agreed quantity of shares at the agreed price sometime in the future. **American-style options** can be exercised by the buyer at any time up to the expiry date, whereas **European-style options** can only be exercised on a predetermined future date. Just to confuse everybody, the distinction has nothing to do with geography: most options traded in Europe are American-style options.

Call option holders (call option buyers)

Now let us examine the call options available on an underlying share, Cadbury Schweppes, on 31 October 2002. There are a number of different options available for this share, many of which are not reported in the table presented in the *Financial Times*, which is reproduced as Exhibit 8.1.

	Call option prices (premiums) pence		
Exercise price	**January**	**April**	**July**
390p	41.5	48.5	54.5
420p	24.5	32.5	39.5
Share price on 31.10.02 = 416p			

Exhibit 8.1 Call options on Cadbury Schweppes shares, 31 October 2002

Source: *Financial Times*, 1 November 2002

So, what do the figures mean? If you wished on 31 October to obtain the right to buy 1,000 shares on or before late January 2003[1] at an **exercise price** of 420p, you would pay a premium of £245 (1,000 × 24.5p). If you wished to keep your option to purchase open for another 3 months you could select the April call. But this right to insist that the writer sells the shares at the fixed price of 420p on or before a date in late April will cost another £80 (the total premium payable on one option contract is £325 rather than £245). This extra £80 represents additional **time value**. Time value arises because of the potential for the market price of the underlying to change in a way that creates **intrinsic value**. The intrinsic value of an option is the payoff that would be received if the underlying were at its current level when the option expires. In this case, there is currently (31 October) no intrinsic value because the right to buy is at 420p whereas the share price is 416p. However, if you look at the call option with an exercise price of 390p then the right to buy at 390p has intrinsic value because if you purchased at 390p by exercising the option you could immediately sell at 416p in the share market: the intrinsic value is therefore 26p per share, or £260 for 1,000 shares. The longer the time over which the option is exercisable, the greater the chance that the price will move to give intrinsic value. Time value is the amount by which the option premium exceeds the intrinsic value.

The two exercise price (also called strike price) levels presented in Exhibit 8.1 illustrate an **in-the-money option** (the 390 call option) and an **out-of-the-money option** (the

[1] Expiry of options is on the third Wednesday in expiry month.

420 call option). The underlying share price (416p) is above the strike price of 390 and so the 390p call option has an intrinsic value of 26p and is therefore in-the-money. The right to buy at 420p is out-of-the-money because the share price is below the call option exercise price and therefore has no intrinsic value. The holder of a 420p option would not exercise this right to buy at 420p because the shares can be bought on the stock exchange for 416p. (It is sometimes possible to buy an **at-the-money option**, which is one where the market share price is equal to the option exercise price.)

To emphasise the key points: The option premiums vary in proportion to the length of time over which the option is exercisable (e.g. they are higher for an April option than for an January option). Also, call options with a lower exercise prices will have a higher premiums.

Suppose on 31 October you are confident that Cadbury Schweppes shares are going to rise significantly over the next 3 months to 700p and you purchase a January 390 call at 41.5p.[2] The cost of this right to purchase 1,000 shares is £415 (41.5p × 1,000 shares). If the share rises as expected then you could exercise the right to purchase the shares for a total of £3,900 and then sell them in the market for £7,000. A profit of £3,100 less the option premium of £415 (i.e. £2,685) is made before transaction costs (the brokers' fees, etc. would be in the region of £20–£50). This represents a massive 647 per cent rise before costs.

However, the future is uncertain and the share price may not rise as expected. Let us consider two other possibilities. First, the share price may remain at 416p throughout the life of the option. Second, the stock market may have a severe downturn and Cadbury Schweppes shares may fall to 300p. These possibilities are shown in Exhibit 8.2.

	Assumptions on share price in January at expiry		
	700p	**416p**	**300p**
Cost of purchasing shares by exercising the option	£3,900	£3,900	£3,900
Value of shares bought	£7,000	£4,160	£3,000
Profit from exercise of option and sale of shares in the market	£3,100	£260	Not exercised
Less option premium paid	£415	£415	£415
Profit (loss) before transaction costs	£2,685	–£155	– £415
Percentage return over 3 months	647%	– 37%	– 100%

Exhibit 8.2 Profits and losses on the January 390 call option following purchase on 31 October

[2] For this exercise we will assume that the option is held to expiry and not traded before then. However, in many cases this option will be sold on to another trader long before expiry date approaches.

In the case of a standstill in the share price, the option gradually loses its time value over the 3 months until, at expiry, only the intrinsic value of 26p per share remains. The fall in the share price to 300p illustrates one of the advantages of purchasing options over some other derivatives: the holder has a right to abandon the option and is not forced to buy the underlying shares at the option exercise price – this saves £900. It would have added insult to injury to be compelled to buy at £3,900 and sell at £3,000 after having already lost £416 on the premium for the purchase of the option.

Exhibits 8.3 and 8.4 show the extent to which the purchase of an option gears up the return from share price movements: a wider dispersion of returns is experienced. On 31 October 2002, 1,000 shares could be bought for £4,160. If the value rose to £7,000, a 68 per cent return would be made, compared with a 647 per cent return if options are bought. We would all like the higher positive return on the option than the lower one available on the underlying – but would we all accept the downside risk associated with this option? Consider the following possibilities. If the share price remains at 416p, the return if shares are bought is 0 per cent, while the return in one 390 January call option is bought is –37 per cent (the £415 paid for the option declines to its intrinsic value of only £260).[3] If the share prices falls to 300p, then the return if shares are bought is –28 per cent, while the return if one 390 January call option is bought is –100 per cent (the option is worth nothing).

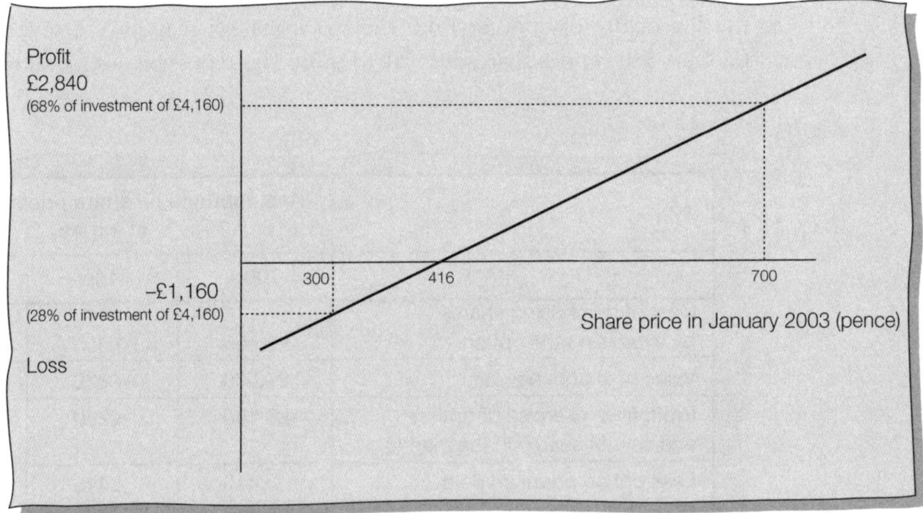

Exhibit 8.3 Profit if 1,000 shares in Cadbury Schweppes are bought on 31 October 2002 at 416p

The holder of the call option will not exercise unless the share price is at least 390p. At a lower price it will be cheaper to buy the 1,000 shares on the stock market. Break-even does not occur until a price of 431.5p because of the need to cover the cost of the pre-

[3] £260 is the intrinsic value at expiry: (416p – 390p) × 1,000 = £260.

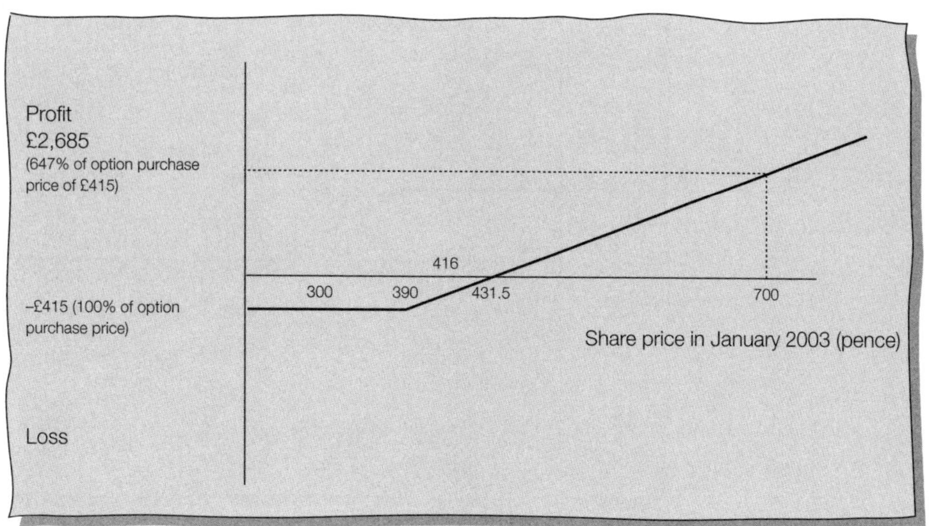

Exhibit 8.4 Profit if one 390 January call option contract (for 1,000 shares) in Cadbury Schweppes is purchased on 31 October 2002 and held to maturity

mium (390p + 41.5p). However, at higher prices the option value increases, penny for penny, with the share price. Also the downside risk is limited to the size of the option premium.

Call option writers

The returns position for the writer of a call option in Cadbury Schweppes can also be presented in a diagram (see Exhibit 8.5). With all these examples remember that there is an assumption that the position is held to expiry.

If the market price is less than the exercise price (390p) in January the option will not be exercised and the call writer profits to the extent of the option premium (41.5p per share). A market price greater than the exercise price will result in the option being exercised and the writer will be forced to deliver 1,000 shares for a price of 390p. This may mean buying shares on the stock market to supply to the option holder. As the share price rises this becomes increasingly onerous, and losses mount.

Note that in the sophisticated traded option markets of today very few option positions are held to expiry. In most cases the option holder sells the option in the market to make a cash profit or loss. Option writers often cancel out their exposure before expiry – for example, they could purchase an option to buy the same quantity of shares at the same price and expiry date.

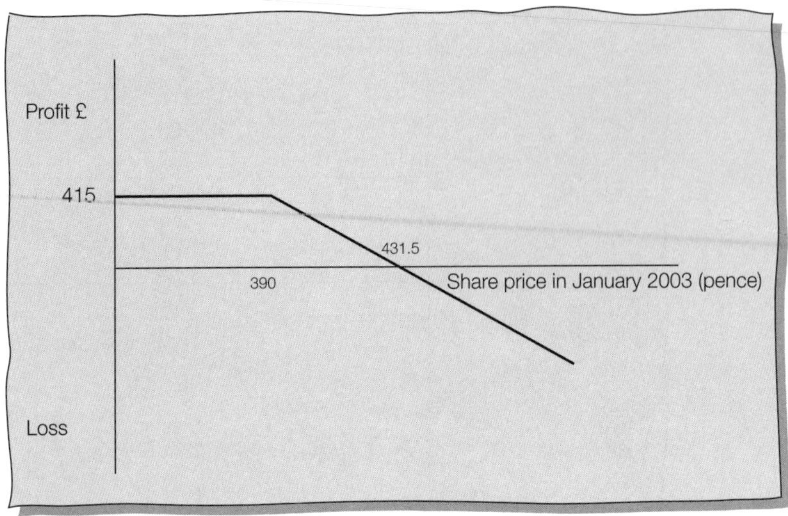

Exhibit 8.5 The profit to a call option writer on one 390 January call contract written on 31 October 2001

An example of an option writing strategy

Joe has a portfolio of shares worth £100,000 and is confident that, while the market will go up steadily over time, it will not rise over the next few months. He has a strategy of writing out-of-the-money (i.e. no intrinsic value) call options and pocketing premiums on a regular basis. Today (31 October 2002) Joe has written one option on July calls in Cadbury Schweppes for an exercise price of 420p (current share price 416p). In other words, Joe is committed to delivering (selling) 1,000 shares at any time between 31 October 2002 and near the end of July 2003 for a price of 420p at the insistence of the person who bought the call. This could be very unpleasant for Joe if the market price rises to, say, 500p. Then the option holder will require Joe to sell shares worth £5,000 to him/her for only £4,200. However, Joe is prepared to take this risk for two reasons. First he receives the premium of 39.5p per share up front – this is 9.5 per cent of each share's value, equivalent to three times the annual dividend. This £395 will cushion any feeling of future regret at his actions. Second, Joe holds 1,000 Cadbury Schweppes shares in his portfolio and so would not need to go into the market to buy the shares to then sell them to the option holder if the price did rise significantly. Joe has written a **covered** call option – so-called because he has backing in the form of the underlying shares. Joe only loses out if the share price on the day the option is exercised is greater than the strike price (420p) plus the premium (39.5p). He is prepared to risk losing some of the potential upside (above 420p + 39.5p = 459.5p) to gain the premium. He also reduces his loss on the downside: if the shares in his portfolio fall he has the premium as a cushion.

Some investors engage in **uncovered (naked)** option writing. This is not recommended for beginners as it is possible to lose a great deal of money – a multiple of your current resources if you write a lot of option contracts and the price moves against you.

Imagine if Joe had only £10,000 in savings and entered the options market by writing 30 Cadbury Schweppes July 2003 420 calls receiving a premium of 39.5p × 30 × 1,000 = £11,850.[4] If the price moves to £5 Joe has to buy shares for £5 and then sell them to the option holders for £4.20, a loss of 80p per share: 80p × 30 × 1,000 = £24,000. Despite receiving the premiums Joe has wiped out his savings.

LIFFE share options

The *Financial Times* lists about 70 companies' shares in which options are traded – some are shown in Exhibit 8.6.

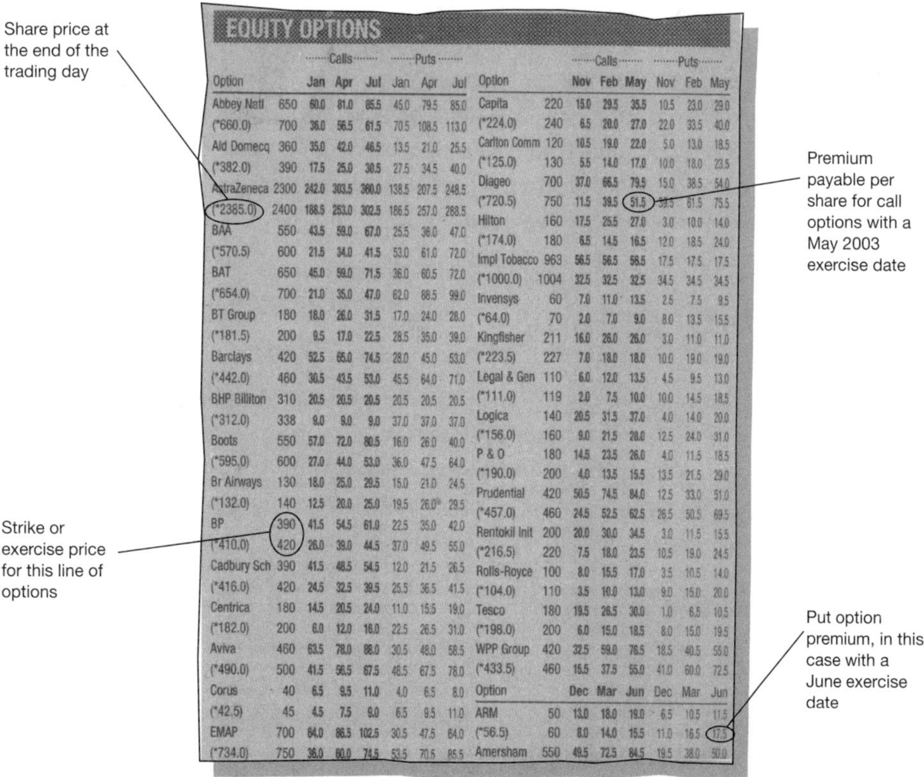

EQUITY OPTIONS

Option		Calls Jan	Calls Apr	Calls Jul	Puts Jan	Puts Apr	Puts Jul
Abbey Natl	650	60.0	81.0	85.5	45.0	79.5	85.0
(*660.0)	700	36.0	56.5	61.5	70.5	108.5	113.0
Ald Domecq	360	35.0	42.0	46.5	13.5	21.0	25.5
(*382.0)	390	17.5	25.0	30.5	27.5	34.5	40.0
AstraZeneca	2300	242.0	303.5	360.0	138.5	207.5	248.5
(*2385.0)	2400	188.5	253.0	302.5	186.5	257.0	288.5
BAA	550	43.5	59.0	67.0	25.5	36.0	47.0
(*570.5)	600	21.5	34.0	41.5	53.0	61.0	72.0
BAT	650	45.0	59.0	71.5	36.0	60.5	72.0
(*654.0)	700	21.0	35.0	47.0	62.0	88.5	99.0
BT Group	180	18.0	26.0	31.5	17.0	24.0	28.0
(*181.5)	200	9.5	17.0	22.5	28.5	35.0	39.0
Barclays	420	52.5	65.0	74.5	28.0	45.0	53.0
(*442.0)	460	30.5	43.5	53.0	45.5	64.0	71.0
BHP Billiton	310	20.5	20.5	20.5	20.5	20.5	20.5
(*312.0)	338	9.0	9.0	9.0	37.0	37.0	37.0
Boots	550	57.0	72.0	80.5	16.0	26.0	40.0
(*595.0)	600	27.0	44.0	53.0	36.0	47.5	64.0
Br Airways	130	18.0	25.0	29.5	15.0	21.0	24.5
(*132.0)	140	12.5	20.0	25.0	19.5	26.0	29.5
BP	390	41.5	54.5	61.0	22.5	35.0	42.0
(*410.0)	420	26.0	39.0	44.5	37.0	49.5	55.0
Cadbury Sch	390	41.5	48.5	54.5	12.0	21.5	26.5
(*416.0)	420	24.5	32.5	39.5	25.5	36.5	41.5
Centrica	180	14.5	20.5	24.0	11.0	15.5	19.0
(*182.0)	200	6.0	12.0	16.0	22.5	26.5	31.0
Aviva	460	63.5	78.0	88.0	30.5	48.0	58.5
(*490.0)	500	41.5	56.5	67.5	46.5	67.5	78.0
Corus	40	6.5	9.5	11.0	4.0	6.5	8.0
(*42.5)	45	4.5	7.5	9.0	6.5	9.5	11.0
EMAP	700	64.0	86.5	102.5	30.5	47.5	64.0
(*734.0)	750	36.0	60.0	74.5	53.5	70.5	85.5

Option		Calls Nov	Calls Feb	Calls May	Puts Nov	Puts Feb	Puts May
Capita	220	15.0	29.5	35.5	10.5	23.0	29.0
(*224.0)	240	6.5	20.0	27.0	22.0	33.5	40.0
Carlton Comm	120	10.5	19.0	22.0	5.0	13.0	18.5
(*125.0)	130	5.5	14.0	17.0	10.0	18.0	23.5
Diageo	700	37.0	66.5	79.5	15.0	38.5	54.0
(*720.5)	750	11.5	39.5	51.5	[illegible]	61.5	75.5
Hilton	160	17.5	25.5	27.0	3.0	10.0	14.0
(*174.0)	180	6.5	14.5	16.5	12.0	18.5	24.0
Impl Tobacco	963	56.5	56.5	56.5	17.5	17.5	17.5
(*1000.0)	1004	32.5	32.5	32.5	34.5	34.5	34.5
Invensys	60	7.0	11.0	13.5	2.5	7.5	9.5
(*64.0)	70	2.0	7.0	9.0	8.0	13.5	15.5
Kingfisher	211	16.0	26.0	26.0	3.0	11.0	11.0
(*223.5)	227	7.0	18.0	18.0	10.0	19.0	19.0
Legal & Gen	110	6.0	12.0	13.5	4.5	9.5	13.0
(*111.0)	119	2.0	7.5	10.0	10.0	14.5	18.5
Logica	140	20.5	31.5	37.0	4.0	14.0	20.0
(*156.0)	160	9.0	21.5	28.0	12.5	24.0	31.0
P & O	180	14.5	23.5	26.0	4.0	11.5	18.5
(*190.0)	200	4.0	13.5	15.5	13.5	21.5	29.0
Prudential	420	50.5	74.5	84.0	12.5	33.0	51.0
(*457.0)	460	24.5	52.5	62.5	26.5	50.5	69.5
Rentokil Init	200	20.0	30.0	34.5	3.0	11.5	15.5
(*216.5)	220	7.5	18.0	23.5	10.5	19.0	24.5
Rolls-Royce	100	8.0	15.5	17.0	3.5	10.5	14.0
(*104.0)	110	3.5	10.0	13.0	9.0	15.0	20.0
Tesco	180	19.5	28.5	30.0	1.0	6.5	10.5
(*198.0)	200	6.0	15.0	18.5	8.0	15.0	19.5
WPP Group	420	32.5	59.0	76.5	18.5	40.5	55.0
(*433.5)	460	15.5	37.5	55.0	41.0	60.0	72.5
Option		**Dec**	**Mar**	**Jun**	**Dec**	**Mar**	**Jun**
ARM	50	13.0	18.0	19.0	6.5	10.5	11.5
(*56.5)	60	8.0	14.0	15.5	11.0	16.5	17.5
Amersham	550	49.5	72.5	84.5	19.5	38.0	50.0

Exhibit 8.6 LIFFE equity options prices in the *Financial Times*

Source: *Financial Times* 1 November 2002

[4] This is somewhat simplified. In reality Joe would have to provide margin of cash or shares to reassure the clearing house that he could pay up if the market moved against him. So it could be that all of the premium received would be tied up in margin held by the clearing house (the role of a clearing house is explained in the next chapter).

Put options

A **put option** gives the holder the right, but not the obligation, to sell a specific quantity of shares on or before a specified date at a fixed exercise price.

Imagine you are pessimistic about the prospects for Cadbury Schweppes on 31 October 2002. You could purchase, for a premium of 12p per share (£120 in total), the right to sell 1,000 shares before late January 2003 at 390p (see Exhibit 8.6). If a collapse in price subsequently takes place, to 350p, say, you can insist on exercising the right to sell at 390p. The writer of the put option is obliged to purchase shares at 390p while being aware that the put holder is able to buy shares at 350p on the stock market. The option holder makes a profit of 40p per share less the 12p premium (28p per share or £280 in total), a 233 per cent return (before costs).

As with calls, in most cases the option holder would take profits by selling the option on to another investor via LIFFE rather than waiting to exercise at expiry.

For the put option holder, if the market price exceeds the exercise price, it will not be wise to exercise as shares can be sold for a higher price on the stock market. Therefore the maximum loss, equal to the premium paid, is incurred. The option writer gains the premium if the share price remains above the exercise price, but may incur a large loss if the market price falls significantly.

Traditional options

The range of underlyings available on LIFFE and other exchanges is limited. Traditional options, on the other hand, are available on any security, but there is usually no choice on the strike (exercise) price: this is set as the market price on the day the option is bought (or close to it). Also all options expire within 3 months (traded options have up to 9 months to expiry) and the option cannot be sold on to another investor: it has to be either exercised by the original purchaser (it can be exercised at any time before expiry) or left to lapse. The purchaser may close a position during the life of an option by doing the reverse (e.g. if he has bought a call option he could sell a call option at the same strike price).

How to trade options

Your existing share dealing broker will probably be able to offer an option (and futures) dealing facility, with or without advice. If not, ask another broker. Minimum commissions are generally £20, but brokers do go lower in special promotional periods when in search of business. Expect to pay a bid–offer spread of between 1p and 3p per share on the premiums. So if a premium were quoted at 35p in the *Financial Times*, this will be a mid-price between the price you would pay if you were buying (offer price), say 36p, and the price you would receive if you were selling (bid price), say 34p.

Traded option prices are carried on LIFFE's website, *www.liffe.com*, continuously updated with a 15-minute delay. The site also carries a list of approved brokers. Traders can set limits on the price to pay when making an order. The price limits can be **good for the day** (if not fulfilled in a day, the order is cancelled) or **good till cancelled**.

Gains from option trading are taxable as capital gains. No stamp duty is levied on purchases.

Using share options to reduce risk: hedging

Hedging with options is especially attractive because they can give protection against unfavourable movements in the underlying while permitting the possibility of benefiting from favourable movements. Suppose you hold 1,000 shares in Cadbury Schweppes on 31 October 2002. Your shareholding is worth £4,160. There are rumours flying around the market that the company may become the target of a takeover bid. If this materialises, the share price will rocket; if it does not, the market will be disappointed and the price will fall dramatically. What are you to do? One way to avoid the downside risk is to sell the shares. The problem is that you may regret this action if the bid does subsequently occur and you have forgone the opportunity of a large profit. An alternative approach is to retain the shares and buy a put option. This will rise in value as the share price falls. If the share price rises you gain from your underlying shareholding.

Assume a 390 April put is purchased for a premium of £215 (see Exhibit 8.6). If the share price falls to 320p in late April you lose on your underlying shares by £960 ((416p – 320p) × 1,000). However the put option will have an intrinsic value of £700 ((390p – 320p) × 1,000), thus reducing the loss and limiting the downside risk. Below 390p, for every 1p lost on the share price, 1p is gained on the put option, so the maximum loss is £475 (£260 intrinsic value + £215 option premium).

This hedging reduces the dispersion of possible outcomes. There is a floor below which losses cannot be increased, while on the upside the benefit from any rise in share price is reduced due to the premium paid.

Using options to reduce losses

A simpler example of risk reduction occurs when an investor is fairly sure that a share will rise in price but is not so confident as to discount the possibility of a fall. Suppose that the investor wished to buy 10,000 shares in Diageo, currently priced at 720.5p (on 31 October 2002) – see Exhibit 8.6. This can be achieved either by a direct purchase of shares in the market or through the purchase of an option. If the share price does fall significantly, the size of the loss is greater with the share purchase – the option loss is limited to the premium paid.

Suppose that ten February 750 call options are purchased at a cost of £3,950 (39.5p × 1,000 × 10). Exhibit 8.7 shows that the option is less risky because of the ability to abandon the right to buy at 750p.

Diageo share price falls to	Loss on 10,000 shares	Loss on 10 call options
700	£2,050	£3,950
650	£7,050	£3,950
600	£12,050	£3,950
550	£17,050	£3,950
500	£22,050	£3,950

Exhibit 8.7 Losses on alternative buying strategies

Index options

Options on whole share indices can be purchased: for example, Standard and Poor's 500 (USA), FTSE 100 (UK), CAC 40 (France), DAX (Germany). Large investors usually have a varied portfolio of shares so, rather than hedging individual shareholdings with options, they may hedge through options on the entire index of shares. Also speculators can take a position on the future movement of the market as a whole.

A major difference between index options and share options is that the former are '**cash settled**' – so for the FTSE 100 option, there is no delivery of 100 different shares on the expiry day. Rather, a cash difference representing the price change changes hands.

If you examine Exhibit 8.8, you will see that the index is regarded as a price and each one-point movement on the index represents £10. So if you purchased one contract in December expiry 4,125 calls (C) you would pay an option premium of 136 index points × £10 = £1,360. Imagine that the following day, 1 November 2002, the FTSE 100 moved from its closing level on 31 October 2002 of 4,040 to 4,127 and the option price on the 4,125 call moved to 225 index points (2 points of intrinsic value and 223 points of time value). To convert this into money you could sell the option at £10 per point per contract (225 × £10 = £2,250). In 24 hours your £1,360 has gone up to £2,250, a 65 per cent rise. Large gains can be made when the market moves in your favour. If it moves against you, large percentage losses will occur in just a few hours.

FTSE 100 INDEX OPTION (Euronext.liffe) £10 per full index point — 31 Oct

	3725		3825		3925		4025		4125		4225		4325		4425	
	C	P	**C**	P	**C**	P	**C**	P	**C**	P	**C**	P	**C**	P	**C**	P
Nov	**319**	24½	**235½**	41	**162½**	68	**102½**	108	**56½**	162	**28**	233	**11½**	316½	**4**	409
Dec	**388½**	87½	**315**	113½	**247½**	145½	**187**	184½	**136**	233	**93½**	289½	**61½**	357½	**37½**	432½
Jan	**429½**	120	**356**	146	**289½**	178½	**229½**	217½	**176½**	263½	**131**	317½	**95**	380½	**65½**	450½
Feb	**472½**	156½	**403½**	187½	**339½**	223½	**279½**	263½	**227**	311	**180½**	364½	**140½**	424½	**106**	490
Mar	**477**	194	**410**	225½	**346½**	260	**287½**	300	**233**	344	**186½**	395½	**144½**	452½	**111**	517½

Calls 47,687; Puts 43,334 . * Underlying index value. Premiums shown are based on settlement prices.

Exhibit 8.8 FTSE 100 index option prices

Source: *Financial Times* 1 November 2002

Hedging against a decline in the market using index options

An investor with an £80,000 broadly spread portfolio of shares is concerned that the market may fall over the next 4 months. One strategy to lower risk is to purchase put options on the share index. If the market does fall, losses on the portfolio will be offset by gains on the value of the index put option.

First the investor has to calculate the number of option contracts needed to hedge the underlying. With the index at 4,040 on 31 October 2002 and each point of that index settled at £10, one contract has a value of 4,040 × £10 = £40,400. To cover an £80,000 portfolio two contracts are needed (investors can trade in whole contracts only). The investor opts to buy two February 4,025 puts for 263.5 points per contract.[5] The premium payable is :

$$263.5 \text{ points} \times £10 \times 2 = £5{,}270$$

This amounts to a 6.6 per cent 'insurance premium' (£5,270/£80,000) against a downturn in the market.

Consider what happens if the market does fall by a large amount, say, 15 per cent, between 31 October and February. The index falls from 4,040 to 3,434, and the loss on the portfolio is

$$£80{,}000 \times 0.15 = £12{,}000$$

If the portfolio is unhedged, the investor suffers from a market fall. However, in this case the put options gain in value as the index falls because they carry the right to sell at

[5] This is not a **perfect hedge** as there is an element of the underlying risk without offsetting derivative cover.

4,025. If the investor closed the option position by buying at a level of 3,434, with the right to sell at 4,025, a 591-point difference, a gain is made :

Gain on options (4,025 – 3,434) × 2 × £10	=	£11,820
Less option premium paid		£ 5,270
		£6,550

A substantial proportion of the fall in portfolio value is compensated for through the use of the put derivative.

Further reading

D. Blake, *Financial Market Analysis*, 2nd edn (Wiley, 2000). Some very useful material – but your maths has to be up to scratch!

B. A. Eales, *Financial Risk Management* (McGraw-Hill, 1995). Introductory material on derivatives.

L. Galitz, *Financial Engineering*, 2nd edn (Financial Times Prentice Hall, 1998). A clearly written and sophisticated book on use of derivatives. Aimed at a professional readership, but some sections are excellent for the novice.

F. Taylor, *Mastering Derivatives Markets*, 2nd edn (Financial Times Prentice Hall, 2000). A good introduction to derivatives instruments and markets.

R. Vaitilingam, *The Financial Times Guide to Using the Financial Pages*, 4th edn (Financial Times Prentice Hall, 2001). Explains the tables displayed by the *Financial Times* and some background about the instruments – for the beginner.

S. Valdez and S. Woods, *An Introduction to Global Financial Markets*, 4th edn (Palgrave Macmillan, 2003). Very good introductory description of instruments, with a description of markets around the world.

Websites

www.bloomberg.com	Bloomberg
www.reuters.com	Reuters
www.money.cnn.com	CNN Financial News
www.wsj.com	Wall Street Journal
www.ft.com	Financial Times
www.fow.com	Futures and Options World
www.liffe.com	London International Financial Futures and Options Exchange
www.liffeinvestor.com	Information and learning tools from LIFFE to help the private investor
www.liffe-style.com	Prices on LIFFE

9

Futures

Futures are contracts between two parties to undertake a transaction at an agreed price on a specified future date. In contrast to buying options, which give you the choice to walk away from the deal, with futures you are committed and are unable to back away. This is a very important difference. In purchasing an option the maximum you can lose is the premium paid, whereas you can lose multiples of the amount you employ in taking a futures position.

A simple example will demonstrate this. Imagine a farmer wishes to lock in a price for his wheat, which will be harvested in 6 months. You agree to purchase the wheat from the farmer 6 months hence at a price of £60 per tonne. You are hoping that by the time the wheat is delivered the price has risen and you can sell at a profit. The farmer is worried that all he has from you is the promise to pay £60 per tonne in 6 months, and if the market price falls you will walk away from the deal. To reassure him you are asked to put money into what the farmer calls a **margin account**. He asks and you agree to deposit £6 for each tonne you have agreed to buy. If you fail to complete the bargain the farmer will be able to draw on the money from the margin account and then sell the wheat as it is harvested at the going rate for immediate ('**spot**') delivery. So as far as the farmer is concerned the price of wheat for delivery at harvest time could fall to £54 and he is still going to get £60 for each tonne: £6 from what you paid into the margin account and £54 from selling at the spot price.

But what if the price falls below £54? The farmer is exposed to risk – something he had tried to avoid by entering a futures deal. It is for this reason that the farmer asks you to top up your margin account on a daily basis so that there is always a buffer. He sets a **maintenance margin** level of £6 per tonne.

You have to maintain at least £6 per tonne in the margin account. If, the day after buying the future, the harvest-time price in the futures market falls to £57 you have only £3 per tonne left in the margin account as a buffer for the farmer. You agreed to buy at £60 but the going rate is only £57. To bring the margin account up to a £6 buffer you will be required to put in another £3 per tonne. If the price the next day falls to £50 you will be required to put up another £7 per tonne. You agreed to buy at £60; with the market price at £50 you have put a total of £6 + £3 + £7 = £16 into the margin account. By providing top-ups as the price moves against you there will always be at least £6 per tonne providing security for the farmer. Even if you go bankrupt or simply renege on the deal he will receive at least £60 per tonne, either from the spot market or from a combination of a lower market price plus money from the margin account. As the price fell to £50 you have a £10 per tonne incentive to walk away from the deal except for the fact that you have put £16 into an account that the farmer can draw on should you be so stupid or unfortunate. If the price is £50 per tonne at expiry of the contract and you have put £16 in the margin account, you are entitled to the spare £6 of margin.

It is in the margin account that we have the source of multiple losses in the future markets. Suppose your life savings amount to £10 and you are convinced there will be a drought and shortage of wheat following the next harvest. In your view the price will rise to £95 per tonne. So, to cash in on your forecast you agree to buy a future for 1 tonne of wheat. You have agreed with the farmer that in 6 months you will pay £60 for the wheat, which you expect to then sell for £95. (The farmer is obviously less convinced that prices are destined to rise than you.)

To gain this right to buy at £60 you need only have £6 for the **initial margin**. The other £4 might be useful to meet day-to-day **margin calls** should the wheat price fall from £60 (temporarily, in your view). If the price does rise to £95 you will make a £35 profit having laid out only £6 (plus some other cash temporarily). This is a very high return of 483 per cent over 6 months. But what if the price at harvest time is £40? You have agreed to pay £60, therefore the loss of £20 wipes out your savings and you are made bankrupt. You lose three times your initial margin. That is the downside to the gearing effect of futures.

The above example demonstrates the essential features of futures market trading. In reality, however, participants in the market do not transact directly with each other, but go through a regulated exchange. Your opposite number, called a **counterparty**, is not a farmer but an organisation that acts as counterparty to all futures traders, buyers or sellers, called the **clearing house**. This significantly reduces the risk of non-compliance with the contract for the buyer or seller of a future, as it is highly unlikely that the clearing house will be unable to fulfil its obligation.

COMMODITY PRICES

		Change
Alum HG (cash, t)	$1430-30.5	+6.0
Alum Alloy (cash, t)	$1407-409	+10.5
Copper Gr A (cash, t)	$1814.5-15	+6.3
Lead (cash, t)	$540-1	+0.3
Nickel (cash, t)	$10315-20	+112
Tin 99.85% (cash, t)	$4940-45	+22.5
Zinc SHG (cash, t)	$836-6.5	+13.8
Gold close (troy oz)	$385.60-386.10	+0.6
Gold am fix (troy oz)	$385.25	-1.2
Gold pm fix (troy oz)	$385.00	+0.4
Gold - GOFO, 3mth	0.12	nc
Silver fix (troy oz)	522.50c	-3.0
Platinum (troy oz)	$704.0	-3.0
Palladium (troy oz)	$218.0	+4.0
Oil- Brent blend (Oct)	$26.79-6.85	+0.7
Unleaded Gas (95R)	$266-268	+7.0
Gas Oil (German Htg)	$229-231	+5.0
Heavy Fuel Oil	$141-143	+5.0
Naphtha	$248-250	+8.0
Jet fuel	$253-255	+5.0
Diesel (French)	$237-239	+5.0
NBP Gas (Oct)	18.90-19.00	-0.4
Euro Gas (Zeebrugge)	20.25-20.35	+0.1
UKPX Spot Index £/Mwh	16.63	+2.1
Conti Power Index €/Mwh	39.2131	+5.2
globalCOAL RB Index™ †	$36.25	nc
Barley (Eng. feed)	69.50	nc
Maize (US No3 Yellow)	62.60	nc
Wheat (US Dark Nth)	100.0	nc
Rubber (KL RSS no1, c/kg)	427.5	+4.5
Palm Oil (Malay) ‡	450.0	nc
Soyabeans (US)	188.0	-2.0
Cotton A Index (per lb)	66.05c	nc
Wooltops (Super, p/kg)	546.0	nc
Coffee fut (Sep)	$717	+9
Cocoa fut (Dec)	1017	+16
Sugar fut (white, Dec)	$183.5	-1

Sources: LME/Amalgamated Metal Trading, lbma.org.uk/NM Rothschild, Petroleum Argus, UK power exchange, Platts, Global Coal, Reuters and Euronext.liffe. † US $ per metric tonne, week to date. ‡ CIF Rotterdam.

Exhibit 9.1 Commodity spot and futures prices in the *Financial Times*

Source: *Financial Times* 25 September 2003

The exchange provides standardised legal agreements traded in highly liquid markets. The fact that the agreements are standardised allows a wide market appeal because buyers and sellers know what is being traded: the contracts are for a specific quality of the underlying, in specific amounts with specific delivery dates. For example, for sugar traded on LIFFE (see Exhibit 9.1) one contract is for a specified grade of sugar and each contract is for a standard 50 tonnes with fixed delivery days in late August, October, December, March and May.

In examining Exhibit 9.1, it is important to remember that it is the contracts themselves that are a form of security bought and sold in the market. Thus the December future priced at $183.5 per tonne is a derivative of sugar and is not the same thing as sugar. To buy this future is to enter into an agreement with rights. It is the rights that are bought and sold, not the commodity. But when exercise takes place, it is sugar that is bought. However, as with most derivatives, usually future positions are cancelled by an offsetting transaction before exercise.

Marking to market and margins

With the clearing house being the formal counterparty for every buyer or seller of a futures contract, an enormous potential for credit risk is imposed on the organisation given the volume of futures traded and the size of the underlying they represent (LIFFE has an average daily volume of around £500 billion). If only a small fraction of market participants fail to deliver, this could run into hundreds of millions of pounds. To protect itself the clearing house operates a margining system. The futures buyer or seller has to provide, usually in cash, an **initial margin**. The amount required depends on the futures market, the level of volatility of the underlying and the potential for default; however, it is likely to be in the region of 0.1–15.0 per cent of the value of the underlying. The initial margin is not a 'down-payment' for the underlying; the funds do not flow to a buyer or seller of the underlying, but stay with the clearing house. It is merely a way of guaranteeing that the buyer or seller will pay up should the price of the underlying move against them. It is refunded when the futures position is closed.

The clearing house also operates a system of daily **marking to market**. At the end of every trading day each counterparty's profits or losses created as a result of that day's price change are calculated. Any counterparty that has made a loss has his/her **member's margin account** debited. The following morning, the losing counterparty must inject more cash to cover the loss if the amount in the account has fallen below a threshold level, called the **maintenance margin**. An inability to pay a daily loss causes default and the contract is closed, thus protecting the clearing house from the possibility that the counterparty might accumulate further daily losses without providing cash to cover them. The margin account of the counterparty that makes a daily gain is credited. This may be withdrawn the next day. The daily credits and debits to members' margin accounts are known as **variation margin**.

Worked example showing margins

Imagine a buyer and seller of a future on Monday with an underlying value of £50,000 are each required to provide an initial margin of 10 per cent, or £5,000. The buyer will make profits if the price rises while the seller will make profits if the price falls. In Exhibit 9.2 it is assumed that counterparties have to keep the entire initial margin permanently as a buffer.[1] (In reality this requirement may be relaxed by an exchange.)

	Day				
£	**Monday**	**Tuesday**	**Wednesday**	**Thursday**	**Friday**
Value of future (based on daily closing price)	50,000	49,000	44,000	50,000	55,000
Buyer's position					
Initial margin	5,000				
Variation margin (+ credited, – debited)	0	–1,000	–5,000	+6,000	+5,000
Accumulated profit or loss	0	–1,000	–6,000	0	+5,000
Seller's position					
Initial margin	5,000				
Variation margin (+ credited, – debited)	0	+ 1,000	+ 5,000	–6,000	–5,000
Accumulated profit (loss)	0	+ 1,000	+ 6,000	0	–5,000

Exhibit 9.2 Example of initial margin, variation margin and marking to market

At the end of Tuesday the buyer of the contract has £1,000 debited from her member's account. This will have to be handed over the following day or the exchange will automatically close the member's position and crystallise the loss. If the buyer does provide the variation margin and the position is kept open until Friday the account will have an accumulated credit of £5,000. The buyer has the right to buy at £50,000 but can sell at £55,000. If the buyer and the seller closed their positions on Friday the buyer would be entitled to receive the initial margin plus the accumulated profit, £5,000 + £5,000 = £10,000, whereas the seller would receive nothing (£5,000 initial margin minus losses of £5,000).

[1] Initial margin is the same as maintenance margin in this case.

This example illustrates the effect of leverage in futures contracts. The initial margin payments are small relative to the value of the underlying. When the underlying changes by a small percentage the effect is magnified for the future, and large percentage gains and losses are made on the amount committed to the transaction:

Underlying change (Monday–Friday): $\frac{£55,000 - 50,000}{£50,000} \times 100 = 10\%$

Percentage return to buyer of future: $\frac{£5,000 \times 100}{£5,000} = 100\%$

Percentage return to seller of future: $\frac{-£5,000 \times 100}{£5,000} = -100\%$

Clearly playing the futures market can seriously damage your wealth. This was proved with a vengeance by Nick Leeson of Barings Bank. He bought futures in the Nikkei 225 index – the main Japanese share index – in both the Osaka and the Singapore derivatives exchanges. He was betting that the market would rise as he committed the bank to buying the index at a particular price. When the index fell margin payments had to be made. Leeson took a double or quits attitude: 'a lot of futures traders when the market is against them will double up'.[2] He continued to buy futures. To generate some cash, to make variation margin payments, he wrote combinations of call and put options ('straddles'). This compounded the problem when the Nikkei 225 index continued to fall in 1994. The put options became an increasingly expensive commitment to bear – counterparties had the right to sell the index to Barings at a price much higher than the prevailing price. Over £800 million was lost.

Settlement

Historically the futures markets developed on the basis of the **physical delivery** of the underlying. If you had contracted to buy 40,000 lb. of lean hogs, you would receive the meat as settlement. However, in most futures markets today (including that for lean hogs) only a small proportion of contracts result in physical delivery. The majority are **closed out** before the expiry of the contract and all that changes hands is cash. Speculators certainly do not want to end up with 5 tonnes of coffee or 15,000 lb. of orange juice and so will **reverse their trade** before the contract expires; for example, if they originally bought 50 tonnes of white sugar they later sell 50 tonnes of white sugar for the same future delivery date.

[2] Nick Leeson in an interview with David Frost reported in the *Financial Times*, 11 September 1995.

A hedger, say a confectionery manufacturer, may sometimes take delivery from the exchange but in most cases will have established purchasing channels for sugar, cocoa, etc. In these cases they may use the futures markets not as a way of obtaining goods but as a way of offsetting the risk of the prices of goods moving adversely. So a confectionery manufacturer may still plan to buy, say, sugar, at the spot price from its long-standing supplier in 6 months and simultaneously, to hedge the risk of the price rising, will buy six-month futures in sugar. The position will then be closed before expiry. If the price of the underlying has risen the manufacturer pays more to the supplier but has a compensating gain on the future. If the price falls the supplier is paid less and so the confectioner makes a gain here, but, under a perfect hedge, the future has lost an equal value.

As the futures markets developed it became clear that most participants did not want the complications of physical delivery and this led to the development of futures contracts where cash settlement takes place. This permitted a wider range of futures contracts to be created. Futures contracts based on intangible commodities such as a share index or a rate of interest are now important financial instruments. With these, even if the contract is held to the maturity date one party will hand over cash to other (via the clearing house system).

For example, FTSE 100 futures (see Exhibit 9.3) are notional futures contracts. If not closed out before expiry they are settled in cash based on the average level of the FTSE 100 index between stated times on the last trading day of the contract. Each index point is valued at £10.

Exhibit 9.3 shows futures in indices from stock markets around the world for 24 September 2003. We will focus on the line for the FTSE 100 index future. This is very much a cut-down version of the futures available to traders. As well as the December delivery future shown, LIFFE also offers traders the possibility of buying or selling futures that 'deliver' in March, June and September.

EQUITY INDEX FUTURES

Sep 24		Open	Sett	Change	High	Low	Est. vol.	Open Int.
DJIA	Dec	9530.0	9393.0	-134.0	9555.0	9381.0	11,905	30,928
DJ Euro Stoxx‡	Dec	2517.0	2469.0	-27.0	2527.0	2459.0	436,643	1241,508
S&P 500	Dec	1025.60	1007.30	-18.10	1028.20	1006.30	45,655	568,699
Mini S&P 500	Dec	1025.50	1007.25	-18.25	1028.25	1006.25	623,754	367,830
Nasdaq 100	Dec	1388.50	1337.50	-51.50	1393.50	1337.00	18,568	69,342
Mini Nasdaq	Dec	1389.50	1337.50	-51.50	1393.50	1339.50	307,358	161,344
Russell 2000	Dec	520.00	506.25	-13.10	520.25	506.25	1,584	22,069
CAC 40	Sep	3260.5	3264.0	-3.0	3301.5	3229.5	91,460	655,958
DAX	Dec	3455.5	3363.5	-60.0	3468.5	3351.0	106,810	245,451
AEX	Oct	325.25	322.75	-0.55	326.20	322.25	13,120	43,485
MIB 30	Dec	25720.0	25655.0	+71.0	25790.0	25570.0	17,140	14,355
IBEX 35	Oct	6950.0	6890.0	-43.5	6977.0	6874.0	7,882	51,707
SMI	Dec	5227.0	5238.0	+21.0	5257.0	5210.0	27,833	123,593
FTSE 100 •	Dec	4256.0	4255.5	+12.0	4281.5	4224.0	58,013	403,863
Hang Seng	Sep	11000.0	11341.0	+371.0	11358.0	10978.0	47,163	76,565
Nikkei 225†	Dec	10520.0	10460.0	+20.0	10640.0	10340.0	62,777	218,068
Topix	Dec	1045.5	1037.0	-2.5	1053.0	1026.5	36,196	264,889
KOSPI 200	Dec	93.05	93.25	+0.55	93.60	92.20	320,549	81,367

North American close . The contracts shown are among the 20 most traded based on estimates of average volumes in the first half of 2002. Previous day's Open Interest. † Osaka contract. ‡ Eurex contract.

Exhibit 9.3 Equity index futures table in the *Financial Times*

Source: *Financial Times* 25 September 2003

The exhibit shows the first price traded at the beginning of the day (Open), the settlement price used to mark to market (usually the last traded price), the change from the previous day, highest and lowest prices during the day, the number of contracts traded that day (Est. vol.) and the total number of open contracts (these are trading contracts opened over the last few months that have not yet been closed by an equal and opposite futures transaction).

Worked example: Hedging with a share index future

It is 24 September 2003 and the FT 100 is at 4,236. An investor wishes to hedge a £120,000 fund against a decline in the market. A December FTSE 100 future is available at 4,255.5 – see Exhibit 9.3. The investor retains the shares in the portfolio and *sells* three index futures contracts. Each futures contract is worth £42,555 (4,255.5 points × £10). So three contracts are needed to cover £120,000 (£120,000/(£10 × 4255.5)).

For the sake of argument assume that in December the index falls by 10 per cent to 3,812, leaving the portfolio value at £108,000. The closing of the futures position offsets this £12,000 loss by buying three futures at 3,812 producing a profit of:[3]

Able to sell at 4,255.5 × 3 × £10	=	£127,665
Able to buy at 3,812 × 3 × £10	=	£114,360
		£ 13,305

These contracts are settled in cash, so £13,305 will be paid, and the investor gets back margin, less broker's fees.

Buying and selling futures

A trader in futures must deal through a registered broker. Many brokers will not accept private clients. Those who will accept them insist that traders have enough capital to be able to set aside a proportion for risky futures trading. They will often require a minimum of £20,000 to be set aside, and this is to be no more than 10 per cent of your investment assets (excluding your house) so you have to be fairly wealthy to play in these markets. Euronext.liffe provide a list of designated brokers (these follow rules and codes of conduct imposed by the regulators and the exchange).

Gone are the days of open pit trading and those brightly coloured jackets in the UK. Trades are now conducted over a computer system on LIFFE (LIFFE CONNECT™). You can place a **price limit** for your trade or make an **at-the-market order**, to be executed immediately at the price determined by current supply and demand conditions. The

[3] Assuming that the futures price is equal to the spot price of the FTSE 100. This would occur close to the expiry date of the future.

buyer of a contract is said to be in a **long position** – he/she agrees to receive the underlying. The seller who agrees to deliver the underlying is said to be in a **short position**.

If the amount in the trader's account falls below the maintenance margin the trader will receive a demand to inject additional money. This may happen every day so the trader cannot buy/sell a future and then go on holiday for a month (unless he/she leaves plenty of cash with the broker to meet margin calls). Prices are set by competing market makers on LIFFE CONNECT. Real-time market prices are available on the Internet, as well as historical prices (e.g. *www.liffe-style.com*).

Universal stock futures (single stock futures)

As well as being able to buy or sell futures on commodities or entire share indices, you can trade futures in a particular company's shares. You can agree to buy 1,000 shares (one future contract)[4] in, say, Vodafone 2 or 3 months from now at a price that is agreed now. Exhibit 9.4 shows some of the universal stock futures (USFs) traded on Euronext.liffe.

Suppose you want to speculate that Vodafone will fall in price between 24 September 2003 (now) and the third Wednesday in November (the delivery date for the November futures shown in Exhibit 9.4). You could sell, say, 100 contracts (100,000 shares for delivery in November) at a price of 126.50p. Imagine now that the November futures price falls to 95p on 15 November; you could close your position by buying 100 futures. Your profit would be £126,500 – £95,000 = £31,500, less dealing costs. You could have made this profit by putting down a margin of only about £15,000,[5] thus more than doubling your money in 2 weeks.

On the other hand, if the December futures rose to 145p and you closed your position for fear of the price rising further, then the loss of £126,500 – £145,000 = £18,500 would wipe out your initial margin. (Note: there are a variety of other delivery days over the following 4–6 months that are not shown in the *Financial Times* – go to *www.liffe.com* to find these.)

[4] Some contracts are for 100 shares.

[5] Initial margin varies depending on the volatility of the share, but it is generally in the range of 5–20 per cent of overall contract value.

STOCK FUTURES

Sep 24		Open	Sett price	Change	High	Low	Est. vol	Open int.
BP	Oct		27.16	-1.01			0	0
ENI Spa	Nov		12.67	-0.18			0	0
HSBC Hldgs	Oct		20.79	-0.66			0	50
ING	Nov		52.80	-1.05			0	0
Nokia	Nov		7.50	-0.10			0	0
Royal Dutch	Oct		4.11	+0.01			0	0
Siemens	Nov		4.11	+0.01			0	0
San-Paolo-IMI	Nov		10.42	-0.22			0	0
Total SA	Nov		52.31	+0.81			0	0
Vodafone	Nov		126.50	+2.50			0	0

The stocks shown are a selection made by Euronext.liffe. UK and Italian companies 1000 shares - others 100 shares. A full list of Euronext.liffe Universal Stock Futures is available at www.liffe.com

Exhibit 9.4 Universal stock futures table in the *Financial Times*

Source: *Financial Times* 25 September 2003

The cost of trading single stock futures is less than the cost of trading shares, not least because they are free from stamp duty. If single stock futures are held to the delivery date then they are usually settled in cash rather than by the delivery of shares (i.e. if you have made a gain you receive it in cash). However, a few (e.g. Nokia, Norsk Hydro) are settled with physically delivered shares. You may be liable for capital gains tax on USFs. An example of USF use: suppose you hold 30,000 Vodafone shares with a current market price of 126p. You bought these for 76p and therefore your capital gain is 50p per share, or £15,000. You are convinced the market is due for a fall. To protect yourself you could sell the Vodafone shares. However, this will result in capital gain tax payable at up to 40 per cent.

An alternative is to sell 30 USFs in Vodafone at 126.50p while holding onto the shares. If the market does fall you are protected on the downside. The gain made on the USFs offsets the loss on the underlying shares. So, if the underlying and the future price falls to 95p the loss on the shares, £9,300, is largely offset by the gain on the USFs.

Sold for 126.50p	=	£37,950
Bought for 95p	=	£28,500
		£ 9,450

This USF gain can be taken over into another tax year to use the capital allowance (see Chapter 17). So, in effect, you have delayed capital gain realisation, thereby legitimately avoiding tax while locking in your gain during the market fall.

For further reading and a list of websites, see Chapter 8.

10

Spread betting, contracts for difference and warrants

Spread betting

You can bet on the future movements of shares (and other securities) in a similar way to betting on horses. If the share moves the way you said it would, you gain. However, unlike with horses, if it moves against you the loss can be a multiple of the amount you first put down – you lose money for every 1p adverse movement in a share price. So, if you bet that Marks & Spencer's share price will rise, and you punt £10 for every penny rise, if M&S increases by 30p you win £300. However, if M&S falls 30p you have to hand over £300. This is the basic principle, but the actual operation is slightly more complicated. If you believe that the price is destined to rise you will contact (by telephone or using the Internet) one of the **spread betting companies**. They will quote you two prices (the **spread**), say, 348p–352p, for M&S. The first is called the '**bid**' price and is the relevant price if you are '**selling**'. The second is the '**offer**' price and is the relevant price if you are '**buying**'.

Given your optimism about M&S, the relevant price is 352p. You agree to bet £10 per 1p rise in the price. You '**buy**' at 352p. Now imagine that you were correct and the spread on M&S moves to 375p–379p. You can close your position by telephoning the spread dealer and '**selling' to close**. The relevant price for you (betting on a rise) on the close is the lower of the two quoted: 375p. So you have made a gain of 23p (375p–352p), which translates into £230 given a bet of £10 per penny.

If you had been pessimistic about M&S when the spread quote was at 348p–352p you would have bet by 'selling' at 348p. A movement up to 375p–379p would result in a loss of 31p (379p – 348p) – £310 at £10 per penny. However, if the spread quote moves to 320p–324p the gain is 348p less 324p = 24p (or £240 if you bet £10 per penny move).

You can see how the spread betting company can make money from the spread: you sell and buy at the least advantageous price on the spread. Presumably there are other investors doing the opposite, if you are 'buying' at 352p they are 'selling' at 348p. The spread betting company's books are balanced but a 4p gain is made. The size of these spreads varies depending on volume of trade and degree of competition between spread betting firms.

Money up-front

The bookmaker (spread betting company) will require you to demonstrate that you are able to pay should the bet go against you. When you lay a bet you will be asked for a sum of money called the **notional trading requirement** or 'deposit'. This will obviously be a larger sum if you are betting £10 per penny (point) rather than £5 per penny (point) movement in the underlying share (or index), or if the share (or index) is particularly volatile.

Furthermore, if the bet starts to go against you and the position is held open over a number of days you will be asked to top up the funds deposited with the spread betting company through margin calls. Naturally, these will be returned to you if there are moves in your favour.

Imagine you placed an 'up bet' on Vodafone when the spread quote is 103p–104p. You therefore 'buy' at 104p, betting £100 per penny movement. The maximum possible loss occurs when Vodafone goes to zero: 104p loss at £100 per penny is equal to £10,400. The spread betting company requires 10 per cent of this maximum loss (in this particular case), so you deposit £1,040.[1] If the Vodafone spread falls by 5p to 98p–99p the next day, your account will be debited £500 (5 × £100 = £500). The spread betting company then asks you to top up your account by paying an additional margin of £500. For the next two weeks Vodafone oscillates greatly. On some days your account is credited, on others you are asked for more margin through **'cash calls'**. After 14 days you close your position by telephoning the spread betting company and telling the dealer that you would like to sell Vodafone 'to close'. It is important to make it clear that you are not selling Vodafone 'to open' as that means a fresh separate bet on Vodafone falling.

The spread quoted is 108p–109p. You have gained £400 (sold at 108p and bought at 104p, i.e. a 4p rise at £100 per penny). This is a good return on an initial cash injection of £1,040 (plus a few cash calls during the two weeks). However, the potential risk of it all going wrong was also very high.

An alternative to betting and then being subject to a series of cash calls is to place a 'stop-loss' at the time of the bet. Under a stop-loss the spread betting company closes your position for you if the underlying share moves to the stated stop-loss price. At the time that you place the bet you hand over margin to the spread betting company equal to the maximum loss that could occur should the stop-loss be triggered. For example, if you make an up bet on Berkeley when the spread quote is 780p–800p at £10 per penny and you set a stop-loss at 640p (i.e. 20% below the bet level) the maximum loss if the stop-loss is triggered is 160 × £10 + £1,600, so you will be asked to provide £1,600 of margin. This cash may already be in a special account opened when you registered with the spread betting company, or could be transferred by debit card over the telephone.

There are two types of stop-loss order. A 'standard' stop-loss is one where the company will *try* to close your position, but if the market is falling like a stone it may not be able to close it before the market price has zoomed past the stop-loss limit. With a 'guaranteed' ('controlled risk') stop-loss the spread betting company will close at the agreed stop-loss price even if the market price has moved beyond this before they were able to act. To have a guarantee you will have to pay a wider spread at the time that the bet is placed. A standard stop-loss does not require a wider spread.

Types of bet

There are three types of share or index bet. An **intraday (cash or spot) bet** is one that starts and is closed in the same trading day. A **futures-based bet** is one on the price of shares (index) on the next quarter day or the one after that (quarter days are in late March, June, September and December). So in the above Vodafone example the spread

[1] The notional trading requirement can be as low as 3 per cent for bets on a share index and 5 per cent for individual share bets, but is more usually 20 per cent.

quotes would have been based on the future price for a Vodafone share on the next quarter day. This price is made by the spread betting company but cannot deviate too far from prices in the market place (otherwise arbitrageurs will be given an invitation to make money risk-free by doing opposite transactions in the market and with spread betting companies).

Traditionally, futures-based betting was the way to spread a bet over a few days or weeks. However, spread betting companies have recently introduced **rolling cash spread betting**. This is betting on the cash price of the share (not on what the share price will be at the end of the quarter). The spread better 'rolls' his/her position overnight to the next day.

Uses of spread betting

Spread betting can be used as a kind of insurance. For example, when you hold the underlying shares and you think it possible that the price will fall substantially in the short term, but a potential capital gains tax causes you to hesitate in selling the underlying shares, you could place a bet such that you gain if the share price falls. You will stabilise your position: if the share falls your portfolio declines but you win (an equal amount) on the bet; if the share rises you gain on the portfolio but lose on the bet. You can then select the time when you sell the shares – it might good to wait a few months until the next tax year when you can use your annual capital gains tax allowance (see Chapter 17).

Spread betting can also be used to take highly leveraged positions where a small movement in the underlying leads to a large percentage gain on the amount initially committed to the bet – as in the Vodafone example.

Finally, spread betting allows you to gain from share (index) falls. You are restricted from shorting shares – selling shares you don't own in anticipation of closing your position by buying the same quantity at a lower price later – in the stock market, but spread betting makes this easy, at least for movements over a few months.

Further points

- All spread bet winnings are free from both income and capital gains tax. No stamp duty is payable, nor are broker's fees (the spread betting companies make their money from the spread).
- With the market being regulated by the Financial Services Authority the investor has some further reassurance.
- In addition to spread betting on shares and share indices, you can spread-bet commodities, bonds, interest rates, currencies, options, and even the outcomes of sporting events.
- Spread betting companies regularly advertise their services in the *Financial Times* and *Investors Chronicle*.

Contracts for difference

Trading in contracts for difference (CFDs) is very similar to spread betting. However, with CFD there is no settlement date – your open position can continue until you choose to close it (or it is closed for you because you have failed to provide margin).

In a CFD contract the buyer and seller agree to pay, in cash, at the closing of the contract, the difference between the opening and closing price of the underlying shares, multiplied by the number of shares in the contract.

For example, imagine that you have a deposit account with a CFD broker. You have placed £20,000 in this account. You are pessimistic about Vodafone's shares and ask for a price quote from the broker. She replies with: '102 bid and 103 offer'. You agree to sell CFDs for 160,000 shares in Vodafone at a price of 102p. Note that with the amount of cash you have (£20,000) you would not be able to purchase this many shares. It is because the CFD brokers permit trading on margins of around 10–20 per cent that you can leverage up the use of the £20,000. If we assume that the CFD broker requires 10% as margin then just over £16,000 of the deposit money will now be held as margin (and not simply as a deposit), leaving you with just under £4,000 as **free equity**. It is good to have some free equity as you might have to meet margin calls if the price starts to move against you. If the shares now fall to 92 bid and 93 offer you will be showing a gain on your margin account of 102p – 93p = 9p per share, or £14,400. If you close your position your deposit account will then contain the original £20,000 plus £14,400.

On the other hand if Vodafone's share price moves to 113p–114p you lose and the CFD broker will require additional margin. If you close your position at this point your loss will be 114p – 102p = 12p per share or 0.12 × 160,000 = £19,200.

Additional points

- No stamp duty is charged but you are liable for capital gains tax.
- Some brokers quote a narrower spread, but then charge up to 0.25 per cent of the trade value on both the opening and closing transactions.
- Stop-losses can be set up.
- When you sell a CFD as your opening position any dividend due during your period of ownership will be taken from your margin account. Those with a buy ('long') position will receive a payment equivalent to the net dividend.
- The amount you need to deposit with a CFD broker tends to be at least £10,000 – significantly more than with spread betting.
- If you take a long position (buy) the CFD trader will charge you interest during the period of holding the CFD (typically LIBOR plus 2–3 per cent). If you sell (go short), interest will be added to your account.

- CFD brokers require you to show you are an experienced trader who understands the gearing (leverage) and other risks of CFD.
- You must carefully monitor your position on a day-to-day basis as you may have to meet margin calls and/or close out positions.

Warrants

Warrants give the holder the right to subscribe for a specified number of shares at a fixed price during or at the end of a specific time period. So, the holder has the right, but not the obligation, to buy shares. Does this sound familiar? It should. Warrants are very closely related to call options (see Chapter 8). The main difference is that a warrant is issued by the company whose shares you would be entitled to buy, whereas options are written by people and organisations unconnected with the company.

Imagine that a company with shares currently trading at 75p chooses to sell warrants, each of which grants the holder the right to buy a share for £1 over the next five years. If the warrant is exercised the company will issue new shares at the exercise price (£1) and so raise additional finance.

The amount you pay for a warrant depends on demand from investors. Let us assume in this case that you purchase one warrant for 20p, which gives you the right to buy a share for £1. If the share price rises to £1.50 (a 100% rise from the current price of 75p), the right you hold to buy at £1 now has an intrinsic value of 50p – you can sell a share for £1.50 in the market that you can purchase for £1. The warrant value has risen by 150 per cent, from 20p to 50p; it might even be worth more than 50p if there is still some time before expiry. If the share price trebles to £2.25 the warrant's intrinsic value rises to £1.25, a 525 per cent gain on the 20p originally paid. This demonstrates the gearing effect of warrants relative to shares. Of course, this works the other way. If the share price falls (stays the same, or even rises a little) the warrant might expire worthless – a loss of 100 per cent of your investment.

There is no requirement for you to hold the warrant until you exercise or it expires. You can sell warrants to other investors in an active secondary market on the London Stock Exchange. Current prices are shown together with the share prices on the inside back page of the *Financial Times* (they are described as 'wts'). Most of them are issued by investment trusts (investment companies). A major advantage of warrants over traded or traditional options is that they usually hold the right to purchase over many years rather than a few months. Thus you can have a geared exposure to a company's fortune over a much longer time frame.

Note that investors need to keep track of warrants they own, especially those nearing expiry, because if they fail to exercise them the investment becomes worthless.

Covered warrants

Covered warrants are the same as the warrants described in the previous section, except that financial institutions issue them rather than the company itself. The financial institution receives payment (a '**premium**') selling a warrant in, say, BP shares, and in return grants the warrant holder the right, but not the obligation, to buy or sell an underlying asset (BP shares) at a specified price during, or at the end of, a specified time period. They are '**covered**' because the financial institution (usually an investment bank) that issues them covers its exposure by buying (or selling) the underlying security in the open market – there are now over 500.

In 2002 the London Stock Exchange launched its new covered warrant market so that even private investors could buy (sell) covered warrants (it was previously a market for professionals only, unless you could prove you understood the risks). Initially 160 covered warrants were made available on leading UK and international companies and international indices – there are now over 500.

You can purchase either a call or a put covered warrant. A call gives the right to buy a share. A put gives the right to sell a share. The put rises in value when the share falls – see the description of put options in Chapter 8.

You also have a choice of contract styles. A European-style covered warrant can only be exercised (i.e. share purchase or sale made) at expiry (say, after a year). An American-style covered warrant allows exercise at any time up to expiry.

Exhibit 10.1 shows how covered warrant prices are presented in the *Financial Times*.

Example of covered warrant use – releasing cash while maintaining exposure to a share

You own 10,000 shares in Barclays plc, currently priced at 479p, and need to release cash to put a deposit on a house. However, you feel that Barclays are destined to rise over the next few months. You could sell the Barclays shares, releasing £47,900, while simultaneously buying 10,000 Barclays covered warrants, giving the right to buy at 550p. These will expire in 9 months. You pay 26.3p for the right to buy one share at 550p – a cost of £2,630. The total cash released is thus £45,270.

If, by expiry of the warrants, Barclays shares have moved to £6, the covered warrants are worth £5,000 (£6 – £5.50 = £0.50 × 10,000). Note the gearing effect; the share moves by 25 per cent but the warrant rises by 90 per cent. You could, of course, sell the covered warrants when they still had time value at any point prior to expiry.

If you are wrong and the Barclays share price stays under £5.50, the covered warrants expire worthless and your loss is limited to £2,630.

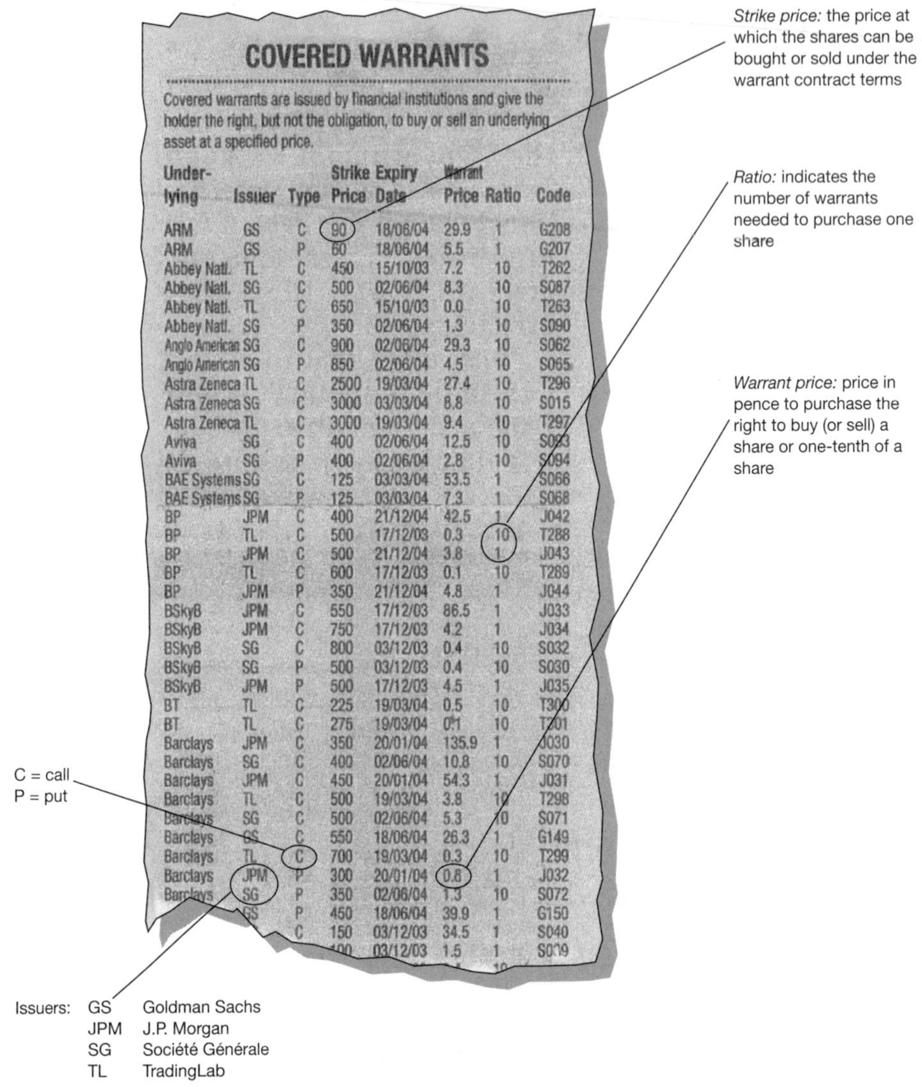

COVERED WARRANTS

Covered warrants are issued by financial institutions and give the holder the right, but not the obligation, to buy or sell an underlying asset at a specified price.

Underlying	Issuer	Type	Strike Price	Expiry Date	Warrant Price	Ratio	Code
ARM	GS	C	90	18/06/04	29.9	1	G208
ARM	GS	P	60	18/06/04	5.5	1	G207
Abbey Natl.	TL	C	450	15/10/03	7.2	10	T262
Abbey Natl.	SG	C	500	02/06/04	8.3	10	S087
Abbey Natl.	TL	C	650	15/10/03	0.0	10	T263
Abbey Natl.	SG	P	350	02/06/04	1.3	10	S090
Anglo American	SG	C	900	02/06/04	29.3	10	S062
Anglo American	SG	P	850	02/06/04	4.5	10	S065
Astra Zeneca	TL	C	2500	19/03/04	27.4	10	T296
Astra Zeneca	SG	C	3000	03/03/04	8.8	10	S015
Astra Zeneca	TL	C	3000	19/03/04	9.4	10	T297
Aviva	SG	C	400	02/06/04	12.5	10	S093
Aviva	SG	P	400	02/06/04	2.8	10	S094
BAE Systems	SG	C	125	03/03/04	53.5	1	S066
BAE Systems	SG	P	125	03/03/04	7.3	1	S068
BP	JPM	C	400	21/12/04	42.5	1	J042
BP	TL	C	500	17/12/03	0.3	10	T288
BP	JPM	C	500	21/12/04	3.8	1	J043
BP	TL	C	600	17/12/03	0.1	10	T289
BP	JPM	P	350	21/12/04	4.8	1	J044
BSkyB	JPM	C	550	17/12/03	86.5	1	J033
BSkyB	JPM	C	750	17/12/03	4.2	1	J034
BSkyB	SG	C	800	03/12/03	0.4	10	S032
BSkyB	SG	P	500	03/12/03	0.4	10	S030
BSkyB	JPM	P	500	17/12/03	4.5	1	J035
BT	TL	C	225	19/03/04	0.5	10	T300
BT	TL	C	275	19/03/04	0.1	10	T301
Barclays	JPM	C	350	20/01/04	135.9	1	J030
Barclays	SG	C	400	02/06/04	10.8	10	S070
Barclays	JPM	C	450	20/01/04	54.3	1	J031
Barclays	TL	C	500	19/03/04	3.8	10	T298
Barclays	SG	C	500	02/06/04	5.3	10	S071
Barclays	GS	C	550	18/06/04	26.3	1	G149
Barclays	TL	C	700	19/03/04	0.3	10	T299
Barclays	JPM	P	300	20/01/04	0.8	1	J032
Barclays	SG	P	350	02/06/04	1.3	10	S072
	GS	P	450	18/06/04	39.9	1	G150
		C	150	03/12/03	34.5	1	S040
			100	03/12/03	1.5	1	[illegible]

Exhibit 10.1 Covered warrants listing in the *Financial Times*

Source: *Financial Times* 26 September 2003

Additional points

- Those covered warrants granting rights on overseas shares can be traded in sterling, thus reducing concern about exchange rate risk.
- Covered warrants have an average life of 6–12 months, but they can be up to 5 years.
- You buy/sell through an ordinary broker in the same way as buying/selling shares. Market makers provide bid and offer prices on a continual basis.

- You can either insist on delivery of shares when you exercise or settle for cash – the investor receives cash from the issuer representing the profit they would have made through physical exercise (they are normally settled in cash because this avoids stamp duty).
- Potential losses are limited to the amount paid as a premium unlike spread betting, futures and CFDs, where potential losses can be unlimited.
- There is no daily mark-to-market or need to provide margin. You can therefore take a longer-term view – you can go on holiday and not have to keep an eye on the market.
- Covered warrants that are worth something on expiry date are automatically exercised, so you will not lose out if you forget to exercise.
- The Financial Services Authority oversees the market, regulating advisers, issuers and brokers.

Further reading

D. Blake, *Financial Market Analysis*, 2nd edn (Wiley, 2000). Some very useful material – but your maths has to be up to scratch!

C. Vintcent, *How to Win at Financial Spread Betting* (Financial Times Prentice Hall, 2002). A brief introduction to spread betting.

Websites

www.londonstockxchange.com	London Stock Exchange
www.bloomberg.com	Bloomberg
www.reuters.com	Reuters
www.ft.com	Financial Times

PART 3

Company analysis

11

Company accounts

Investment in shares requires analysis of companies. To avoid analysis is to end up speculating in shares in an uninformed manner. There is a world of difference between a speculator and an 'investor'.

A subtle blend of two elements is needed for successful analysis: quantitative and qualitative data. An assessment of the company's current financial position, its history of profit growth and other measures of performance are essential quantitative data used to inform the investor trying to gauge future prospects. We compare the current value of projected future business income (per share) with the current share price to draw conclusions about whether the market is over- or undervaluing a company.

Note from this that historical facts about the company are not interesting in and of themselves. They are used to provide clues to enlighten our focus on the *future*: directors' performance in using resources in the past (their '**stewardship' role**) may help assess the likelihood of good managerial performance *in the future*; the level of debt relative to the amount of the equity capital in the business may provide a clue on the *future* risk of bankruptcy; the analysis of past cash flow may assist us to assess the extent to which *future* revenues are likely to be swallowed up by investment in plant and machinery rather than being available for distribution to shareholders.

Quantitative data provide a firm factual base to make these future-orientated judgements, but this is far from sufficient. The really important factors that contribute to future profits of a company are not expressed on a balance sheet, profit and loss account or cash flow statement. These qualitative elements cover a multitude of attributes but can be summarised under the following headings:

- The nature of the industry in which the company is operating, as defined by strategic analysis.
- The competitive strength of the company within its industry, as defined by its possession (or not) of extraordinary resources that can lead to above industry average returns on capital invested – does the company have a strong business franchise surrounded by a deep and dangerous moat to deter competitors?
- The honesty and competence of the managerial team. Competence on its own is not enough. Honesty is essential, too. You can't, as an investor, sleep easy if you have the most intelligent, experienced and wise managerial team in the world and yet doubt their honesty and sincerity in focusing on shareholder value.

Newspaper articles sometimes have a bias towards providing the reader with a glimpse of some of the key qualitative elements. For example:

> Sir John Wiseman, the well-respected, highly experienced chief executive of Entrenched plc, yesterday announced the results of his strategic review of the company. It holds a 30% market share in Europe and is building rapidly from its 17% share in the North American market. It is well known that Entrenched has a great deal of power over its customers, the retail chains, because the company's profits are 'must have' brands for the supermarkets. The company has also been very careful in sourcing supplies from a wide

> variety of companies, reducing the potential for a supplier to increase prices in what for the supplier is a highly competitive market. Entrenched has decided not to take over any more competitors but to concentrate on increasing the strength of its brand and raising the research and development budget to £1.1bn per year. This will make it hard for its competitors to challenge Entrenched, either on cost or in its roll-out of innovative products. The management team has recently been strengthened by the appointment of Mike Robinson as finance director, a key figure in the accounting profession's drive for clear and simple accounting and Pat Davis as director with special responsibility for shareholder value management development programme throughout the organisation. In May Entrenched completed a £700m share buy-back. Sir John said that the company is throwing off cash and shareholders could probably use the money more effectively than the company. 'We do not want to grow the business just for the sake of growth – we must generate a return greater than our investors could obtain investing elsewhere with that money to justify any expansion.'

On other occasions the journalist concentrates on the quantitative. For example:

> Entrenched plc, the consumer products company, reported turnover up from £8.4bn to £9.8bn in the year to the end September. Pre-tax profits have accelerated to £1.8bn, a rise of 10% on last year. This is double the profit of only five years ago. Earnings per share rose from 10p to 11p, which places the shares at their current price of 220p on a price–earnings ratio of 20. This is above the industry average, but, given the strengths of the firm, is regarded as justified.

Many of the technical terms, such as price–earnings ratio, mentioned in these articles will be explained in this part of the book, as will numerous other factors that the serious investor should look for.

The vital factors in company analysis are dealt with as follows. Quantitative analysis is presented in Chapters 11, 12 and 13. The analysis of industries is the subject of Chapter 14. This is followed by the description of a framework for analysing the competitive strength of a company within its industry in Chapter 15.

Oh no! Not numbers again!

Some share pickers never look at the accounts. They are complex and impenetrable, full of jargon and numbers. The prospect of reading such a boring document is daunting – guaranteed to cure your insomnia.

It has to be admitted that there are more fun ways of spending time, but reading a set of accounts (and the report that goes with them) is a necessary task for an investor. They are a primary source of information permitting company analysis. If you were thinking of buying a corner shop as a going concern you would not see the accounts as a boring irrelevance. Indeed, you would be very keen to know all sorts of things: from the growth in sales to the proportion of sales income that turns into take-away profit; from the market value of the building to the cost of acquiring the stock held in the shop. You could probably think of a dozen fascinating accounting questions before breakfast. What level of debt is the business carrying? Is the profit trend upward or downward? Which areas of the business create profit? And so on. The price you offer for the business would be intimately connected with the numbers you observe in the accounts. And so it is with the price you would pay for shares in larger companies. Firms quoted on stock exchanges present similarly crucial fundamental data. It is just that it looks far more complicated when first encountered.

The key elements of accounting are simple. It really is not necessary for investors to deal with the more complex and obtuse accounting issues in order to understand the profit performance of a business or the value of the firm's assets. Indeed, the most successful investor in the history of the world, Warren Buffett, declares that accounts should be easy to follow. If they are presented in such a way that you are finding them difficult then it is probably because the management do not want you to understand. Such a company should be struck from your list of prospective investments simply because you cannot trust the managers.

It is vital that you gain confidence in interpreting the essential financial data. After reading this chapter and the next two you will be ready to have a go, and you will gradually gain the confidence to answer key questions. Be prepared for some work, if you want to reduce the chance of making unwise investment decisions.

Be aware that you need to develop a healthy sense of scepticism when examining accounts because, even though they are all drawn up under accounting guidelines, there is plenty of room when compiling the numbers for interpretation, approximation and estimation. The guidelines limit the wriggle-room, but there are still plenty of opportunities for subjectivity and flattery by the managers and their accountants. Despite the element of spurious precision in accounting numbers the report and accounts provide a lot of useful information.

How to obtain reports

Getting hold of a company's report and accounts is very easy these days. For a start, all registered shareholders will generally receive a copy of the annual report and accounts automatically. The word 'generally' is used because some companies produce both a full version and **a cut-down version, the annual review and summary financial statement**. Shareholders then have a choice as to which they would like to receive. The summary rarely contains enough information for investors trying to assess the company, and so reading the full version is necessary.[1]

[1] If you hold shares through a nominee account (see Chapter 4), the report and accounts will be sent to the nominee company. If the terms of the nominee account allow, they will be passed on to you – for which there may be a charge.

If you are not a shareholder, you'll need to contact the company. You can telephone or write to the **company secretary**, or simply telephone the head office switchboard. Even if you do not hold any shares in the company, nine times out of ten you'll receive a copy of the report and accounts within a week, at no cost. Another possibility is to go to the **company website**, where you'll be able to download not only the most recent figures but also 5 or more years of data. These *can* be very detailed and include a full set of **notes to the accounts**, but in other cases some elements could be missing. If in doubt, obtain the paper version with a full set of notes.

The *Financial Times*, in partnership with WILink, provides a free report and accounts service for hundreds of quoted companies. They will send one or more reports and accounts absolutely free the next business day, and you don't even have to pay for postage. If you look at the list of quoted companies in the *Financial Times* you will find some have a ♣ symbol next to the name; report and accounts are available for those companies. The service also available online (*http://ft.ar.wilink.com*), or by telephone (020 8391 6000).

It is also possible to obtain reports and accounts from Companies House (*www.companieshouse.gov.uk*) for all companies, whether quoted or not. A small fee (£4 at the time of writing) is charged. Some websites provide summary accounting information for some companies that is useful if you are carrying out an initial analysis as a filtering exercise (e.g. Hemscott, *www.hemscot.com*; Carol, *www.carol.co.uk*).

Of course, you could go about things the old-fashioned way and ask your broker to forward reports and accounts to you, but this seems a cumbersome method in the communication and information age.

The report and accounts

UK companies are required by law to publish a set of accounts annually. They are not obliged to have a December **year-end** to match the calendar year or a 5 April **year-end** to match the tax year. Sometimes the year-end is determined by when the company was originally registered. Other companies opt for a year-end that helps the accounts to look healthy – for example, an agricultural business would choose a date just after harvest when debts are low and cash holdings are high.

Registered shareholders are sent the report and accounts a few weeks before the **annual general meeting**, together with details of the meeting and issues on which a vote is required (voting forms are included in case the shareholder cannot attend the AGM). The law requires that the following information be provided in the reports and accounts:

1. A directors' report.
2. A profit and loss account.
3. A balance sheet.
4. An auditor's report.
5. Notes to the accounts.

The **accounting standards** set by the accounting profession clarify the rules and conventions governing the report and accounts. They also require the publication of some other documents such as a cash flow statement for all public companies. Furthermore, the United Kingdom Listing Authority insists that quoted companies[2] provide more information. First, an **interim profit statement (interim report)** describes the company's activities and profit and loss for the first 6 months of each financial year. Frequently companies also comply with what is considered **best practice**,[3] which means they usually include a balance sheet, a cash flow statement and some comment on trading and prospects for the company. They also generally go to the expense of having the figures **reviewed** by auditors. This is less thorough than the normal audit as it concentrates mainly on whether the numbers have been prepared in a manner consistent with the annual accounts. Best practice also insists that interim reports are made available within 60 days of the half-year-end. **Interim dividends** are also announced at this time. The Saturday edition of the *Financial Times* lists all the quoted companies which have published interim reports in the previous week – see Exhibit 11.1.

Figure in brackets is pre-tax profit for the same period last year. 'L' signifies loss

● Last week's interim results

Company	Sector	Pre-tax profit (£m)	Interim dividends* per share (p)
Abingdon Capital	AIM	0.228L (0.534L)	0.1 (nil)
Advanced Tech	AIM	2.18L (1.76L)	- (-)
Alpha Airports	Trns	7.9 (10.7)	1 (1)
Amco Corporation	AIM	0.628L (1.12)	nil (nil)
Andrews Sykes	AIM	5.61 (4.55)	nil (nil)
Arcon Intl €	Mine	4.96L (5.48L)	- (-)
Ardagh €	-	2.19L (11.7L)	nil (nil)
Arko Energy $	Uqtd	3.46 (1.66)	- (-)
Ashtenne	Real	9.18 (5.74)	3.8 (3.5)
Barr (AG)	Bev	7.18 (6.18)	8.5 (7.35)
Beazley	Insc	2.54 (0.596)	0.25 (-)
BNB Resources	Uqtd	4.58L (0.668L)	nil (nil)
Boot (Henry)	CBld	25.9 (5.12)	4 (3.6)
Brit Insurance	Insc	31 (4.28L)	nil (nil)
CA Coutts	AIM	0.101 (0.21L)	1.35 (1.25)
Capital Management	AIM	7.26L (0.545)	

The total interim dividend in pence per share

Exhibit 11.1 Interim results shown in the *Financial Times*

Source: *Financial Times* 27/28 September 2003

[2] All quoted companies are public, but not all public companies are quoted.

[3] This is voluntary, but companies are frowned upon by the Accounting Practices Board and the UKLA if they ignore it. An offender can be ostracised by the financial community.

Second, the UKLA insists on publication of **preliminary annual results (prelims)** for the year. These appear a few weeks after the year-end and provide shareholders with key data such as profits for the year a month or more before the full report and accounts are presented. (The annual report must be issued within 6 months of the year-end.) The prelims usually receive a great deal of publicity. Be aware, however, that they do not have to be audited, nor do they contain the notes to the accounts, which provide so much vital detail for the investor. The preliminary results announced during the week are listed in the Saturday edition of the *Financial Times* – see Exhibit 11.2. *Financial Times* articles during the week would have provided more detail and some discussion of the prelims.

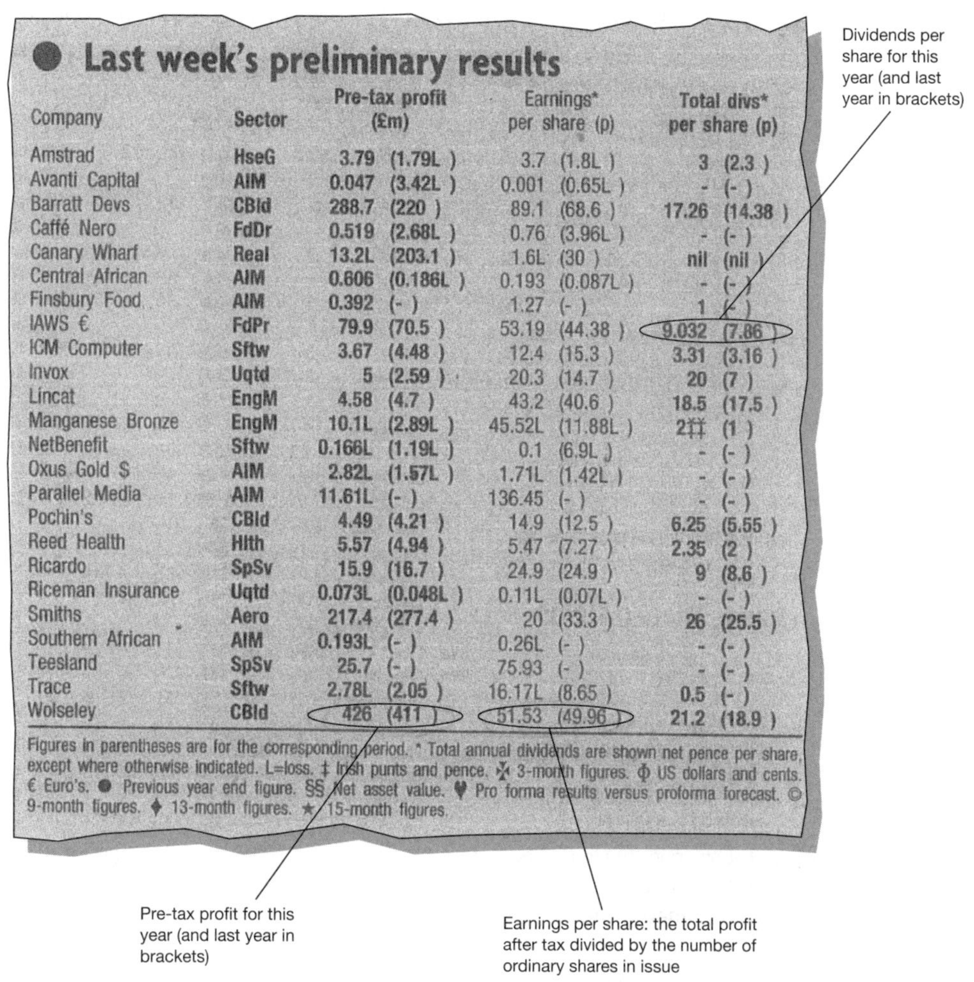

● **Last week's preliminary results**

Company	Sector	Pre-tax profit (£m)	Earnings* per share (p)	Total divs* per share (p)
Amstrad	HseG	3.79 (1.79L)	3.7 (1.8L)	3 (2.3)
Avanti Capital	AIM	0.047 (3.42L)	0.001 (0.65L)	- (-)
Barratt Devs	CBld	288.7 (220)	89.1 (68.6)	17.26 (14.38)
Caffé Nero	FdDr	0.519 (2.68L)	0.76 (3.96L)	- (-)
Canary Wharf	Real	13.2L (203.1)	1.6L (30)	nil (nil)
Central African	AIM	0.606 (0.186L)	0.193 (0.087L)	- (-)
Finsbury Food	AIM	0.392 (-)	1.27 (-)	1 (-)
IAWS €	FdPr	79.9 (70.5)	53.19 (44.38)	9.032 (7.86)
ICM Computer	Sftw	3.67 (4.48)	12.4 (15.3)	3.31 (3.16)
Invox	Uqtd	5 (2.59)	20.3 (14.7)	20 (7)
Lincat	EngM	4.58 (4.7)	43.2 (40.6)	18.5 (17.5)
Manganese Bronze	EngM	10.1L (2.89L)	45.52L (11.88L)	2‡‡ (1)
NetBenefit	Sftw	0.166L (1.19L)	0.1 (6.9L)	- (-)
Oxus Gold $	AIM	2.82L (1.57L)	1.71L (1.42L)	- (-)
Parallel Media	AIM	11.61L (-)	136.45 (-)	- (-)
Pochin's	CBld	4.49 (4.21)	14.9 (12.5)	6.25 (5.55)
Reed Health	Hlth	5.57 (4.94)	5.47 (7.27)	2.35 (2)
Ricardo	SpSv	15.9 (16.7)	24.9 (24.9)	9 (8.6)
Riceman Insurance	Uqtd	0.073L (0.048L)	0.11L (0.07L)	- (-)
Smiths	Aero	217.4 (277.4)	20 (33.3)	26 (25.5)
Southern African	AIM	0.193L (-)	0.26L (-)	- (-)
Teesland	SpSv	25.7 (-)	75.93 (-)	- (-)
Trace	Sftw	2.78L (2.05)	16.17L (8.65)	0.5 (-)
Wolseley	CBld	426 (411)	51.53 (49.96)	21.2 (18.9)

Figures in parentheses are for the corresponding period. * Total annual dividends are shown net pence per share, except where otherwise indicated. L=loss. ‡ Irish punts and pence. ✠ 3-month figures. ɸ US dollars and cents. € Euro's. ● Previous year end figure. §§ Net asset value. ♥ Pro forma results versus proforma forecast. © 9-month figures. ♦ 13-month figures. ★ 15-month figures.

Exhibit 11.2 Preliminary results shown in the *Financial Times*

Source: *Financial Times* 27/28 September 2003

Third, companies are **required by the Listing Rules** to include in the annual report much more than unlisted companies: a brief biography of each non-executive director, details of directors' interests in the company's shares and options on shares, information on shareholdings greater than 3 per cent of the shares, particulars of significant contracts and details of share repurchases. Some companies choose to report quarterly to provide investors with more up-to-date information. Companies on techMARK are compelled to report quarterly.

Profit and loss account

The profit and loss account (also called an **income statement**) records whether the company's sales revenue was greater than its costs. It allows you to compare the latest profit with previous year's profits, or with other companies. It also states what happened to the profit: the proportions that were paid out in tax, in dividends, or retained within the business.

Exhibit 11.3 shows a typical profit and loss account. The layout and terminology may change from one company to another, but the exhibit captures the key figures you are likely to come across. The 'Notes' column points out where in the notes to the accounts to look for more detailed information about a particular item. Brackets are placed around negative numbers.

	Notes	2003 £m	2002 £m
Turnover	1	230	200
Cost of sales	2	(140)	(120)
Gross profit	3	90	80
Distribution costs	4	(15)	(11)
Administrative costs	5	(10)	(9)
Other costs	6	(10)	(10)
Operating profit		55	50
Less Interest payable	7	(6)	(5)
Profit on ordinary activities before tax		49	45
Less Tax on ordinary activities	8	(14)	(13)
Profit after tax		35	32
Less minority interests	9	(1)	(1)
Less dividends	10	(17)	(15)
Retained profit for the year		17	16
Earnings per share	11	68p	62p
Dividends per share	12	34p	30p

Exhibit 11.3 Typical consolidated profit and loss account

The accounts of quoted companies with subsidiaries are described as **consolidated**. This means that all the income, costs, assets and liabilities of all group companies, whether **wholly owned** or **partially owned**, are brought together in the group's consolidated accounts.[4] Quoted companies often operate through dozens of other companies. In most cases they set up these companies and own 100 per cent of the ordinary shares (wholly owned). In other cases they may have acquired, say, 60 per cent of the shares (partially owned), leaving **minority shareholders** with the other 40 per cent. Each of these wholly owned or partially owned subsidiaries will have its own accounts, but when the figures are brought together in the consolidated accounts 100 per cent of the income, costs, assets and liabilities are thrown in, even if the controlling company owns only, say, 60 per cent of the subsidiary's shares. A deduction is made later (minority interests) to allow for the 40 per cent owned by outside shareholders.

Each of the entries in Exhibit 11.3 will be explained in turn:

- **Turnover.** This is money received or to be received by the company from the sale of goods or services during the year. Other terms used are '**revenue**' and '**sales**'. This figure is stated net of VAT or sales taxes. Accounting standards require that profit and loss accounts separate the turnover of continuing operations from activities discontinued during the year and from joint ventures (businesses operated in partnership with other companies). The notes to the accounts will usually give a more detailed breakdown of where sales came from. For example, Boots plc separates turnover from Boots The Chemists, Boots Healthcare International, and Wellbeing Services.

  Accounts usually show the previous year's figures as well as the latest, which makes comparison over time easier. This is further helped by the five-year summary (described later in this chapter), usually placed at the back of the report. In the example shown, turnover has risen by an apparently healthy 15 per cent, but the analyst would like to know what proportion of that rise was achieved by the existing operations, by new companies acquired in the year, or by **organic** (that is, non-acquisition) capital growth. (For example, did the company borrow a massive amount to open up 100 more shop branches, leading to sales growth? If so, you may be less impressed by a mere 15 per cent rise.) You might also want to take inflation into account when examining change over time.
- **Cost of sales.** The expense incurred for bought-in raw materials or components, and the costs of bringing materials to saleable condition.
- **Gross profit.** Turnover less cost of sales.
- **Distribution costs, administration expenses and other costs.** This covers a lot of items, from the expense of employees in head office to the rent paid for a building. **Depreciation** of plant, machinery and other capital items will be included in this

[4] This applies to companies where more than 50 per cent of the shares are held by the parent, or if less than 50 per cent of the shares are held the parent company still exercises control over the majority of director appointments, or exercises a dominant influence over the undertaking.

section. Depreciation represents the reduction in the stated carrying value of fixed assets in the balance sheet. The method of depreciation will be described in the notes to the accounts.

- **Operating profit (operating income).** This is the income remaining after paying all costs other than interest. It thus focuses on the underlying business return, without the distortionary effect of allowing for how the business was financed (i.e. high or low levels of debt). This may be split between continuing and discontinued operations. At this point, many accounts show an adjustment for **exceptional items**. These are gains or costs which are part of the company's ordinary activities but are either unusual in themselves or have an exceptionally large impact on profits that year. These one-off items may distort profits in a particular year, so accounts often show results both before and after exceptional items. Examples might include the windfall profits on the sale of an office block, or the exceptional cost of closing down a business activity (e.g. the redundancy costs of closing a subsidiary).
- **Profit on ordinary activities before taxation.** Interest paid is deducted, or interest received is added, to arrive at the key profit figure: the one that often receives a lot of attention in the press. This is also referred to as the **pre-tax profit**. In the case of Exhibit 11.3 net interest paid has risen from £5 million to £6 million between 2002 and 2003. Perhaps interest rates rose and/or the amount borrowed increased in 2003. The notes to the accounts will show a breakdown of borrowings – for example, it will lay out the proportion that is repayable within 1 year, 5 years, etc.; the amounts borrowed in different currencies; and the amounts borrowed through various bond issues or bank loans.

  An analyst might notice that while the turnover of the firm in Exhibit 11.3 has risen by 15 per cent, costs have grown by a larger percentage, so that pre-tax profit rose by only 9 per cent from £45 million to £49 million.
- **Taxation. Corporation tax** is payable by UK resident companies on all income and capital gains after all costs. Dividends paid out to ordinary shareholders are not costs, they are a distribution of profits to the owners, the shareholders. The rate of corporation tax varies, depending on the size of the company. In the case of the large company in our example the top rate of 30 per cent will be payable. Note, however, that the company is not due to pay 30 per cent of £49 million, (which is £14.7 million) in tax. The exact proportion of reported profit paid in tax depends on a number of factors, such as whether tax was paid abroad on income earned abroad. Some companies can pay a very low tax relative to current year earnings because they have tax losses due to trading and other losses made in previous years. When they move into profit they may not have to pay tax for many years. The notes to the accounts (in this case note 8) should provide details on the computation of tax.
- **Profit after tax.** This is also called **net profit**. If there are no minority interests then we can call this the **equity earnings** of the company, which belong to the shareholders. However, in this case one or more of the company's subsidiaries is partly owned by someone else. It is therefore necessary to deduct their slice of the profits. This is

shown by the £1 million minority interest figure. The subsidiary that is only partially owned by our large firm has all its revenues and costs included in the figures presented in the upper half of the profit and loss accounts, and it is only at this point in the accounts that we acknowledge that a proportion of the profits actually belong to outsiders. So, after deducting minority interests (and possibly dividends on **preference shares**) the **profit attributable to the shareholders** of the example company is £34 million in 2003. This is often called the **'bottom line' figure**. The **dividend** figure shows the total amount of both the **interim** (paid months ago) and the **final** dividend. When this is deducted we are left with the funds which have been ploughed back into the business – **the retained earnings** (or retentions).

- **Earnings per share.** This is the profit attributable to ordinary shareholders (i.e. after minority interests and preference dividends) divided by the number of ordinary shares in issue. The company has issued 50 million shares and so we have earnings per share of £34m/50m = 68p. Earnings per share are a key measure of a company's performance. They allow investors to observe the growth in profits for each share held (it is easy for management to raise total profits if they keep issuing more shares and thereby bring more money into the business; it is not so easy to raise the earnings on each existing share). They are also a measure of the company's ability to pay dividends in a sustainable manner.

  Earnings per share may be presented both before and after exceptional items. There are many adjustments that can be made to earnings per share figures – see Chapter 12 for more details.

- **Dividends per share.** The total amount paid or due to be paid in dividends for the year (interim and final dividend) divided by the number of shares in issue. For 2003 this is £17m/50m = 34p per share.

Balance sheet

The balance sheet provides a snapshot of what the company owned[5] and is owed on a particular day in the past: usually the last day of the financial year (or last day of the first half of the year). The balance sheet summarises the **assets** and the **liabilities** of the business. The difference between the assets and liabilities is the **shareholders' funds**.

In reports and accounts you will often see two balance sheets. The first is for the **parent company (holding company)**. This company's numerous wholly or partly owned subsidiaries will be represented on the parent company's balance sheet but not in consolidated form, so this is of limited use for financial analysis. The attention of the investor should be directed at the second balance sheet – the **consolidated (or group) balance sheet**. This includes all the assets and liabilities of the subsidiary companies and the

[5] Or, in some cases, controlled, as with some leased assets.

holding company, whether the parent holds 60, 70 or 100 per cent of the shares in the subsidiary. To explain the terms in a balance sheet we will work through the items shown in Exhibit 11.4.

	Notes	2003 £m	2002 £m
Fixed assets			
Tangible assets	13	82	80
Intangible assets	14	18	20
Investments	15	5	5
		105	105
Current assets			
Stock	16	35	20
Debtors	17	60	40
Current asset investments and deposits	18	20	20
Cash at bank and in hand	19	10	10
		125	90
Current liabilities			
Creditors' amounts due within one year	20	(62)	(49)
Net current assets		63	41
Total assets less current liabilities		168	146
Creditor amounts due in more than one year	21	(25)	(20)
Provisions for liabilities and charges	22	(14)	(14)
Net assets		129	112
Capital and reserves			
Called-up share capital	23	5	5
Share premium account	24	50	50
Revaluation reserve	25	23	23
Profit and loss account	26	46	29
Equity shareholders' funds		124	107
Minority interests	27	5	5
Total capital employed		129	112

Exhibit 11.4 Typical consolidated balance sheet at 31 March 2003

- **Fixed assets.** The assets are separated into long-term assets (fixed assets) and short-term assets (current assets). Fixed assets are those that are not held for resale, but for use in the business. The fixed assets are generally displayed under three categories:
  - **Tangible assets.** Assets used to earn revenue that have a physical presence (e.g. land, buildings, factories, machinery and vehicles).

- **Intangible assets.** Things you cannot touch, but which have a long life (longer than 1 year). Included here would be copyright and other publishing rights, licences, patents, trademarks, goodwill, etc.
- **Investments.** These assets are expected to be held for the long term. Included here would be shareholdings in other companies (except subsidiary holdings), works of art, and gilts.

Most long-term assets wear out, and so allowance has to be made for this. Tangible and intangible assets are therefore recorded at **net book value**, which is the original cost of the assets, minus the accumulated depreciation for tangibles, or minus amortisation in the case of intangibles, since their acquisition. Accounting standards require all fixed assets except land to be depreciated (or amortised). Some assets rise in value. If this happens, companies have the possibility of **revaluing assets** in the balance sheet. This is shown in the **revaluation reserve**. The revaluation reserve represents the accumulated revaluations of fixed assets. In this way a company does not credit the fortuitous increase in value of a fixed asset to the profit and loss account, because this would distort the picture of underlying profitability.

Investments are generally shown at cost, but investments in stock market quoted securities are often shown at market value in the notes to the accounts.

- **Current assets.** These comprise cash and assets that can be rapidly turned into cash. Stocks of raw materials, partially finished or finished goods are included here as well as the value of **debtors (receivables)** – that is, amounts owed to the business, usually by customers. Investments expected to be sold within the next year are included under current assets (these are shown at the lower of cost or net realisable value).
- **Liabilities. Current liabilities** are amounts owed that the company expects to have to pay within the next year. Bank loans with less than a year to repayment and overdrafts will be included here, as will outstanding trade creditors (suppliers allowing the firm to pay later for goods supplied) and corporation tax due but not yet paid. The difference between current assets and current liabilities is **net current assets** (commonly known as **working capital**). In our example, on 31 March 2003 it amounts to £63 million. If we now add on the value of the fixed assets we have the figure of £168 million for the **total assets less current liabilities**.
- **Net assets.** The net assets figure is the total assets minus all the liabilities. Included in liabilities are those creditor amounts due to be paid after more than a year (e.g. long-term bank loans or bonds), and **provisions for liabilities and charges**. A provision is an allowance for a liability if you are unable to be precise about either the amount or when it will be paid. Provisions are often included for items such as pension obligations, restructuring costs (e.g. staff retraining or relocation), environmental damage or litigation.
- **Capital and reserves.** The net assets of the company are owned by the shareholders. However, there are two groups of shareholders that we have to allow for in a consolidated balance sheet. Recall that for partially owned subsidiaries we boldly

included 100 per cent of the assets and liabilities in the top half of the balance sheet. Some of these net assets are attributable to the holders of the minority fraction of the subsidiaries and not to the holding company shareholders. This amount is represented by the figure for **minority interests**. The remainder is the net assets attributable to the holding company's shareholders. This is termed '**equity shareholders' funds**', or '**shareholders' funds**' for short. In the example equity shareholders' funds are allocated to four categories. The first is **called-up share capital**. If we looked up note 23 we will observe two share capital numbers. The first is the **authorised share capital**. This is the nominal (par) value of the shares that were created when the company was established, or which were subsequently created (with shareholder approval). The nominal value of each share might be, say, 5p,10p, 25p, 50p or any amount the original founders decided upon. The second is **issued (or called-up) share capital**. This is the total value of the shares issued (sold or allotted to investors) when expressed at nominal value. It is normal to observe a company having many more shares authorised than have actually been sold (issued). The notes usually state both the total number of shares, the nominal value of each share and the total nominal value of all the shares. In this case there are 50 million shares in issue ('called up'), each with a nominal value of 10p at the end of the 2003 financial year, thus we see a figure of £5 million (the total nominal value) shown in the balance sheet. When shares are sold they rarely sell at nominal value. We saw earlier in the chapter that our example company is now producing earnings per share of 68p and paying a dividend of 34p. Clearly if the company issued more shares they could sell them for more than 10p – I'd be first in the queue with my 10p if I could get an annual dividend of 34p! Even when a company is first established the nominal value is often set below the amount received from the sale of the shares. The **share premium account** records the additional amount (above the nominal value) that shares were sold for.

The **profit and loss account** entry in the balance sheet represents the accumulated retained profits for all the years of the company's existence. Notice that this figure rose by £17 million between 2002 and 2003, reflecting the retention of the profits made in 2003. This is the only one of the reserves that can be dipped into to pay dividends. So if our company has a loss-making year in 2004 and still wishes to pay a dividend it could do so up to an amount of £46 million.

Cash flow statement

One of the main reasons why companies go into liquidation is that they run out of cash. It is possible for profits to be on a rising trend and yet to see the company going under. The prospect of liquidation is one of the reasons why the analyst needs to examine the cash inflows and outflows of the business over the year.

In addition to assessing the likelihood of corporate failure, examining cash flow statements is very useful for filling in some of the gaps in the picture of the company's performance and strength left after analysing the profit and loss and the balance sheet. It helps answer some key questions such as: what proportion of any increase in profit is swallowed up by ever larger investments in fixed assets, debtors and stocks needed to maintain earnings growth? If all the cash is being absorbed, what is going to be left for dividends? If investment in assets year after year is greater than cash generated by operations, will the directors have to keep asking shareholders for more money or will they borrow more? If borrowings are increasing how does that affect the risk of the ordinary shares? Does the company generate enough cash to pay its interest? And so on.

Furthermore, the cash flow statement is much more difficult for managers to manipulate than the profit and loss account and balance sheet because it is a measure of actual cash movements. It identifies where the company gets its money from and what it spent that money on.[6]

Exhibit 11.5 shows a typical cash flow statement. This is for the same company as the profit and loss and balance sheet shown earlier in the chapter. It is divided into eight areas:

- **Net cash flow from operating activities.** This includes the cash received from the firm's customers in the year (excluding sales made for which cash has not yet been received and sales taxes, e.g. VAT). Cash paid to suppliers, employees, etc., has been deducted. In the reconciliation between the profit and loss and the cash flow statement there will be a recognition that the depreciation expensed in the profit and loss is not a cash outflow. This boosts cash flow compared with profit. However the additional expenditure on more stock (£15 million – see balance sheet change between 2002 and 2003 in Exhibit 11.4) and on debtors (£20 million) reduces cash flow relative to profit. If net cash from operating activities is negative we might start to worry because the company is not selling its goods and services for more than they cost or is pumping vast amounts into working capital to keep up its sales level.

[6] In addition to the cash flow statement there will be a **reconciliation of operating profit reported in the profit and loss and the net cash flow from operating activities**. This will disclose separately the movements in stocks, debtors and creditors. There will also be a note **reconciling the movement of cash with the movement in net debt**.

	Notes	£m
Net cash inflow from operating activities	28	26
Returns on investment and servicing of finance		
Interest paid	7	(6)
Dividends paid to minority interests	9	(1)
Taxation		(13)
Capital expenditure and financial investment	13	(5)
Acquisitions and disposals		0
Equity dividends paid	10	(15)
Net cash inflow (outflow) before financing		(14)
Financing		
Issue of ordinary shares		0
Increase (decrease) in debt	20, 21	14
Increase (decrease) in cash in the year		0

Exhibit 11.5 Typical cash flow statement for the year ending 31 March 2003

- **Returns on investment and servicing of finance.** This shows interest earned or paid. In this case only interest of £6 million is paid as no return was received on investment. Dividend payments made by the holding company to its shareholders might also be here, but our example shows them separately lower down the cash flow statement.
- **Taxation.** Much of the tax for one year is usually paid during the next accounting year, so the figure shown for 2003 does not match the tax owed on 2003.
- **Capital expenditure and financial investment.** This section includes cash used to pay for the acquisition of fixed assets and/or cash generated by the sale of fixed assets. In this case a net £5 million was spent on long-lived assets – vehicles, equipment, buildings, etc.
- **Acquisition and disposals.** Cash can also be used to purchase subsidiaries or some of the shares in subsidiaries – cash inflow can increase if these assets are sold. Of course, if shares in the holding company were issued to buy a subsidiary no cash outflow would be recorded (however, there may be the receipt of the subsidiaries' cash balances).
- **Equity dividends paid.** Some of the dividends shown as being due to be paid in one year's profit and loss account may not be paid until the following year, and so the cash outflow differs from the profit and loss entry for the year.
- **Net cash inflow (outflow) before financing.** The first six items show how much net cash the business generated, how much was paid in interest and how much was reinvested in the business to help drive future growth. The net cash inflow before financing figure shows whether the company is throwing off cash or has a desper-

ate thirst for cash. On this score our example company is not doing very well – the company needs an injection of cash to pay for its investment in current and fixed assets.

- **Financing.** The company obtained the extra cash it needs (£14 million) from an increase in debt to leave cash balances shown in the balance sheet at £10 million at the start and end of the year. Our example is unusual in showing zero overall cash movement for the year. Most will show a significant positive or negative cash balance change. The statement that **reconciles the movement of cash with the movement of net debt**, which follows the cash flow statement, will provide more detail on the financing of net cash out flow (not shown here).

Note in all this that '**cash**' means notes and coins as well as deposits repayable on demand in financial institutions (it includes foreign currencies). '**Cash flow**' includes payments by cheque, etc.

Example of a *profitable* company forced into liquidation

ABC plc starts the year by obtaining equity capital of £1 million by selling shares, and it borrows £1.5 million from the bank on 1 January. It buys £2 million of machinery and hires 25 workers. The machinery is expected to have a useful life of 10 years and is depreciated (an expense) at a rate of £200,000 per year. In the first year the company is profitable (Exhibit 11.6).

Despite reporting a profit, the company runs out of cash and is forced by its bank into liquidation. It ran out of cash because of a number of factors. It granted its customers the right to pay for goods 60 days after delivery. In the meantime, ABC had to pay its raw

	£
Sales	5,000,000
Cost of sales	(4,000,000)
Gross profit	1,000,000
Costs	
Labour	(400,000)
Factory and other costs	(300,000)
Depreciation on machine	(200,000)
Operating profit	100,000
Less interest payable	(80,000)
Profit on ordinary activities before taxation	20,000

Exhibit 11.6 ABC plc profit and loss account

material suppliers, labour, machinery and distribution costs while production was taking place. Many customers either paid late (after 60 days) or did not pay at all. Also another machine was purchased half way through the year for £250,000. The cash flow statement for the year in this simple case looks far worse than the profit and loss account (Exhibit 11.7). This company started the year with zero cash and ended with negative £530,000 cash – clearly unsustainable (even if it did manage to limp to the end of the year).

	£
Net cash flow from operating activities[a]	(700,000)
Interest paid	(80,000)
Taxation	0
Capital expenditure	(2,250,000)
Equity dividends paid	0
Cash inflow (outflow) before financing	(3,030,000)
Financing: Issue of shares	1,000,000
Increase in debt	1,500,000
Increase (decrease) in cash in the year	(530,000)

[a] Cash received from customers (£4m) minus cash flowing out for operations (£4.7m).

Exhibit 11.7 ABC plc cash flow statement

Chairman's statement

The law does not require a chairman's statement, but most companies include one. It can be useful because it helps to put the accounting numbers into context. Events might have occurred which have a significant effect on the profit and loss, balance sheet and cash flow statement, and it is often the chairman's statement that flags these. For example, a major acquisition may have taken place, together with a rights issue and a rise in borrowing impacting on the accounts. Without the comment from the chairman it may not be possible to understand why the accounts show dramatic change from one year to the next.

The statement is also a personal comment from the chairman that will attempt to enlighten the shareholders on the general trading environment that the company coped with in the past and is now faced with. It may also break down the overall performance into constituent parts (e.g. by product line, division or geography) and comment on future prospects for these. Major action, such as factory closures or large investments in new technology, may be referred to. Also some comment will be made on the overall corporate strategy.

Some chairmen take their role as overseer of the company's direction and performance seriously. They examine the firm's actions purely from a shareholder's perspective. They then report to the shareholders in a frank and critical fashion about the quality of stewardship by the directors of shareholders' money and about the future prospects. Unfortunately, all too many chairmen see their role as cheerleaders for the executives, and the statement can appear to be a public relations exercise: long on presenting the positives of executive action and short on balanced critical content. The investor then has to read the statement with particular care and a degree of cynicism. Reading between the lines is the order of the day. Examine the statement not for what it contains, but for what it leaves out.

Chief executive's review

In addition to the chairman's statement (or sometimes instead of one) there is the chief executive's review or operational review. The **chief executive officer (CEO)** is the most powerful director. In the UK this would normally be the managing director. The review will provide more detail on performance, strategy and managerial intentions for each division.

Directors' report

This is required by law, but directors frequently supply much more information and commentary than either statutes or the Stock Exchange insist on. It must contain the following:

- a review of activities during the year and discussion of likely future developments;
- important events affecting the company, which have occurred since the year-end;
- details of share buy-backs;
- technical information, e.g. names of directors and their shareholdings, political or charitable contributions made by the company.

To assist the understanding of the financial statement the directors might choose to provide the following:

- an outline of the principal activities of the business;
- a description of research and development activity;
- policies on employment, supplier relationships and the environment.

Financial review

The financial review tries to explain financial performance and strategy. For example, what led to the charging of 'exceptional' costs in the profit statement? Why did debt increase? In what way were the results influenced by foreign exchange rate changes? How does the company limit its risk exposure to interest rates, commodities and currencies? Why is the company embarked on so much capital expenditure? The 'operating and financial review' is not yet compulsory, but the government is pushing for it.

Auditors' report

The auditors are appointed by the shareholders at the AGM to hold office until the next AGM. It is a legal requirement to appoint auditors (except for very small companies). Their role is to determine whether the company's financial statements are misleading – whether the accounts show a '**true and fair view**'. It is an offence for directors to give false or misleading information to auditors. Auditors have the **right of access** to the books and accounts at all times. They can insist on additional information and explanations from managers to try to obtain an understanding of the financial position.

If auditors have doubts about the quality of record keeping or they detect a discrepancy between the books and the accounts, or the information and explanations they demand are not forthcoming, they will state the difficulty in their report. That is, they **qualify their report**. Alarm bells should start to ring when an investor reads the accounts have been qualified.

Auditors also comment on whether the company complies with the code of practice relating to **corporate governance** – that is, the system of management and control of the corporation. Guidelines of best practice were issued by the **Cadbury, Greenbury, Hampel and Hicks committees**, now consolidated in the **Combined Code of Corporate Governance**. Directors have to state in the accounts how the principles of the code have been applied. If the principles have not been followed they have to state why. Among these principles are the following: there should be transparency on directors' remuneration, requiring a remuneration committee consisting mainly of non-executive directors; directors should retire by rotation at least every 3 years; the chairman should not also be the chief executive officer to avoid domination by one person (in exceptional circumstances this may be ignored, if a written justification is presented to shareholders); the **audit committee** (responsible for validating financial figures, e.g. by appointing effective external auditors) should consist mainly of independent[7] non-executive directors and not executive directors, otherwise the committee would not be able to act as a check and

[7] To be independent the non-executive directors should not, for example, be a customer, supplier, or a friend of the founding family or the chief executive.

balance to the executive directors; at least half the members of the board, excluding the chairman, should be independent non-executive directors; the accounts must contain a statement by the directors that the company is a going concern, that is, it will continue for at least another year; and a senior independent director should be appointed to listen to the views of a range of shareholders and communicate those views to the board.

Five-year summary

Usually placed at the back of the report and accounts is a very useful 5- or 10-year summary of key financial data. It is here that you can observe the historic pattern of growth in sales, profits, dividends, earnings per share, and a host of other important variables. An erratic pattern may be less attractive than a smooth one. Fast sales and profit growth with zero earnings per share growth will probably indicate large-scale acquisition of companies combined with regular issuance of shares. This is likely to be less attractive than more pedestrian organic sales and profit growth combined with rising earnings per share.

Beware of relying too much on these summary tables without understanding the detail behind them. Distortions over time can arise because of changes in accounting practice policies, or even accounting standards. Another major source of confusion is the inclusion or exclusion of discontinued activities.

Further reading

G. Holmes, A. Sugden and P. Gee, *Interpreting Company Reports and Accounts*, 8th edition (Financial Times Prentice Hall, 2002).

W. McKenzie, *The Financial Times Guide to Using and Interpreting Company Accounts*, 3rd edition (Financial Times Prentice Hall, 2003).

These books provide easy-to-follow introductions to reports and accounts that are much more detailed than provided in this chapter. Up-to-date information in the various accounting standards is available from the Accounting Standards Board website (*www.asb.org.uk*).

12

Key investment ratios and measures

This chapter explains the jargon used by the financial press when it reports on the performance or the financial health of a company. The investor is bombarded with a bewildering variety of summary statistics about companies. Here we describe the most commonly used and important. So if you don't know your acid test from your EBITDA, or your PER from your ROCE then this is the chapter for you.

At the end of it you will not only be able to understand company data in the *Financial Times* but will be capable of calculating for yourself ratios and other measures from the base data – usually the annual report and accounts. You will then be in a position to analyse a company by focusing on those elements that seem particularly important to you. In other words, you don't have to be reliant on other people's judgement as to which measures are most significant, or how they are calculated (with some measures there is room for selection as to which component numbers to include).

The value of these ratios and other measures is that they help to put into perspective the numbers reported in the profit and loss account, balance sheet and cash flow statements. They often relate one aspect of the accounts (e.g. profits) to another (e.g. the value of all the assets the company is using). For example, if you were told that company A made £10 million profit whereas company B made £20 million, would you automatically conclude that B is the better company? Perhaps you would like to compare the return per pound used by each business. If A had net assets of £40 million at the start and end of the year, while B had £200 million of net assets you would have some useful information about the efficiency with which each company used the assets available to it. Company A produces a 25p profit for every £1 of capital, a 25% return on capital (profit/net assets = £10m/£40m = 0.25) whereas B produces a mere 10p for every £1 of capital it uses (£20m/£200m = 0.10).

These ratios and measures, as well as displaying the relationship between pairs of figures and permitting comparison with other companies, allow an investor to develop a more informed perspective on the firm's performance and financial standing across time. The way in which ratios change over a period of 5 or 10 years can help to build up a picture of the company's progress or decline.

In this chapter the investment ratios and measures are presented in four sections:

- Measures that are given daily (or at least weekly) in the financial press. These mostly relate to the share price.
- Statistics that measure the company's performance in terms of profit, profitability and efficiency.
- Financial health ratios and measures. This section examines the level of debt and solvency ratios.
- Forward-looking measures that help in the valuing of shares based on the income flows that a shareholder is forecast to receive.

From the financial pages

Price–earnings ratio

The **price–earnings ratio or PER (also abbreviated as 'P/E ratio')** compares a company's share price with its latest earnings per share (eps). The eps is the profit attributable to shareholders, as shown in the profit and loss, divided by the number of shares in issue (see Chapter 11).

$$\text{PER} = \frac{\text{Current market price of share}}{\text{Last year's earnings per share}}$$

So, for example, if a company has a current market price of £9 for one of its shares and the earnings per share shown in the latest accounts are 68p the PER (**earnings multiple**) is:

$$\text{PER} = \frac{900\text{p}}{68\text{p}} = 13.2$$

The eps figure assumed here came from the profit and loss account shown in Chapter 11 (Exhibit 11.3). The profit attributable to the shareholders is £34 million (after subtracting £1 million for minority interests from the profit after tax figure) and the number of shares in issue is 50 million, giving eps of 68p.

The PER shown above should strictly be called the '**historic PER**' because it is based on earnings that have already happened. This is the PER that receives most attention in the press. However, quite often investors are interested in knowing how high the share price is in relation to the level of projected earnings for next year. This is the **prospective PER** or **forward PER**:

$$\text{Prospective PER} = \frac{\text{Current market price of share}}{\text{Next year's expected earnings per share}}$$

Exhibit 12.1 shows the historic PER for a number of retailers. The PER changes daily as the share price moves up or down. The previous day's PER is shown in the Tuesday to Saturday editions of the *Financial Times*. The Monday edition shows other company/market statistics.

An examination of Exhibit 12.1 shows that investors are willing to buy Carphone Warehouse shares at 23.3 times last year's earnings, compared with only 14.7 times last year's earnings for Boots. One explanation for the difference in PERs is that companies with higher PERs are expected to show faster growth in earnings in the future. Carphone

Warehouse may appear expensive relative to Boots based on historical profit figures, but the differential may be justified when forecasts of earnings are made. If a PER is high, investors expect profits to rise. This does not necessarily mean that all companies with high PERs are expected to perform to a high standard, merely that they are expected to do significantly better than in the past.

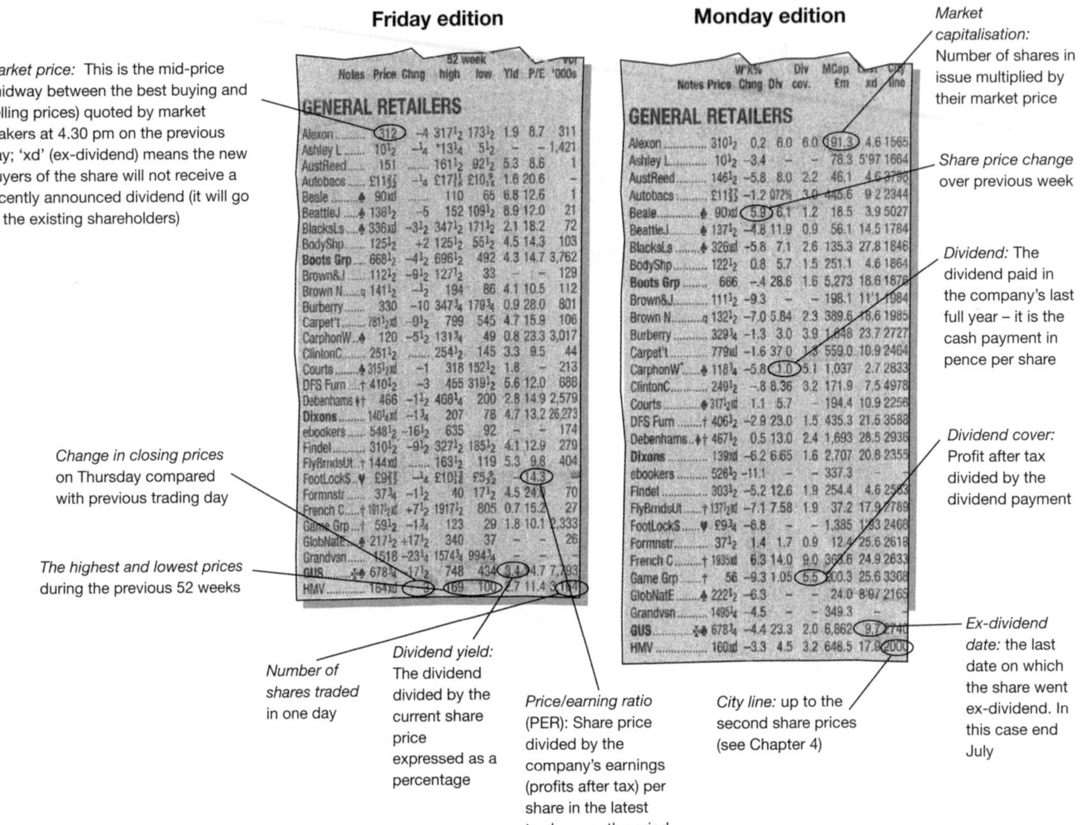

Friday edition

GENERAL RETAILERS

	Notes	Price	Chng	52 week high	52 week low	Yld	P/E	Vol '000s
Alexon		312	–4	317½	173½	1.9	8.7	311
Ashley L		10½	–¼	*13¾	5½	–	–	1,421
AustReed		151	......	161½	92½	5.3	8.6	1
Autobacs		£11 27/32	–¼	£17 11/16	£10 9/16	1.6	20.6	–
Beale	♠	90xd	......	110	65	6.8	12.6	1
BeattieJ	♠	136½	–5	152	109½	8.9	12.0	21
BlacksLs	♠	336xd	–3½	347½	171½	2.1	18.2	72
BodyShp		125½	+2	125½	55½	4.5	14.3	103
Boots Grp		668½	–4½	696½	492	4.3	14.7	3,762
Brown&J		112½	–9½	127½	33	–	–	129
Brown N	q	141½	–½	194	86	4.1	10.5	112
Burberry		330	–10	347¾	179¾	0.9	28.0	801
Carpet't		781½xd	–9½	799	545	4.7	15.9	106
CarphonW	♠	120	–5½	131¾	49	0.8	23.3	3,017
ClintonC		251½	......	254½	145	3.3	9.5	44
Courts	♠	315½xd	–1	318	152½	1.8	–	213
DFS Furn	†	410½	–3	455	319½	5.6	12.0	688
Debenhams	♦†	466	–1½	468¼	200	2.8	14.9	2,579
Dixons		140¼xd	–1¾	207	78	4.7	13.2	26,273
ebookers		548½	–16½	635	92	–	–	174
Findel		310½	–9½	327½	185½	4.1	12.9	279
FlyBrndsUt	†	144xd	......	163½	119	5.3	9.8	404
FootLockS	♥	£9 27/32	–¼	£10 11/16	£5 9/32	–	14.3	–
Formnstr		37¾	–1½	40	17½	4.5	24.[illegible]	70
French C	†	1917½xd	+7½	1917½	805	0.7	15.2	27
Game Grp	†	59½	–1¾	123	29	1.8	10.1	2,333
GlobNatE	♠	217½	+17½	340	37	–	–	26
Grandvsn		1518	–23¼	1574¾	994¾	–	–	–
GUS	♣♠	678¾	–17½	748	434	3.4	14.7	7,793
HMV		164xd	–3	169	100	2.7	11.4	3,164

Monday edition

GENERAL RETAILERS

	Notes	Price	W'k% Chng	Div	Div cov.	MCap £m	Last xd	City line
Alexon		310½	0.2	6.0	6.0	191.3	4.6	1565
Ashley L		10½	–3.4	–	–	78.3	5'97	1664
AustReed		146½	–5.8	8.0	2.2	46.1	4.6	3798
Autobacs		£11 27/32	–1.2	072%	3.0	445.6	9 2	2344
Beale	♠	90xd	5.9	6.1	1.2	18.5	3.9	5027
BeattieJ	♠	137½	–4.8	11.9	0.9	56.1	14.5	1784
BlacksLs	♠	326xd	–5.8	7.1	2.6	135.3	27.8	1846
BodyShp		122½	0.8	5.7	1.5	251.1	4.6	1864
Boots Grp		666	–.4	28.6	1.6	5,273	18.6	1876
Brown&J		111½	–9.3	–	–	198.1	11'1	1984
Brown N	q	132½	–7.0	5.84	2.3	389.6	18.6	1985
Burberry		329¾	–1.3	3.0	3.9	1,648	23.7	2727
Carpet't		779xd	–1.6	37.0	1.3	559.0	10.9	2464
CarphonW*	♠	118¾	–5.8	1.0	5.1	1,037	2.7	2833
ClintonC		249½	–.8	8.36	3.2	171.9	7.5	4978
Courts	♠	317½xd	1.1	5.7	–	194.4	10.9	2256
DFS Furn	†	406½	–2.9	23.0	1.5	435.3	21.5	3588
Debenhams	♦†	467½	0.5	13.0	2.4	1,693	28.5	2936
Dixons		139xd	–6.2	6.65	1.6	2,707	20.8	2355
ebookers		526½	–11.1	–	–	337.3	–	–
Findel		303½	–5.2	12.6	1.9	254.4	4.6	2563
FlyBrndsUt	†	137½xd	–7.1	7.58	1.9	37.2	17.9	2789
FootLockS	♥	£9¾	–6.8	–	–	1,385	1'93	2468
Formnstr		37½	1.4	1.7	0.9	12.4	25.6	2618
French C	†	1935xd	6.3	14.0	9.0	368.6	24.9	2633
Game Grp	†	56	–9.3	1.05	5.5	300.3	25.6	3308
GlobNatE	♠	222½	–6.3	–	–	24.0	8'97	2165
Grandvsn		1495¼	–4.5	–	–	349.3	–	–
GUS	♣♠	678¾	–4.4	23.3	2.0	6,862	9.7	2740
HMV		160xd	–3.3	4.5	3.2	648.5	17.9	2000

Exhibit 12.1 London share service extracts: general retailers

Source: *Financial Times* 26 September 2003 and 29 September 2003

Some analysts prefer to swap the top and bottom of the PER ratio to create the **earnings yield**. This shows the profits attributable to each £1 invested buying a share:

$$\text{Earnings yield} = \frac{\text{Earnings per share}}{\text{Current market price of share}}$$

So, to take our earlier example, for every £1 spent buying a share last year's company profits are 7.56p (historic earnings yield):

$$\text{Earnings yield} = \frac{68\text{p}}{900\text{p}} = 7.56\%$$

Historic PERs reported in the financial press are usually based on the latest annual reports and accounts, and are updated on interim figures. So if earnings for the first 6 months of the year have just been reported these are used instead of the earnings for the first 6 months of the last full year to calculate the latest 12 months of earnings.[1]

The eps figures used by the press are usually **'basic' earnings** (or '**FRS 3' earnings**, after the reporting standard). These include a deduction from profit of one-off exceptional items and goodwill amortisation (goodwill is discussed in Chapter 13), so they present a warts-and-all picture.

Companies sometimes report **diluted** earnings per share. This takes into account any additional shares that may be issued in the future under executive share option schemes, convertible bonds, convertible preference shares and warrants. The word 'diluted' indicates that the earnings are spread over a larger number of shares so the fully diluted eps will be less than the normal eps reported.

Companies often like to present the largest eps figure possible and so they highlight the **headline**, **underlying**, **adjusted** or **normalised** eps, which excludes one-off costs, exceptional items and goodwill amortisation. These figures are supposed to show the underlying trend, but some companies seem to have a habit of showing large, supposedly one-off, costs every year. The reassuring titles of these earnings figures belie the fact that directors are able to flatter the company's performance by emphasising these numbers – they neatly sidestep some harsh facts, such as major losses in some of the business's operations.

If shares are issued during the year so there are more at the end than at the beginning, a **weighted average** number of shares will be used to calculate eps. This gives more weight to those issued earlier in the year – as they were in existence longer.

The PER on its own does not tell you whether a share is appropriately valued. It merely tells you the profit growth that investors are generally expecting. This can then be compared with your estimate of growth to judge whether the market is being realistic, over-pessimistic or over-optimistic. Perhaps your judgement will be influenced by the PERs of other companies, such as those in the same sector, or the PER for the market as a whole. The *Financial Times* publishes industry group and market-wide PERs every day except Monday.

Dividend yield

The dividend yield is the amount of dividend paid on each share as a percentage of the share price:

$$\text{Dividend yield} = \frac{\text{Dividend per share (pence)}}{\text{Current share price (pence)}} \times 100$$

[1] A rolling method is used: take the latest full year's earnings, add on the latest 6 months' figures and deduct the earnings for the 6 month period a year ago.

So, in the case of a company where the dividend paid is 34p per share and the current share price is 900p,

$$\text{Dividend yield} = \frac{34\text{p}}{900\text{p}} \times 100 = 3.78\%$$

The dividend figure is the total of all dividend payments declared for the year. There may be two payments: an interim dividend (say, 14p per share) following the first half of the year, and the final dividend (say, 20p). There may be four payments in the case of those companies declaring dividends quarterly.

In Exhibit 12.1 the dividend yield ('yield') includes all the dividends for the last 12 months, which means they are updated for interim (or quarterly) dividends. Suppose a company is more than half way through a financial year and has paid the following dividends:

Last complete financial year dividend payment	22p
Latest interim dividend	7p
Previous interim dividend	6p
Current share price	500p

Then:

$$\text{Adjusted dividend} = 22\text{p} + 7\text{p} - 6\text{p} = 23\text{p}$$

$$\text{Dividend yield} = \frac{23}{500} \times 100 = 4.6\%$$

Dividend yields can be calculated on **historic** figures (based on the most recent 12 months of dividends) or on a **prospective** basis, which makes use of the forecast for the next year.

Dividend yield is important because it is the return you are actually receiving from a company. You may hope to make capital gains as well, but this is somewhat theoretical – dividend income is real. The yield offered on a share can be compared with other shares, sectors or the market as a whole. It can also be compared with other investments such as government bonds or building society accounts. Government bonds usually give a higher yield than shares. This is acceptable to shareholders despite the higher risk on shares because there is an anticipation that the yield on shares will grow significantly over the years as profits rise, while coupon payments on bonds are normally a constant amount. Those companies expected to grow their profits at a fast rate will have low dividend yields because investors tend to bid up the share price. These **lower-yield** shares are often labelled 'growth shares'. **Higher-yield** (or simply **yield**) **stocks** are expected to have low profits growth and are labelled 'value shares'.[2] Shares offering very high yields often indicate market consensus that the dividend will fall as the company heads into difficulties.

[2] This is an unforgivably crude definition of 'growth' and 'value' shares and should not be taken too seriously – see Glen Arnold, *Valuegrowth Investing* (Financial Times Prentice Hall, 2002) for the poor quality of thinking demonstrated by crudely classifying shares as value or growth.

Managers often use dividends to signal to shareholders their confidence in the firm's future. In years when losses are made dividends are often maintained, or even increased, to signal that the firm had an unusually bad year and all will be well soon.

Dividend cover, payout ratio and retention ratio

Dividend cover is the ratio of profit attributable to ordinary shareholders to dividends. It can be calculated by dividing the earnings per share by the dividend per share:

$$\text{Dividend cover} = \frac{\text{Earnings per share}}{\text{Dividends per share}}$$

Or, for the company as a whole:

$$\text{Dividend cover} = \frac{\text{Profit attributable to ordinary shareholders}}{\text{Total dividend payment}}$$

So, if eps are 68p and the dividend per share is 34p (Exhibit 11.3) the dividend cover is 2.

Dividend cover highlights the affordability of the current level of dividends. It shows the number of the current dividend payments that could be made out of current after-tax profits. The higher the proportion of profits paid out, the less is available for business investment and growth. Switching around the top and bottom of the ratio gives the **payout ratio**. This is the percentage of after-tax profit paid to shareholders in dividends. What is left in the company is the **retention ratio**:

$$\text{Retention ratio} = \frac{\text{Retained profits}}{\text{Profits attributable to ordinary shareholders}}$$

Companies, on average, maintain payout ratios of around 45–50 per cent, therefore dividend covers are typically around 2 or slightly higher (although they dipped to around 1.5 in 2002–2003 as companies maintained dividends in difficult times). However, there is a wide range around this average, as you can see from the Monday *Financial Times* extract in Exhibit 12.1. Some companies pay out all profit and more (see Beattie), others only pay out a small fraction of profits (see French Connection).

Market capitalisation

The market capitalisation of a company is the number of shares in issue multiplied by the market price. **Market capitalisation** is useful for comparing the size of companies. Exhibit 12.1 shows that the total value of the ordinary shares in Laura Ashley is only £78.3 million compared with £6,862 million for GUS. Note that companies may issue two or more types of shares (e.g. ordinary shares with votes and ordinary shares without votes). These will be quoted separately in the *Financial Times*. The value of the two types would need to be added together to calculate the company's total market capitalisation.

Net asset value

Net asset value (NAV) is the total assets of a company minus all its liabilities. The NAV is often viewed as the break-up value of the company.[3] Should the company be wound up *and* its assets sold at the balance sheet value *and* the liabilities remain as shown on the balance sheet, then the NAV represents the amount available for shareholders after all other claims have been met.

The NAV figure provides a useful indicator of the value of assets underpinning the shares. However, most shares are rarely valued on NAVs because investors are not looking to liquidate the company, but are anticipating a flow of income from holding shares, and this income flow forms the basis for valuation.

Market to book ratio

The market to book ratio is the share price divided by net assets per share (book value). This ratio is used by some analysts as an indicator of over- or undervaluation. If the balance sheet assets per share are much larger than the share price, this is taken to be a buy signal. Share prices significantly above net assets values might indicate over-excitement. However, this type of analysis relies on balance sheets providing useful and accurate valuations – close to sale value or the value of replacing the assets. As discussed in the next chapter, balance sheets are not designed for this.

$$\text{Market to book ratio} = \frac{\text{Current market price of share}}{\text{Book value (net asset value) per share}}$$

For the example company in Chapter 11, assets are £129 million and the NAV per share is £2.58 (£129m/50m). Thus the market to book ratio can be calculated as

$$\frac{900\text{p}}{258\text{p}} = 3.49$$

A more sophisticated method would be to deduct the £5 million of net assets attributable to minority shareholders (see Exhibit 11.4), leaving net assets of £124 million and a market to book ratio of 3.63. Some analysts would deduct goodwill as well.

If the NAV is high relative to a share's current market value it gives the shareholder some reassurance about the downside of the share. Of course, this only applies if you can trust the balance sheet values. The chances of being able to sell the assets at the balance sheet values are pretty slim for most companies.

[3] The financial press often uses a different 'break-up value'. This is based on the amount that could be raised by selling the various subsidiaries (rather than individual assets) to other companies, and is usually considerably more than the NAV.

Enterprise value

Enterprise value (EV) is the total of equity market capitalisation and all of the company's debt minus cash the company holds:

$$\text{EV} = \text{Market capitalisation} + \text{total debt} - \text{cash}$$

So, for our example company in Chapter 11, with 50 million shares in issue each trading at 900p, we have total capitalisation of £450 million. The balance sheet shows total debt of £87 million (£62 million due within 1 year and £25 million due after 1 year) and £10 million in cash. Thus:

$$\text{EV} = £450\text{m} + £87\text{m} - £10\text{m} = £527\text{m}$$

Analysts use EV when comparing relative profit or cash flow. If the profit or cash flow is expressed before deduction of interest payments, then you can compare the company's profits before interest with the total value of the equity and debt held by the business. (In the EV calculation, some analysts add pension provisions, minority interests and other claims on the business.)

Performance ratios and measures

Profit margins

There are different profit margins, and it is important to know which one is being referred to in a particular context.

Gross profit margin (or **gross margin**) is defined as sales minus cost of sales, expressed as a percentage of sales:

$$\text{Gross profit margin} = \frac{\text{Gross profit}}{\text{Sales}} \times 100$$

$$= \frac{\text{Sales} - \text{Cost of sales}}{\text{Sales}} \times 100$$

So, for the example used in Chapter 11, where sales are £230 million in 2003 (£200 million in 2002), and the cost of sales £140 million (£120 million in 2002), the gross profit margins are:

$$\text{For 2003: } \frac{90}{230} \times 100 = 39.1\%$$

$$\text{For 2002: } \frac{80}{200} \times 100 = 40\%$$

A complication can arise in the definition in the cost of sales. While most companies include the expense of bought-in raw materials/components, as well as employee remuneration and overheads directly related to production (i.e. the costs of bringing materials to a saleable condition), others simply include the expense of bought-in raw materials/components. The lesson is to read the notes to the accounts and take care when comparing one company with another.

Gross profit margin can be used to compare the performance of a company with that of its competitors. If it is low, investigate the reason. It may simply be that the company has a mix of products that have a high level of bought-in raw material costs. It could be that the management are less efficient, or, perhaps, pricing power in the market place is low. Observations of gross profit over time can likewise prompt further investigation.

Operating profit margin (or **operating margin** or **trading margin)** is operating profit as a percentage of sales. The profit figure used here is profit before interest and tax (PBIT) is deducted. It allows for all the expenses of manufacture, distribution, administration, R&D, depreciation, etc., but not for the financing costs or tax.

$$\text{Operating profit margin} = \frac{\text{Operating profit}}{\text{Sales}} \times 100$$

$$= \frac{\text{Sales} - \text{All operating expenses}}{\text{Sales}} \times 100$$

In our example:

$$\text{For 2003:} \quad \frac{55}{230} \times 100 = 23.9\%$$

$$\text{For 2002:} \quad \frac{50}{200} \times 100 = 25\%$$

If the company has a declining operating profit margin over time and/or relative to its competitors, this may be a sign of serious trouble – cost control or pricing power may be deteriorating.

Pre-tax profit margin (or **pre-tax margin**) is profit after all expenses including interest, expressed as a percentage of sales:

$$\text{Pre-tax profit margin} = \frac{\text{Profit on ordinary activities before taxation}}{\text{Sales}} \times 100$$

In our example:

$$\text{For 2003:} \quad \frac{49}{230} \times 100 = 21.3\%$$

$$\text{For 2002:} \quad \frac{45}{200} \times 100 = 22.5\%$$

Again the profit margin worsens over time.[4] This piece of information needs to be combined with others to build up a picture of the company. It must be noted that a pre-tax profit margin of over 20% is still high compared with most firms (mind you, this depends on the industry), so perhaps our company is fundamentally sound but has had a minor downturn in fortunes. We are unable to draw conclusions yet, but we are gaining insight as we gather information.

Return on capital employed

The return on capital employed (ROCE) measures the return (operating profit) per pound invested in assets within the business.

$$\text{ROCE} = \frac{\text{Profit before interest and tax (operating profit)}}{\text{Capital employed}} \times 100$$

There is no hard-and-fast rule to define capital employed. It may be defined as the total of equity shareholders' funds plus all borrowings. If we assume, for the sake of simplicity, all liabilities are borrowings for our example company then:

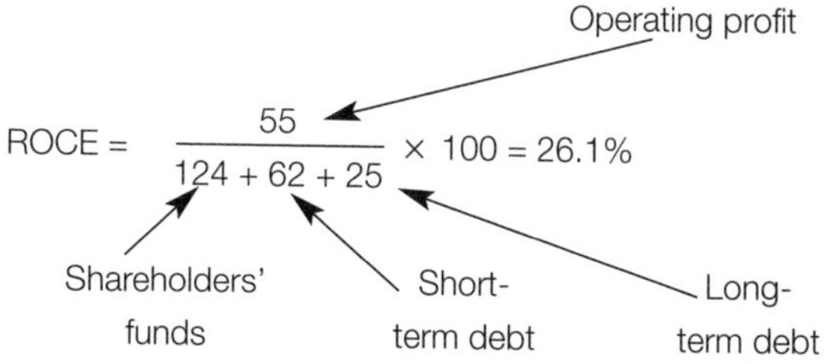

Alternatively, capital employed can be defined as equity shareholders' funds plus long-term loans only. Other analysts throw in provisions for liabilities and charges, minority interests and a host of other factors as part of the capital figure. Clearly, you need to know just what definition was used if you are taking someone else's calculation for ROCE. You also need to ensure consistency when comparing figures over the years or between companies.

ROCE measures how successfully a company is at investing the money it takes from investors (and lenders) in real assets. Our example company produces a relatively high ROCE. A return of 26 per cent is likely to be significantly above any cost of borrowing that money or the return that shareholders could get elsewhere for the level of risk associated with holding the shares. If ROCE were less than 8–10 per cent we would worry, as this is likely to be below the returns achieved by other companies or available elsewhere in the financial markets.

[4] We would normally observe margin changes over at least 5 years to avoid drawing conclusions from a period that is too short.

You may observe in practice that some ROCE calculations don't use the end-of-year balance sheet values for capital employed but use an average of two consecutive balance sheets. This is to reflect the fact that the profits were earned over a period of a year – using the quantity of assets available at different points in the year and not just using the assets the company happened to have right at the end of the year. Apart from anything else, the end-of-year balance sheet is likely to be boosted by the retained profits for the year, so the ROCE is unreasonably reduced by the benefit of having lots of retained profits that year.

It might be interesting to look at the return generated for every pound of *equity capital* – leaving out the return to debt holders and the money put in by lenders. This is achieved by calculating the **return on equity (ROE)**:

$$\text{ROE} = \frac{\text{Profit attributable to shareholders}}{\text{Equity shareholders' funds}} \times 100$$

Profit attributable to shareholders is profit after the deduction of interest, tax, minority interests and preference share dividends. Equity shareholders' funds are calculated after the deduction of minority interests and preference share capital. So, for our example company:

$$\text{ROE} = \frac{34}{124} \times 100 = 27.4\%$$

The ROE may be affected by unusual tax conditions outside management control, and so in using this measure as a comparator care must be taken. Note that some analysts may leave minority interests in the numerator and denominator – if a consistent approach is taken this is not a problem.

Other variations on the theme of profit per pound of capital include **return on capital, return on net assets** and **return on shareholders' funds**. Definitions of these vary and often overlap with the measures we have already looked at.

EBITDA

EBITDA (pronounced 'e-bit-dah') became a very popular measure of a company's performance in the late 1990s. It was especially popular with managers of firms that failed to make a profit. EBITDA means '**earnings before interest, taxation, depreciation and amortisation**'. Managers liked to emphasise this measure in their communications to shareholders because large positive numbers could be shown. Some cynics have it renamed it 'earnings before I tricked the dumb auditor'.

If you run an internet company that makes a £100 million loss and the future looks pretty dim unless you can persuade investors and bankers to continue their support, perhaps you would want to add back all the interest (say, £50 million), depreciation on assets that are wearing out or becoming obsolete (say, £40 million), and the declining value of intangible assets, such as software licences and goodwill amortisation (say, £65 million), so that you could show a healthy positive number on EBITDA of £55 million. And if your loss seems to get worse from one year to the next as your acquisition strategy fails to pay off, it is wonderfully convenient to report and emphasise a stable or rising EBITDA.

The use of EBITDA by company directors makes political spin doctors look amateurs by comparison. EBITDA is not covered by any accounting standards, so companies are entitled to use a variety of methods – whatever shows the company in the best light.

In the real world directors (and investors) cannot ignore the cost of using up and wearing out equipment and other assets or the fact that interest and tax need to be paid, however much they would want to. Warren Buffett made the comment: 'References to EBITDA make us shudder – does management think the tooth fairy pays for capital expenditures?'[5]

Free cash flow

Free cash flow is a useful measure of the company's cash flow available to return to lenders and shareholders. It takes into account the fact that tax payments and investments in working capital and long-lived assets represent cash that is then not available to return to lenders and shareholders. For our example company we calculate the free cash flow as follows:

	£m
Operating profit	55
plus depreciation and other non-cash items	5
minus cash tax paid	(13)
Cash profits	47
minus investment in fixed assets	(5)
minus investment in working capital	(35)
Free cash flow	7

Out of a company's free cash flow it will have to make interest payments, which may or may not leave some free cash flow available for shareholders.

Small, rapidly expanding companies frequently fail to produce positive free cash flow. This may be good if the company is investing for the future by buying lots of assets to permit growth. However, a mature business with few avenues for profitable capital investment should not show negative cash flow. It should be throwing off cash for shareholders to invest elsewhere.

Also note that if fixed asset (long-lived asset) expenditure is significantly less than depreciation the company may be stinting on investment. This may boost short-term appearances with a nice positive free cash flow – and even high dividends – but in the long run serious damage may be done to the business as it falls behind competitors.

[5] Chairman's letter accompanying the 2000 annual report of Berkshire Hathaway Inc.

Owner earnings

Whereas free cash flow reports the *actual* expenditure on new business assets, owner earnings force the analyst to think about the *necessary* level of expenditure *in the future* on these items needed to maintain the firm's competitive position, its unit volume and to invest in all new projects that create value for shareholders. This investment figure is inevitably subjective and imprecise, but then we must acknowledge that the most important aspects of investment are not the quantifiable elements – I'd rather be roughly right than precisely wrong.

Owner earnings represent what can be taken out of the business by shareholders without damaging the company's economic franchise. Owner earnings are defined as:

(a) reported earnings after tax;

(b) *plus* depreciation, depletion (e.g. of natural resources such as oil reserves), amortisation of intangible assets and certain other non-cash charges;

(c) *less* the amount of expenditure for plant and machinery, etc., that the business requires to fully maintain its long-term competitive position, its unit volume and its investment in all new value-creating projects;

(d) *less* any extra amount for working capital that is needed to maintain the firm's long-term competitive position, unit volume and its investment in all new value-creating projects.[6]

An example of share valuation using owner earnings is shown later in this chapter – in the intrinsic value calculation.

Financial health ratios and measures

Gearing

We need to avoid some of the confusion possible when using the word 'gearing'. First, we should make a distinction between operating gearing and financial gearing.

Operating gearing refers to the extent to which the firm's total costs are fixed. The profits of firms with high operating gearing, such as car or steel manufacturers, are very sensitive to changes in the sales level. They have high **break-even points** (the turnover level at which profits are achieved) but when this level is breached a large proportion of any additional sales revenue turns into profit because of the relatively low **variable costs** (costs that go up and down as company output and sales change).[7]

Financial gearing concerns the proportion of debt in the capital structure. Net income (after interest) to shareholders in firms with high financial gearing is more sensitive to changes in operating profits. There are two ways of putting in perspective the levels of

6 For more detail see Chapter 8 of Glen Arnold, *Valuegrowth Investing*.

7 Most practitioners use the terms gearing and leverage interchangeably, although leverage is used more in America.

debt that a firm carries. **Capital gearing** focuses on the extent to which a firm's total capital is in the form of debt. **Income gearing** is concerned with the proportion of the annual income stream (i.e. the pre-interest profits) devoted to the prior claims of debt holders, in other words, what proportion of profits is taken by interest charges.

There are alternative measures of the extent to which the capital structure consists of debt. One popular approach is the ratio of long-term debt to shareholders' funds (the **debt to equity ratio**). The long-term debt is usually taken as the balance sheet items 'amounts falling due after more than one year'.

$$\text{Capital gearing (1)} = \frac{\text{Long-term debt}}{\text{Shareholders' funds}}$$

This ratio is of interest because it may give some indication of the firm's ability to sell assets to repay debts. For example, if the ratio stood at 0.3, or 30 per cent, lenders and shareholders might feel relatively comfortable as there would be, apparently, over three times as much in net assets (i.e. after paying off liabilities) as long-term debt. So, if the worst came to the worst, the company could sell assets to satisfy its long-term lenders. A figure of over 100 per cent would be a matter of concern (for most types of company/industry).

There is a major problem with relying on this measure of gearing. The book value of assets can be quite different from the saleable value. This may be because the assets have been recorded at historical purchase value (perhaps less depreciation) and have not been revalued over time. It may also be due to the fact that companies forced to sell assets to satisfy creditors often have to do so at greatly reduced prices if they are in a hurry. Also, this measure of gearing can have a range of values from zero to infinity, and this makes inter-firm comparisons difficult. The measure shown below puts gearing within a range of zero to 100 per cent as debt is expressed as a fraction of all long-term capital:

$$\text{Capital gearing (2)} = \frac{\text{Long-term debt}}{\text{Long-term debt + Shareholders' funds}}$$

Many firms rely on overdraft facilities and other short-term borrowing. Technically these are classified as short-term. In reality, many firms use the overdraft and other short-term borrowing as a long-term source of funds. Furthermore, if we are concerned about the potential for financial distress, then we must recognise that an inability to repay an overdraft can be just as serious as an inability to service a long-term bond. The third capital gearing measure, in addition to allowing for long-term debt, includes short-term borrowing:

$$\text{Capital gearing (3)} = \frac{\text{All borrowing}}{\text{All borrowing + Shareholders' funds}}$$

To add sophistication to capital gearing analysis it is often necessary to take into account any cash (or marketable securities, e.g. gilts) holdings in the firm. These can be used to offset the threat that debt poses.

The capital gearing measures rely on the appropriate valuation of net assets either in the balance sheet or in a revaluation exercise. Furthermore, capital gearing measures focus on a worst-case scenario: 'What could we sell the business assets for if we had to, in order to pay creditors?'

It may be erroneous to focus exclusively on assets when trying to judge a company's ability to repay debts. Take the example of a successful advertising agency. It may not have any saleable assets at all, apart from a few desks and chairs, and yet it may be able to borrow hundreds of millions of pounds because it has the ability to generate cash to make interest payments. Thus, quite often, a more appropriate measure of gearing is one concerned with the level of a firm's income relative to its interest commitments, the **interest cover**:

$$\text{Interest cover} = \frac{\text{Profit before interest and tax}}{\text{Interest charges}}$$

The lower the interest cover ratio the greater the chance of interest payment default and liquidation. The inverse of interest cover measures the proportion of profits paid out in interest – this is known as **income gearing**. As a crude rule of thumb, an interest cover of less than 3 would be a worry unless the company had exceptionally stable cash flows.

Watch out for interest being 'capitalised' on a balance sheet rather than being treated as an expense and therefore charged to the profit. This can make interest payments seem low when in reality large sums are paid out to lenders. You can check up on this practice by observing cash outflow for interest payments in the cash flow statement and related notes. Capitalisation of interest is discussed in more detail in the next chapter.

Current ratio

It is useful to know if a company has enough cash and other short-term assets that can fairly quickly be turned into cash to meet its short-term liabilities. Can the company pay its near term bills? The current ratio measures this:

$$\text{Current ratio} = \frac{\text{Current assets}}{\text{Current liabilities}}$$

In the case of our example company

$$\text{Current ratio} = \frac{125}{62} = 2.01$$

indicating that it has significantly more short-term assets than short-term liabilities – this would be considered prudent (a current ratio less than 1 is cause for worry).

Quick ratio

A large element of the current assets, that is, stock (of raw material, half-finished goods, etc.), may not be easy to quickly convert to cash so a tighter measure of **solvency** (the ability to pay debts when they become due) is used, called the **quick ratio** or **acid test**:

$$\text{Quick ratio} = \frac{\text{Current assets} - \text{stock}}{\text{Current liabilities}}$$

So, for our example company:

$$\text{Quick ratio} = \frac{125 - 35}{62} = 1.45$$

If the quick ratio is less than 1 the company could not meet all its current liabilities should they be due immediately. Comparison across an industry is useful for putting the quick ratio figure in perspective. For example, supermarkets frequently show a quick ratio of around 0.2 – for these firms this is acceptable given that so much of their current assets are rapidly moving stock items matched by high levels of trade creditors (a current liability).

Forward-looking measures

Dividend valuation model

To value a share, analysts often estimate all the future dividends. They are not able to simply add these together to calculate a share's value, because a dividend of 34p to be received in 5 years is not worth the same to the investor as a dividend of 34p received now. Most people, given the choice between the receipt of a sum of money now and the same sum in the future will say 'I'd rather have it now'. Thus money has a **time value**. Given the existence of the time value of money, it makes sense to allow for the fact that people will need to be compensated for giving up money now.

There are three reasons why investors prefer £1 now rather than £1 in the future and therefore three things that have to be compensated for:

- **Inflation**. If there is inflation, then investors need additional compensation over time for giving up money now.
- **Risk**. If there is a risk that the future payout may not take place or will be less than promised, then investors will want a greater return on their money (greater compensation over time). Company shares carry greater risk than, say, government bonds, and offer a significantly higher rate of return.

- **Impatience to consume.** People like to consume. Compensation will be required for a delay in gratification even in a world without the first two factors, inflation and risk.

Let us assume that the company shares we are analysing present a risk level to investors which means they require an annual rate of return of 10 per cent which incorporates all these elements of compensation (impatience to consume, inflation and risk). Now, if you asked someone who required a 10 per cent rate of return what is the sum of money to be received in 1 year that is sufficient for you to give up £100 now, they will reply £110. They are indifferent between holding on to the £100 now and giving it up and receiving £110 in 12 months' time. The relationship is explained in the compounding formula:

$$\text{Future value} = \text{Present value } (1 + \text{rate of return})^{\text{number of years}}$$

$$£110 = £100\,(1 + 0.10)^1$$

We could use the formula to ask other questions. For example, what sum of money do investors need in 3 years' time to compensate them for the sacrifice of £100 now if the required rate of return is 10 per cent per year? The answer is:

$$£100(1 + 0.1)^3 = £100 \times 1.10 \times 1.10 \times 1.10 = £133.10$$

Investors in this risk class of shares are indifferent between receiving £133.10 in 3 years' time and keeping £100 because they get a 10 per cent rate of return. If they received £150 in 3 years the rate of return would be more than 10 per cent and investors would be delighted to receive a surplus above the minimum required.

An alternative way of using the formula is to estimate the future income and then turn it into an equivalent value now. That is, calculate its **present value**. So, if you estimate income of £133.10 in 3 years and the required rate of return on an investment of that risk is 10 per cent the equivalent present value is £100:

$$\frac{£133.10}{(1 + 0.10)^3} = \frac{£133.10}{1.10 \times 1.10 \times 1.10} = £100$$

This is called '**discounting**' the future income flow. If you estimate the future income to be £150 in 3 years, the present value is more than £100 because you still discount at 10 per cent (the discount rate is determined by the risk class):

$$\frac{£150}{(1 + 0.10)^3} = £112.70$$

If someone asks you to pay £100 now for an investment that pays £150 in 3 years snatch it quick as its equivalent present value is £112.70 (assuming a time value of 10 per cent per year – more risky investments require higher rates of return).

With shares the dividends are not all received at one point in the future. Rather, they arrive at fairly regular intervals. When calculating a share's value we can use the **dividend**

valuation model. For the sake of simplicity we will assume dividends are received annually, with the first one due in a year from now. Let us assume that each of the future dividends (which occur every year for ever) will be 34p. Then we can value a share (assuming a 10 per cent discount rate) as follows:

Time dividend received:

	in 1 year		*in 2 years*		*in 3 years*	
Share value =	$\frac{34p}{1+0.10}$	+	$\frac{34p}{(1+0.10)^2}$	+	$\frac{34p}{(1+0.10)^3}$	+ . . . + . . .
Present value =	30.91p	+	28.10p	+	25.5p	+ . . . + . . .

Notice the decline in the present value of the dividend the further from the present time it is received.

These dividends stretch to an infinite horizon and so this calculation could take a long time – if we do it this way. Fortunately, we can be rescued from the dire prospect of lengthy calculations because the formula simplifies down to the following if the dividends are constant and are at annual intervals for ever:

$$\text{Share value} = \frac{\textit{Dividend}}{\textit{Discount rate}} = \frac{34p}{0.10} = £3.40$$

Note here that even though only one year's dividend has gone into the formula it represents all the future dividends – for ever.

Dividends are rarely constant year after year. Managers often make great efforts to provide a steadily rising annual dividend. If dividends grow over time by a constant amount each year, say 4.5 per cent per year, then the following formula can be used:

$$\text{Share value} = \frac{\text{Next year's dividend}}{\text{Discount rate} - \text{Growth rate}}$$

If the recently paid dividend is 34p and the next to be paid, in one year, is bigger by 4.5 per cent then next year's dividend is 35.53p (34p × 1.045). The share value is now:

$$\frac{35.53p}{0.10 - 0.045} = £6.46$$

Notice that even a modest rate of growth in the dividend results in the share value almost doubling from the constant (no-growth) dividend case – from £3.40 to £6.46.[8]

The major difficulty with the discounted valuation method is the estimation of the growth rate. The chapters on industry and strategic analysis (Chapters 14–15) will help

[8] For more on discounted cash flow and the dividend valuation model, see Chapters 2, 16 and 17 of Glen Arnold, *Corporate Financial Management* (Financial Times Prentice Hall, 2002).

you to search for the right factors, but it remains a difficult and uncertain task. One pointer is that companies as a whole do not grow dividends at a faster rate than the economy grows over the long run. So if, say, real economic growth is 2.5 per cent and inflation is 2 per cent don't expect the average company to grow profits at more than 4.5 per cent per year except in short-term bursts (which are likely to be corrected in the next downturn). City analysts often bring out absurd estimates for the corporate sector expecting double-digit growth for many years ahead. If this happened over the long run then corporate profits and dividends would become larger than the entire economy!

Intrinsic value

The intrinsic value of a share is the discounted value of all the owner earnings that can be taken out of the business during its remaining life. Future owner earnings are determined by the strength and durability of the economic franchise (see Chapters 14 and 15), the quality of the management and the financial strength of the business.

Each of the estimated future annual owner earnings figures needs to be calculated and then discounted. When these are all totalled we have intrinsic value. So, if our example company has reported earnings after tax attributable to shareholders[9] of £34 million and in calculating that figure the non-cash item depreciation (£5 million) was deducted we can *estimate* last year's owner earnings. This can only be an estimate because items (c) and (d) in the owner earnings calculations (see page 198) are largely subjective. For example, we may estimate that the level of investment needed in fixed capital equipment to maintain long-term competitive position, unit volume and investment in new projects is £5 million per year, but we cannot be mathematically precise. Likewise we may judge that £8 million will be needed for working capital investment.[10] Despite the uncertainty inherent in such judgements these elements are vital and this method preferable than merely using reported historical cash flow. With the assumption that total expenditure on fixed capital assets and working capital is £13 million we have owner earnings of £26 million:

		£m
(a)	Reported earnings after tax	34
	Plus	
(b)	Depreciation, depletion, amortisation and other non-cash charges	5
		39
	Less	
(c)	and (d) Expenditure on plant machinery, working capital, brand maintenance, etc., required to maintain long-term competitive position, unit volume and investment in new projects	13
		26

[9] After minority interests.

[10] Notice that this figure is a lot les than that shown in the example company's cash flow statement. This is because owner earnings estimate the *necessary future* expense, not the *actual* expense in the last reported figures.

If we now make the simplifying assumption that the owner earnings will be the same in all future years we can calculate intrinsic value:

$$\text{Intrinsic value} = \frac{\text{Annual owner earnings}}{\text{Discount rate}}$$

If the appropriate discount rate is 10 per cent, then the intrinsic value is

$$\text{Intrinsic value} = \frac{£26\text{m}}{0.1} = £260m$$

or £260m/50m = £5.20 per share.

These shares are currently trading in the stock market at £9, so we would not be buyers based on this calculation.

However, it is possible we have been too pessimistic in assuming that the company will not grow its owner earnings over time. Let us now assume that the company has a series of new projects that will generate returns greater than 10 per cent (the required rate of return for this risk class of shares). By investing in these projects, owner earnings will rise by 5 per cent in each future year (on the one hand, owner earnings are decreased by the need for additional investment in fixed and working capital, but, on the other, reported earnings after tax are boosted to produce a net 5 per cent growth). With a constant future growth rate we can use the formula:

$$\text{Intrinsic value} = \frac{\text{Owner earnings next year}}{\text{Discount rate} - \text{Growth rate}}$$

$$\text{Next years' owner earnings} = £26\text{m} \times (1+0.05) = £27.30\text{m}$$

$$\text{Intrinsic value of company} = \frac{£27.30\text{m}}{0.10 - 0.05} = £546\text{m}$$

$$\text{Intrinsic value per share} = \frac{£546\text{m}}{50\text{m}} = £10.92$$

Under these circumstances the share does not look overvalued. However, given the uncertainties in the calculation I would want to see a larger 'margin of safety' between my calculated value and the current share price before buying.

Further reading

Good descriptions of ratios are given by G. Holmes, A. Sugden and P. Gee, *Interpreting Company Reports and Accounts*, 8th edition (Financial Times Prentice Hall, 2002) and

B. Vause, *Guide To Analysing Companies*, 2nd edition (The Economist Books/Profile Books, 1999). Typical ratios for companies in various sectors are published by ICC (*www.icc.co.uk*). Dun and Bradstreet publish key company statistics (*www.dnb.com*). Other electronic sources of ratios and measures include Datastream (*www.datastream.com*), Fame (*www.fame.bvdep.com*) and Hemscott (*www.hemscot.net*).

13

Tricks of the accounting trade

Financial statements are supposed to show the underlying economic performance of a company. The profit and loss account shows the difference between total revenue and total expenses. The balance sheet displays the assets, liabilities and capital of the business at a snapshot moment. What could be simpler than adding a few numbers to get a trustworthy and definitive conclusion? Well, drawing up a set of accounts is far from simple, or unambiguously precise. It is nowhere near as scientific and objective as some people would have you believe. There is plenty of scope for judgement, guesswork or even cynical manipulation. Despite the mountain of accounting rules and regulations there are numerous opportunities to flatter the figures, or at least to offer two or three legitimate estimates of the value of something or the profit generated by an activity. Imagine the difficulty facing the company accountant and auditors of a clothes retailer when trying to value a dress which has been on sale for 6 months. Let us suppose the dress cost the firm £50. Perhaps this should go into the balance sheet and the profit and loss account would not be affected. But what if the store manager says that he can only sell the dress if it is reduced to £30, and contradicting him the managing director says that if a little more effort was made £40 could be achieved? Which figure is the person who drafts the accounts going to take? Profits can vary significantly, depending on a multitude of small judgements like this.

Consider another simple example. Suppose that there are two identical companies except that during the last year one bought a £10 million factory, while the other spent £10 million on advertising. How are you going to value the assets at the end of the year? The company that acquired the £10 million factory has something tangible to show. Perhaps we should say the year-end value of the asset is £10 million. On the other hand, you may think the asset has decreased in value since it was purchased. Perhaps it should now be valued at only £9 million. So what do you do with the £1 million write-off? Should that be regarded as a cost of doing business and deducted from profit? Or, if the £1 million reduction in value is due to a general downturn in property values, is it best to account for it by stating a separate exceptional charge? The second firm's accounts are even more subject to judgement. Presumably the management believed that expenditure on advertising would create something of value – an enhanced brand, for example. This asset may be more valuable than the physical assets bought by the first company, and yet, because intangibles are usually valued at zero, the entire expenditure becomes a cost for the year, reducing the profit significantly.

Given that accounts are malleable, investors need to be alive to three possibilities:

- Directors and accountants are trying hard to present a picture of the firm's performance and financial standing that is true and fair but are forced to make numerous judgements along the way. They are trying to apply the rules to produce accurate figures. However, if another equally honest and meticulous accountant were making the judgements the figures would look different simply because some of these judgement calls are finely balanced. We do not live in a mathematically precise world – the investor needs to accept that the accounts merely provide no more than ballpark figures. Having said this, for most firms, with accountants conscientiously trying to avoid tipping the balance either way between favourable and unfavourable reporting, the room for judgement should not make more than about 10–20 per cent difference.

- The second possibility is **creative accounting**, in which the letter of the accounting standards is abided by, but there is a deliberate attempt to flatter the figures. When judgement calls are required there is a bias to show a favourable figure. The accounting regulators periodically try to close loopholes to bring accounts back to a true and fair view, but many managers and their accountants are adept at outwitting the rule setters. Every now and again there is the deafening sound of stable doors being slammed long after the horses have bolted.
- Fraud occasionally occurs in which the rules are completely flouted. WorldCom is probably a record holder for both the amount involved and for its brass-necked boldness in committing such a simple fraud. All it did was declare that $3.8 billion of operating expenses were not expenses at all and claim this money went to create assets of ongoing value to the company – see Exhibit 13.1.

Experts amazed at simplest trick in the accounts book

by **Andrew Hill** in New York

Do not expect to see any complex Enron-style diagrams detailing the alleged accounting fraud at WorldCom: judged on the available information, accounting experts agree that what the telecommunications company did was one of the simplest accounting tricks in the book.

Robert Willens, accounting analyst at Lehman Brothers, said yesterday: 'There is no great issue as to the proper treatment of these items. The thing that has to bother you was how in the world this was missed. This is the most fundamental accounting issue: whether to capitalise or expense an outlay.'

According to WorldCom, some $3.8bn was transferred from 'line cost expenses' to capital in 2001 and the first quarter of this year.

This has several flattering effects on the key measures of the company's performance at a point at which it was under intense scrutiny as the telecoms bubble of the late 1990s deflated.

- Assets can be depreciated over a long period, therefore WorldCom avoided having to record an immediate cash cost, and inflated net income.
- The depreciating cost of these 'assets' did not show up in earnings before interest, tax and depreciation (ebitda), one of the most important measures of WorldCom's financial health. After the restatement, 2001 ebitda was $6.3bn rather than the $10.5bn declared, and in the first quarter of 2002 it was $1.4bn rather than $2.2bn.
- Capital expenditure was inflated by the transfer of expenses to assets.
- On the other hand, line costs were obviously higher than reported. In 2001, WorldCom said it had edged up from 40 per cent to 42 per cent of revenues. But in reality they had leapt to 50 per cent of revenues.

Accountancy experts agree that there are grey areas in accounting standards on how to capitalise spending. As a result, the literature lists numerous cases of aggressive and improper capitalisation of expenses.

... the company said in its 2001 annual report that the 'principal components of line costs are access charges and transport charges' – essentially payments for the use of other companies' telecoms networks.

Mr Carcello says: 'That's paying for a service during a particular period. I don't know how you argue that that's part of a physical asset that's going to have a 10, 20 or 30-year life.'

Second, according to WorldCom's brief account of what happened, the expenses were not wrongly classified as capital assets, they were 'transferred' to capital accounts. That suggests that these were costs formally recorded as expenses and then simply switched to the capital line when the accounts were drawn up.

Exhibit 13.1 How WorldCom cooked the books

Source: *Financial Times* 27 June 2002

This chapter cannot protect you against out-and-out fraud, but it can explain a number of areas of accounting in which judgement calls have to be made and where there is sufficient lack of clarity in the rules for a potential bias to creep in and open up the possibility of producing artificially increasing profits, or higher asset levels than are truly warranted. Following this chapter you should understand the high degree of flexibility in accounting data and the potential for enhancing companies' reported performance through circumventions of the spirit of the accounting regulations. You will view accounts with a questioning mind and make sure you are aware of the company's accounting policies and the implications behind them. Remember: if it looks too good to be true, then it probably is.

Goodwill

When one company acquires another there is usually a difference between the fair value of the assets acquired and the price paid. The difference is termed **goodwill**. The significance of this is best explained through an example. Imagine that Stephenson Brunel Ltd has been operating for 50 years and is making profits of £20 million per year. The assets on its balance sheet have a **stated** and a **fair value**[1] of £100 million after subtracting all liabilities (i.e. £100 million represents the net assets).

You and I are owners of a railway company in another part of the country and we decide to offer £220 million to buy all the shares in Stephenson Brunel. Our offer price is based primarily on the earnings potential of the business, not on its net assets. The offer is accepted. We have paid £120 million above the asset value. This is motivated by our high regard for the company's economic franchise – for example, it has a near monopoly position (economic franchises are discussed in Chapter 15).

Stephenson Brunel now becomes a subsidiary of our company, and consolidated accounts are prepared. But how do we draw up a balance sheet? Prior to the acquisition we held £220 million in cash as one of our assets in the balance sheet. We exchanged this for £100 million of assets. There is a gap of £120 million. To solve this problem the accountant places in the balance sheet a £120 million asset called 'goodwill'. Now the books will balance: £220 million buys £100 million of tangible assets plus £120 million of the intangible asset called goodwill.

Goodwill = Price paid – Fair value of assets acquired.

What happens next can make a huge difference to the balance sheet, the profit and loss account and to various measures of performance. In the UK, until 1998 companies were permitted to write off purchased goodwill through the balance sheet. Immediately goodwill seemed to simply vanish from the accounts.[2] Managers liked this approach for

[1] The stated value is the value derived from the accounts. The fair value is the amount an asset could be exchanged for in an arm's-length transaction between informed and willing parties.

[2] However, the rules insisted that some note on accumulated goodwill write-offs be presented in the notes to the accounts.

two reasons. Firstly, because profits in the year of acquisition and all future profits do not have to suffer the burden of an annual expense of writing off a portion of the goodwill through the profit and loss accounts year by year; it was all written off in one year – moreover, it was written off via the balance sheet, so the profits did not take a hit. Secondly, reducing the net assets of the firm by £120 million makes managers look good when they are judged by a return-on-capital measure, such as return on capital employed. The denominator (capital) is reduced while the numerator (profit) does not suffer. Managers begin to look like geniuses because they appear to be making high profits on a lower capital base.

Accountants pondered these distortions and concluded that, generally, acquired goodwill does in fact decline in value over time, and so needs to be **amortised** (depreciated) in a similar fashion to tangible assets, such as machinery. It should not be assigned a zero value in the year of acquisition. The new (since 1998) rule is that purchased goodwill should be **capitalised** (i.e. placed in the balance sheet at its purchase value) and then amortised over the asset's useful economic life, up to a maximum of 20 years in most cases.

Now imagine you are a director needing to show good profit figures and you know that £120 million of purchased goodwill has to be apportioned as an expense to the profit and loss account over 'its useful economic life'. You can see there is considerable room for debate on the length of time representing this asset's useful economic life. Would you tend to plump for a write-off over, say, 6 years, so that £20 million comes off your profit in each of the next 6 years? Or would you go for the longest period possible, 20 years, in which case only £6 million is amortised each year? Well now, guess what the vast majority of firms 'estimate' the length of 'useful economic life' to be. Yes, it's 20 years! Does this reflect reality in terms of the true value of the intangible assets over time? I doubt it. Obsolescence, competitor action, and changes in the market environment can have a devastating impact, and many firms lose their business franchises in as little as 2–3 years.

Also, under the new rules, companies can amortise over more than 20 years, or even not amortise at all, if they can show that the balance sheet entry shows a reasonable valuation. (However, if they choose either of these methods the assets must be reviewed each year to see if it is being impaired.) If it has been impaired then the goodwill must be written down in the balance sheet and the loss is shown separately in the profit and loss account (as **a goodwill impairment charge**). This is all very reasonable. The problem is that the numbers used are based on estimates and forecasts made by the *company*. Many firms claim values for purchased goodwill that you or I might question.

All the discussion so far applies to purchased ('acquired') goodwill. What about **goodwill** that is **generated internally**? Most company's shares are worth a lot more than the net assets total shown in the balance sheet. The stock market values a company on the basis of its future earnings, which, in turn, come from *all* its 'assets', including those not measured in a balance sheet, such as extraordinarily good reputations or strong relationships with customers. This internally generated goodwill cannot be shown in the accounts – any figure selected would be too subjective. Stock market investors are left to value this on their own.

There are, however, some intangible assets that can be valued on the balance sheet. These are intangibles for which it is possible to get a reasonably firm grasp on the cost of creating or buying them. For example, while most **research and development (R&D) expenditure** is written off in the year in which it occurs (i.e. the profit figure is reduced) it is possible for a UK company to argue that the R&D expense is for a separately identifiable project for which there is almost complete assurance of continued success. In this case the expenditure can be **capitalised**, that is, shown as an asset on the balance sheet, and then the expense to the profit and loss account (amortisation of the asset) is spread out over many years. **Copyrights**, **licences** (e.g. book makers' licence to operate), **patents**, **brands** and **trademarks** may also be capitalised and amortised over their useful lives.[3] With all of these intangibles there is considerable room for disagreement about appropriate values over time and the amount that should be deducted from the profit and loss account each year.

Points to watch out for when viewing goodwill and other intangibles in accounts include the following:

- Amortisation generally takes place by an arbitrary amount over an arbitrary time period. However, as a safeguard, the policy adopted must be clearly stated in the accounts.
- Goodwill and other intangibles are frequently **not depreciating** assets in the everyday sense of really losing value. When analysing a company it might be advisable to add back the amount of amortisation to the year's profit and loss account to obtain a measure of **normalised earnings**. You could also add back goodwill accumulated over many years to obtain a more realistic net asset figure.
- Following an acquisition, expenditures designed to maintain the real underlying goodwill of the business (e.g. by building up a brand) will not be shown as an asset but will be written off as an expense against the year's profit. The analyst may modify this by capitalising some expenditure, thereby obtaining a clearer picture of profit.
- Goodwill amortisation penalises companies that acquire businesses with a higher proportion of intangible assets. Be careful when comparing one company with another.
- In some companies goodwill and other intangibles may be eroding much faster than the amortised rate. The analyst will need to reduce the profit and balance sheet asset figures to account for this.
- A company showing significant regular goodwill impairment charges should be viewed with scepticism. This may indicate that the company has a habit of overpaying for acquisitions. Many technology companies showed a tendency to regularly write off goodwill in the boom.

[3] To be capitalised it must be possible to separate these assets from the rest of the business and sell them. There must be a 'readily ascertainable market' for internally generated assets to be valued in the accounts.

All the above adjustments by the analyst are, of course, subjective and imprecise, but are nevertheless better than simply ignoring the issue. The adjustments can have profound effects on key measures such as net assets, gearing, earnings per share and return on capital employed.

Fair value

When a company is acquired its assets are revalued at fair value on the acquisition date for the purposes of consolidation in the group accounts. In the Stephenson Brunel example we assumed that the fair value of net assets was £100 million (which for the sake of simplicity, is the same as the stated value in Stephenson Brunel's balance sheet). This left £120 million of goodwill. Given the scope for discretion in this area it might be possible for the directors to argue that the assets are in fact worth only £50 million. Auditors might then agree, and £50 million is placed in the consolidated balance sheet. Goodwill in the balance sheet therefore rises to £170 million (£220m – £50m). Perhaps you may say that the directors have acted prudently and made sensible provision for the potential of asset devaluation. But what if next year these assets are sold for £180 million? Well, the profit and loss account gets a boost of £130 million because of the 'profit' on the differences between the 'fair' value of the assets (£50 million) and the sale proceeds (£180 million). Thus profits can be massaged by marking down fair values of acquired assets. There are also (dubious) benefits prior to selling the assets: a lower capital figure in the balance sheet improves the return on capital employed performance measure; depreciation is lower and so less is coming off the profit figure each year; undervaluing stock items reduces future cost of sales to enhance profits; undervaluing debtors will help a later year's operating profit if customers eventually pay more than the stated amount owed.

What was our revenue again?

The trick of bringing forward revenue from future years into this year is an old one. Sales are not easy to define. Do you recognise sales revenue when the order is placed, when you receive cash from the customer, or when the goods or services are delivered to the customer? For a retailer the issue of revenue recognition is usually simple: a sale takes place when the goods are handed over and payment is received. But revenue is more difficult to allocate to particular years when the revenue bridges different years. For example, imagine a long-term contract to build and service a power station. The order is placed in 2001, construction begins in 2002, the first payments are received in 2003 and ongoing annual service activity is expected from 2004. What revenues do you allocate to each year? Xerox faced a similar issue and was heavily criticised by the regulator for wrongly accelerating the recognition of equipment revenue by $3 billion. Further examples are shown in Exhibit 13.2. When there is doubt about the veracity of the figures, the analyst will want to look at cash flow to see when the cash from sales actually turns up.

Opening a blind eye to tech stocks' figure-flattering

Investors and analysts are concerned some companies are exploiting holes in accounting rules, say *Caroline Daniel* and *Michael Peel*

Investors and analysts are growing increasingly concerned that some companies are exploiting holes in accounting rules to give their turnover a more flattering look.

Institutions complain that their search for potential winners in volatile markets is hindered by companies that confuse the issue by booking tomorrow's sales today.

Last month, shares in Lucent, the telecommunications equipment maker, fell sharply after it said it had overstated turnover because of a suspected accounting irregularlity. The company refused to reveal further details of what it called a 'revenue recognition issue' until an investigation had been completed.

... the boundaries become more blurred in sectors such as software, where companies might have ongoing obligations to provide customers with services such as advice and upgrades.

Some software businesses, such as Logica, take a prudent approach and recognise the sales in increments as they complete their contract.

But others take the more adventurous option of booking the full value of the sale as soon as product is handed over, even though their obligations may continue for many months.

Changes in revenue recognition policies can have a big impact, as ITNet, the computer services company, illustrated last month.

The group announced it would take a profits write-off of between £10m and £11m this year as a result of changing its accounting policy for long-term contracts.

Another case in point is Cedar, the software group, which suffered a poor take-up of its rights issue in October after a note from Collins Stewart, the stockbroker, questioned its revenue recognition policy. 'Cedar brought this issue to the fore, but it is by no means unique' said one fund manager. Mike Harrison, chief executive of Cedar, insisted the group's accounting policies were in line with those of other UK software companies.

A key point is that companies taking an aggressive line on accounting are not contravening any regulations, because Britain lacks clear standards on revenue recognition.

Exhibit 13.2 Flattering the figures

Source: *Financial Times* 1 December 2000

■ Exceptional items

When companies issue press releases about their results they tend to emphasise 'profit before exceptional items'. This is, profit that does not take account of items which are the result of ordinary activities but are large and unusual (e.g. a large bad debt, windfall profits, merger bid defence costs or losses on the disposal of a subsidiary). Companies are obliged to report both profit before and after deduction of exceptionals. It makes some sense to exclude unusual events so that the underlying trend can be seen. However, directors tend to want to direct your attention to the figure that puts them in the best light. Profit figures feed through to reported earnings per share and if directors can get investors to focus on the 'sustainable', 'maintainable' or 'normalised' earnings which exclude exceptionals then the share price might increase.

There is also the problem of defining what is an exceptional occurrence. It is funny how directors can be persuaded to include or exclude an exceptional item depending on whether it will have a positive or negative impact on reported figures. Dixons included a £9.5 million profit on the disposal of property as a non-exceptional item and was heavily criticised for it – see Exhibit 13.3.

Dixons comes under fire over property gains

By Peter Smith

Dixons yesterday came under fire for its accounting practices, as the electricals retailer reported an underlying annual profits increase of 7 per cent.

JP Morgan's retail analysts yesterday said UK profits had been helped by property disposals and provisions. 'Overall we were disappointed with Dixons results,' they said in a circular to clients.

Dixons yesterday reported group profits before exceptionals up 7 per cent to £297m. However, this included a £9.5m profit on disposal of developed properties. Excluding that gain meant Dixons' UK profits fell slightly to £244.1m, rather than increasing by 4 per cent to £253.6m.

One Dixons shareholder said yesterday it was 'not happy' about the accounting for property gains.

Exhibit 13.3 Accounting for property gains

Source: *Financial Times* 27 June 2002

The case of Unilever demonstrates the flexibility management have over presenting figures and highlights the focus of analysts on profits after exceptional items, the amortisation of goodwill and other intangibles – see Exhibit 13.4.

Unilever acts on revamping

By Adam Jones, Consumer Industries Correspondent

Unilever is to tighten its treatment of restructuring costs, after it completes its current burst of plant closures and job shedding.

In a move that continues the debate on the appropriate use of exceptional charges, the maker of Lipton tea and Dove soap said that, from 2005, restructuring costs would be included in a key performance measure. It said the aim was to present a clear and simple picture to investors and to keep management on its toes.

Unilever's preferred measure of operating profit margin currently excludes restructuring costs, because it has been closing dozens of factories and shedding thousands of jobs as part of its 'Path to Growth' programme and the integration of Bestfoods. The costs are disclosed separately.

'We had a genuinely exceptional period,' said Niall FitzGerald, co-chairman. The new approach, which will apply after 'Path to Growth' concludes at the end of 2004, will mean that as much as €500m (£322m) a year of restructuring costs will no longer be excluded from its benchmark calculation of operating margin.

Rudy Markham, finance director, said this means future restructuring projects may have to compete with each other, because Unilever may not be able to fund them all while sticking to its target of a 16 per cent-plus operating margin.

Yesterday, shares in the Anglo-Dutch consumer products group rose 9 per cent to 562½p after it reported better-than-forecast second quarter profit.

Excluding exceptional items, amortisation of goodwill and intangibles – the measure favoured by analysts – earnings per share rose 32 per cent in the second quarter at constant exchange rates, significantly more than the rise of about 20 per cent forecast by the company a month ago.

Sales of its leading brands rose 4.4 per cent in the quarter and underlying sales rose 3.3 per cent. Unilever said it was now expecting 'mid teens' percentage growth in underlying earnings per share, compared with its earlier estimate of low double digits.

In the half year to June 30, sales fell 1 per cent to €25.6bn at constant exchange rates. Pre-tax profit rose 12 per cent to €2.3bn. Earnings per share rose 1 per cent to 16.77 cents.

Exhibit 13.4 What price restructuring?

Source: *Financial Times* 1 August 2002

Stock (inventory) valuation

Year-end stock displayed in a company's balance sheet normally consists of a mixture of raw materials, work in progress (incomplete items still being worked on) and finished goods ready for sale. The rule on stock valuation is that it should be shown on the balance sheet at cost or net realisable value (what someone might reasonably expect to pay for it), whichever is lower.

Identifying the cost of some items of stock is relatively easy. If the company buys 100 tonnes of steel as a raw material input to its processes then it has invoices to look at. But consider the difficulty of valuing an incomplete car half way down an assembly line. You might be able to isolate the costs of the material actually used, but how much of the factory overheads and the company's general overhead should be allocated to the cost calculation for the car? **Overheads** are business expenses that range over the operations as a whole and are not directly chargeable to a particular part of the work or product. So the costs of the factory managers and the factory rent relate to the costs of all cars produced in the year and not to any particular one. The accountant, when valuing a half-finished car, will add together the easily identifiable direct costs with the difficult-to-apportion production overhead costs. With overhead allocation there is much room for disagreement and also much room for putting on a positive gloss. The higher the year-end value, the lower the cost of manufacturing the cars sold during the year and therefore the higher the profit figures. A £1,000 increase in year-end stock value feeds into a £1,000 rise in profits. Also the balance sheet can be shown in a healthier light, with more assets relative to debts.

For retailers and wholesalers the valuation of stocks should be easy – they buy finished goods – but even here serious errors can be made, as the example of T.J. Hughes shows – see Exhibit 13.5. We are not told the exact problems in this case, but one of the difficulties for retailers is to know when to classify stock items as 'dead', that is, as having become an irrecoverable cost that should be charged to revenue. The carrying forward of 'dead' stock at the amount it cost is a classic way of artificially boosting profits – or rather, failing to recognise losses.

Stock discrepancy knocks TJ Hughes

By David Blackwell

The finance director of TJ Hughes resigned yesterday as the rapidly expanding chain of discount stores warned that a discrepancy in its stock valuation would knock up to £3m from last year's profits.

The shares tumbled 114p to 206p as analysts lopped forecasts for the year to January 31 from £8m to £5m.

The overstatement of the value of the stock emerged as the company switched over to its fully integrated electronic point of sale computer system, which became fully functional at the beginning of this year. KPMG has been appointed to review both the management information systems and the stock valuation.

'We are selling at a lower margin than we thought,' said George Foster, chief executive. 'The shortfall goes back several years, and that has compounded to reach this amount.' He said about £700,000 related to last year and described the £3m as a one-off hit. But, going forward, gross margins would be down from 32 to 31 per cent.

Exhibit 13.5 A company takes stock

Source: *Financial Times* 9 March 2001

Depreciation

Imagine that your company has just purchased a state-of-the-art computer-controlled machine for its manufacturing operations at a price of £20 million. The managing director estimates that it will have a useful economic life of 10 years and at the end have a second-hand sale value of £1 million. She is in favour of **straight-line depreciation**, which means that the same amount is charged each year to the profit and loss account for the cost of using the machine.[4] The cost less the residual value is £19 million. This is divided by 10 years to give a depreciation charge of £1.9 million per year.

The production director, on the other hand, thinks that the machine will wear out much more quickly. He prefers to use the **declining (reducing) balance method of depreciation.** He thinks the appropriate rate in this case is 25 per cent per year. Thus the machine will be depreciated each year by 25 per cent of the balance sheet value at the start of the year. In the first year £5 million is charged to the profit and loss (25 per cent × £20 million). In the second year 25% of £15 million (balance sheet value at end of first year) is charged (£3.75 million). In the third 25% of £11.25 million is charged (£2.81 million) and so on.

Both methods are permitted under the accounting rules, and yet choosing one rather than the other can have a dramatic effect on profit and asset levels. Imagine that profit before the depreciation expense is charged is £8 million per year, the machine represents the only asset the firm has and there is no debt. Then the profit patterns under these two methods look quite different (Table 13.1). Profit appears to be on a rising trend in the second case – it will soon overtake the static profit in the first case.

After 4 years the asset value is still over £12.4 million under the straight-line method, but only £6.33 million under the declining balance method. Imagine that the numbers in Table 13.1 represent two identical firms, and that the only difference is the method used for depreciation of fixed assets. If you were analysing these four years you would need to dig out the notes to the accounts in the hope that you could find the basis on which depreciation was calculated and then make adjustments in order to compare the performance and balance sheet strength of the two. Of course, you should discover that the two, at base, are identical, but frequently there is insufficient information to reach that conclusion and the superficial appearance of the profit and loss account and balance sheet persuades investors that one company is more sound than the other when the only difference is the optimism/pessimism of the management about a long-term asset that may or may not have a 10-year life.

Even worse, although the two depreciation methods shown are the most commonly used, they are not the only ones permitted – there are at least four other methods for managers to choose from at their discretion. In addition, companies can play tricks by being more optimistic on the **residual value** (the sale value of the asset when the com-

[4] The term 'depreciation' is generally applied to tangible fixed assets, whereas 'amortisation' is used for intangible assets.

Table 13.1 Two methods of depreciation

Year	1	2	3	4
	£m	£m	£m	£m
Straight-line method				
Profit before depreciation	8.0	8.0	8.0	8.0
Straight-line depreciation charge	(1.9)	(1.9)	(1.9)	(1.9)
Profit after straight-line depreciation	6.1	6.1	6.1	6.1
Declining balance method				
Profit before depreciation	8.0	8.0	8.0	8.0
Declining balance depreciation charge	(5.0)	(3.75)	(2.81)	(2.11)
Profit after declining balance depreciation	3.0	4.25	5.19	5.89
Effect on the balance sheet at end of year:				
Value of asset under straight-line depreciation	18.1	16.2	14.3	12.4
Value of asset under declining balance method	15.0	11.25	8.44	6.33

pany has finished with it). The potential for manipulation is huge, and all within the rules of the game.

Managers sometimes change the depreciation policy, sometimes for legitimate reasons (e.g. the asset suddenly has a new lease of life and should be depreciated in a different way), sometimes simply to make the accounts look better. So what is the investor to do? The answer is to examine the statement on depreciation methodology in the report and accounts. You can also derive evidence on depreciation policy change by comparing the amount of depreciation with the value of assets: do the proportions change over time? A fall from 12 per cent to 5 per cent, for instance, may set alarm bells ringing, as managers may be deliberately underestimating wear and tear and obsolescence of assets.

Capitalisation

When a company spends money on something there are two possible consequences: either an asset is acquired which then goes into the balance sheet; or there is an expense to be charged to the profit and loss. It is possible to boost profit and the balance sheet asset values by taking the view that a greater proportion of spending is for the acquisition of assets rather than for expenses. With assets such as buildings there is little problem with stating a capital value in the balance sheet. However, with spending on items like research and development we have the potential for rose-tinted spectacle distortion. As stated earlier, companies are allowed to capitalise R&D expenditure for clearly defined projects with near-certain commercial success – that is, show it on the balance sheet as an asset. This subjective test is all the flexibility that creative accountants need. Alongside R&D expenditure managers are permitted to capitalise interest on a project during construction. So a property construction company that paid £100,000 for building land, £900,000 to build and £200,000 of interest during construction may have a stated balance sheet value for that property of £1.2 million. Under the rules capitalisation of interest is supposed to stop after completion of the building. However, some companies have been known to extend this period of 'construction' over a considerable time period, thus tying up more interest as an 'asset' in the balance sheet. Supermarkets often capitalise the interest incurred while building a supermarket. This is then written off gradually under the company's normal depreciation policy. Capitalisation of interest has also been used by ship and aircraft manufacturers, and producers of whisky (a 'good' that takes a long time to 'construct'). The problem is that some managers and acquiescent accountants/auditors have taken the process too far.

The analyst needs to take particular care when calculating the interest cover ratio (see Chapter 12) for a company with a propensity to capitalise interest. The interest paid and charged to the profit and loss can be a small fraction of that sent straight to the balance sheet to be capitalised. You need to add both interest figures together to get a view on the level of payments to lenders relative to profits.

It is also considered acceptable to capitalise some starting-up costs (e.g. costs of running in new machinery or testing equipment). Again the absence of precise definitions for what can and can't be capitalised provides the loophole some managers and accountants are looking for.

The decision whether to capitalise an item seems to be influenced by the financial strengths of the company. Take the case of BSkyB (financially strong) on the one hand, and NTL and Telewest (no profits and very weak balance sheets) on the other. BSkyB writes off the cost of supplying set-top boxes as an operating expense, whereas NTL and Telewest declare that they have a capital value and are shown on the balance sheet. Perhaps the fact that their boxes are leased (and so can be returned) rather than given to customers justifies this accounting treatment. Have a look at Exhibit 13.6 to judge for yourself whether managers are clutching at accounting straws to save their companies, or are objectively using prudent accounting policies.

Off-balance sheet items

Investors may be worried not about the treatment of items that are actually shown in the balance sheet, but about commitments the company has entered into, but which are *not* shown in the balance sheet. These off balance sheet items can seem to appear out of the blue to destroy a company. For example, Enron, the disgraced Texas energy trader, used **special-purpose entities** to manipulate its profits and the appearance of its balance

Renewed scrutiny for cable industry

By Carlos Grande and Juliana Ratner

The debt-laden cable companies, NTL and Telewest, could have to justify the long-standing industry practice of treating the provision of set-top boxes to customers as a capital cost.

BSkyB, the satellite operator, treats the cost of boxes and installations as operating expenses it incurs as soon as customers start receiving its service.

But if the cable operators followed BSkyB's method, the result would be to depress reported earnings before interest, tax, depreciation and amortisation. Analysts said the impact of that change would stretch from missed targets for bank covenants and credit ratings to management bonus schemes.

Cable executives, however, said targets rendered impossible by accounting treatments such as writing off boxes as expenses were unlikely to be agreed.

As market sentiment has turned against the loss-making cable operators, ebitda has in practice been largely ignored by investors focused on the real cash position of companies.

Sceptics point out that NTL continued to meet or exceed its ebitda targets even when it was close to bankruptcy. Telewest has also outperformed ebitda targets, yet equity and bond investors have sent its shares and bonds crashing.

Executives from both companies have also been criticised by investors for receiving and accepting cash bonuses – some based on ebitda – for 2001 despite collapsing share prices.

Both cable operators have high capital expenditure. Telewest reported capital expenditure of £653m in 2001, and NTL UK £1.1bn.

Much of this was spent on building and upgrading fixed line cable networks, which most analysts agreed was capital spending on an asset. Programming costs were treated as expenses.

Analysts and independent consultants accepted there was also a rationale for treating some cable costs differently from those at BSkyB. Cable boxes are leased to customers. If customers opt to stop taking services or move out of a cable area, the operator will take the boxes back.

By contrast, BSkyB does not recoup boxes. It views an installation as a one-off customer cost. One exception was when Telewest wrote off the cost of all its old analogue boxes.

Analysts add that the capital required to provide cable service – from digging up roads, to running cable into homes and installing boxes – is greater than that needed by satellite companies. One analyst said: 'There is no right or wrong to this. The issue is how much you capitalise.'

Exhibit 13.6 What shall we do with the set-top boxes?

Source: *Financial Times* 27 June 2002

sheet. Special-purpose entities are set up as separate organisations and their accounts are not consolidated with the rest of the group – which can be useful if you want to hide a vast amount of debt or expenses. Not all special-purpose entities should be viewed with suspicion; some have legitimate uses, for example, to finance a research and development partnership with another company, or for repackaging some of the company's assets and then selling these on to investors **(securitisation)**. However, special-purpose entities are a useful tool in the hands of dishonest managers.

In the UK there have been fewer scandals with special-purpose entities and other off balance sheet financing techniques than in the US. Perhaps this is due to the accounting rules insisting that, regardless of the technical position, managers and accountants are required to report the substance of a transaction. Accounts are supposed to reflect the underlying reality of the situation. Having said that, some grey areas remain. For example, banks take on numerous risks in the derivatives markets. They might have to face significant liabilities if certain events come to pass (e.g. interest rates rise or fall by large amounts. Many of these risks do not appear in the accounts).

Another grey area is the presentation of **lease commitments**. Take a company needing to acquire the use of a new machine. It could go out and buy the machine for £1 million, using a bank loan to do it. A disadvantage of this is that the debt–equity ratio (gearing) rises because of the new loan. An alternative is to lease the machine for say, £10,000 per month. The company has not borrowed £1 million and so the balance sheet is not burdened. However, with many of these lease agreements the company is making a strong a legally binding commitment to make regular payments: at least as strong as it would if it was paying off a bank loan. So the substance is much the same, whether the asset is leased or bought with a bank loan. Back in the 1980s the accounting profession made a big step in closing this loophole. If the lease transfers substantially all the risks and rewards of ownership of an asset to the company over the course of the lease then it has to be classified as a **finance lease**, which means the machine is recorded as an asset and the obligation to pay future rentals is recorded as a liability on the balance sheet.

Other leases are referred to as **operating leases**. The assets and liabilities under operating leases do not have to be displayed on the balance sheet. While many lease obligations are made explicit to investors, this remains a tricky area because it is often very difficult to declare one lease as 'transferring substantially all the risk and rewards of ownership' and another lease as not doing so. Airlines, for example, are very adept at signing up for aircraft rentals that just fall into the category of operating leases and thereby clear their accounts of large numbers of aircraft as assets, and the associated leases as liabilities.

Another off balance sheet liability is the amount companies owe to the **pension scheme** set up for employees. Much heated discussion is currently taking place as to whether companies should place this as a liability on their balance sheet. The case for ignoring it is that the amount owed varies from one year to the next and so the accounts would become volatile for reasons unconnected with underlying trading. Investors would then be confused by the extra information, and this would lead to wrongly priced shares. This is a self-serving argument in most cases. Some companies have pension liabilities that dwarf the assets of the business. British Airways, for example, has been described as a pension fund with an interesting sideline in flying.

■ Share (stock) options

Imagine you own 50 per cent of the shares in X plc. There are 10 million shares in issue. The company has a share option scheme in which directors are entitled to buy, in 3 years' time, 1 million shares at £1 each (the same as the current share price). Now imagine that the 3 years have passed and the share price has risen to £3. The directors have a bonanza. They can now exercise the option to purchase £3 million worth of shares for a third of the price.

This type of scheme is quite common and can be useful to incentivise managers. However, the difficulty comes in accounting for share options. Suppose the company at the end of the 3 years is making annual profits of £2 million, so before the exercise of the options you, as a 50 per cent shareholder, have a £1 million claim on the profits – 20p per share. If the options are exercised the number of shares in issue rises to 11 million. Then each share has a claim on only £2m/11m = 18.18p. Your claim is 5m × 0.1818 = £909,090. You have lost out because the directors now have a claim on 9 per cent of the company's profits.[5] This is a cost to you, the shareholder.

Most companies fail to properly acknowledge share options as a cost to the shareholders – the best that is offered is a note in the accounts. Thousands of directors have become very wealthy as a result of share option schemes. That wealth has come from somewhere, and yet rarely is the cost to shareholders properly recorded. Sure, the earnings per share figure can be 'diluted' to allow for the possibility of the issue of additional shares, but the headline profit reported on the face of the accounts generally ignores the cost.

If managers had been incentivised through a cash bonus scheme of £2 million, this would have been a highly visible and profit would have been depressed. Given this, why not express share option-based transfer of shareholder wealth as a cost? The accounting regulators are currently battling with directors over this issue – as you will occasionally see in the press. Until the issue is resolved the investor is advised to pay close attention to diluted earning per share calculations.

Other tricks

- In the dot.com boom directors got into the habit of emphasising '**pro-forma**' accounting numbers when announcing results. This was a deliberate distraction tactic employed by companies that made accounting losses. Pro-forma numbers remove many negative items from the profit and loss account in a manner that may not, in any way, comply with the accounting rules. Pay no attention to pro-forma figures.
- Companies sometimes try to load losses on to **operations** that are going to be **discontinued**. Because continuing businesses and discontinued businesses are separated in the profit and loss account, it becomes possible to direct investors' attention to the continuing business and then bury losses in the non-continuing businesses section.
- Firms sometimes fail to **write-off worthless assets**.

[5] Admittedly, directors have boosted the company's cash by £1 million, but this is insufficient to offset the loss.

- Fun and games can also be had with **changes in foreign exchange rates** impacting on assets, liabilities, revenues and costs, but that is a complication too far for an introductory investment book.

Concluding comment

So what is the time-pressed investor to do, given all this potential for trickery? First of all, don't panic. The vast majority of managers are honest and like to present an accurate picture of the state of affairs of the company. Even those tempted to flatter the figures will be restrained by the accounting standards and the necessity of adding a note to the accounts where they have viewed an element in a particularly favourable light. They are also inclined to integrity by the fact that a lot of the tricks will be revealed to investors over the medium term – they might get away with it for a year or two but eventually the truth will out. Smart managers, with a long-term career to think about, recognise the necessity of straight dealing. Most try to avoid weaving tangled webs.

Having said that, not all managers and accountants are as straight as we would like, so here is a list of what you can do to avoid being taken for a ride:

- **Pay close attention to the notes to the accounts.** Many analysts read the accounts backwards working from the notes, through the cash flows, balance sheets and profit and loss until finally reaching the points that were supposed to impress (and possibly mislead) them at the front of the annual report and accounts. Reading the notes first will highlight issues tucked away, such as goodwill, amortisation, exceptional items and capitalised interest that will not be presented in the profit and loss, balance sheet and cash flows. When you reach the main accounts you will have the information to allow you to make adjustments so that ratio analysis is more meaningful. When reading the accounts ask yourself which numbers you would manipulate if you wanted to bias the figures.
- **Get data from other sources.** Brokers' reports can give a critical appraisal of the company's accounts. You can obtain information about the directors' past lives by, say, conducting an Internet search – tap their names into a search engine and see what comes up. Industry analyses are available from the specialist websites ICC (*www.icc.co.uk*), Dun and Bradstreet (*www.dnb.com*), Datastream (*www.datastream.com*) and Fame (*www.fame.bvdep.com*).
- **Focus on cash.** Being creative with cash flow figures is much more difficult than being creative with profits and balance sheets. Be sceptical about companies that show high and rising profits with low cash flow. A very useful measure is the cash return on capital employed in the business. It suffers far less from biased accounting than earnings-based measures.
- **Check accounting policies.** If accounting policies (e.g. on depreciation) have changed from the previous year then watch for the effect on profits. Ask questions

such as: does the reduction in depreciation boost profit artificially, or is it justified? If there is not enough information in the accounts then you could ring the **investor relations department** of the firm to ask for an explanation of the accounting policies.

- **Meet the management.** The issues of creative accounting and fraud are fundamentally issues of trust. If you attend AGMs and regularly scrutinise the directors' public statements you may instinctively sniff out suspicious characters. For instance, if managers one year try to direct your attention to earning per share, and the next to EBITDA, and in the third year they emphasise operating profits, you may start to suspect that they are more interested in short-term appearances than in creating long-term value. They are certainly not interested in communicating their (inevitable bumpy) progress in a frank and unspun way. If year after year the firm comes up with pathetic excuses such as an 'early Easter' or 'bad weather' for poor performance rather than occasionally putting their hands up and saying that the strategy had gone awry, you have reason to doubt the management's honesty – with themselves, let alone with investors.
- **If in doubt, don't take a punt.** If you are not sure about the quality of the numbers, or cannot see clearly what is going on, then don't allocate some of your precious fund to the company. Investors can afford to let many balls go past them until they get a perfect pitch that they can hit cleanly and relatively safely.

Further reading

G. Holmes, A. Sugden and P. Gee *Interpreting Company Reports and Accounts*, 8th edition (Financial Times Prentice Hall, 2002) and T. Smith, *Accounting for Growth*, 2nd edition (Random House Business Books, 1996) provide plenty of detail on accounting trickery.

14

Analysing industries

The examination and analysis of the report and accounts tells us a lot about the company's past performance. The questions we must now ask are: How sustainable is that past performance? What potential is there for improvement in the future? The answers to these questions depend not only on the financial strength of the company, but also on the type of industry or industries in which the company operates, its possession or otherwise of extraordinary resources allowing it to perform well in the industry (i.e. to achieve returns on capital invested in real assets significantly above the industry average) and the honesty and competence of the managerial team. This chapter focuses on the first of these factors: the analysis of industries.

There are some crucial factors that determine the average long-run rate of return on capital employed by firms in an industry. This chapter provides a framework for identifying these factors.[1]

The competitive floor

In a **perfectly competitive industry** structure, where outside firms can enter the industry at will, companies can only achieve a **'normal' rate of return**. That is, shareholders receive a rate of return that only just induces them to put money into the firm and hold it there. If returns dropped by 0.1 per cent then investors would withdraw capital from the firm and invest in an alternative with the same risk level providing the full 'normal' rate of return – eventually the firm would go out of business. With perfect competition the rate of return cannot rise above the normal level to give a **supernormal return**. Imagine if an industry did give a very high rate of return temporarily because of, say, a rise in the price of the product. **New entrants** to the industry, or additional investment by existing competitors, would quickly result in any supernormal return being competed away to take the industry back to the point where the return available is merely that appropriate for the risk level.

Obviously, a perfectly competitive industry is not attractive for investors. Investors need to search for an industry displaying a wide gap between the price of the product and its cost – one producing a high rate of return on the capital taken from shareholders and used by managers. The problem is that competitive forces within industries tend to continually narrow the gap between price and cost – to push it towards **the competitive floor** – and thus put downward pressure on the rate of return on invested capital.

However, there are some industries in which the **competitive forces** are weak, permitting supernormal returns to persist over a long period. The investor needs to search out those industries in which the average firm has a high degree of **durable pricing power**.

[1] Much of the material for this chapter is taken from G. Arnold, *Valuegrowth Investing* (Financial Times Prentice Hall, 2002).

The five competitive forces

Michael Porter produced a framework for analysing the forces driving returns to the perfectly competitive level. It goes way beyond simply analysing the degree of rivalry between existing competitors and the potential for entry of new competitors. He pointed out that customers, suppliers, and substitutes are also 'competitors' to the firms in an industry in the sense that they impose constraints on the firms achieving supernormal returns. For example, Heinz has few direct competitors, because its brand sets it apart and it has an unrivalled distribution system. It faces little threat from the entry of new competitors because the new entrant would need decades to build the necessary brand image and distribution capability. However, Heinz's management is worried because of the increasing power of its customers, the major supermarket chains. The giant food retailers are in a position to ask for more of the value generated by the sale of the product – to put it more crudely, they can hammer Heinz on price. Take another case: the music distribution industry (record producers and retailers) chief executives here are scared. It is not that particularly strong current competitors are taking greater market share and thereby becoming stronger. This is happening, but it is not the main cause of sleepless nights. Nor are they worried about the entry of new record labels and retail chains. These have come and gone before, and industry returns have remained high. No, their nightmare comes in the form of a new technology that allows consumers to download music by file-swapping on the Internet for virtually nothing. Thus a substitute distribution system is a competitive threat to the entire industry.

In a perfectly competitive situation entry is free and existing firms have no bargaining power over suppliers or customers. In addition, rivalry between existing firms is fierce because products are identical. In reality, few industries resemble perfect competition. As J.K. Galbraith once observed, the greatest source of insecurity in business is competition, and so managers strive constantly to move as far away from perfect competition as possible. How far they travel is determined by the strength of the five forces shown in Exhibit 14.1.

The five forces determine the industry structure, which in turn determines the long-run rate of return for the industry. Some industries have an appalling position *vis-à-vis* the five forces and thus make very poor returns. Take steel production in western Europe, for example. Here are some of the largest and most efficient plants in the world. As things stand, the steel firms could hire the best team of managers in the world but they would still not make good rates of return. All the five forces are against them. The suppliers of raw materials tend to be large groups with strong bargaining power (three producers dominate the world's iron-ore business, for instance). Many of their customers are enormous groups (particularly the big six car makers who are quite prepared to switch steel supplier unless the keenest prices are offered). There are dozens of low-cost new entrants in Asia and eastern Europe eager to take market share. Within Europe there is intense rivalry between the existing players because of the need for each participant to produce at a high volume due to the necessity of spreading high fixed costs. This is exacerbated by the difficulty of achieving **exit** from the industry: many companies are seen a national champions and important employers; they thus receive more than just a sympathetic ear from government. On top of all of this there is continual threat of **substitutes** – for example, the aluminium producers are a constant worry.

An industry that has proven to be even worse than steel is airlines. It is astonishing to discover that, after years of management initiatives, cost-cutting, mergers, massive marketing campaigns and all the rest, the cumulative earnings of the industry over its entire history are negative. The fact that passenger numbers grow at a rate other industries would die for (4–5 per cent per year) seems to count for nothing in terms of profitability. Suppliers are often powerful (e.g. pilot unions). Also, if an airline establishes a profitable market segment it is quickly swamped by new entrants, and by existing airlines moving planes from one part of the globe to another. Over-capacity and low prices are the result. Airlines find it difficult to shed capacity in a hurry; they buy aircraft that fly for decades. When passenger demand falls they simply cannot reduce the supply of aircraft. Exit from the industry is also inhibited by national pride, which leads to suspension of normal commercial logic allowing unprofitable companies to die.

It is worth remembering two points before we look in more detail at the framework for the analysis of industry structure. The first is that industries can change. An industry with a poor structure offering low returns can be transformed into an industry with a high rate of return on invested capital. This may come about for any number of reasons, ranging from a technological innovation that alters the entire economics of the industry (e.g. mobile phones and the Internet in the case of telecommunications) to government policy (e.g. allowing mergers to take place in the airline industry that were previously prohibited). We therefore need to obtain a dynamic rather than a static view when enquiring into an industry structure.

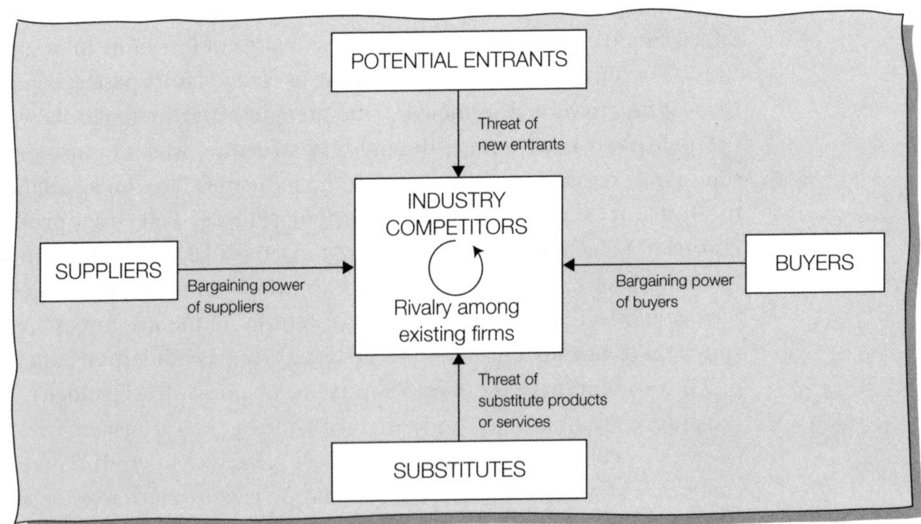

Exhibit 14.1 The five forces driving industry competition

Source: Michael Porter, *Competitive Strategy* (Free Press, 1980), p. 4.

Second, when we are talking about **rates of return on invested capital** we are referring to the rate expected **over the long term**. Transient boosts to or dampenings of profitability – from an economic boom or recession, for example – should be distinguished from the long-term underlying nature of the industry and its consequent rate of return.

The strength of each of the five forces is influenced by a number of factors. The most important of these are discussed below. This discussion will provide a checklist of factors that the investor needs to investigate.

Threat of entry

If an industry is generating a return above that available in other industries (of comparable risk) it acts as a honey pot – a swarm of hungry insects will try to enter to take away some of the honey. New entrants add to the capacity of the industry as they make a grab for market share. The result is falling prices for every firm in the industry, or the costs of the original industry players rise as they try to maintain sales by spending on marketing, favourable credit terms for customers, etc.

New entry is definitely something that the incumbent firms abhor. There are two things that can stop, or at least slow down, the advance of the insects to the honey pot. First, there could be **barriers** put in the path of the outsiders. Second, a clear message could go out to the aspiring entrants that if they did dare to cross the threshold then they would be subject to a **massive retaliatory attack** until they were driven out again. Of course, in many industries these two disincentives work in tandem.

Credibility is key to using the threat of retaliation to deter entrants. The following enhance this credibility:

- If the incumbents have shown themselves to be vigorous defenders of their honey pot in the past.
- If the incumbents have a large stock of resources with which to fight (cash, borrowing capacity, strong relationships or power over suppliers and customers, etc.).
- If the incumbents are clearly committed to the industry (e.g. the assets employed within it have few alternative uses).

Examples of industries with strong retaliatory threats include PC software and soft drinks.

Barriers to new entry come in a variety of forms – these may occur singly or in combination:

- **Large economies of scale and high capital costs.** In some industries firms operating on a small scale are at a competitive disadvantage because the average cost of their product is higher than for those companies producing at the **most efficient scale**. The aspiring entrant therefore knows that the only way it can survive in the industry is to invest massively. This narrows the field of potential entrants down to a few firms with the required financial resources. If one of these large firms did dare to commit so much money it would risk a severe reaction from the existing firms. Examples of industries protected to some degree by scale economies include brewing, aircraft engines and mid-market automobile assembly. To overcome established brands such as Mars, Coca-Cola or Nike would cost a vast amount in marketing expense. Some industries are also protected by **economies of scope** – that is, the ability to reap economies by sharing costs between a number of product lines. For example, food manufacturers can add additional product lines that make use of the same logistical network, influence with retailers and production equipment. This is one of the main motivators for mergers in this industry.

- **High risks associated with imitation.** It is not always easy to identify how it is that a successful business manages to do what it does to elevate it above the also-rans. The incumbent(s) may have special capabilities that are very difficult to emulate even if they could all be observed. The **uncertainty of being able to imitate** inhibits firms from entering the competitive arena. For example, it would be very difficult to imitate, in a credible fashion, the McKinsey method or the Goldman Sachs approach.
- **Access to distribution channels.** The obvious distribution channels are usually tied up by the existing firms. The newcomer will need to somehow break into these relationships to try to secure distribution for its product. This can be very costly. Buyers are likely to ask for substantial price-cutting and other benefits if they are to welcome a new supplier. New food manufacturers, for example, find it very difficult to attract the attention of the large retailers. Incumbents often have strong relationships and a long experience of adapting to customer demands to provide a specialist, high-quality service. These can form a very high barrier to entry. Often the only option open to an outsider is to find a completely new distribution channel (e.g. the Internet)
- **Switching costs.** It may be prohibitively expensive for the buyers of a firm's output to switch to another supplier. For example, the purchasers of aircraft spend a substantial amount training employees to fly and service the aircraft. They may invest in ancillary equipment to maintain and make best use of the planes. It would be costly to switch to another airplane manufacturer in terms of staff training and equipment. New entrants have to make an offer that is so good that it overcomes these switching costs. It would be very expensive for organisations to switch from using Microsoft's operating system and the Office suite. Any potential entrant would need to offer something very special to encourage a switch. Merely offering slightly better performance and a slightly lower price is not good enough.
- **Differentiation.** Differentiation means that the product offers something of higher value than the competition. The additional features of the offer are valued more highly than the additional cost of those features charged to the customer. For example, there are many chocolate bars on the market, but only one Dairy Milk. Once a reputation is established it is very difficult for others to usurp that position.

- **Experience.** Over time incumbents learn a great deal about their industry, their suppliers' and their buyer's industries. They develop specialist technical knowledge and a culture adapted to operating in the industry. The experienced firm can often make the product better or more cheaply then anyone else. Intel, for example, has decades of experience in developing microprocessors, which makes it very difficult for new entrants to catch up.
- **Government legislation and policy.** Patents are the most obvious barriers to entry erected by governments, but there are others. For example, restrictions on take-off and landing slots at airports, controls on over-the-counter pharmaceuticals, tariff and quota barriers keeping out foreign competition, government subsidies to favoured sectors, licensing which forecloses entry, regulation of pricing, fishing quotas, and purchase of defence equipment from domestic suppliers.
- **Control over raw materials or outlets.** The firms in the industry may have favourable access or outright control over key inputs and outlets. For example, De Beers has tremendous power to insist that diamond miners sell through them.

Intensity of rivalry of existing companies

Investors must concern themselves with the degree of **rivalrous behaviour** between the existing industry competitors. The more in-fighting there is between the companies for market share and profits, the more rates of return will be depressed. Intense rivalry can erode profits in a number of ways, as firms compete fiercely on price (any move made by one player is quickly matched by rivals), there is a tendency to spend a great deal on marketing, and firms are impelled regularly to improve the product and to introduce new products to try and stay one step ahead.

In highly rivalrous industries there is always at least one maverick trying to get ahead of competitors. They see an opportunity and go for it with all their might. Unfortunately, the advantage is short-lived as other firms follow the price reductions, marketing innovation or new improved product with their own versions. At the end of the process the whole industry can end up less profitable than before.

In industries with few companies competitors usually start to recognise their mutual interdependence and so restrain their rivalry. If the industry develops a dominant competitor, rather than a set of equally balanced competitors, rivalry is reduced – the dominant firm has a strong influence on industry prices and is able to discipline the mavericks. For highly rivalrous industries the financial press is likely to use phrases such as 'cut-throat competition' or 'price wars'. Less rivalrous industries will be described as 'stable', even 'boring' or 'gentlemanly'. Some of the factors that intensify rivalry and which can therefore be taken as bad signs for investors are:

- **Many equally balanced competitors.** Where there is no dominant player there will be fierce fighting for market share and profits. This is great for customers, but the industry would be much more profitable with a dominant player.
- **Slow industry growth.** When an industry is growing fast firms can increase sales without necessarily taking sales from other firms. In a slow-growing industry there is a tendency to intense market share rivalry. The mass-market automobile industry is a prime example – car assemblers rarely achieve a good rate of return on their massive investment; much of the time they make losses.
- **High fixed costs.** Firms with high fixed costs[2] need to have a high volume of output to spread costs over a lot of units. There is a high breakeven point. Rivals will cut prices to achieve the turnover required. Paper-making and steel manufacturers are industries that suffer from this problem. A similar tendency to slash prices to achieve rapid throughput is present in industries producing goods and services that are difficult to store (e.g. fruit, air travel).
- **Products are not differentiated.** If the product (or service) is seen as commodity-like (it is identical to that supplied by other firms) buyers will be attracted purely by price and ancillary services. Margins will be cut and rates of return constrained. For example, bricks, fertiliser and various plastics have been **commoditised**.
- **Extra capacity is added in large increments.** In some industries small increases in capacity are not possible (e.g. bulk chemicals, steel). When a large-scale plant is added chronic industry disruption can occur. Companies are tempted to fill the capacity by reducing prices. Many industries are subject to recurring bouts of over-capacity (e.g. paper, oil and plastics) as new plant is brought on-stream – usually at the peak of business cycles.
- **When rivals have different strategies, origins, personalities and relationships.** Firms in an industry may have completely different objectives, targets and strategies depending on their background, parent-company goals and corporate personalities. What seems rational action to one appears irrational industry-damaging to others. In their competitive acts they 'continually run head on into each other in the process'.[3] Family-owned firms might have a completely different attitude to public companies or foreign rivals. Tacit collusion becomes extremely difficult as they have great difficulty reading each other's signals. Rules of the game do not become established to allow each firm to earn a high return.
- **High exit barriers.** In a low return industry the logical response from managers should be to exit the market and use the resources thus released in another industry where the returns are higher. The reduced supply will benefit the firms that remain and rates of return will rise. In reality, there are often factors that prevent the exit of firms despite sub-normal returns. **Exit barriers** come in many forms:

2 Those costs that do not change as quantity produced rises.

3 Porter, M (1980) p.19.

- *Specialised assets.* If the assets of the business are useful in the one business but have no or little value in any other there may be little incentive to quit. Investment in plant, machinery, and so on may be regarded as sunk and therefore does not contribute to the economic cost of running the business. The textile industry in Europe and North America suffered from the unwillingness of firms to exit that were using increasingly old machinery – the fifty-year shake-out is continuing.
- *Fixed costs of exit.* There may be substantial costs imposed on firms when they exit an industry. For example, they may be obliged to pay large amounts under labour agreements (this is particularly the case in many countries in Europe); the divestment process itself is costly in terms of managerial time, lawyers and accountants; customers may have entitlement to after-sales service or spare parts for many years; employees may need to be retrained and reassigned; and supplier compensation may be payable for broken contracts.
- *Strategic loss.* The business may be part of an overall strategic plan. Its removal might have a severe impact on other parts of the business. Perhaps the business, although not profitable in itself, adds greatly to the image of the firm or the quality of its relationships with customers, suppliers or government, so it is well worth retaining (e.g. newspapers often make a loss, but the political leverage they bring to owners may be useful for other businesses in the group). It may share facilities that would become uneconomic for the parent without the business. Key raw material suppliers to the group may become unwilling to supply in the absence of the subsidiary. The business may be an important link in a vertically integrated chain. For example, the major oil companies have exploration operations, extraction divisions, refining business and retail outlets. One of these businesses could be underperforming (often the retail side), yet it is kept within the fold out of wider strategic considerations.
- *Emotional barriers.* In a stand-alone business the managers will tend not to exit even in the face of economic adversity. They are likely to have an emotional attachment to the business. They take pride in the quality of the product and in the efficiency of the operation. It is a business they know and love – it often has a rich history and tradition. The managers realise that they are ill suited for any other trade. These emotional ties can be especially strong in family-owned firms.
- *Government and social barriers.* Governments often step in to prevent the closure of businesses because of their concern for jobs and the community. As a result, the required capacity reduction in the industry does not take place and companies grimly hang on and battle away. The result is persistent low returns for the entire industry.

The threat from substitutes

The threat from substitutes dampens profit potential. **Substitutes** are products or services that perform the same function (at least in approximate terms). The returns available in the beverage packaging industry have a ceiling because the buyers are able to switch between steel, aluminium, glass and plastic. Book retailers' margins are under threat because the Internet has provied a substitute method of obtaining books. The threat of substitutes is worse if the cost to buyers of switching is low, and the ratio of price to performance is better. That is, the substitute may not be as good at serving the function as the existing product or service, but it is a lot cheaper (e.g. low-cost airlines); or the substitute is slightly more expensive, but significantly more effective.

Buyer (customer) power

Buyer power gives customers the potential to squeeze industry margins by forcing down prices, or pressing for higher quality or more services. Wal-Mart has achieved a great deal of buyer power. It is able to exert huge pressure on the firms in the industries producing food, clothes, garden equipment and toys. Buyers are in a strong bargaining position if one or more of the following applies:

- **There is a concentration of buyers.** If there are a few large firms responsible for the majority of market purchases then their power is likely to be enhanced *vis-à-vis* suppliers. The major automobile assemblers have a great deal of power over component suppliers. The supplier can be threatened with a loss of business if they refuse to co-operate. They are usually desperate to avoid losing a substantial proportion of their sales.
- **The product is standardised or undifferentiated.** If the product is much the same as that supplied by other companies, then buyers will be confident that they will always be able to obtain the product if a particular supplier refuses to reduce prices or add service features. They are then in a position to play one company against another. This is a particular problem for suppliers of some raw materials.
- **If the product accounts for a large proportion of buyers' costs.** Purchasers are likely to expend more energy driving down the price of larger-cost items than the price of a product that has an insignificant effect on their overall costs. Buyers are less price-sensitive with incidental products.
- **If the buyer has low switching costs.** If it is costly for buyers to change suppliers then the suppliers' bargaining power is enhanced.
- **Buyers suffer from low profitability.** Vehicle assemblers frequently announce that they have developed a plan for survival and for a return to profitability. Invariably, as part of the package of measures, they declare that they have reached an 'agreement' with their suppliers to cut billions of pounds from the components bill. One can only guess at the negotiating stance taken, but it probably goes along the line of 'If you don't reduce prices then we will shut down plant, and even go bankrupt, and you will lose an important customer.' If buyer firms are highly profitably they are less likely to be focused on cost-cutting and may take a greater interest in preserving the long-run health of their suppliers.

- **If buyers can integrate backwards.** If buyers can credibly threaten to make the product themselves they may have greater leverage over the suppliers. Paint manufacturers are often in a position to manufacture resin themselves should they choose to do so. If the 'make or buy' decision is finely balanced, suppliers have little room for bargaining.
- **The consequences and risks of product failure are low.** If the quality of the product is crucial to buyers' systems of operations then they are likely to pay less attention to fine-tuning the price. For example, equipment that is used to prevent oil-rig blow-outs is so vital and costs such a small amount compared with the costs of a blow-out that buyers are willing to pay a little extra to be absolutely sure of complete safety. Similar logic applies to medical equipment, legal advice and corporate finance guidance. If quality is unimportant, buyers will be more price-sensitive and shop around among suppliers.
- **Buyers have plenty of information.** Buyers' leverage can be enhanced if they know a lot about suppliers' margins, costs, and order books. Suppliers will be unable to kid the buyers into thinking that they have inflicted real pain by bargaining down the price when in reality the price agreed is above the suppliers' minimum bargaining price. The old lines such as 'you've cut my prices to the bone' and 'at this rate I'll be losing money on the deal' will not work if the buyer knows the reality of the supplier's costs.

Supplier power

In many ways supplier power is the mirror image of buyer power. Powerful suppliers are able to set prices that are much greater than their production costs; they are able to appropriate a substantial proportion of the value created in the industries they serve. Suppliers exercise the power that they possess by raising prices or reducing the quality of purchased goods and services. Intel is a powerful supplier to the PC assemblers. Sports rights holders and hit TV show producers are powerful suppliers to the TV networks. Coca-Cola sells to an industry (retailers) that is highly fragmented. Most of these buyers have very little power. A few of the large supermarket groups try to exert some authority, but they are up against a powerful brand and a company used to deciding terms (Coke has over 50 per cent of the carbonated soft drinks market worldwide: in Greece it has an amazing 72.7 per cent, in France 55 per cent, in Germany 56.6 per cent, in Spain 56 per cent, and in Italy 44.9 per cent).[4] If the firms in the industry are geared up to obtaining supplies from a particular source and there would be enormous cost of switching suppliers then the supplying firms have power. For example, Judge Thomas Penfield Jackson in his findings on Microsoft in 1999 declared

[4] John Willman and James Blitz, Coca-Cola's style offends European regulators' taste. *Financial Times*, 22 July 1999, p. 2.

> the cost of switching to a non-Intel compatible PC operating system includes the price of not only a new operating system, but also a new PC and new peripheral devices. It also includes the effort of learning to use the new system, the cost of acquiring a new set of compatible applications, and the work of replacing files and documents that were associated with the old applications. . . . users of Intel-compatible PC operating systems would not switch in large numbers to the Mac OS in response to even a substantial, sustained increase in the price of an Intel-compatible PC operating system.[5]

Industry evolution

The five-forces model is essentially static. However, investors need to develop a view of how favourable the industry structure will be years into the future. Industries change as companies, suppliers and buyers undertake strategic actions to enhance their respective degrees of power. They also change as new technology and government policy shift the basic economic facts of life.

Having completed a static evaluation of the industry – a snapshot in time – the investor must consider the factors that are likely to lead to the **evolution of the industry**. A firm that currently has strong pricing power can find it slipping away rapidly – one example is IBM's slide in the late 1980s and early 1990s as the PC was exploited more effectively by competitors; another is the way fixed-line telecom companies have been outwitted by mobile companies.

If you have found an industry with excellent current characteristics then, when completing an industry evolution analysis, you will be looking for the potential for the industry to continue to produce high returns. Stability and invulnerability to attack and change are the desired qualities. On the other hand, if the industry has a 'poor' or 'fair' structure you would be interested in evaluating the potential for change to a durable high-return structure.

Long-range structural analysis is used to forecast the long-term rates of return of an industry. The task is to examine the changing strength of each competitive force and to attempt the construction of a probable profit potential of the industry. Of course, this is easier in less complex industry environments. Investors should not try to analyse an industry with many highly uncertain variables. Concentrate on industries that are relatively easy to follow. (You may ignore this point if you have special knowledge of a hard-to-follow industry – exploit your analytical advantage.)

Changes in the environment of the industry are of significance if they affect the five forces. So an analyst will ask whether the change in technology or government regulations will result in a raising or lowering of entry or exit barriers, and whether a social trend will result in more power accruing to buyers. The driving forces at the root of industry evolution can be classified under the following headings:

[5] See http://usvms.gpo.gov.

- technological change;
- learning within the industry, and by suppliers, buyers and potential entrants;
- economic change;
- government legislation and policy;
- social change.

Technological change

The most visible and pervasive form of change in society is the result of technological developments. New products, processes and materials directly affect people and alter the competitive forces within industries. Just consider the last 100 years. Inventions and innovations in the fields of electricity, communication, transport, pharmaceuticals, computers and satellites, to name a few, have had profound effects on daily lives and industry structure. Given that there are more scientists alive today than have ever breathed in all the previous generations, it seems reasonable to conclude that technological change is more likely to accelerate rather than decline. This presents a serious challenge to the investor in trying to assess the durability of an industry's rate of return. If you really understand an industry subject to unusually rapid technological change, such as one of the information technology or biotechnology industries, then by all means concentrate your resources on estimating likely future profitability. However, most of us will not be able to do this. For us the only hope is to focus on industries that are more predictable. These will still have technological (and social, economic, etc.) change and therefore need an evolutionary assessment; however, the pace of change is likely to be much slower in certain areas. For example, the industry structure for the extraction of rock and gravel is unlikely to alter greatly as a result of invention and innovation. Perhaps new improved and specialist machinery will come along, but there are unlikely to be the seismic shifts that occur in other industries. The production and sale of old favourites such as *The Economist* and Nescafé is likely to continue much as it did before. It is true that all of these firms have to consider developments such as the Internet, but they will be able to adapt without fundamentally changing the method of doing business or, more importantly, the power structure within the industry. The *Financial Times* may develop its website but the paper version will still sell well. Nestlé may use the Internet to co-ordinate suppliers and drive down prices but will still sell through vending machines, stores and fast food outlets, over which it has tremendous power. Of course, we may be surprised by developments in the industry or in adjacent industries that lead to dramatic technological change, and in the five forces. Despite this problem, evolution analysis is still desirable. There are a number of ways in which technology can impact on industry structure. For example, the cost and quality of substitutes can change as a result of invention and innovation. This can affect the demand for the product if the cost falls or the quality improves sufficiently to overcome buyer switching costs. Examples of such change include the switch from the purchase of air travel tickets from travel agents to the Internet, and the switch from traditional brokers to Internet brokers for the purchase of shares.

The sales achieved by a particular industry may be influenced by the cost, quality and availability of **complementary products**. If the complementary product is affected by technological change then the industry under examination may experience a shift in the five forces. For example, advances in computer games affect the demand for games consoles.

Entry barriers have been smashed in a lot of industries as a consequence of using Internet technology. Now small players can establish themselves as music or periodical publishers; a specialist producer of Stilton cheese in England can market the product worldwide, bypassing the powerful retail chains. Rapid and frequent product introduction may create barriers to entry because potential competitors are unable to keep pace with the incumbent firms (e.g. microprocessor design).

New technology can change the way business is conducted. For example, insurance brokers have been squeezed by clients approaching insurance companies directly using new technology (first the telephone and now the Internet). Also, a number of computer manufacturers sell direct to users, bypassing retailers (e.g. Dell).

The methods of producing the output of the industry might change as new technology is introduced. Banks are switching increasing numbers of customers to Internet bank accounts. They are under attack from non-banking firms setting up Internet banking operations now that the barriers to entry have been lowered – an extensive branch network is not required. Technological advancement may lead the industry to change the typical buyers that it serves. For example, mobile telephones were initially very expensive and useful only in a confined geographic area, such as the City of London. Target customers were high-income, time-pressed individuals. Now one of the largest target markets is children who value text messaging as well as chatting.

Technological innovation can change the definition of the industry as industry boundaries can be enlarged or contracted. For example, the TV set is being used for communication and the Internet (particularly via cable systems). The convergence of telecommunications, computer technology and televisions will have a profound impact on these industry structures. New rivals appear, buyer power changes (as well as buyer demands) and content provider power may be enhanced.

Learning

Over time the participants in an industry and those with an interest in an industry (e.g. suppliers) accumulate knowledge that can change the industry power balance. Through the regular purchase of a product, buyers develop knowledge of the product's characteristics and qualities, and the cost of competing products. As buyers become more expert and the volume of sales increases, a product can move from being unusual and differentiated to being more commodity-like. Buyers become increasingly demanding, looking for higher specification, additional service, and lower price. When personal computers were first marketed they were novel and differentiated. As more manufacturers extended the industry and buyers accumulated knowledge, the PC increasingly became a commodity item. Also, buyers insisted on even greater computing power, after-sales service and 'free' software. Now many manufacturers make losses or very poor profits in the PC market.

Some industries are developed on the back of specialist knowledge of business processes or products. The firms in possession of this knowledge will guard it jealously to differentiate their product from the current competitors and to keep out potential entrants. However, gradually, as a technology becomes established, diffusion takes place. This may occur because other firms take apart the product and figure out how it was put together, or they may poach key staff; or customers may help create alternative suppliers by deliberate leaking.

Advantages based on the ownership of special knowledge are likely to be eroded. Advantages based on the ability to continually develop new special knowledge can be sustainable. There must be a dynamic managerial response. If a technology-led company is hiding behind patent protection and is not developing a stream of successor products it will not have the durable competitive advantage that the investor is looking for.

Economic change

A slowdown in the growth rate of an industry can have a dramatic effect on the industry structure. This is a particular problem for durable goods producers. When a durable good is first invented there is initially a slow consumer take-up. There follows a rapid growth phase. This starts to tail off as penetration reaches saturation point. A slowdown in the rate of growth is bad enough for firms that are accustomed to large year-on-year increases. But at least they are selling more each year so they continue to add capacity. Then the crunch comes. Once satiation is reached sales can fall dramatically as consumers shift from first-time buying to replacement purchase – for example, some mobile phone handset providers came close to failure because the anticipated growth in demand did not materialise after they borrowed to grow. With durable goods consumers can put off replacement for many years (even decades). This effect can be exacerbated by recession. The power balance in the growth phase can be completely different from that in the falling sales phase. During growth the industry can absorb entrants while each firm remains profitable. The companies are less concerned with pushing down the price of components from suppliers than with reliability and speed of supply. In the downturn new entrants become a great danger to industry profitability. Suppliers are asked to bear a greater share of the burden of the crisis and buyers gain enormous power as they shop around for bargains.

Changes in the price of input costs as a result of economic developments can affect industry structure. For example, in the last 50 years the cost of shipping goods around the world has fallen a great deal. This has widened the potential market for some producers of exported goods and meant an influx of entrants for incumbents in particular countries. The lowering of telecommunications costs has also had a significant effect on industries. For example, India has an enormous software industry – code can be written in India at a fraction of the cost in Silicon Valley and transmitted instantly to anywhere in the world. Other examples of economic events that influence industry structure and the relative strength of the five forces include the liberalisation of world trade, the rise in labour costs and changes in exchange rates.

Government

Changes in government legislation and policy can lead to significant changes in industry structure. The government's attitude towards competitive practices, for example, can vary over time. What is considered an acceptable level of industry concentration of power in the hands of a few firms at one time is regarded as unacceptable at another, and companies are obliged to subject themselves to greater competition. There are some industries whose prices are regulated by governments or government-appointed agencies. Governments also license some firms to enter industries. The other side of that coin is they restrict the entry of other companies. Product quality and safety are also influenced by government organisations (e.g. in food). The Kyoto conference in 1997 led a number of governments to impose legislation to curtail the emission of greenhouse gases. Industry structure can be greatly influenced by the imposition or removal of tariffs or import quotas.

Industry structures are changed by a whole series of other government moves from labour law and privatisation to patent law and information disclosure. The investor has the difficult task of trying to evaluate the likelihood of a change in government policy having a significant influence on industry profitability through the power relationships of the five forces.

Social change

Demographic change can influence the size of the buyer pool for an industry. For example, as the proportion of the population over the age of 50 in western countries increases, demand for some products will rise (e.g. golf?) and others will fall (e.g. discos?). The ethnic mix of the population can alter the demand for products. This may increase the demand for some products (e.g. certain foods) at the expense of others.

Values and cultures can change. Vegetarianism is growing in popularity, which is bound to affect the meat industry. There is greater equality between the sexes, which will affect industries from employment agencies to childcare providers. Shifts are taking place in the perceived appropriate work–life balance, affecting the demand for leisure activities.

Education and health levels can change over a relatively short period of time, particularly in countries with high economic growth. A more highly educated populace is likely to demand more newspapers, books and training courses. Health can rise in some regards, but decline in others, as incomes increase. Concern about weight has become a fixation – slimming foods and exercise gym businesses have been the beneficiaries.

Income distribution can change over time. For example, the redistribution of income towards the poor can reduce the demand for luxury goods but increase the demand for basics. Even a social issue as simple as the spread of English as the world language can influence industry structure: film and television producers see their buyers and competitors as existing all over the world.

Concluding comments

No industry is perfect for the investor. Each one will be negatively affected to some extent by one or more of the forces described above. The investor should not drop an industry from further consideration just because a negative factor is uncovered. Rather, the investor needs to weigh up the balance of a mixture of positive and negative factors. Some industries display an overwhelming combination of negatives – for example, the firms have low bargaining power over suppliers and customers; they are vulnerable to attack by new entrants; the industry is growing slowly; and it has many aggressively competing players.

On the other hand, there are industries with two or three players who sell to customers unable to easily switch their suppliers. Being the dominant firms, these companies can be very forceful in agreeing terms with suppliers. Prices are kept way above the cost of production, helped by a tacit agreement between the companies that they will not compete on price. Entry by other companies is difficult. Even in an industry with so many positives there may be one or two threats – for example, technological or government rule changes may encourage substitute product makers or encourage entry into the industry.

The investor has to be able to stand back and observe the overall picture. Judgement is required in broad terms rather than in pinpoint precision. Here, we are dealing with subjective probabilities of industry returns on capital in the long term, not definitive objective certainties. Despite the superficial appearance that investment is based on hard numbers, it has to be acknowledged that the key inputs to the process are qualitative, such as the degree of pricing power.

Further reading

Two books that are very easy to read and give more detail on analysing industries are Michael Porter, *Competitive Strategy*, and Glen Arnold, *Valuegrowth Investing*.

15

The competitive position of the firm

The previous chapter dealt with identifying industries offering high returns on capital employed. However, identifying a good industry is only the first step. Investors need to seek out companies that beat the average rates of return on capital employed in a good industry. To beat the averages, companies need something special. That something special comes from the bundle of resources that the firm possesses. Most of the resources are ordinary. That is, they give the firm competitive parity. However, the firm may be able to exploit one or two extraordinary resources – those that give a competitive edge. An **extraordinary resource** is one which, when combined with other (ordinary) resources, enables the firm to outperform competitors and create new value-generating opportunities. Critical extraordinary resources determine what a firm can do successfully.

It is the ability to generate value for customers that is crucial for superior returns. High shareholder returns are determined by the firm's ability to offer either the same benefits to customers as competitors but at a lower price, or unique benefits that more than outweigh the associated higher price.

Ordinary resources provide a threshold competence. They are vital to ensure a company's survival. The problem is that mere competitive parity does not produce the returns looked for by investors. In the food retail business, for example, most firms have a threshold competence in basic activities, such as purchasing, human resource management, accounting control and store layout. However, the large chains have resources that set them apart from the small stores: they are able to obtain lower-cost supplies because of their enormous buying power; they can exploit economies of scale in advertising and in the range of produce offered.

Despite large retailers having these advantages, it is clear that small stores have survived, and some produce very high returns on capital invested. These superior firms provide value to the customer significantly above cost. Some corner stores have a different set of extraordinary resources compared with the large groups: personal friendly service could be valued highly; opening at times convenient to customers could lead to acceptance of a premium price; the location may make shopping less hassle than traipsing to an out-of-town hypermarket. The large chains find emulation of these qualities expensive. If they were to try and imitate the small store they could end up losing their main competitive advantages, the most significant of which is low cost.

The extraordinary resources possessed by the supermarket chains as a group when compared with small shops are not necessarily extraordinary resources in the competitive rivalry *between* the chains. If the focus is shifted to the 'industry' of supermarket chains, factors such as economies of scale may merely give competitive parity – scale is needed for survival. Competitive advantage is achieved through the development of other extraordinary resources – for example, the quality of the relationship with suppliers, the combination of a sophisticated system for collecting data on customers and target marketing, or ownership of the best sites. However, even these extraordinary

Much of the material for this chapter comes from Glen Arnold *Valuegrowth Investing* (Financial Times Prentice Hall, 2002).

resources will not maintain a superior competitive position for ever. Many of these can be imitated. Long-term competitive advantage may depend on the ability of the management team to continually innovate and thereby shift the ground from under the feet of competitors. The extraordinary resource is then the coherence, attitude, intelligence, knowledge and drive of the managers in the organisation setting.

Many successful companies have stopped seeing themselves as bundles of product lines and businesses. Instead they look at the firm as a collection of resources. This helps to explain the logic behind some companies going into apparently unconnected product areas. The connection is the exploitation of extraordinary resources. So, for example, Honda has many different product areas: motor boat engines, automobiles, motorcycles, lawn mowers, and electric generators. These are sold through different distribution channels in completely different ways to different customers. The common root for all these products is Honda's extraordinary resource, which led to a superior ability to produce engines. Likewise, photocopiers, cameras and image scanners are completely different product sectors and sold in different ways. Yet they are all made by Canon, which has extraordinary capabilities and knowledge of optics, imaging and microprocessor controls.

The TRRACK system

The investor should not be looking for a long list of extraordinary resources in any one firm. It is great if you can find one – it only takes one to leap ahead of competitors and produce supernormal returns. If two are found, then that is excellent. It is very unusual to come across a company that has three or more extraordinary resources. Coca-Cola is an exception with an extraordinary brand, an extensive distribution system with its connected relationships, and highly knowledgeable managers (knowledgeable principally about how to work the systems in countries around the world to keep the competition authorities off their backs while they tighten control over distribution and prices – allegedly).

To assist the thorough analysis of a company's extraordinary resource I have developed the TRRACK system. This classifies extraordinary resources into six categories:

T Tangible
R Relationships
R Reputation
A Attitude
C Capabilities
K Knowledge

Notice that the vast majority of extraordinary resources are intangible. They are qualities that are carried within the individuals that make up the organisation, or are connected with the interaction between individuals. They are usually developed over a long time rather than bought. These qualities cannot be scientifically evaluated to provide objective quantification. Despite our inability to be precise, it is usually the case that these people-embodied factors are the most important drivers of value creation and we must pay most attention to them. Good investment hinges on good judgement rather than the ability to plug numbers into a formula.

Tangible

Occasionally physical resources provide a sustainable competitive advantage. These are assets that can be physically observed and are often valued (or misvalued) in a balance sheet. They include property, materials, production facilities and patents. They can be purchased, but if they were easily purchased they would cease to be extraordinary because all competitors would go out and buy. There must be some barrier preventing other firms from acquiring the same or similar assets for them to be truly valuable in the long run.

McDonald's makes sure that it takes the best locations on the busiest highways, rather than settling for obscure secondary roads. Many smaller businesses have found themselves with (or made smart moves to secure) the ownership of valuable land adjacent to popular tourist sites. Pharmaceutical companies, such as Merck, own valuable patents giving some protection against rivalry – at least temporarily.

Relationships

Over time companies can form valuable relationships with individuals and organisations that are difficult or impossible for a potential competitor to emulate. Relationships in business can be of many kinds. The least important are the contractual ones. The most important are informal or implicit. These relationships are usually based on a trust that has grown over many years. The terms of the implicit contract are enforced by the parties themselves rather than through the court – a loss of trust can be immensely damaging. It is in all the parties' interests to co-operate with integrity because there is the expectation of reiteration leading to the sharing of collective value created over a long period.

Buyer–seller relationships differ in quality. Many are simply arm's-length, adversarial and involve serious bargaining. This may make sense when selling incidental items, say pencils, to organisations. It is not worth the expense of establishing a more sophisticated interaction. However, many firms have seen the value of developing close relationships with either their suppliers or customers. For example, Ikea and Wal-Mart are moving towards more collaborative relationships with suppliers to improve delivery mechanisms, through joint planning and scheduling, information system management and co-operation on quality and reliability advances.

South African Breweries (now SAB Miller) has 98 per cent of the beer market in South Africa. It has kept out foreign and domestic competitors because of its special relationships with suppliers and customers. It is highly profitable, and yet for the last two decades it has reduced prices every year – the price of beer has halved in real terms. Most of South Africa's roads are poor and electricity supplies are intermittent. To distribute its beer it has formed some strong relationships. It helps truck drivers, many of whom are former employees, to set up small trucking businesses. *Shebeens* sell most of the beer. These are unlicensed pubs. Often they are tiny – no more than a few benches. SAB cannot sell directly to the illegal shebeens. Instead it maintains an informal relationship via a system of wholesalers. SAB makes sure that distributors have refrigerators and, if necessary, generators. An entrant would have to develop its own special relationship with truck drivers, wholesalers and retailers. In all likelihood it would have to establish a completely separate and parallel system of distribution. Even then it would lack the legitimacy that comes with a long-standing relationship.

Accounting firms, management consultancies and investment banks are particularly keen on 'client-relationship management'. Frequently, it is the quality of the customer relationship that creates the real value for these types of organisations.

Relationships between employees, and between employees and the firm, can give a competitive edge. Some firms seem to possess a culture that creates wealth through the co-operation and dynamism of the employees. Information is shared, knowledge is developed, innovative activity flows, rapid response to market change is natural, and respect for all pervades.

The quality of the relationships with government can be astonishingly important to a company. Many of the defence contractors concentrate enormous resources to ensure a special relationship with various organs of government. The biggest firms often attract the best ex-government people to take up directorships or to head liaison with the government. Their contacts and knowledge of the inside workings of purchasing decisions, with their political complications, can be very valuable. A similar logic often applies to pharmaceutical companies, airlines and regulated (e.g. energy, water) companies.

Reputation

Reputations are normally made over a long period. Once a good reputation is established it can be a source of very high returns (assuming that all the necessary ordinary resources are in place to support it).

In the markets for goods and services consumers constantly come up against the difficulty of judging quality before purchase. This is an ancient problem. In medieval times craftsmen banded together in guilds which then sought to establish a quality reputation for every member of the group. If a member fell below the required standard he would be ejected to prevent the image of the group being sullied permanently. This type of arrangement exists today for builders, plumbers and cabinet-makers. Those who deal in gold and silver found, and still find, it worthwhile to spend time and money demonstrating the purity of the metal. They paid for systems to assay to the declared specification.

Customers are willing to pay a premium for product quality assurance when they cannot easily monitor quality for themselves. This premium is not available to the suppliers in many markets (e.g. coal, electricity, sugar, paper) where the buyer is able to quickly and cheaply gauge quality. But in some industries customers will pay a price premium for the assurance of quality. To appreciate the value of reputation it is worth thinking about goods and services as falling into four categories:

- search goods;
- immediate-experience goods;
- long-term-experience goods;
- no-experience goods.

Reputation is most important in the last two, but it has relevance to many immediate experience goods.

Search goods are those for which the buyer can establish quality by inspection before purchase. So, for example, the quality of bananas can generally be observed in the store. It makes sense for the storekeeper to build up a reputation for quality as this will enable the store to remain on the list of retailers that consumers like to purchase from. But retailers are generally unable to exploit this reputation to charge a significant price premium. If they attempted to do so, consumers would quickly switch to other stores where they could easily assess the quality of the produce.

The second group of products are **immediate-experience goods**. Here quality cannot be established by inspection. So the taste of a soup in a can or the flavour of canned vegetables is only learnt by the consumer after purchase. However, it does not take long to learn about the quality of Campbell's or Heinz soup. Consumers soon develop a knowledge of a manufacturer's quality with immediate-experience goods. Once learned, there tends to be some degree of inertia, leading to consumers being reluctant to switch brands (giving some pricing power).

The value of **long-term-experience goods** can only be determined after extensive personal experience. For example, it takes a long time to establish whether a doctor is very able (given that most ailments clear up spontaneously). Only in the long term do you know, if you are relying on personal experience, whether the cancer treatment is working or the heart pills do not have unacceptable side effects. Reputation established with other patients may be key to your decision to accept the advice and treatment of a doctor. When companies are selecting auditing, accounting and other professional services they rarely have an extensive history of dealing with a range of possible suppliers to be able to choose one on the basis of experience. They generally rely on reputation. With car hire in a foreign country the consumer is unable to assess quality in advance. Hertz provide certification for local traders under a franchise arrangement. These local car hirers would see no benefit to providing an above average service without the certification of Hertz because they would not be able to charge a premium price.[1] It is surprising how much more consumers are willing to pay for the assurance of reliable and efficient car hire when they travel abroad, compared with the hiring of a car from an unfranchised local.

[1] J. Kay *Foundations of Corporate Success* (Oxford University Press, 1993).

There are some goods that are only purchased once (or rarely). These are **no-experience goods**. Examples are funeral services, swimming pools, construction, and specialist legal services. Consumers tend to lean heavily on reputations established with other customers.

The ways in which buyers ascertain the quality of a good (e.g. visual inspection or personal recommendation) can strongly influence the potential for competitive advantage in an industry. The four types of goods and the importance of reputation in attaining reassurance on quality are shown in Table 15.1.

Table 15.1 Type of good and the importance of reputation

Type of good	Information on quality	Examples
Search	Obtained by inspection prior to purchase: reputation is of very little importance	Fresh fruit and vegetables Clothing Some furniture
Immediate experience	Obtained quickly after consumption: reputation is of some importance	Tinned food and drink Newspapers Theme parks
Long-term experience	Obtained only after a long period of individual experience: reputation is therefore very important	Professional advice Some medicines Investment advice
No experience	Not possible to obtain from individual experience: reputation is therefore very important	Investment bank advice Funeral services Life assurance

Branding is designed to represent and enhance reputations. Brands generally provide a degree of quality certification for consumers. For immediate-experience and long-term-experience goods the brand provides the assurance of **consistency**. People buy branded beer because they expect that the next can will taste the same as the ones they bought previously. In many product areas consumers are reluctant to take the risk of buying unbranded products, for fear of inconsistency of quality (e.g. hamburgers, soup, breakfast cereals and shampoo).

The promise of consistency provides a company with a competitive advantage, but the price premium that can be charged for this factor alone is limited because the consistency can be replicated by competitors. There are two other advantages of branded products that permit enhanced pricing power. These are shown in Exhibit 15.1. A firm may have one, two or all three of these advantages. Naturally, the more the better.

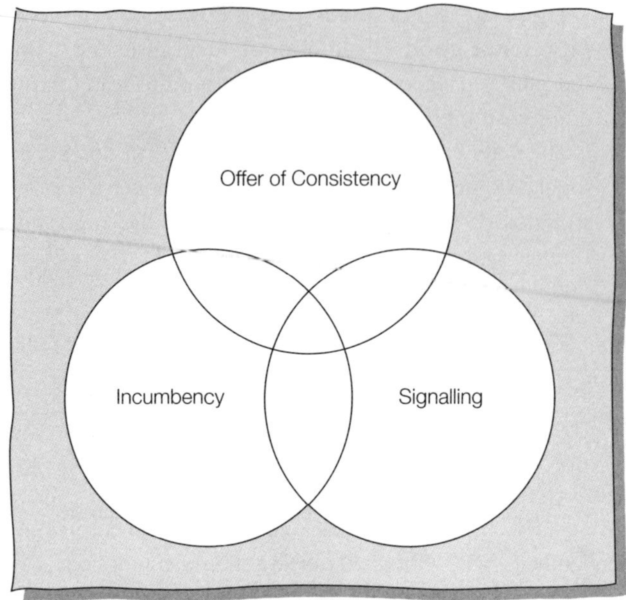

Exhibit 15.1 Three powerful advantages of brands

Incumbency can be a powerful quality of a brand. Once a brand is established in the minds of consumers it is very difficult for a rival manufacturer to successfully introduce an alternative product, even if that product offers better value. For example, a rival to Cadbury's Flake may offer a chocolate bar of equivalent quality at a lower price, but few consumers will switch – at least not without a vast marketing spend and a long period of time. Similarly, consumers are attached to dog food brands, ketchup brands and cleaning product brands. Consumer recognition and acceptance of a new product in the face of a well-establish incumbent is extraordinarily difficult. The combination of consistency and incumbency can lead to very high returns. Coca-Cola is aware of the role of these two factors in its success – Douglas Daft, Chairman and Chief Executive, wrote: 'All our success flows from the strength of our brands, and our ability to relate to people. That's why we have to be the world's best marketers.'[2] He says that Coca-Cola should focus on becoming a 'pure marketing company', presumably in order to entrench the power of consistency and incumbency.

Consumers often use branded products to send **signals** to other people. Nike, Reebok, Levi's and a host of others exploit this element of human nature and receive a premium price. Signals of high status are generally expensive – Rolls-Royce, Moët et Chandon, and Burberry spring to mind. Coca-Cola manages to score on this point as well: in many developing countries its American cultural associations mean that young people, in particular, will pay a premium. A similar advantage has accrued to Marlboro.

[2] D. Daft, Back to basic Coke, *Financial Times,* 27 March 2000, p. 20.

Attitude

Attitude refers to the mentality of the organisation. It is the prevalent outlook. It is the way in which the organisation views and relates to the world. Terms such as 'disposition', 'will' and 'culture' are closely connected with attitude. Every sports coach is aware of the importance of attitude. The team may consist of players with the best technique in the business or with a superb knowledge of the game, they may be the fastest and the most skilful, but without a winning attitude they will not succeed. There must be a will to win.

Some firms develop a winning mentality based on a culture of innovation. Others are determinedly orientated towards customer satisfaction, while some are quality-driven. 3M has a pervasive attitude of 'having a go'. Testing out wild ideas is encouraged. Employees are given time to follow up a dreamed-up innovation, and they are not criticised for failing. Innovations such as Post-it notes have flowed from this attitude.

Capabilities

Capabilities are derived from the company's ability to undertake a *set* of tasks. The term 'skill' can be used to refer to a narrow activity or single task. The word 'capability' is used for the combination of a number of skills. For example, Sony developed a capability in miniaturisation. This enabled it to produce a string of products from the Walkman to the PlayStation. It grew by continually reinforcing the various skills needed for technology-based product innovation. This was complemented by marketing flair and strong brands. Nokia has taken world leadership in the manufacture of mobile telephones as a result of its capability in technical design and marketing.

Frequently, it is extremely difficult for a firm to combine its process skills in such a way as to provide a superior capability. The mere fact that it is difficult gives a competitive advantage to a firm that has achieved it, as the combination becomes difficult for rivals to imitate. Static capabilities are less valuable than the ability to move quickly in product markets.

In the 1940s Caterpillar developed a capability for building roads, airstrips and army bases for the US Department of War. It had to develop a wide range of skills as the military needed one supplier that would take on entire projects. Caterpillar offered a worldwide service and supply network for construction equipment at low cost. Having met the challenge set by the military Caterpillar was in an excellent position after the war to offer a capability rivals could not emulate. It became the dominant firm in the heavy construction equipment industry. Its ability to deliver any Caterpillar part to any location in the world in less than 2 days was an unbeatable offer.

In some industries the capability to be the **lowest-cost producer** is vital for superior profitability. Cost leaders must exploit all sources of cost advantage. They tend to sell standard, undifferentiated products with few or no frills. They must be determined to be *the* lowest-cost producer, not just one of many. In computers, Dell is the classic industry cost leader. It is brutal in cutting prices in order to take market share. Higher market share leads to lower unit costs and a widening gap between Dell and its smaller rivals. Its direct selling model gives a major cost advantage.

Knowledge

The retention, exploitation and sharing of knowledge can be extremely important in the achievement and maintenance of competitive advantage. **Knowledge** is the awareness of information, and its interpretation, organisation, synthesis, and prioritisation, to provide insights and understanding. All firms in an industry share basic knowledge. For example, all publishers have some knowledge of market trends, distribution techniques and printing technology. It is not this common knowledge that I am referring to in the context of extraordinary resources. If a publisher builds up data and skills in understanding a particular segment of the market (say, investments books), then its superior awareness, interpretation, organisation, synthesis and prioritisation of information can create competitive advantage through extraordinary knowledge. The company will have greater insight than rivals into this segment of the market.

There are two types of organisational knowledge. The first, **explicit knowledge**, can be written down and passed on to others relatively easily. This is objective knowledge that can be defined and documented. The second, **tacit knowledge**, is very difficult to define. It is subjective, personal, fuzzy and complex. It is hard to formalise and communicate. An example of explicit knowledge would be how to manufacture a component. Explicit knowledge is unlikely to provide competitive advantage: if it is easily defined and codified it is likely be available to rivals. Tacit knowledge, on the other hand, is very difficult for rivals to obtain. Consider the analogy of football: explicit knowledge of tactics is generally available; what separates the excellent from the ordinary player is the application of tacit knowledge (e.g. the instinctive ability to place the ball and an awareness of other members of the team). Tacit knowledge is transmitted by doing: the main means of transferring knowledge from one individual to another is through close interaction to build understanding, as in the master–apprentice relationship.

Nike was started by Phil Knight in 1964. He had a special knowledge of the needs of runners – in the 1950s he had been a middle-distance runner in the University of Oregon's track team. He felt that runners had been badly served by the existing manufacturers. He designed shoes using his special insight, but had no special knowledge of manufacturing, and so this was contracted to Asian suppliers. His new designs were a great success. In the 1980s the company grew from the specialist sports shoe market to the fashion-conscious teenage and young market. This required an additional set of knowledge attributes. As well as knowledge of how to create innovative sport shoes (e.g. Air Shoes) the company became very knowledgeable about its customers, marketing and distributors. For example, image building was vital to sell to this type of consumer. Michael Jordan was featured in its advertising. The amount spent on sports marketing reached $1 billion in 1995. Tiger Woods and the whole of the Brazilian soccer team were signed up. The company's understanding of its target market was second to none. It projected a cool and competitive image that appealed to the young. Its knowledge of product development was built on – in one year it launched 300 new designs! It developed a knowledge of new materials and fabrics. The easily documented elements of Nike's knowledge base are the least important. The key elements are the knowledge that comes from day-to-day interaction between employees and with customers, suppliers and distributors. This knowledge builds up over time and is diffused throughout the organisation in the heads of thousands of individuals.

What makes resources extraordinary?

It is sometimes difficult to identify the extraordinary resources of a company, if indeed it has any at all. This section may help by summarising the characteristics of extraordinary resources. To achieve *sustainable* competitive advantage, the three characteristics must be **durable**. That is, it is expected that the above average return on capital will persist for a very long time because:

- the resource will be **demanded** (regarded as valuable) by customers far into the future;
- the resource will continue to be **scarce** (i.e. competitors will not be able to imitate the resource or substitute alternative resources to satisfy customers' needs);
- as far as can be seen, the additional net income generated by the use of the extraordinary resource is **appropriable** by the firm and not by another organisation or individual(s).

The challenge for the investor is understanding what distinguishes extraordinary resources from those that merely give competitive parity and to recognise when a resource switches from being extremely valuable to being pedestrian (and the likelihood of that switch occurring in the near future). For example, lower-priced Swiss watch manufacturers discovered that the extraordinary resources of knowledge accumulated over centuries and a high reputation were not enough to induce consumers to pay a premium when cheap digital watches became available. Similarly, IBM found that it could not resist the onslaught in the PC market as the extraordinary resources it offered (technical design, reputation for bespoke solutions, etc.) became regarded as secondary when customers were offered cheaper PCs with a high specification produced as commodity-type products.

Demand

The first question to ask is whether the resource produces something of value to the customer, at a price the customer is more than willing to pay. To be extraordinary the resource must fulfil a customer's need, and the customer must be prepared to pay a premium over the cost to obtain that benefit. At any one time, willingness to pay a premium will depend on the alternatives open to the customer. The resource has to meet current and projected needs that cannot be met by competitors.

Firms frequently see themselves as having extraordinary resources that are still demanded by customers, but, in reality, they are deluding themselves. Their belief is often based success in the past. For example, a manufacturer of metal automobile bumpers may be the best in the world, with the greatest technical design, cheapest operating costs, brilliant plant managers, etc. But if customer demand has moved from metal automobile bumpers to compressible plastic, those resources are no longer in demand and are therefore not valuable. To take another example, the demand for the resources possessed by skilful tailors has all but disappeared.

There are some resources that are more likely to have a long life than others. For example, Disney's extraordinary resource as a family-orientated entertainment brand will, bar managerial stupidity or accident, produce price premiums long into the future. Each of the leading characters (Mickey Mouse, Snow White, etc.) and the library of movies can be considered extraordinary resources with a long shelf life. The theme parks have a special place in the hearts of many people – they are world-renowned leaders in the field. Each generation will want to share with their children the magic of Disney. They offer something special that competitors find hard to beat. CadburySchweppes and *The Economist* have powerful reputations in their respective fields that are likely to be long-lived because they offer to satisfy customer needs better than alternatives. Of course, the management will need to be vigilant and to invest to stay ahead, but they start from an excellent position.

Scarcity

If the resource is widely available it cannot be extraordinary. It must be in short supply to be valuable. If it is commonplace competitors will acquire it and undercut the price premium. The company must have some protection against the actions of rivals attempting to either imitate its advantage or provide a substitute resource to steal away customers. It must have a deep moat around the competitive advantage to make it sustainable. Resources that have built-in inhibitors to imitation fall into four categories:[3]

- **Physically unique**. A company may have ownership of the best real estate. Rivals cannot imitate this. The firm may have the mineral rights over a piece of land that contains the only economically viable quantity of a metal on a continent. Patent rights (e.g. for drugs), can prevent imitation for a while. However, the company must not rest on its laurels, as patent rights can be bypassed by determined rivals fairly quickly. A more durable extraordinary resource is the ability to produce a *stream* of patentable products. That way competitors are always running to catch up. So developing a capability and an attitude that allows rapid knowledge accumulation, innovative thinking, and quick development of products may be sustainable. The physical assets of firms are rarely inimitable. Gillette, for example, took 10 years and spent $1 billion developing its Mach3 triple-blade razor. Within a few months, Asda had produced its own triple-bladed razor selling at a 40 per cent discount. The start-up electronic traders such as

[3] Much of this discussion is inspired by work done by David Collis and Cynthia Montgomery; see D.J. Collis and C.A. Montgomery, *Corporate Strategy* (Irwin, 1997) for more details.

Amazon.com, CDNOW, eToys and E*Trade thought they had developed unique physical resources – a strong presence on the Internet. However, it has become apparent that the 'space' they occupy can be invaded by the traditional retailers, who found it relatively easy to occupy a 'site' adjacent to the brash upstarts. Furthermore, the old firms were able to apply some other significant advantages such as exploiting relationships established with millions of customers over many years, a strong brand name, tried and tested distribution capability and good relationships with suppliers.

- **Path dependency.** This is more likely to produce sustainable extraordinary resource than physical assets. Path-dependent resources are created over a long period of time. They are created because of the route that the firm took to get to where it is today. The history of some firms gives them the idiosyncratic attributes that make them unique. Only they can offer the qualities demanded by the customer. So, a technology firm may develop an extraordinary resource in the creation and exploitation of breakthroughs in a scientific discipline. It is the long history of sequentially overcoming scientific barriers by a tight knit group of scientists that provides the firm with superior knowledge and capabilities leading to products that are cutting-edge. Competitors may try to imitate by hiring hundreds of scientists and providing them with vast financial resources, but the new team will lack the long-term perspective, coherence and tacit knowledge of the established team. It takes a long time to develop strong and loyal networks of relationships with suppliers and customers. For example, South African Breweries is now in a strong position because, over many decades, it worked with suppliers and customers to make the distribution of beer possible in difficult circumstances. Brand name recognition is usually path-dependent. Kellogg's and Heinz have taken over a century to establish themselves in the psyche of consumers. An imitator would find this very difficult to break. Coca-Cola's brand name recognition will not be replicated simply by rival spending vast sums on marketing. Consumers have long experience of drinking Coke, and their association of the drink with every stage of their lives means that they have a path-dependent attachment to it. This presents a deep moat to rivals.
- **Causal ambiguity.** By this is meant uncertainty over what the extraordinary resource is or how it was created. There are two types of causal ambiguity. The first is where the potential imitator is unable to see clearly which resource is giving the sustainable competitive advantage. The second is where it is difficult to identify the way in which the extraordinary resource was created in the first place: the recipe is not obvious. If the sustainable competitive advantage is created by a single skill, relationship or capability then rivals will usually find it relatively easy to understand the causal mechanism leading to market-place success and abnormally high rates of return on capital used. However, in many cases the competitive advantage relies on a complex set of interacting factors and it is very difficult to disentangle the key elements that create resources and to identify those resources that raise the firm above competitive parity. With Sony it is possible to observe the extraordinary resources, therefore the first type of causal ambiguity is no problem. Sony has created a working environment that produces a

seemingly never-ending stream of well-designed consumer-orientated innovations. It has also developed complementary extraordinary resources that lead to superior marketing and brands. While a rival can observe that Sony has these extraordinary resources, it cannot figure out how those resources were created in the first place. A multitude of factors embedded in the company's culture, personal interactions of employees, attitudes and skills base enter the melting pot to produce the special something. It is usually the case that the firm with the causally ambiguous extraordinary resources does not itself understand what it is that gives it an advantage. If it did become obvious to those working for the company then rivals would be able to imitate it by hiring away the well-placed knowledgeable managers. The most common reason for causal ambiguity is that the firm's resources are the result of complex social phenomena. The unique formal and informal social structures and interactions develop in that one environment.

- **Economic deterrence.** Rivals may be able to imitate but choose not to do so because they fear the consequences. For example, some industries consist of a few firms operating with very high fixed (and often sunk) costs in large-scale plant. A potential entrant could build a similar massive plant but that would add a lot of additional supply to the market and result in depressed prices. Furthermore, the existing players often have assets specific to that industry – they cannot be redeployed in another industry. The incumbents therefore offer a very credible threat of retaliation to a new rival, as they are quite prepared, at least in the short run, to sell the product at a very low price.

Appropriability

The resource that is supplying value must be one that allows *the company* to capture the value, rather than allowing it to be captured by another organization or individual(s). In other words, the value is appropriable by the shareholders. For example, movies that are successful at the box office are often financially damaging to the studios. The leading actors are able to bargain for such high fees that they leave little for the company. A similar phenomenon occurs in sport where the clubs fail to hold on to the revenue generated as players appropriate a substantial proportion – witness all the loss-making football clubs as players receive thousands of pounds for every game. In investment banking 'star' mergers and acquisition specialists, equity underwriters and bond managers can ask for multimillion-dollar remuneration packages, siphoning off much (or all) of the value they create.

This distribution-of-rewards question will be resolved in favour of the company if the company, rather than an external party, owns the property rights to the critical resource. For a company like Disney the critical resources are owned by the organization – Snow White, the reputation for family orientated entertainment, library of movies etc. – therefore the company will gain from the exploitation of the resource. From time to time a brilliant director, manager or 'imaginateer' will be found in the organisation, but the value that these individuals can pull away will be small beer compared with the organisation in its entirety.

Another factor influencing appropriability is the degree of bargaining power. The firm's negotiating position will be enhanced if the supplier of a critical resource is one amongst many – then the company can shop around. (In contrast, Intel and Microsoft are able to appropriate much of the value created by PCs. The manufacturers of PCs battle it out in a fierce market, while these two companies coin it in.) Also, if the critical resource owner has few or no alternative uses for the skill, capability, knowledge or whatever, then the company may be able to lower the cost of using that resource.

Sometimes firms seem to give away the value derived from resources. Perhaps, they come under pressure to pay out the supernormal profits by making excessive payments for inputs. The major European telecommunication firms, such as British Telecom, Deutsche Telekom and France Telecom, saw that high revenues could be expected by developing third-generation (3G) mobile telephone networks. They are right; value will be created by this new technology. What is doubtful is whether any of this value will be appropriated by the telecommunications companies. They have already committed themselves to paying over £80 billion to various European governments for licences to set up networks. They will have to spend the same amount again to build the networks. It is hotly debated as to whether all or most of the value to be created by 3G will be captured by governments, consumers and equipment suppliers, with little or nothing going to the operators. It will be many years before the truth is known. However, share and bond investors have already reacted, pushing prices down sharply.

Investment in resources

The investor needs to investigate whether the firm is continuing to invest in its resource base. If it is reporting high current earnings because it is running down the resource base, then the shares should be avoided. A good company needs to maintain an approach of dynamic evolution with regard to its extraordinary resources. It has to recognise that it faces a never-ending struggle for competitive advantage. The firm can never rest from continually trying to offer better service to customers if it is to retain a large gap between price charged and cost. If it does not have this sense of urgency, then rivals will soon take action to erode its advantage.

The resources of a firm have been likened to water in a bathtub. The water represents the current stock of resources. Unfortunately, there is a continual leakage from the bottom as resources depreciate (knowledge becomes less relevant, capabilities decline or reputations and brands become less appealing). It is necessary to continually pump in more to maintain the future value to be generated from a sustainable competitive advantage. Failure to spend more to top-up the resource base (e.g. by not advertising the brand or by cutting R&D) is perfectly possible for a number of years. Profits will receive a short-term boost. But eventually the tub runs out of water – the company has no extraordinary resources to offer customers. It is condemned to either limp along with low returns or head for corporate death.

Changing the metaphor might help to see what a truly good company looks like. Companies can be viewed as organisations existing in a Darwinian ecology of survival of the fittest and natural selection. Those that have reached the top have created extraordinary resources that enable them to dominate and exploit their part of the ecosystem. They have developed superior ways of doing things. Their capabilities, knowledge, attitudes, etc., have allowed them to survive when less well-endowed rivals failed. But the business world is susceptible to much more rapid change than the biological one. If the company becomes too rigid in relying on the ways of doing things that have stood it in good stead for much of its history then it becomes vulnerable to competitors who are better able to adapt to environmental change, ranging from new technology to social trends. Entire species of companies will die unless they adapt. Some are aware enough, and able enough, to respond; others die, sometimes slowly, sometimes quickly, but usually mystified as to why they are being outcompeted when they used to be so strong.

Leveraging resources and over-exploiting them

Some companies have a powerful ability to leverage their resources into other segments or industries. For example, Disney has leveraged its characters into theme parks, promotions at McDonald's, websites and elsewhere.

Many resources not fully utilised in their original settings offer terrific opportunities for being applied to other fields. For example, a firm may have developed strong relationships and/or reputations with customers, governments and suppliers. These could be used by other parts of the organisation at little additional cost and without impairing the resource. Likewise brands may be used for a wider range of products (e.g. chocolate bar brand used for ice cream). Or knowledge could be leveraged (e.g. the use of technological innovation in more than one business sector). Or co-ordination of marketing strategies could create value (e.g. a film division might use music from the back catalogues of the music division). In the case of Time Warner film, paper publishing, Internet and TV divisions can use each other's resources to benefit the whole firm.

The investor needs to watch out for companies diversifying beyond their extraordinary resource base. Between 1958 and 1974 BIC Pen Corporation had a great time leveraging its resources. It had the extraordinary resources of capability and knowledge in plastic injection molding, mass marketing and a reputation through its strong brand. It leveraged from disposable pen production to disposable lighters and then to razors. This leveraging went well because the new product lines could make good use of all three of

BICs extraordinary resources. Then, in 1974 it made a mistake. It entered the hosiery market. None of the extraordinary resources were any use at all in producing or selling stockings. Their plastic manufacturing capability was not relevant, the product sold through completely different outlets, and marketing a fashion item required a different approach than selling disposable pens, lighters and razors.

Also watch out for companies over-exploiting a resource. Gucci is a company that realizes that one of its key resources is its rarity value. It is careful not to grow too big or to stretch the brand too far. Instead of increasing volume it has added new rarity value brands: Yves Saint Laurent, Boucheron, Sergio Rossi and Alexander McQueen. Gucci had learnt the hard way that over-exploitation of a brand is both possible and potentially fatal. In the 1980s it launched an aggressive strategy of rapid sales growth. It added lower-priced goods to its product line and started to sell through department stores and duty-free shops. Its name appeared on a host of products, from sunglasses to perfumes. Sales soared but its image fell, along with sales of its up-market products, reducing overall profitability.

Concluding comments

The investor has quite a long list of factors to consider when trying to identify companies with durable extraordinary resources in an industry with high returns. However, you should not be daunted. A two-stage approach will ease the burden. The first stage is designed to create a short-list of candidates for more in-depth analysis in the second stage. Simply read the financial press on a regular basis, looking out for key phrases that connect with the factors under the TRRACK system. So if you read 'XYZ plc has a dominant market position because of its strong brand' you would recognize that this fits the 'reputation' heading. Cut out the article and place it in a file to be researched later. Also, try to memorise the companies in your short-list file so that you can look out for other articles on them.

The second stage (possibly months or years after the first) is to confirm that the company has the characteristics you are looking for: a presence in an industry with high sustainable returns on capital; at least one durable extraordinary resource; and a management that is competent, honest and reliably shareholder-orientated? Information from many sources needs to be tapped. The Internet can be great for this. Company websites and specialist financial sites, such as *www.hemscot.net*, can provide mountains of information. Websites linked to newspapers, such as *www.ft.com*, will provide articles going back several years. The annual reports of rival companies will also be on the Internet.

If the written information does not put you off, then you might want to see the management face to face. By buying a small number of shares you will be invited to the AGM of the company where you will hear the directors explain their actions and their future plans – you can even question them (after all, they are the shareholders' servants). If you really want to make sure you have dotted all the i's and crossed all the t's you could attend trade shows or go and talk to the firm's competitors, suppliers and customers to build up a detailed picture of the company's strengths and weaknesses.

Given the amount of time and effort required to invest (rather than speculate), the great investors suggest that we do not try to analyse and subsequently keep track of dozens of companies. If we do, we will never attain the required level of depth of knowledge on any of them. On the other hand, retort thousands of professional investors trained in portfolio theory, it is essential to be well diversified so that if some investments turn south you are protected. By this they generally mean at least 20 holdings, possibly 40. The great investors reply that this approach merely results in diversification to mediocrity, and the biggest threat to investor wealth is the failure to understand the companies they own a part of. 'Analysing' 40 companies means not understanding any of them. Besides, if the fund managers cared to look at the research on portfolio theory they would find that the vast majority of the benefits of diversification (lower portfolio volatility) occur up to a diversification level of five or six shares. Going from six to 40 shares has very little effect on volatility, but there is a heavy price to be paid – in terms of moving from buying on intelligence to buying on ignorance.

On top of that we have the phenomenon of **diminishing marginal attractiveness**. Imagine listing all the shares you could buy in order of attractiveness. At the top of the list would go a company in whose prospects and management you feel very confident, and whose share price is well below your calculation of intrinsic value. The next share is very attractive, but not as great as the top one, and so on. The great investors ask: what is the point in investing significant sums in the 40th share on your list when you could move up the diminishing marginal attractiveness curve and buy more of the top five? None of the great investors suggest that we should put all our money in just one or two shares, but they agree that most private investors are unlikely to be able to investigate, understand and follow up the story on more than five to ten companies.

Further reading

Some of the issues discussed in this chapter are explained in more depth in David Collis and Cynthia Montgomery, *Corporate Strategy*. Another useful book is John Kay, *Foundations of Corporate Success*. You could read about this form of analysis in a broader context of disciplined investing in Glen Arnold, *Valuegrowth Investing*.

PART 4

Managing your portfolio

16

Companies issuing shares

Occasionally there are opportunities to buy shares directly from the company, rather than from existing shareholders. The company may be floating its shares for the first time on the stock market and offering new shares to outsiders to, say, raise money for future growth – called a '**new issue**' or '**initial public offering**' **(IPO)**. Alternatively, firms that have been on the stock market for some time may need to raise more money for expansion or to replace debt financing. This can be achieved by selling new shares to existing shareholders in a **rights issue**. Or the company may offer its shares to outsiders in a **placing** or **open offer**. On the other hand, there are times when the directors believe the company has too much equity capital and the best thing to do with the surplus cash is to return it to shareholders by **buying in** some of their **shares**.

This chapter will help you to understand the process of new issues, rights issues, other share sales, scrip issues and share buy-backs. It will alert you to the pitfalls and tackle the bewildering jargon associated with this area of investment.

New issues

In a typical week two or three companies obtain a quotation for their shares on the Official List of the London Stock Exchange. This is often referred to as companies '**going public**'. This term is accurate in the sense that the shares will now be available to a much wider range of people. But it may mislead if it is thought that the companies are changing their status from **private limited companies** ('Ltd') to **public limited companies** ('Plc'). There are many thousands of plcs that choose not to float on the stock market. Being plcs they can, under the law, offer their shares to a wider range of investors than private limited companies. However, plc status on its own does not mean there is a secondary market in the shares on a regulated exchange.

If you are a shareholder in an unquoted plc you will probably find it difficult to sell your shares when you want to. This is one reason why some plcs choose to have their shares quoted on an exchange – it allows existing shareholders to liquidate their holdings (or simply to value their shares). Another reason is to raise money to grow the business.

The sponsor

When the directors decide it is time to **float** the company they will quickly realise that they lack the expertise needed to bring the project to fruition. They need the help of a number of specialists. The key adviser is the sponsor. This may be a merchant bank, stockbroker or other professional adviser (e.g. accountant) approved by the United Kingdom Listing Authority.

The sponsor (sometimes called the **issuing house**) will discuss with the directors the nature of the business and the aspirations of the management team. They will be probing to see if flotation really is the most suitable route for the company to take. The sponsor usually has a high reputation in the City and will be putting this reputation on the line if it recommends a company to investors – sponsors regularly drop unsuitable companies. One of the key things the sponsor will examine is the management team. There must be sufficient range and depth, and a high degree of continuity and stability over recent years. Investors do not like to be reliant on the talents of one individual and so will expect an able team. The sponsor may even – quite forcefully – recommend additional directors, supplementing the team to bring it up to the required standard.

The sponsor will also make sure the company complies with the usual rule of having **three years of accounting figures.**[1] Another key rule is that the company is willing to allow at least **25 per cent** of the **share capital** to be in **public hands**. Additional tasks for the sponsor include drawing up a timetable for the flotation, advising on the method of flotation (e.g. placing or offer for sale): and co-ordinating the activities of a raft of other professional advisers involved in the project.

The prospectus

The most important document in the process is the prospectus. The sponsor helps to draft this alongside the directors (who carry ultimate responsibility for its accuracy). It is designed to reveal a lot of facts about the company to investors. It will probably contain far more information about the firm than it has previously dared to put into the public domain. The UKLA lays down stringent requirements for the content of the prospects. Even without these the company has an interest in producing a stylish and informative document as it acts as a marketing tool attracting investors.

When examining a prospectus, bear in mind the following:

- A trading record of three years is the minimum requirement, but you will often be presented with detailed accounts going back 5 years. Examine these carefully – Chapter 11, 12 and 13 of this book should help.
- Consider the information given about the growth trajectory of the company. Look at its history, its current position and the no doubt rosy picture painted by the directors of its prospects. Do you share their optimism about the industry and about this company's competitive strength within the industry?
- If the company is selling new shares, does it have a sound strategy for spending the money it raises? Or does it sound vague, using phrases such as 'we are raising funds to exploit future business opportunities' or to 'provide working capital'. It could be that the directors are primarily interested in growing the business for themselves (higher status, salaries, etc.) rather than for shareholders and they see a chance of persuading gullible investors to part with their money.
- All businesses face risks. The writing of the prospectus should have forced the directors to think about and list the risks facing the firm. For example, is the firm heavily

[1] This rule is relaxed for scientific research-based companies on techMARK and those undertaking major capital projects (e.g. Eurotunnel) – see Chapter 3.

dependent on one customer? Does it rely too much on overdrafts rather than long-term loans? Does it have too much debt? Are its sales vulnerable to political change in a volatile part of the world? To allow investors to assess these risks, the prospectus will lay out details on types of debt (e.g. repayment at short notice or after 2, 5 and 10 years, bank loans versus bonds, currency of interest and capital payments) and state whether there is sufficient working capital. Also all major contracts entered into in the past 2 years will be detailed. Analysis of sales by geographic area and category of activity will help you assess the riskiness of the businesses, as will the information on research and development and significant investments in other companies. Statements by experts are usually required: valuers confirm the valuation of property, engineers comment on the viability of processes or machinery, accountants comment on profit figures. As a further safeguard, the prospectus is required to bring to the attention of potential shareholders any risk element apparent to the directors or sponsors that has not already been disclosed.

- Who owns the shares in the company? Is there a dominant shareholder? To help you here, the rule is that all persons holding more than 3 per cent have to be named.
- Is the dividend policy acceptable to you? Some companies (e.g. hi-tech firms), have a policy of ploughing back all the money generated (if there is any) and so won't pay dividends for some years.
- Examine the information given on the directors' and senior managers' backgrounds and reward systems. Which other companies have they worked for? Have they set up a number of companies and abandoned them when they faltered? How many were liquidated? How much are they being paid? Are pay and performance linked in a way that means that they do well only if shareholders are doing well? Watch out for three-year rolling contracts, which used to be very popular with directors – they always had 3 years to go on the contract and so they were entitled to massive compensation on loss of office (e.g. following a merger). Does the company do business with another company owned by one or more of the directors (e.g. renting a factory owned by a private company associated with a director)?

Finding out about new issues

Each week the *Financial Times* (Monday's edition) and the *Investors Chronicle* provide a list and some details of companies that are due to float in the following months. A contact telephone number is supplied so that you can obtain a prospectus. Both the *Financial Times* and *Investors Chronicle* display statistics of recent new issues. An example is shown in Exhibit 16.1. The website of the London Stock Exchange (*www.londonstockexchange.com/newissues/*) carries details on the new issues launched in the previous 2 years or so. Subsequent events can be examined on the Regulatory News Services archive of *www.uk-wire.co.uk*. Other websites concerned with new issues include Hemscott (*www.hemscot.net*), Ample (*www.iii.co.uk/newissues*) and Issues Direct (*www.issuesdirect.com*).

Brokers usually offer a new issues service. You will be sent details of all new issues which your broker is willing to apply for. (Many new issues are only open to large buyers, such as pension funds and insurance companies. However, brokers are allowed to collate small-investor applications and then buy shares in bulk in the same way as an institution.)

Recent issues

Name	Business	Date of first trading	Latest market cap	Issue price	High	Low	Latest price
Bristol & London	Vehicle credit hire	Sep 25	**£30.5m**	**130.0p**	**172.5p**	**167.5p**	**167.5p**
America Mineral Fields	Mineral exploration	Sep 26	**£26.0m**	**C$1.10**	**58.5p**	**58.5p**	**58.5p**
Chicago Environmental	Environmental investments	Sep 18	**£15.3m**	**100.0p**	**102.0p**	**102.0p**	**102.0p**
EPIC Reconstruction	Distressed company finance	Sep 16	**£31.5m**	**100.0p**	**105.0p**	**105.0p**	**105.0p**
Incite Holdings	Telecoms	Sep 12	**£19.1m**	**25.0p**	**69.5p**	**35.0p**	**66.0p**

Impending issues

Name	Business	Sponsor	Issue method	Market debut	Expected market cap	Market
Wolfson Microelectronics	Audio technology	Citigroup	Placing	Q4 2003	**£200m**	Main
Creechurch	Insurance	Hoare Govett	Placing	Q4 2003	**£75m**	Aim
Burren Energy	Oil	Seymour Pierce	Placing	Q4 2003	**£130m**	Main
James Hull Associates	Dentistry	Numis Securities	Placing	Q4 2003	**£35m**	Aim
Bema Gold	Mining	Cannaccord Capital	Introduction	Sep 30	**£180m**	Aim
Real Good Food Co	Food producer	JM Finn & Co	Placing	Sep 30	**£5.5m**	Aim

Sources: Digital Look; Thomson Datastream

UK RECENT EQUITY ISSUES

Issue date	Issue price p	Sector	Stock code	Stock	Close price p	+/-	High	Low	Volume 000's	Mkt cap (£m)
25/9	§130	AIM	BTL	Bristol & London	172½		172½	159	-	0.40
25/9	§	AIM	AMF	America Minl Fld	56		56	51½	-	-
18/9	§1	AIM	CEV	Chicago Environm	102		102	102	-	-
18/9	-	Util	UU.A	Utd Utilities A	277½	+3½	281½	267	4530	858.3
16/9	§100	AIM	ERN	Epic Construction	105		105½	104¼	-	31.5
16/9	§	SpFn	IPXA	Impax 5.5% Cnv Ln	105		105	105	-	2.66
15/9	*	Sftw	CRP	CryptoLogic	612½	-5	695	612½	-	75.1
12/9	*25	AIM	INC	Incite Hldgs	66½	-3	73½	32½	402	19.4
8/9	§	AIM	RBUY	Readybuy	54½		54½	52½	5	9.81
28/8	§	AIM	CP	Corpora	35		45	35	-	4.90
12/8	§	AIM	DVS	Designer Vision	16½		17½	12	-	8.25
4/8	*	AIM	CBM	Cambrian Mining	44	-½	48½	32½	6	8.36
30/7	-	AIM	AEY	Antrim Energy	52½		52½	35½	10	10.5
29/7	§48	AIM	CLK	CityBlock	51½		51½	51½	-	11.2
16/7	*	AIM	OHT	Orad Hi-Tec	98½		104	88½	-	10.5
10/7	285	Med	YELL	Yell	300½	-4½	326½	276	10176	2,109
8/7	§91	AIM	CUS	CustomVis	69½		94½	67½	-	24.1
1/7	§100	AIM	MSG	Milestone	85½	+4	104½	54½	33	18.5
30/6	-	E&EE	RXOP	Roxboro Red Pf	75		76	74½	-	42.6
27/6	103.5	AIM	FPM	Faroe Petroleum	81		115½	78	-	34.5

§ Placing price. * Introduction. ‡ When issued. For a full explanation of all other symbols please refer to the London Share Service notes.

Exhibit 16.1 New issue tables in the *Financial Times*

Source: *Financial Times* 29 September 2003 and 26 September 2003

Underwriting

The sponsor generally **underwrites** the issue. In return for a fee, underwriters guarantee to buy any shares not taken up by the market. This is a kind of insurance for the company – come what may, it will raise the money it needs to fulfil its strategic objectives.

The sponsor generally charges a fee of 2 per cent of the issue proceeds and then pays part of that fee, say 1.25 per cent, to **sub-underwriters** (usually large financial institutions) who each agree to buy a certain number of shares if called on to do so. In the vast majority of cases the underwriters do not have to purchase any shares and so walk away with thousands or millions of pounds in fees. However, there are occasional flops when they are forced to buy shares no one else wants, resulting in the shares **overhanging the market**. Attempts have been made by some companies to go below the standard 2 per cent cost of underwriting but the majority continue to accept this as the going rate. It is a 'nice little earner' for the City institutions, and they like to keep it that way.

The role of the corporate broker

Brokers play a vital role in advising on share market conditions and the likely demand from investors for the company's shares. They also represent the company to investors to try to generate interest. When debating issues such as the method to be employed, the marketing strategy, the size of the issue, the timing or the pricing of the shares, the company may value the market knowledge the broker has to offer. Brokers can also organise sub-underwriting, and in the years following the flotation may work with the company to maintain a liquid and properly informed market in its shares. When a broker is employed as a sponsor the two roles can be combined. If the sponsor is a merchant bank, the UKLA requires that a broker also be appointed.

After flotation

The UKLA insists on listed companies having '**continuing obligations**'. The intention is to ensure that all price-sensitive information is given to the market as soon as possible and that there is '**full and accurate disclosure**'. Information is price-sensitive if it might influence the share price or the trading in the shares. Investors need to be sure that they are not disadvantaged by market distortions caused by some participants having the benefit of superior information. Public announcements will be required in a number of instances, for example: the development of major new products; the signing of major contracts; details of an acquisition; a sale of large assets; a change in directors; a decision to pay a dividend. The website *www.uk-wire.co.uk* shows all major announcement made by companies going back many years.

Methods of flotation

The sponsor will look at the motives for wanting a quotation, at the amount of money that is to be raised, at the history and reputation of the firm, and will then advise on the best method of issuing the shares. There are various methods, ranging from a full-scale offer for sale to a relatively simple introduction. The final choice often rests on the costs of the method of issue, which can vary considerably. Here are the main options:

- **Offer for sale.** The company sponsor offers shares to the public by inviting subscriptions from institutional and individual investors. Sometimes newspapers carry a prospectus and an application form. However, most investors will need to contact the sponsor or the broker to obtain an application form. Normally the shares are **offered at a fixed price** determined by the company's directors and their financial advisers. A variation of this method is **an offer for sale by tender**. Here investors are invited to state a price at which they are willing to buy (above a minimum reserve price). The sponsor gathers the applications and then selects a price which will dispose of all the shares – the strike price. Investors bidding a price above this will be allocated shares at the strike price – not at the price of their bid. Those who bid below the strike price will not receive any shares. This method is useful in situations where it is very difficult to value a company – for instance, where there is no comparable company already listed or where the level of demand may be difficult to assess. Many investors are put off offers for sale by tender because they do not want the onerous task of estimating the share's value.
- **Introduction.** Introductions do not raise any new money for the company. If the company's shares are already quoted on another stock exchange or there is a wide spread of shareholders, with more than 25 per cent of the shares in public hands, the Stock Exchange permits a company to be 'introduced' to the market. This method may allow companies trading on AIM to move up to the Official List or foreign corporations to gain a London listing. This is the cheapest method of flotation since there are no underwriting costs and relatively small advertising expenditures.
- **Offer for subscription.** An offer for subscription is similar to an offer for sale, but it is only partially underwritten. This method is used by new companies which state at the outset that if the share issue does not raise a certain minimum the offer will be aborted. This is a particularly popular method for new investment trusts: if the fund managers do not raise enough to create a large investment company which will be able to pay them large ongoing management fees, then they can abandon the whole idea.
- **Placing.** In a placing, shares are offered to the public but the term 'public' is narrowly defined. Instead of engaging in advertising to the population at large, the sponsor or broker handling the issue sells the shares to its own private clients – usually institutions such as pension and insurance funds. The costs of this method are considerably lower than those of an offer for sale. There are lower publicity and legal costs. A drawback of this method is that the spread of shareholders is going to be more limited. To alleviate this problem the Stock Exchange does insist on large number of placees holding shares after the new issue. In the 1980s the most frequently used method of new issue was the offer for sale. This ensured a wide spread of share ownership and thus a more liquid secondary market. It also permitted all investors to participate in new issues. Placings were only permitted for small offerings when the costs of an offer for sale would have been prohibitive. Today any size of new issue can be placed. As this method is much cheaper and easier than an offer for sale, companies have

naturally switched to placings. The majority now choose to use the placing method, thus excluding small investors from most new issues.

- **Intermediaries offer**. This method is often combined with a placing. Shares are offered for sale to financial institutions such as stockbrokers. Clients of these intermediaries can then apply to buy shares from them.
- **Book-building.** Selling new issues of shares through book-building is a popular technique in the USA. It is starting to catch on in Europe. Under this method the financial advisers to an issue contact major institutional investors to get from them bids for the shares. The investors' orders are sorted according to price, quantity and other factors such as 'firmness' of bid (e.g. 'we will buy regardless of market conditions'). This information may then be used to establish a price for the issue and the allocation of shares.

Timetable for a new offer

The various stages of a new share issue will be explained using the example of the flotation of easyJet on the Official List. This timetable is set out in Exhibit 16.2.

- **Pre-launch publicity.** For many years before the flotation, easyJet raised its profile with the public with exciting news stories. It even allowed a television company to make a fly-on-the-wall documentary about the firm's operations. This was shown weekly for many weeks, almost like a soap opera.
- **Technicalities.** UBS Warburg and Credit Suisse First Boston were co-leading sponsors, with Merrill Lynch and Schroder Salomon Smith Barney assisting as co-managers. It was decided to float by way of a placing. Having many leading City institutions managing the issue with their extensive range of contacts with fund managers was valuable for placing the shares. On 9 November a price range of 280p–340p was indicated. This was a narrower range than that announced the previous week (250p–350p). By announcing a price range the sponsors and fund managers can gauge reaction from potential buyers before selecting the final single price.

  It was decided that the company would sell 63 million shares (25.1 per cent of the enlarged capital). A further 9.45 million shares were put aside for a '**greenshoe**' or **over-allotment issue**. This means that the company reserved the right to sell these additional shares if there was sufficient demand. Doing so would raise the final **free-float** (shares not associated with a person closely connected with the business, e.g. dominant shareholder) to 27.8 per cent of the enlarged capital.[2]

  During 2000 easyJet had been gathering a distinguished group of non-executive directors to supplement its board, with the task of looking after the interests of all the shareholders. Tony Illsley, the former chief executive of Telewest Communications,

[2] The greenshoe shares must be issued at the offer price within 30 days of admission to the Official List.

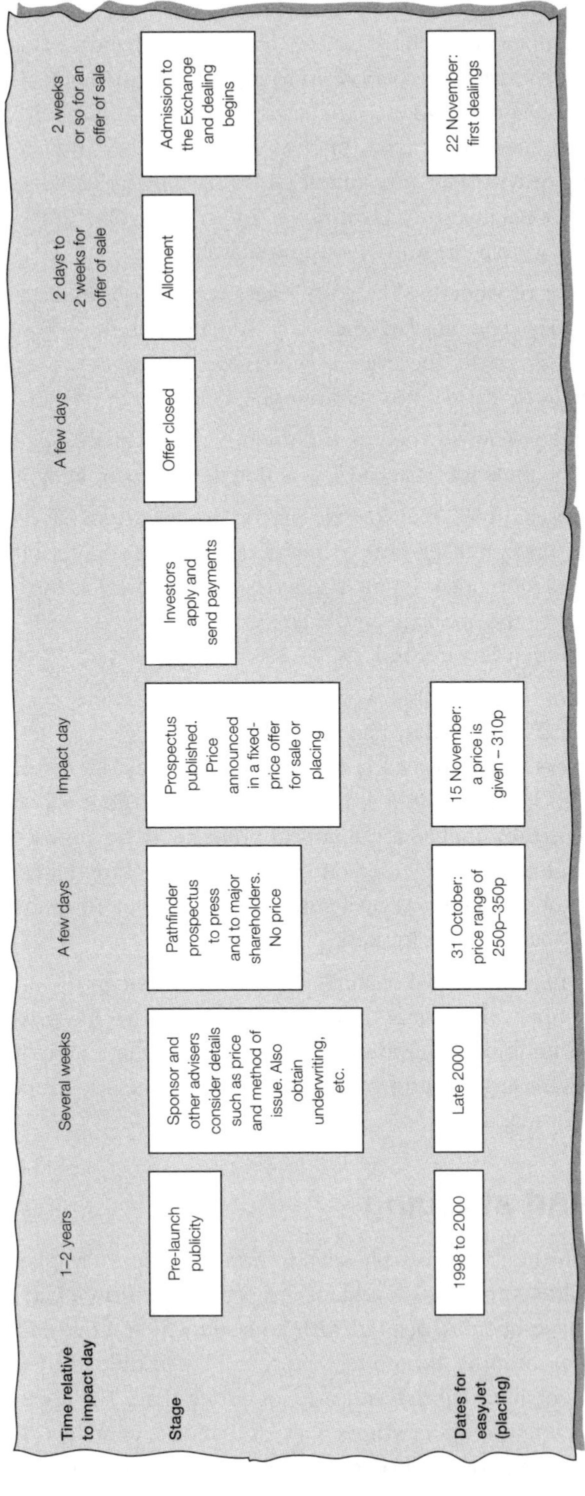

Exhibit 16.2 Timetable of an offer for sale and a placing

was hired in May, Colin Day, chief financial officer of Reckitt Benckiser, was appointed in September and John Quelch, dean of the London Business School, joined in November. During the period up to **impact day** the auditors were very busy and the sponsoring banks marketed the issue forcefully. 'Auditors have been working hard to get the figures into shape for the prospectus, but in the meantime analysts from easyJet's heavyweight investment banks have been intensely marketing this research to institutional investors' (*Financial Times*, 25 October 2000, p. 3). It was decided that no shares were to be sold by existing shareholders.

- **Pathfinder prospectus.** The pathfinder prospectus is made available a few days before the sale. This contains background information on the company, but does not tell the potential investors the price at which the shares are to be offered. The pathfinder prospectus for easyJet was sent out on 31 October.
- **Impact day.** The prospectus is launched at this stage, together with the price. For easyJet the price was set at 310p, valuing the company at £778 million.
- **Offer closes.** In an offer for sale up to 2 weeks are needed for investors to consider the offer price and send in payments. There is a fixed cut-off date for applications. In the case of a placing the time needed is much shorter as the share buyers have already indicated to the sponsors and managers their interest and transactions can be expedited between City institutions.
- **Allotment.** More shares were applied for than were available – they were **oversubscribed** – and so they had to be allocated. This can be achieved in a number of different ways. A **ballot** means that only some investors receive shares (recipients are selected at random). In a **scale-down** applicants generally receive some shares, but fewer than they applied for. A **cut-off point** might be imposed by which applicants for large quantities are excluded. Money not used to buy shares is returned to investors. easyJet's share offer was over-subscribed by about 10 times. It is not clear how the available shares were allocated.
- **Dealing begins.** Formal dealing in the shares through the Stock Exchange started on 22 November. The shares traded 10 per cent above the placing price at 342p, giving investors an immediate profit. Between 15 November and 22 November some shares had been trading in a **grey market** off the exchange – see Exhibit 16.3 for a description of the grey market.

Underpricing and stagging

The company floating is usually keen to have the offer fully taken up by public investors. To have shares left with the underwriters gives the firm a bad image because it is perceived to have been associated with an issue which 'flopped'. Furthermore, over the following few months, the underwriters will try to offload their shares, and this action has the potential to depress the price for a long time. The sponsor also has an incentive to avoid leaving the underwriters with large blocks of shares. The sponsoring organisation consists of people who are professional analysts and deal makers, and an issue

Everything you wanted to know about the grey market.

Norma Cohen puts her grey matter to good use

Q. So what's this grey market I keep reading about?

A: In short, it is the market where shares that do not yet exist are traded.

Huh? How can you trade in shares that don't exist?

Well, that's because you are quite certain that they will soon exist and, moreover, you have a fairly good idea of a range of prices at which investors are prepared to buy them.

Why does anyone want to buy – or sell – shares before they exist?

Institutions might want to use the grey market because they fear they will not get as large a share of the IPO as they wanted. Alternatively, they may think they paid too much and want to get rid of some before the price sinks further. Investment banks may want to use the market to hedge a long or short position, and the dentist in Bromley may just want a quick punt without having actually to buy the shares or pay tax on winnings.

Is there just one big grey market?

No. In fact, 'grey market' is a kind of shorthand for three different kinds of trading. The first of these is London Stock Exchange trading in initial public offerings, or rights issues, and is known as When-Issued Trading.

The second is the real grey market. It works through brokers – Tullett & Tokyo Liberty is the UK market leader – and participants sign contracts promising to buy or sell unissued shares at set prices. Neither the buyer nor the seller know each other's identity and the broker takes a fee to act as middleman.

Oh. So if the price collapses before the shares are issued, can I tear up my contract?

Absolutely not. These are binding contracts and brokers have been known to pursue counterparties in the law courts, even in East Asia. But you haven't let me finish.

The third route into the grey market is via spread betting firms. These allow punters to take a bet on where the price of an IPO will be. The spread betting firm takes a view on the shares and punters offer their own views. It's not a bad way to gauge demand for an IPO before the shares even emerge.

The difference is that in WI and grey market trading, counterparties actually buy and sell stock. In spread betting, you never buy or sell stock; you only take or pay cash based upon how right or wrong you were.

So this is legal?

Sure. And not only is it legal, but much of it is highly regulated. WI trading, for instance, is conducted under the auspices of the LSE and all its rules apply. Grey market trading contracts themselves are not regulated, but many brokers are. They frequently provide information on trades to regulators when asked. Spread betting is regulated.

Is there grey market trading in all new stocks?

No. The LSE will only offer WI activity when a member firm applies to have it available. Typically, it will not offer it for issues with a free float of less than £100m, and it will not allow it until the listing particulars have been published and the advisers have announced the opening share price.

In the grey market, brokers will offer facilities for smaller issues, with a minimum free float of €25m. They will broker deals once the listing particulars are available, generally up to 10 business days before the shares are traded, and will do so without actually knowing the final price of the offering. Spread betting firms are reluctant to make a book on IPOs smaller than £50m.

If I buy non-existent shares, can I pay with non-existent money?

Don't be ridiculous. Of course you have to pay. How much and when depends on which bit of the market you've used. For WI trading, shares settle on the day actual trading begins.

In the grey market, payment becomes due also on the day trading begins although there can be difficulties in getting hold of stock and this causes delays. In spread betting, of course, you pay – or take a cheque – on the agreed contract date. But you have to put up a percentage of the value of your deal when you open the contract, and if the price appears to be going against you, you will have to make a further deposit.

Exhibit 16.3 The grey market

Source: *Financial Times* 10 May 2002

which flops can be very bad for their image. It might indicate that they are not reading the market signals correctly and that they have overestimated demand. They might have done a poor job in assessing the firm's riskiness or failed to communicate its virtues to investors. These bad images can stick, so both the firm and the sponsor have an incentive to err on the side of caution and price a little lower to make sure that the issue will be fully subscribed. A major problem in establishing this **discount** is that in an offer for sale the firm has to decide the price one or two weeks before the close of the offer. In the period between impact day and first trading the market may decline dramatically. This makes potential investors nervous about committing themselves to a fixed price. To overcome this additional risk factor the issue price may have to be significantly less than the expected first day's trading price. Giving this discount to new shares deprives the firm of money which it might have received in the absence of these uncertainties, and can therefore be regarded as a cost to the firm but an opportunity for buyers in a new issue. They can buy the shares from the company and then sell immediately following receipt. This is called **stagging**. In the case of easyJet the shares moved to a first-day premium of 10 per cent. It could be argued that the existing shareholders sold a piece of the business too cheaply at the issue price.

Stagging for private investors is rarely possible these days as most new issue shares go to institutions in a placing. However there are occasional opportunities in intermediaries offers or (rare) offers for sale.

How does an AIM flotation differ from one on the Official List?

The AIM's rules are kept as relaxed as possible to encourage a wide variety of companies to join and keep costs of membership and capital raising to a minimum. However, it is felt necessary to have some vetting process for firms wishing to float on the AIM. This policing role was given to **nominated advisers** who are paid a fee by the company to act as unofficial 'sponsors' in investigating and verifying its financial health. When the nominated adviser's fee is added to those of the stock exchange, accountants, lawyers, printers and so on, the cost can be as much as 10–12 per cent of the amount being raised. The AIM was designed so that the cost of joining was in the region of £40,000–£50,000. But, this figure has now risen so that frequently more than £300,000 is paid. The nominated advisers argue that they are forced to charge firms higher fees because they incur more investigatory costs due to the emphasis put on their policing role by the Stock Exchange.

Rights issues

A rights issue is an invitation to existing shareholders to purchase additional shares in the company. This is a very popular method of raising new funds. It is easy and relatively cheap (compared with new issues). Directors are not required to seek the prior consent of shareholders, and the London Stock Exchange will only intervene in larger issues (to adjust the timing so that the market does not suffer from too many issues in one period). The UK has particularly strong traditions and laws concerning **pre-emption rights**. These require a company raising new equity capital by selling shares to offer those shares to the existing shareholders first. The owners of the company are entitled to subscribe for the new shares in proportion to their existing holding. This will enable them to maintain their existing percentage ownership of the company – the only difference is that each slice of the company cake is bigger because it has more financial resources under its control.

The shares are usually offered at a significantly **discounted price** from the market value of the current shares – typically 10–20 per cent. This gives the illusion that shareholders are getting a bargain. But, as we shall see, the benefit from the discount given is taken away by a decline in value of the old shares.

Shareholders can either buy these shares themselves or **sell the 'right'** to buy to another investor. For further reassurance that the firm will raise the anticipated finance, rights issues are usually underwritten.

Example

Take the case of the imaginary listed company, Getbigger plc, with 100 million shares in issue. It wants to raise £25 million for expansion but does not want to borrow it. Given that its existing shares are quoted on the stock market at 120p, the new rights shares will have to be issued at a lower price to appeal to shareholders because there is a risk of the market share price falling in the period between the announcement and the purchasing of new shares. (The offer must remain open for at least 3 weeks.) Getbigger has decided that the £25 million will be obtained by issuing 25 million shares at 100p each. Thus the ratio of new shares to old is 25 : 100. In other words, this issue is a 'one-for-four' rights issue. Each shareholder will be offered one new share for every four already held. The discount on these new shares is 20p or 16.7 per cent.

If the market price before the issue is 120p, valuing the entire company at £120 million and another £25 million is pumped into the company by selling 25 million shares at £1, it logically follows that the market price after the rights issue cannot remain at 120p (assuming all else equal). A company that was previously valued at £120 million which then adds £25 million of value to itself (in the form of cash) should be worth £145 million. This company now has 125 million shares, therefore each share is worth £1.16 (i.e. £145 million divided by 125 million shares).

An alternative way of calculating the **ex-rights** price is as follows:

Four existing shares at a price of 120p	480p
One new share for cash at 100p	100p
Value of five shares	580p
Value of one share ex-rights = 580p/5	116p

The shareholders have experienced a decline in the price of their old shares from 120p to 116p. A fall of this magnitude necessarily follows from the introduction of new shares at a discounted price. However, the loss is exactly offset by the gain in share value on the new rights issue shares. They cost 100p but have a market price of 116p. This can be illustrated through the example of Sid, who owned 100 shares worth £120 prior to the rights announcement. Sid loses £4 on the old shares – their value is now £116. However, he makes a gain of £4 on the new shares:

Cost of rights shares (25 × £1)	£25
Ex-rights value (25 × £1.16)	£29
Gain	£4

When journalists talk glibly of a rights offer being 'very attractively priced for shareholders' they are generally talking nonsense. Whatever the size of the discount the same value will be removed from the old shares to leave the shareholder no worse or better off. Logically value cannot be handed over to the shareholders from the size of the discount decision. Shareholders own all the company's shares before and after the rights issue – they can't hand value to themselves without also taking value from themselves. Of course, if the prospects for the company's profits rise because it can now make brilliant capital expenditures, which lead to dominant market positions, then the value of shares will rise – for both the old and the new shares. But this is value creation that has nothing to do with the level of the discount.

What if a shareholder does not want to take up the rights?

As owners of the firm, all shareholders must be treated in the same way. To make sure that some shareholders do not lose out because they are unwilling or unable to buy more shares, the law requires that shareholders have a third choice, other than to buy or not buy the new shares. This is to sell the rights on to someone else on the stock market – **selling the rights nil paid**. Take the case of the impoverished Sid, who is unable to find the necessary £25. He could sell the rights to subscribe for the shares to another investor and not have to go through the process of taking up any of the shares himself. Indeed, so deeply enshrined are pre-emption rights that even if the shareholder does nothing the company will sell his rights to the new shares on his behalf and send the proceeds to him. Thus, Sid would benefit to the extent of 16p per share or a total of £4 (if the market price stays constant), which adequately compensates for the loss on the 100 shares he holds. But the extent of his control over the company has been reduced – his percentage share of the votes has decreased.

The **value of a right** on one new share is:

Theoretical market value of share ex-rights – Subscription price = 116p – 100p = 16p.

Ex-rights and cum-rights

Shares bought in the stock market and designated **cum-rights** carry with them the right to subscribe for the new shares in the rights issue. After a cut-off date the shares go **ex-rights**, which means that any purchaser of old shares during that period will not have the right to purchase any new shares in the rights issue – they remain with the former shareholder.

The price discount decision

Rights basis	Number of new shares (m)	Price of new shares (p)	Total raised (£m)
1 for 4	25	100	25
1 for 3	33.3	75	25
1 for 2	50	50	25
1 for 1	100	25	25

Exhibit 16.4 Comparison of different rights bases

It does not matter greatly whether Getbigger raises £25 million on a one-for-four basis at 100p or on a one-for-three basis at 75p per share, or on some other basis. As Exhibit 16.4 shows, whatever the basis of the rights issue, the company will receive £25 million and the shareholders will see the price of their old shares decrease, but this will be exactly offset by the value of the rights on the new shares. However, the ex-rights price will change. For a one-for-three basis it will be £108.75:

Three old shares at 120p	360p
One new share at 75p	75p
Value of four shares	435p
Value of one share = 435p/4	108.75p

If Getbigger chose the one-for-one basis this would be regarded as a **deep-discounted rights issue** (current share price 120p, new shares sold at 25p). With an issue of this sort there is only a minute probability that the market price will fall below the rights offer price and therefore there is almost complete certainty that the offer will be taken up. It seems reasonable to suggest that the underwriting service provided by the institutions is largely redundant here and the firm can make a significant saving. Yet most rights issues are underwritten, usually involving between 100 and 400 sub-underwriters. In the 1990s the underwriting fees used to be a flat 2 per cent of the offer. However, fees have fallen recently and can be as little as 0.75 per cent for a low-risk deep-discounted issue. Note that a deep discount can sometimes be a disadvantage for private investors – for instance, if they sell the rights nil-paid they may face a capital gains tax bill.

Information on rights issues

The *Financial Times* carries a table showing recent rights issues and the current trading prices of nil paid rights. The *Investors Chronicle* provides details of recently announced issues.

Other equity issues

Some companies argue that the lengthy procedures and expense associated with rights issues (e.g. a minimum three-week offer period) frustrate directors' efforts to take advantage of opportunities in a timely fashion. Firms in the USA have much more freedom to bypass pre-emption rights. They are able to sell blocks of shares to securities houses for distribution elsewhere in the market. This is fast and has low transaction costs. If this were permitted in the UK there would be a concern for existing shareholders: they could experience a dilution of their voting power and/or the share could be sold at such a low price that a portion of the firm is handed over to new shareholders too cheaply. The UK authorities have produced a compromise, under which firms must obtain shareholders' approval through a **special resolution** (a majority of 75 per cent of those voting) at the company's AGM, or at an EGM, to **waive the pre-emption right**. Even then the shares must not be sold to outside investors at more than a 5 per cent discount to the share price. This is an important condition. It does not make any difference to existing shareholders if new shares are offered at a deep discount to the market price as long as they are offered to them. If external investors get a discount there is a transfer of value from the current shareholders to the new.

Placings and open offers

In **placings**, new shares of companies already quoted on the stock market are sold directly to a narrow group of external investors. The institutions, as existing shareholders, have produced guidelines to prevent abuse, which normally allow a placing of only a small proportion of the company's capital (a maximum of 5 per cent in a single year, and no more than 7.5 per cent is to be added to the company's equity capital over a rolling three-year period) in the absence of a **claw-back**. Under claw-back existing shareholders have the right to reclaim the shares as though they were entitled to them under a rights issue. They can buy them at the price they were offered to the external investors. With a claw-back the issue becomes an '**open offer**'. The major difference compared with a rights issue is that if they do not exercise this claw-back right they receive no compensation for any reduction in the price of their existing shares – there are no nil-paid rights to sell. Shareholders on the share register at the time of the announcement of an open offer will receive a document indicating how many shares they can apply for and a timetable. Shareholders generally have 3 weeks to complete application forms and make payments. Trading in the new shares will start a week or so after the final deadline for applications. *Investors Chronicle* carries details of recent and proposed open offers.

Vendor placing

If a company wishes to pay for an asset such as a subsidiary of another firm or an entire company with newly issued shares, but the vendor does not want to hold the shares, the purchaser could arrange for the new shares to be bought by institutional investors for cash. In this way the buyer gets the asset, the vendor (e.g. shareholders in the target company in a merger or takeover) receive cash and the institutional investor makes an investment. There is usually a claw-back arrangement for a vendor placing (if the issue is more than 10 per cent of market capitalisation of the acquirer). Again, the price discount can be no more than 5 per cent of the current share price.

Bought deal

Instead of selling shares to investors, companies are sometimes able to make an arrangement with a securities house whereby it buys all the shares being offered for cash. The securities house then sells the shares on to investors included in its distribution network, hoping to make a profit on the deal. Securities houses often compete to buy a package of shares from the company, with the highest bidder winning. The securities houses take the risk of being unable to sell the shares for at least the amount that they paid. Bought deals are limited by the 5 per cent pre-emption rules.

Information on share issues

The London Stock Exchange (*www.londonstockexchange.com*) provides information on new issues and further issues by established quoted companies.

Scrip issues

Scrip issues do not raise new money: a company simply gives shareholders more shares in proportion to their existing holdings. The value of each shareholding does not change, because the share price drops in proportion to the additional shares. They are also known as **capitalisation issues** or **bonus issues**. The purpose is to make shares more attractive by bringing down the price. British investors are thought to consider a share price of £10 and above as less attractive than one in single figures. So a company with shares trading at £15 on the market might distribute two 'free' shares for every one held – a two-for-one scrip issue. Since the amount of money in the firm and its economic potential are constant, the share price will theoretically fall to £5. Scrip issues are often regarded as indicating confidence in future earnings increases. If this new optimism is expressed in the share price it may not fall as much as theory would suggest.

A number of companies have an annual scrip issue while maintaining a constant dividend per share, effectively raising the level of profit distribution. For example, if a company pays a regular dividend of 20p per share but also has a one-for-ten scrip, the annual income will go up by 10 per cent. (A holder of 10 shares who previously received 200p now receives 220p on a holding of 11 shares.)

Scrip dividends are slightly different: shareholders are offered a choice between receiving a cash dividend and receiving additional shares. This is more like a rights issue because the shareholders are making a cash sacrifice if they accept the scrip shares.

A **'share split'** (stock split) means that the **nominal value** of each share is reduced in proportion to the increase in the number of shares, so the total book value of shares remains the same. So, for example, a company may have 1 million shares in issue with a nominal value of 50p each. It issues a further 1 million shares to existing shareholders with the nominal value of each share reducing to 25p, but total nominal value remains at £500,000. Of course, the share price will halve – assuming all else is constant.

If the share price goes too low, say 15p, companies may decide to **consolidate** its shares. This is the opposite of a split: the number of shares is reduced and the nominal value of each remaining share rises. If the nominal (par) value is 5p the company could consolidate on the basis of five shares for one. A 25p nominal share would replace five 5p nominal shares and the new share would then trade in the market at 5 × 15p = 75p (or slightly more if investors are more attracted to shares within a 'normal' price range).

Share buy-backs and special dividends

Occasionally directors conclude that the company has too much equity capital and that it would be appropriate to hand back some of the cash to shareholders. It could be that the company is able to generate higher returns on each remaining share by borrowing more to reduce the number of shares by self-purchase. It could be that the directors think the shares are undervalued, and by reducing the quantity on the market the price will rise. It could be that the directors are aware of the tendency of companies to squander surplus cash on value-destroying mergers, and they want to avoid the temptation.

Buy-backs may also be a useful alternative when the company is unsure about the sustainability of a possible increase in the normal cash dividend. A stable policy may be pursued on dividends, and then shares are repurchased as and when surplus cash is available. This two-track approach avoids sending an over-optimistic signal about future growth through changing underlying dividend levels.

It is necessary for companies to ask shareholders' permission to buy back shares. Many companies now regularly vote at AGMs to allow buy-backs of up to 10 per cent of share capital in the following 12 months. The directors then have the freedom to choose when, and if, they will buy in shares. The shares bought by the company are cancelled and therefore cannot be resold.

A second possible approach to returning surplus funds is to pay a **special dividend**. This is the same as the normal dividend, but bigger and paid on a one-off basis. A special dividend has to be offered to all shareholders. However, a share repurchase may not always be open to all shareholders as it can be accomplished in one of three ways:

- purchasing shares in the stock market;
- all shareholders are invited to tender some or all of their shares;
- an arrangement with particular shareholders.

Companies purchasing their own shares are listed in *Investors Chronicle* each week.

Many experienced investors, such as Warren Buffett, take buy-backs as an indicator of a management team that is owner-orientated because they are volunteering to reduce the size of their empire. They would rather hand back cash for shareholders to employ elsewhere than go on investing in projects and acquisitions producing ever smaller returns. Other less thoughtful commentators see buy-backs as an admission of managerial failure to develop avenues for expansion. Personally, I would rather back a management team that sticks to where it has a competitive advantage and refuses to expand beyond its circle of competence than one that is so full of hubris that it can always find a use for any amount of shareholders' money.

However, buy-backs can be taken too far. Directors can become a little too macho when it comes to borrowing more to hand out the cash to shareholders. Many companies in the US in the 1990s found that the stock market applauded each buy-back with a share price rise. However, there came a point when the solvency of the business was threatened, especially as the economy turned down. The interest burden just became too great. So when viewing (and voting on) buy-backs, consider the overall debt levels that would result.

17

Taxation and investors

If you are fortunate enough to receive income or capital gains from your investments then the Inland Revenue will be interested in hearing about it. It is illegal to **evade** tax (i.e. deliberately making a false statement or omitting a relevant fact) so you need to keep careful records and declare gains at the appropriate time (e.g. on an annual self-assessment tax return).

The heart sinks at the prospect of handing over large sums, but don't despair. There are many ways of **avoiding** tax – 'avoiding' is OK, it's legal. You can take advantage of various tax breaks introduced by government – usually to encourage people to act in particular ways (e.g. to save more, or to buy shares in companies just starting up). Thus, there are 'tax-efficient' actions that investors can take to reduce the size of the cheque sent to the Inland Revenue. Be careful though: some of these tax wrappers and other structures can cost more than they are worth. In other words, don't let the tax tail wag the investment dog. This chapter describes the main forms of taxation investors have to bear, as well as methods of reducing tax, together with some thoughts on whether these breaks are worth taking advantage of.

Tax rules and allowances change from year to year. The material below is informed by the 2003–04 tax year rules. You might like to consult an expert to understand your position in another year. The Inland Revenue website (*www.inlandrevenue.gov.uk*) can be useful for keeping you up to date.

■ Stamp duty

A tax that you have to pay regardless of whether you are a successful investor is stamp duty. A charge of 0.5 per cent of the value of share purchases (and other marketable securities) is levied at the time of purchase. The tax is automatically added to the bill that you receive from your broker.

Some people get quite hot under the collar about stamp duty, saying that it discourages investment in UK shares, is unfair because it is not based on income, eats into pensions and makes the cost of equity capital greater for companies. The government raises around £4,000 million per year from it and has shown little interest in abolishing it.

■ Tax on dividends

Dividends are subject to income tax. When the company sends you a dividend it has already deducted 10 per cent for taxes – you simply receive the net amount after tax.[1] Unfortunately, if you are not a taxpayer you are unable to reclaim the tax paid. If you are a standard rate tax payer (22 per cent tax rate) you will have no further tax to pay on the dividend.

[1] The 10 per cent tax paid on dividends is counted as part of the company's corporation tax liability for the year.

If you are a higher rate taxpayer (40 per cent marginal rate in 2003–04) you will be chargeable for tax on dividends at a rate of 32.5 per cent. Because 10 per cent has already been paid you will have to pay the difference, i.e. 22.5 per cent, at a later date (after completing your tax return).

You will receive a voucher with the dividend payment showing the tax paid. Hold on to the voucher because you will be asked to declare dividend income and tax payments made on your tax return. It is your responsibility to contact the Inland Revenue if you believe you have taxable income (or gains) to declare.

If you choose to receive shares instead of a cash dividend (called a '**scrip dividend**' or '**stock dividend**' – see Chapter 16) the shares are valued as income equal to the alternative cash dividend for income tax purposes. If there is no cash alternative to the scrip the market value is used. If the cash alternative differs from the market value of the shares by 15 per cent or more the market value will be used. Again, tax is deemed to have been paid at the 10 per cent rate, so if you are a basic rate taxpayer no more tax is payable. A higher rate taxpayer will have to pay more.

Let us take an example: Martin receives a dividend of 20p per share on his 1,000 shares, a total of £200. He also receives a tax credit for 10 per cent of the gross amount of the dividend amounting to £22.22. This represents 10 per cent of the gross dividend which is £222.22: £200 + £22.22 = £222.22.

Martin is a higher rate taxpayer and will have to pay tax of 32.5 per cent of the gross dividend: £222.22 × 0.325 = £72.22. He is deemed to have paid £22.22 of this already (the company did it on his behalf) so he has to pay a further £50. Martin therefore walks away with £150.

Capital gains tax

If you sell an asset for more than it cost, you may be liable for capital gains tax (CGT). However, you will not be liable for tax on all the difference between the purchase price and the sale value. For a start you can deduct various expenses (e.g. stamp duty and brokers' fees). Second, you can set losses made in the same year (or carried forward from an earlier year) on other assets against the gain. Third, and perhaps most importantly, you are permitted to make annual gains of £7,900 (in 2003–04) tax free (called a 'capital gains **tax allowance**') – so you only pay tax on gains made above this figure. Fourth, you are entitled to **taper relief**.

Under taper relief the amount you pay in CGT reduces the longer you have held the shares. If you have held the shares for less than 3 years then you pay CGT (after allowance for expenses, deduction for capital losses and tax-free allowances) at the full rates. These rates depend on your marginal income tax rate as any chargeable gains are added to your income for the tax year and taxed as though they were the top slice of your income. If your income and chargeable capital gains combined put you into the higher tax band you will pay 40 per cent on the gains. If you are a standard rate taxpayer the chargeable gain is taxed at the standard income tax rate for savings, which is 20 per cent (not 22 per cent, which is the standard income tax rate for other income). If your marginal income tax rate is 10 per cent and the chargeable capital gain does not push you into standard rate, you will pay CGT at 10 per cent.

Taper relief decreases the amount of chargeable gain if the asset has been held for 3 years or more for holding periods that started after 5 April 1998. Taper relief applies to **net** gains – that is, after deduction of expenses and capital losses realised in the same year or brought forward from previous years. The rates of taper relief for investors are shown in Table 17.1. Note that you have to hold the asset for **complete tax years**. So, for example, if you bought in September 1998 and sold in February 2003 you have held for 4 years, 5 months, but this counts as only three complete tax years (5 April 1999 to 5 April 2002).

Table 17.1 Rates of taper relief for stock market investors

Number of complete years after 05.04.98 the asset was held	Percentage of chargeable gains subject to tax
Less than 3	100
3	95
4	90
5	85
6	80
7	75
8	70
9	65
10 or more	60

If you bought the asset before 5 April 1998, then you are permitted to reduce the gain made prior to April 1998 by an **indexation allowance** so that you do not have to pay tax on gains made simply due to inflation before 1998. The details of this are a complication too far for this book – seek specialist advice or obtain a tax book.[2]

Example

In 2003–04 Frank has taxable income, after personal allowances, of £26,000. He also makes capital gains on shares bought in 2002, after expenses and offsetting losses, of £16,000. We deduct his £7,900 annual CGT exemption to arrive at the chargeable gain of £8,100. In 2003–04 the basic rate band extended up to a taxable income (after personal allowances, etc.) of £30,500. The CGT payable will be at two rates. The first £4,500 will be taxed at 20 per cent (taking income plus chargeable capital gains up to £30,500), with the remainder taxed at 40 per cent.

[2] See A. Foreman and G. Mowles, *Zurich Tax Handbook* (Financial Times Prentice Hall, 2003); for a book on tax, this is fairly easy to follow.

			£
£30,500 – £26,000	= £4,500 at 20 per cent	=	900
£8,100 – £4,500	= £3,600 at 40 per cent	=	1,440
Total CGT payable			2,340

Tips on reducing CGT

For the majority of private investors the annual allowance of £7,900 will be more than enough to avoid paying any CGT. However, if you are fortunate enough to make substantial gains you might like to know about tax-efficient steps you can take :

- If you are married you could **transfer shares** to your spouse who could then make use of his/her annual £7,900 allowance. You have £15,800 of allowance between you. Transfers between spouses are not taxed.
- '**Bed and breakfasting**' used to be a very popular way of reducing CGT. If you expected to hold shares for a long time there might be many years when you are not using up the annual CGT allowance. Then, when you do sell, the (say) £50,000 capital gain can be offset against only the final year's allowance – so you face a large tax bill. To get around this investors would sell shares to realise a capital gain (bed) and then repurchase these the next day (breakfast) in each of the intervening years (or at least those when they made a gain). Then the capital gain in the final year is the gain made over merely the last 12 months or so. The loophole is now closed. You now have to leave a gap of 30 days before repurchasing if you wish the Inland Revenue to crystallise the capital gain. The exposure to share price change over this month reduced the attractiveness of this technique. The 30-day rule does not apply if you sell the shares and then buy identical shares within an individual savings account ('**bed-and-ISA**'). Alternatively you can reduce your risk exposure over the 30 days by buying a derivative instrument, the value of which goes up and down with the underlying share price (e.g. traded option, universal stock future, spread bet, contracts for difference – see Chapters 8, 9 and 10 for details). A further possibility is to sell your shares in the market to crystallise a loss, and then your spouse could reacquire them. This is called '**bed and spousing**'. The disadvantage of this is that you stop and restart the taper relief clock.
- If your losses in a tax year outweigh your gains, make sure you keep a careful record. You have to let the Inland Revenue know that you are offsetting **carry-forward losses** against gains in later years. Note you cannot offset capital losses against income – only against capital gains.
- **Accelerated taper relief** applies to shares of companies on the AIM or OFEX. CGT only applies to 25 per cent of any gain if the shares have been held for two years or more.[3] This creates, in effect, a CGT rate of 10 per cent on these gains for taxpayers who normally pay at the 40 per cent rate.

[3] Business asset taper relief after one year of holding is 50%, i.e. a gain of £50,000 is taxed as though it is £25,000.

One trick you cannot get away with is to give away the shares or sell them at an artificially low price to an accomplice who then sells them for you. The Inland Revenue are on to this one – they will value the disposal at the proper market price for CGT purposes.

Interest-bearing instruments

Interest from bank and building society accounts is taxed at 20 per cent unless you are liable for higher rate tax. Higher rate tax payers are required to declare this income and it will be subject to 40 per cent tax. The 20 per cent tax will be deducted **at source** by the bank and passed on to the Inland Revenue. (You can fill in a form to stop these deductions if you are unlikely to be a taxpayer.) Interest on gilts is subject to income tax deducted at source (at 20 per cent). You can request that this be paid gross. Private investors pay no tax on capital gains made on gilts. Interest on corporate bonds is normally subject to deduction of tax at source (at 20 per cent).

Inheritance tax

Inheritance tax (IHT) is a tax payable on transfers made on an individual's estate at the time of death (it also covers some gifts made during the individual's lifetime). Transfers of less than £255,000 are free of tax. For every £1 over this threshold 40 per cent goes in tax. Prior to death, gifts can be made to survivors – these are subject to a maximum of £3,000 per donor per year. Gifts made within 7 years of death are taxed at the death rates reduced by the following percentages:

Years before death	0–3	3–4	4–5	5–6	6–7	more than 7
Reduction in tax on gifts	0%	20%	40%	60%	80%	100%

Note that the tax is deducted from the estate before the residual is passed on to heirs. The total exemption is £255,000 on the estate; not £255,000 per heir.

Transfers to spouses are exempt from IHT. Setting up a trust is another way to gain exemption, but requires specialist knowledge – consult a professional (e.g. solicitor). Shares in companies listed on AIM or OFEX are exempt from IHT after a two-year holding period. Gifts to charities – given either while you are alive or in your will – are exempt from IHT and reduce your taxable estate.

Individual savings accounts, ISAs

ISAs should not be viewed as investments in themselves: they are 'wrappers' or 'baskets' which contain the underlying investments. These tax shelters protect your investments from income tax and CGT. The underlying investments fall into three categories :

- **Cash**. With a cash ISA your money is placed in deposit accounts (e.g. with banks or building societies) or National Savings products.
- **Life insurance policies**. These are investment products with some life insurance component (see Chapter 5).
- **Stocks and shares**. This covers shares, unit trusts, investment trusts, open-ended investment companies, corporate bonds, and gilts.

The tax benefits of ISAs are as follows:

- There is no capital gains tax to pay on investments held in the ISA.
- Tax is not deducted from interest paid from, say, bank accounts.

Unfortunately, from 6 April 2004 one of the benefits of ISAs will be removed: from that date dividends on shares (and unit trusts etc.) will be taxable in the normal way for a basic rate taxpayer. That is, the 10 per cent tax paid on dividend income from the company cannot be reclaimed. However, higher rate taxpayers will still be exempt from paying additional tax on dividend income from ISA investments – thus saving an amount equal to 22.5 per cent of the gross dividend.

There is a peculiar structure to ISAs. They are split into two types: the **maxi-ISA** and the **mini-ISA**. Each individual is allowed, on an annual basis, **either to place up to £7,000 in a maxi-ISA**, or to place up to £7,000 in three separate mini-ISAs run by different managers. With the mini-ISA option you cannot place more than £3,000 each tax year in a stocks and shares mini-ISA, more than £1,000 each year in a life-insurance mini-ISA or more than £3,000 in a cash mini-ISA. You cannot have both a maxi-ISA and three mini-ISAs and so the maximum you can invest each tax year is £7,000. The ISA allowance cannot be carried over to the following tax year.

It gets even more absurdly complicated: if you have opted for the maxi-ISA the plan manager can invest the full £7,000 in the stocks and shares type option or can offer to you the possibility of splitting the money between stocks and shares option, the cash option (up to a maximum of £3,000) and life insurance (up to £1,000) – see Exhibit 17.1.

You do not have to invest the full amount all in one go – you can make regular payments or irregular lump sums through the year, just so long as the total does not breach the annual limits. The amount you can put into ISAs each year is not increased if you also withdraw some money in the same tax year. So, if you put £3,000 into a cash ISA in November and then withdraw £1,800 in December, you cannot put another £1,800 in that tax year – you have already used your £3,000 allowance for the tax year. You are permitted to withdraw from an ISA at any time without incurring a tax charge; however, the ISA provider may impose penalties or restrict your freedom of action.

You cannot set up an ISA on your own. It is necessary to purchase the ongoing wrapper service from an ISA provider. Fund supermarkets (see Chapter 5) provide ISA wrappers within which it is possible to invest in many funds run by different managers. Overseas shares on main national exchanges can be held. The Financial Services Authority provides a good independent guide to ISAs, available free at *www.fsa.gov.uk*.

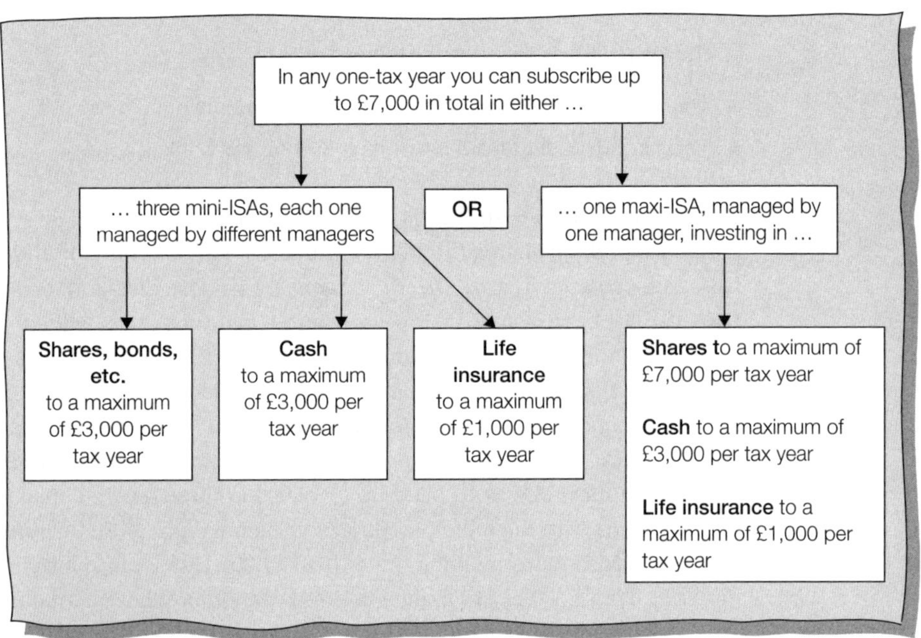

Exhibit 17.1 Types of ISA

Another option is a **self-select ISA**. Here you decide which shares, gilts, OEICs, corporate bonds, etc. should be bought for your funds. Not all ISA managers offer this option, so you may have to shop around. Be wary of the charges levied by the providers of self-select ISAs. In addition to dealing charges for buying the shares, etc., an initial charge (typically 1–6 per cent of the amount put in) can be followed by an annual fee linked to the value of the fund (0.5–1.75 per cent per annum). Alternatively a flat annual management charge will be made. There may also be a charge for dividend collection. You are permitted to deposit unlimited amounts of cash in the self-select ISA. However, the interest rate is usually less than a pure cash ISA and is taxed at 20 per cent. Note that AIM shares cannot be held in a self-select ISA.

The government has introduced a **CAT standard** for ISAs and other financial products. CAT stands for 'Charges, Access and Terms'. To gain CAT accreditation the ISA has to have low charges (e.g. a maximum 1 per cent annual management charge for equity ISAs), allow you to access your account easily (e.g. withdraw money from cash ISAs with no more than 7 days' notice) and have good terms (e.g. must not apply a penalty if you close your account). The CAT mark does not mean the managers are going to give you a high return, simply that they abide by minimum standards in the operation of the account.

Many people doubt the wisdom of holding share ISAs, especially with the withdrawal of the basic rate tax benefit on dividends in 2004. Most private investors are unlikely to be caught by CGT given the £7,900 annual allowance. Buying an equity ISA wrapper for your share investments can therefore mean paying an initial management fee and then annual management charges of 0.5–1.75 per cent for the minor tax advantage that if you are a higher rate taxpayer you will pay a maximum of 10 per cent on dividend income. If dividend income is around 4 per cent of the value of your holding, saving 22.5 per cent[4] of that (i.e. 0.9 per cent) will often be outweighed by the management charges.

Cash ISAs, on the other hand, are regarded as a good home for temporary cash holdings. No charges are applied and you can usually get at your money within a day or so. It is also a very competitive market, so the interest rates offered are good.

Personal pensions

Personal pensions are very tax-efficient if you are saving/investing for the long term:

- The money you put in (your **contributions**) qualify for full tax relief. This means that if you contribute say £2,808 from taxed earnings the government then adds back tax (at 22 per cent) to the fund amounting to £792, meaning that £3,600 is added to your pension pot. Higher rate taxpayers get additional tax relief.
- Once the money is in the fund it can grow without tax being levied on interest income, or on capital gains (however, dividend income is taxed).
- When you reach retirement you can take 25 per cent of the fund in cash, tax-free. (The rest has to be put into a fund that will provide you with an **annuity** – regular payments for the rest of your life.[5] '**Drawdown**' is an alternative to an annuity for 50–74-year-olds – consult a specialist book. Drawdown allows people to draw an income from the pension fund and invest the rest as they choose, e.g. in the stock market.)

[4] That is, 32.5% tax rate payable by higher rate taxpayers on dividends minus the 10% deducted at source, which cannot be reclaimed.

[5] The rules on annuities are to be rewritten shortly if the open debate initiated by the government is anything to go by.

You are permitted to start receiving the pension after the age of 50. You are compelled to do so at the age of 75. Between 50 and 75 you can keep your options open (unless you specified a retirement date when you started the plan). Opening a number of schemes allows you to begin drawing benefits at different points. You do not have to stop work to start receiving benefits under these schemes.

There is a wide range of type of funds: shares (UK or overseas, passive/tracker funds or actively managed), corporate bonds and gilts, cash. You can put money into a fund that invests in a mixture of securities – for example, a **lifestyle** scheme invests mostly in equities when you are many decades away from retirement and then gradually switches to cash and bonds when you are less than 10 years away.

You can save a regular amount into a personal pension (the mimimum is usually £20 a month) or pay in lump sums on an *ad hoc* basis. There are limits on the proportion of your annual income you can save which depend on your age – see Table 17.2.

Table 17.2 Contribution limits to personal pensions

Age	Maximum per cent of earnings
Below 36	17.5
36–45	20
46–50	25
51–55	30
56–60	35
61–74	40

A major disadvantage with personal pensions as investment vehicles is that you cannot get your money back quickly – at least not until you are 50. Even when you start to make use of the savings you are compelled to put most of the fund (75 per cent) into an annuity rather than having the flexibility to do what you wish with it. Drawdown allows a little more flexibility, but you still have to continue investing via the scheme and there are tight limits on how much can be taken out each year to be used elsewhere.

Stakeholder pensions are similar to standard personal pensions except that you pay low management charges (no more than 1 per cent of the value of the pension fund). Contributions can be very small (minimum contribution no higher than £20) and you can move the scheme to another provider without penalty. The most significant advantage is that whatever you pay in (which is a maximum of £3,600 grossed-up contributions per year) is treated as though it has been subject to basic rate tax. The stakeholder scheme provider can claim this back for you even if you are a non-taxpayer (e.g. non-working spouse) and therefore did not actually have tax deducted in the first place. Higher rate taxpayers can claim extra relief. To make use of stakeholder pensions your income has to be less than £30,000 a year.

A disadvantage of standard personal pensions is that you have no choice over the specific investments held in the fund – this is left up to the fund manager. If you are confident about your share selection capabilities then you may like to opt for a **self-invested personal pension (SIPP)**. These allow you to instruct the fund administrator to buy and sell shares and other investments on your behalf within the SIPP wrapper. You gain the same tax advantages as for a standard personal pension and you have control over the investment performance. The disadvantage is that you are likely to pay much more in charges.

SIPP administrators often insist on a high minimum initial investment: £25,000 is fairly typical, but it can be lower. The charging structure varies enormously. Some SIPP providers do not levy an initial charge for putting money into the fund (a 'set-up charge') but then charge you a 'trail commission' of about 0.5–1.5 per cent of the fund per year, with a minimum of between £200 and £400 per year. Other providers will charge you £200–£500 for setting up the account followed by fixed annual fees of £200–£300. Each deal buying or selling securities within the fund would also be subject to brokers' fees of £20–£30.

You can opt for advisory or discretionary SIPP funds, where a broker would either give advice on investments or take responsibility for making investment decisions. These accounts are more expensive than execution-only. Charges are typically £300–£700 to set up, followed by annual management fees of £300–£500.

Online SIPP providers offer a low-cost execution-only dealing service with flat rate charges that can be as low as £75 per year. The online providers will also accept lower minimum initial investments (sometimes as low as £5,000).

SIPPs can invest in domestic or international shares, gilts, corporate bonds, unit trusts, OEICs, investment trusts, insurance company funds, exchange traded derivatives and deposit accounts. They can even invest in commercial property. So you could, for example, use SIPP money to buy an office which you then rented out (maybe even to yourself) on a commercial basis, building up tax-free rental income and capital gains in your retirement fund. (You can borrow 75 per cent of the money for the property purchase and use other assets in the SIPP fund as security for the borrowing.) SIPPs have been particularly popular with doctors, lawyers and accountants to purchase the properties they occupy. The rent paid is a tax-deductible expense of their businesses. The rent received by the SIPP is not taxed in the fund. You cannot use a SIPP to buy residential property.

You can invest in SIPPs after retirement until you are 75. The rule that 25 per cent of a pension pot can be taken as cash-free lump sum applies to SIPPs as well.

SIPPs can be taken out for a non-tax-paying relative – the Inland Revenue will top up the fund at the basic rate of tax. The limit for this is a grossed-up £3,600 per year – so you would put in a maximum of £2,808. The maximum contributions you can make each year in SIPPs are as stated in Table 17.2.

Pay heed to the following warnings on pensions:

- Equities are riskier then bonds or cash, so it can be dangerous to be only 5–10 years away from retirement and be holding your entire pension fund in a handful of shares. To avoid the possibility of retiring just after a collapse in share prices it makes sense to shift the weighting of your fund gradually towards bonds and cash-type (e.g. deposit account) holdings, with perhaps a proportion of the fund in property.

- Be careful that you don't lose half of your fund in management charges of one sort or another. For example, you could end up paying high charges to a unit or investment trust manager as well as fees to the SIPP provider.
- Don't trade frequently. You are likely to lose a tremendous amount in dealing costs for little gain.
- Providers can, and sometimes do, introduce new charges on SIPPs.
- Make sure that it is relatively cheap and painless to transfer your pension to another provider if the service is poor.
- Interest rates on cash balances held by SIPP provider may be low. Shop around and ask before you sign up.
- If you are a member of an occupational pension scheme you can only have a personal pension (including SIPPs and stakeholder) if your pay is less than £30,000. If it is less than £30,000 then the maximum you can put into the personal pension is £3,600 in the relevant tax year.
- If you have income from two sources (e.g. employed income and self-employed income) you can pay into a personal pension up to the age-defined limits (e.g. 20 per cent of earnings at age 36–45) from the self-employed earnings, even if you are a member of an occupational pension scheme.

Enterprise Investment Scheme

The Enterprise Investment Scheme (EIS) is a government initiative to encourage the flow of risk capital to smaller companies. Income tax relief at 20 per cent is available for investments of up to £200,000 made directly into qualifying company shares. By putting £10,000 into an EIS qualifying company an investor will pay £2,000 less tax, so the effective cost is only £8,000. There is also capital gains tax relief,[6] and losses within EIS are allowable against income tax. Furthermore, the value of EIS investments is not counted for inheritance tax after only 2 years.

'Direct investment' means investing when the company issue shares. It does not mean buying shares in the secondary market from other investors. The tax benefits are lost if the investments are held for less than 3 years. To raise money from this source the firm must have been carrying out a 'qualifying activity' for 3 years – this generally excludes financial investment and property companies. The company must not be quoted on the Official List

[6] CGT on any gains realised in the period up to 36 months prior to, and 12 months after, the EIS shares are allotted can be deferred. This applies to gains up to the amount put into the EIS fund. If you made a chargeable gain of £20,000 on some other investment and put £18,000 into the EIS, then you are liable to CGT on only £2,000.

and the most it can raise under the EIS in any one year is usually £1 million. Alternative Investment Market companies frequently qualify for EIS. The company must not have gross assets worth more than £15 million. Funds investing in a range of EIS companies are springing up to help investors spread risk (minimum investment £500–£3,000).

Many of the companies that sell shares to investors under the EIS are high-risk ventures. You must assess the viability of the underlying business and not be mesmerised by the tax reliefs. Only invest if you can afford to lose the lot.

Once the shares are bought you may find yourself with a financial asset that is difficult to sell. This can be the case if the company is on the AIM or OFEX, let alone a company with no secondary market trading facility for its shares.

Venture capital trusts

Venture capital trusts (VCTs) are quoted companies that gather together a pot of investment money by selling their shares to investors. This pot of money is then used to buy shares in smaller unquoted trading companies. They operate in a similar way to investment trusts – see Chapter 5.

There are four tax breaks for investors putting money into VCTs. There is an immediate relief on their current year's income at 20 per cent. Also capital gains tax can be deferred on other investments if the gains are put into a VCT. (The Chancellor has proposed replacing this benefit with an additional 20% income tax relief going directly to the VCT fund in April 2004.) The returns (income and capital gains) on a VCT are free of tax for investments. Individuals claiming tax relief for money put into a VCT are limited to a maximum of £200,000 placed with VCTs per year. Furthermore, these benefits are only available to investors buying new VCT shares (not VCT shares bought from other investors in the secondary market) who hold the investment for at least 3 years. The VCT managers can only invest in companies worth less than £15 million, and the maximum amount a VCT is allowed to put into each unquoted company's shares is £1 million per year. (For VCTs the term 'unquoted' is used rather loosely and includes AIM companies.) A maximum of 15 per cent of the VCT fund can be invested in any one company. Up to half of the fund's investment in qualifying companies can be in the form of loans.

These trusts offer investors a way of investing in a broad spread of small firms with high potential, but with greater uncertainty, in a tax-efficient manner. They also offer the possibility of being able to sell the VCT shares in the secondary market on the London Stock Exchange – however, for some VCTs there is little demand and so you may have difficulty selling. VCTs can have several charges applied including an initial charge, an annual management charge, additional expenses and incentive bonuses to the fund manager. Total fees are around 3.5 per cent per year.

Note that **venture and development capital investment trusts (VDCITs)** are different from VCTs. VDCITs are standard investment trusts with a focus on risky developing companies. They do not carry the same tax breaks as VCTs, but they are allowed to invest in companies of any size – not just those worth less than £15 million. They also have a much more liquid secondary market.

Offshore investment

It is possible to put money into an offshore (i.e. outside of the UK tax regime) fund. **Offshore roll-up funds** keep the interest/dividends within the fund until you partially or wholly encash it. While the roll-up continues you are not subject to UK tax. When you do encash you may be liable for a lower rate of tax than you were earlier. For example, previously you might have been a higher rate taxpayer; now, as a retired person, you pay tax at basic rate. Alternatively, you may retire abroad to a lower tax regime.

Other types of offshore funds that pay regular income are unsuitable for most British investors living in Britain as the tax benefits are low, the management fees can be high and interest rates much the same as at home. Income received will generally be treated for tax under the UK rules. You are required to declare the income on the annual tax returns. Expatriates who are non-residents may have reason to go offshore, but most of us we are better off taking advantage of the tax breaks discussed earlier in this chapter.

18

Mergers and takeovers

This chapter examines the reasons why the managers of your company may want to merge it with another, and the ways in which mergers are financed. Then the merger process itself is described, along with the rules and regulations designed to prevent unfairness to shareholders. A major question to be addressed is: who gains from mergers? Is it shareholders, managers, advisers, etc? Shockingly, the evidence suggests that in less than half of corporate mergers do the shareholders of the acquiring firm benefit.

Many people, for various reasons, differentiate between the terms '**merger**', '**acquisition**' and '**takeover**' – for example, for accounting and legal purposes. However, like most commentators, this book will use the three terms interchangeably, and with good reason. It is sometimes very difficult to decide if a particular unification of two companies is more like a merger – in the sense of being a coming together of roughly equal sized firms on roughly equal terms, in which the shareholders remain as joint owners and both teams of managers share in the managerial duties – or whether the act of union is closer to what some people would say is an acquisition or takeover – a purchase of one firm by another with the associated implication of financial and managerial domination.

Merger motives

In the interests of shareholders

Firms decide to merge with other firms for a variety of reasons. The classic word associated with merger announcements is '**synergy**'. The idea underlying this is that the combined entity will have a value greater than the sum of its parts. The increased value comes about because of boosts to revenue and/or the cost base. Perhaps complementary skills or complementary market outlets enable the combined firms to sell more goods. Sometimes the ability to share sources of supply or production facilities improves the competitive position of the firm. One of the most important forces driving mergers is the attempt to increase **market power**. This is the ability to exercise some control over the price of the product. It can be achieved through either (a) monopoly, oligopoly (a small number of producers) or dominant producer positions, etc., or (b) collusion between the firms in the industry. If a firm has a large share of a market it often has some degree of control over price. It may be able to push up the price of goods sold because customers have few alternative sources of supply. Even if the firm does not control the entire market, a reduction in the number of participating firms to a handful makes collusion easier. Whether openly or not, the firms in a concentrated market may agree amongst themselves to charge customers higher prices and not to undercut each other. The regulatory authorities are watching out for such socially damaging activities and have fined a number of firms for such practices – for example, in the cement, steel and chemicals industries.

An important contributor to synergy is the ability to exploit **economies of scale**. Larger size often leads to lower cost per unit of output. Rationalising and consolidating manufacturing capacity at fewer, larger sites can lead to production utilising larger machines. Economies in marketing can arise through the use of common distribution channels or joint advertising. There are also economies in administration, research and development, purchasing and finance.

If a firm has chosen to enter a particular market but lacks the right know-how, the quickest way of establishing itself may be through the purchase of an existing player in that product or geographical market. To grow into the market organically – by developing the required skills and market strength through internal efforts alone – may mean that for many years the firm will not have the necessary critical size to become an effective competitor. Furthermore, creating a new participant in a market may result in over-supply and excessive competition, leading to the danger of a price war and thus eliminating profits.

One of the primary reasons advanced for **conglomerate** mergers (involving unrelated business areas) is that the overall income stream of the holding company will be less volatile if the cash flows come from a wide variety of products and markets. At first glance the pooling of unrelated income streams would seem to improve the position of shareholders. They obtain a reduction in risk without a decrease in return. The problem with this argument is that investors can obtain the same risk reduction in an easier and cheaper way. They could simply buy a range of shares in the independent, separately quoted firms. In addition, it is said that conglomerates lack focus – with managerial attention and resources being dissipated.

A further reason for mergers which favours shareholders is that the management of firm X may be more efficient than the management of firm Y, resulting in a gain produced if X's management is dominant after the unification.

Many people believe that stock markets occasionally underestimate the true value of a share and so bargains appear for managers of other firms on the prowl for targets. It may well be that the potential target firm is being operated in the most efficient manner possible and productivity could not be raised even if the most able managerial team in the world took over. Such a firm might be valued low by the stock market because the management are not very aware of the importance of a good stock market image. Perhaps they provide little information beyond the statutory minimum and in this way engender suspicion and uncertainty. Investors hate uncertainty and will tend to avoid such a firm. On the other hand, the acquiring firm might be very conscious of its stock market image and put considerable effort into cultivating good relationships with the investment community.

Managerial motives

The reasons for merger described in this section are often just as rational as the ones which have gone before, except, this time, the rational objective may not be shareholder wealth maximisation but manager wealth maximisation.

One group that seems to do well out of merger activity is the management team of acquiring firms. When all the dust has settled after a merger they end up controlling a larger enterprise. And, of course, having responsibility for a larger business means that the managers *have* to be paid a lot more money. Not only must they have higher monthly pay to induce them to give of their best, they must also have enhanced pension contributions and myriad perks. Being in charge of a larger business and receiving a higher salary also brings increased status. Some feel more successful and important, and the people they rub shoulders with tend to be in a more influential class.

As if these incentives to grow rapidly through mergers were not enough, some people simply enjoy putting together an empire – to create something grand and imposing gives a sense of achievement and satisfaction. To have control over ever larger numbers of individuals appeals to basic instincts – some measure their social position and their stature by counting the number of employees under them. Warren Buffett comments:

> The acquisition problem is often compounded by a biological bias: Many CEO's [chief executive officers] attain their positions in part because they possess an abundance of animal spirit and ego. If an executive is heavily endowed with these qualities – which, it should be acknowledged, sometimes have their advantages – they won't disappear when he reaches the top. When such a CEO is encouraged by his advisors to make deals, he responds much as would a teenage boy who is encouraged by his father to have a normal sex life. It's not a push he needs.[1]

John Kay points out that many managers enjoy the excitement of the merger process itself:

> For the modern manager, only acquisition reproduces the thrill of the chase, the adventures of military strategy. There is the buzz that comes from the late-night meetings in merchant banks, the morning conference calls with advisers to plan your strategy. Nothing else puts your picture and your pronouncements on the front page, nothing else offers so easy a way to expand your empire and emphasise your role.[2]

These first four managerial motives for merger – empire building, status, power and remuneration – can be powerful forces impelling takeover activity. But, of course, they are rarely expressed openly, and certainly not shouted about during a takeover battle.

The fifth reason, hubris, is also very important in explaining merger activity. It may help particularly to explain why mergers tend to occur in greatest number when the economy and companies generally have had a few good years of growth, and management are feeling rather pleased with themselves.

[1] Chairman's letter accompanying the 1994 annual report of Berkshire Hathaway Inc. Reprinted by kind permission of Warren Buffett. © Warren Buffett.

[2] John Kay, Poor odds on the takeover lottery, *Financial Times*, 26 January 1996.

'Hubris' means over-weaning self-confidence or, less kindly, arrogance. Managers commit errors of over-optimism in evaluating merger opportunities due to excessive pride or faith in their own abilities. The suggestion is that some acquirers do not learn from their mistakes and may be convinced that they can see an undervalued firm when others cannot. Also, that they have the talent, experience and entrepreneurial flair to shake up almost any business, and generate improved profit performance. Here's what Warren Buffett has to say on the subject of hubris:

Exhibit 18.1 Warren Buffett on hubris:

On Toads and Princesses

Many managements apparently were overexposed in impressionable childhood years to the story in which the imprisoned handsome prince is released from the toad's body by a kiss from the beautiful princess. Consequently, they are certain their managerial kiss will do wonders for the profitability of the Company T(arget).

Such optimism is essential. Absent that rosy view, why else should the shareholders of Company A(cquisitor) want to own an interest in T at the 2X takeover cost rather than at the X market price they would pay if they made direct purchases of their own?

In other words, investors can always buy toads at the going price for toads. If investors instead bankroll princesses who wish to pay double for the right to kiss a toad, those kisses better pack some real dynamite. We've observed many kisses but very few miracles. Nevertheless, many managerial princesses remain serenely confident about the future potency of their kisses – even after their corporate backyards are knee-deep in unresponsive toads.[3]

Note that the hubris hypothesis does not require the conscious pursuit of self-interest by managers. They may have worthy intentions but can make mistakes in judgement.

It is generally observed that mergers tend to take place with a large acquirer and a smaller target. Potential target managements may come to believe that the best way to avoid being taken over and then sacked or dominated is to grow large themselves, and to do so quickly. Thus mergers can have a self-reinforcing mechanism or positive feedback loop – the more mergers there are the more vulnerable managements feel and the more they are inclined to carry out mergers. Firms may merge for their survival of the management team and not primarily for the benefit of shareholders.

Third-party motives

There are many highly paid individuals who benefit greatly from merger activity. Advisers charge fees to the bidding company to advise on such matters as identifying targets, the

[3] Chairman's letter accompanying the 1981 annual report of Berkshire Hathaway Inc. Reprinted by kind permission of Warren Buffett. © Warren Buffett.

rules of the takeover game, regulations, monopoly references, finance, bidding tactics, stock market announcements, and so on. Advisers are also appointed to the target firms. Other groups with a keen eye on the merger market include accountants and lawyers. It seems reasonable to suppose that professionals engaged in the merger market might try to encourage or cajole firms to contemplate a merger and thus generate turnover in the market. Some provide reports on potential targets to try and tempt prospective clients into becoming acquirers. Of course, the author would never suggest that such esteemed and dignified organisations would ever stoop to promote mergers for the sake of increasing fee levels alone. You may think that, but I could not possibly comment.

There is also the press, ranging from tabloids to specialist publications. Even a cursory examination gives the distinct impression that they tend to have a bias of articles emphasising the positive aspects of mergers. It is difficult to find negative articles, especially at the time of a takeover. They like the excitement of the merger event and rarely follow up with a considered assessment of the outcome. Also the press reports generally portray acquirers as dynamic, forward-looking and entrepreneurial.

Financing mergers

In order that the acquiring company can take control of the destiny of the target company it needs to buy the majority of its shares. To induce the target shareholders to sell their shares it usually offers cash, newly minted shares in the acquirer, or some other financial security, such as convertible bonds. Sometimes the acquirer offers a package of cash and/or shares and/or other securities.

Cash

One of the advantages of using cash for payment is that the acquirer's shareholders retain the same level of control over their company. That is, new shareholders from the target do not suddenly take possession of a proportion of the acquiring firm's voting rights, as they would if the target shareholders were offered shares in the acquirer. Sometimes it is very important to shareholders that they maintain control over a company by owning a certain proportion of the firm's shares. Someone who has a 50.1% stake may resist attempts to dilute that holding to 25% even though the company may more than double in size.

The second major advantage of using cash is that its simplicity and preciseness give a greater chance of success. The alternative methods carry with them some uncertainty about their true worth. Cash has an obvious value and is therefore preferred by vendors, especially when markets are volatile.

From the point of view of the target's shareholders, cash has the advantage – in addition to being more certain in its value – that it allows the recipient to spread their investments through the purchase of a wide-ranging portfolio. The receipt of shares or other securities means that the target shareholder either keeps the investment or, if diversification is required, has to incur transaction costs associated with selling the shares.

A disadvantage of cash for the target shareholders is that they may be liable for capital gains tax. This is payable when a gain is 'realised'. If the target shareholders receive cash on shares which have risen in value they may have to pay tax. If, on the other hand, the target shareholders receive shares in the acquiring firm then their investment gain is not regarded as being realised and therefore no capital gains tax is payable at that time. The tax payment will be deferred until the time of the sale of the new shares – assuming an overall capital gain is made.

Shares

The main advantage for target shareholders of receiving shares in the acquirer rather than cash, apart from postponement of capital gains tax, is that they maintain an interest in the combined entity. If the merger offers genuine benefits, the target shareholders may wish to own part of the combined corporation.

To the acquirer an advantage of offering shares is that there is no immediate outflow of cash. In the short run this form of payment puts less pressure on cash flow. However, the firm may consider the effect on the capital structure (amount of debt relative to share capital) of the firm and the dilution of the position of existing shareholders.

A second reason for using shares as the consideration is that the **price–earnings ratio (PER) game** can be played. Through this companies can increase their earnings per share (eps) by acquiring firms with lower PERs than their own. The share price can rise (under certain conditions) despite there being no economic value created from the merger.

Imagine two firms, Crafty plc and Sloth plc. Both earned £1 million last year and had the same number of shares. Earnings per share on a historic basis are therefore identical. The difference between the two companies is the stock market's perception of earnings growth. Because Crafty is judged to be a dynamic go-ahead sort of firm with management determined to improve eps by large percentages in future years, it is valued at a high PER of 20. Sloth, on the other hand, is not seen as a fast-moving firm by investors. It is considered to be rather sleepy. The market multiplies last year's eps by only a factor of 10 to determine the share price – see Table 18.1.

Table 18.1 The price–earnings ratio game

	Crafty	*Sloth*	*Crafty post merger*
Current earnings	£1m	£1m	£2m
Number of shares	10m	10m	15m
Earnings per share	10p	10p	13.33p
Price–earnings ratio	20	10	20
Share price	£2	£1	£2.67

Because Crafty's shares sell at a price exactly double those of Sloth it would be possible for Crafty to exchange one of its shares for two of Sloth's. (This is based on the assumption that there is no bid premium, but the argument that follows works just as well even if a reasonable bid premium is paid.) If Crafty buys all the shares in Sloth its share capital rises by 50 per cent, from 10 million shares to 15 million shares. Earnings per share are one-third higher. If the stock market still puts a high PER on Crafty's earnings, perhaps because investors believe that Crafty will liven up Sloth and produce high eps growth because of their more dynamic management, then the value of Crafty increases and Crafty's shareholders are satisfied.

Each old shareholder in Crafty has experienced an increase in eps and a share price rise of 33 per cent. Also, previously Sloth's shareholders owned £10 million of shares in Sloth; now they own £13.33 million of shares in Crafty (see Table 18.1).

This all seems rational and good, but shareholders are basing their valuations on the assumption that managers will deliver on their promise of higher earnings growth through, for example, operational efficiencies. Managers of companies with high PER may see an easier way of increasing eps and boosting the share price. Imagine you are managing a company that enjoys a high PER. Investors in your firm are expecting you to produce high earnings growth. You could try to achieve this through real entrepreneurial/managerial excellence – for example, by product improvement, achieving economies of scale, or increased operating efficiency, etc. Alternatively, you could buy firms with low PERs and not bother to change operation. In the long run you know that your company will produce lower earnings because you are not adding any value to the firms that you acquire, you are probably paying an excessive bid premium to buy the present earnings and you probably have little expertise in the new areas of activity.

However, in the short run, eps can increase dramatically. The problem with this strategy is that in order to keep the earnings on a rising trend you must continue to keep fooling investors. You have to keep expanding at the same rate to receive regular boosts. One day expansion will stop; it will be revealed that the underlying economics of the firms bought have not improved (they may have even worsened as a result of neglect), and the share price will fall rapidly. The Americans call this the **bootstrap game**. It can be very lucrative for some managers who play it skilfully. However, there can be many losers – society, shareholders and employees.

Other types of finance

Alternative forms of payment for target shares – corporate bonds, convertible bonds and preference shares – are relatively unpopular largely because of the difficulty of establishing a rate of return on these securities which will be attractive to target shareholders. Also, these securities often lack marketability and voting rights over the newly merged company.

The rules of the takeover game

The regulatory bodies

The City Code on Takeovers and Mergers provides the main governing rules for companies engaged in merger activity. The actions and responsibilities of quoted and unlisted public companies have been laid down over a period of 30 years. The Code has been developed in a self-regulatory fashion by City institutions, notably the London Stock Exchange, the Bank of England, the investment institutions, companies, banks, the Financial Services Authority and the accounting profession. It is administered on a day-to-day basis by the **Takeover Panel Executive** of the City Panel on Takeovers and Mergers.

Statutory law is relatively unimportant in the regulation of mergers – its main contribution is to require that directors carry out their duty without prejudice in a fiduciary manner, showing trustworthy and faithful behaviour for the benefit of shareholders equally.

The self-regulatory, non-statutory approach is considered superior because it can provide a quick response in merger situations and be capable of regular adaptation to changed circumstances. There are frequent occurrences where companies try to bend or circumvent the rules, so it is useful to have a system of regulation which is continually reviewed and updated as new loopholes are discovered and exploited.

The Code may not have the force of law, but the Panel does have some powerful sanctions. These range from public reprimands to the shunning of Code defiers by the regulated City institutions – the FSA requires that no regulated firm (e.g. bank, broker, adviser) should act for client firms that seriously break the Panel's rules.

The fundamental objective of the Takeover Panel regulation is to ensure fair and equal treatment for all shareholders. The main areas of concern are:

- shareholders being treated differently (e.g. large shareholders getting a special deal);
- insider dealing (this is assisted by statutory rules);
- target management action that is contrary to its shareholders' best interests (e.g. the advice to accept or reject a bid must be in shareholders' best interest not their own);
- lack of adequate and timely information released to shareholders;
- artificial manipulation of share prices (e.g. an acquirer offering shares cannot make the offer more attractive by getting friends to push up its share price);
- the bid process dragging on and thus distracting management from their proper tasks.

The **Office of Fair Trading (OFT)** also takes a keen interest in mergers to ensure that they do not produce 'a substantial lessening of competition'. An OFT initial screening may or may not be followed by a Competition Commission investigation. This may take several months to complete, during which time the merger bid is put on hold. More recently, another hurdle has been put in the path of large mergers, with intra-European Union mergers being considered by the European Commission in Brussels. This is becoming increasingly influential.

Pre-bid

Exhibit 18.1 shows the main stages of merger. The acquiring firm usually employs **advisers** to help make a takeover bid. Most firms carry out mergers infrequently and so have little expertise in-house. The identification of suitable targets may be one of the first tasks of the advisers. Once identified, there would be a period of appraising the target. The strategic fit would be considered, alongside a detailed analysis of what would be purchased. The product markets and types of customers could be investigated, and there would be financial analysis showing sales, profit and rates-of-return history. The assets and liabilities would be assessed, as would assets that are truly valuable but are never recorded on a balance sheet (e.g. employees' extraordinary abilities when working as a team).

If the appraisal stage is satisfactory, the firm may approach the target. Because it is often cheaper to acquire a firm with the agreement of the target management, and because the managers and employees have to work together after the merger, in the majority of cases discussions take place that are designed to produce a set of proposals acceptable to both groups of shareholders and managers.

During the negotiation phase the price and form of payment have to be decided upon. In most cases the acquirer has to offer a **bid premium** – this tends to be in the range of 20 per cent to 100 per cent of the pre-bid price. The average is about 30–50 per cent. The timing of payment is also considered – for example, some mergers involve '**earn-outs**' in which the selling shareholders (usually the same individuals as the directors) receive payment over a period of time dependent on the level of post-merger profits. The issue of how the newly merged entity will be managed will also be discussed – who will be chief executive? Which managers will take particular positions? The pension rights of the target firm's employers and ex-employees have to be considered, as does the issue of redundancy, especially the removal of directors – what pay-offs are to be made available?

If agreement is reached then the acquirer formally communicates the offer to the target's board and shareholders. This will be followed by a recommendation from the target's board to its shareholders to accept the offer.

If, however, agreement cannot be reached and the acquirer still wishes to proceed, the interesting situation of a **hostile bid battle** is created. One of the first stages might be a '**dawn raid**'. This is where the acquirer acts with such speed in buying the shares of the target company that the raider achieves the objective of obtaining a substantial stake in the target before the target's management have time to react. The acquirer usually offers investors and market makers a price which is significantly higher than the closing price on the previous day. This high price is only being offered to those close to the market and able to act quickly and is therefore contrary to the spirit of the Takeover Panel's rules because not all shareholders can participate. It breaks the rules in another way: the sellers in a 'dawn raid' are not aware of all relevant information, in this case that a substantial stake is being accumulated. The Takeover Panel insists that the purchase of 10 per cent or more of the target shares in a period of 7 days is not permitted if this would take the

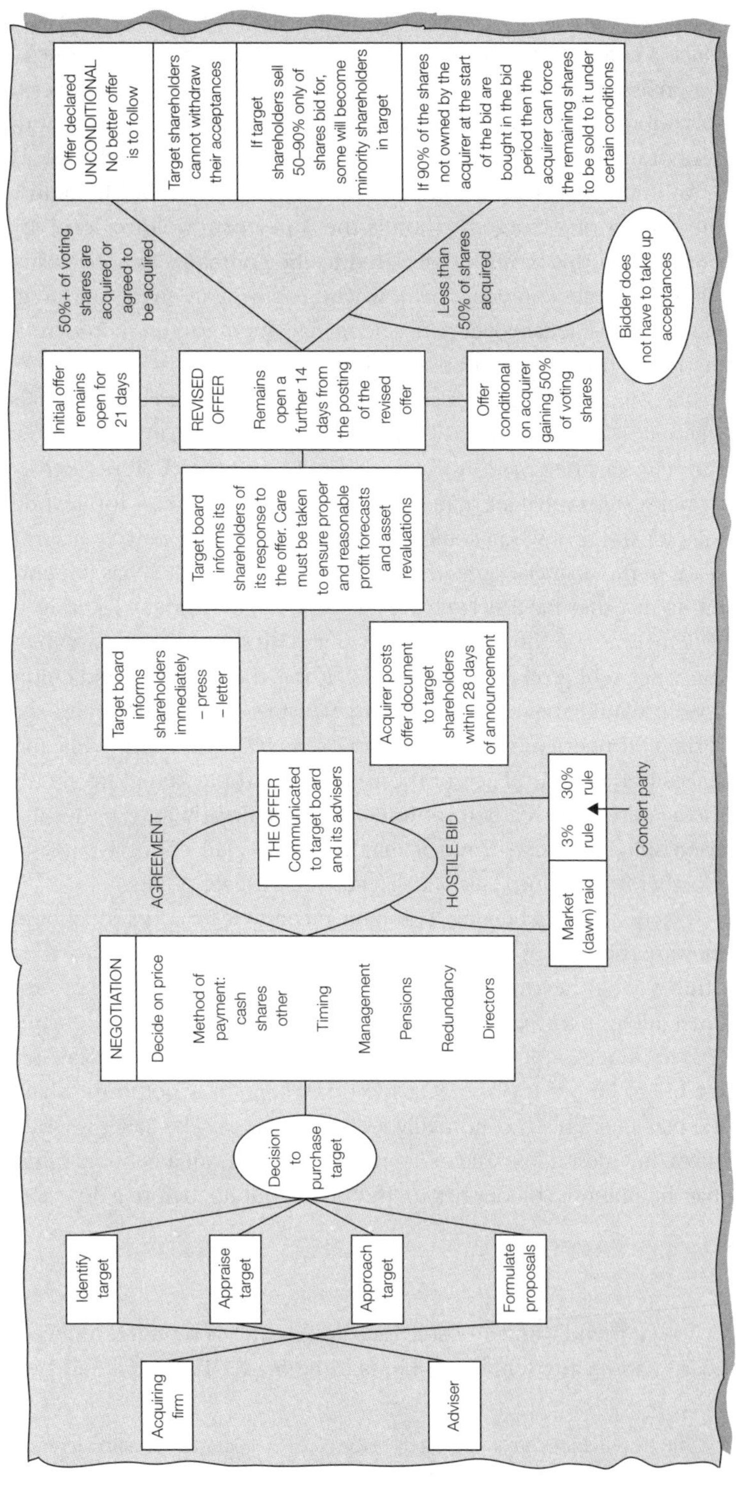

Exhibit 18.1 The merger process

holding to more than 15 per cent (unless the shares are purchased from a single seller).[4] Once a company becomes a bid target, any dealings in the target's shares by the bidder (or an associate) must be publically disclosed no later than 12 noon on the business day following the transaction. Furthermore, once an offer is underway, any holder of 1 per cent or more must disclose dealings by midday of the next business day.

An important trigger point for **disclosure of shareholdings in a company**, whether the subject of a merger or not, is the **3 per cent** holding level. If a 3 per cent stake is owned then this has to be declared to the company. This disclosure rule is designed to allow the target company to know who is buying its shares and to give it advanced warning of a possible takeover raid. The management can then prepare a defence and present information to shareholders should the need arise.

If a company builds up a stake of more than **30 per cent**, the Takeover Panel rules usually oblige it to make a bid for all of the target company's shares (a '**mandatory bid**') at the highest price paid in the previous 12 months. A 30 per cent stake often gives the owner a substantial amount of power. It is very difficult for anyone else to bid successfully for the firm when someone already has 30 per cent. It is surprising how often one reads in the financial press that a company or individual has bought a 29.9 per cent holding so that they have as large a stake as possible without triggering a mandatory bid.

Sometimes, in the past, if a company wanted to take over another to avoid declaring at the 3 per cent level (or 5 per cent as it was then), or to avoid bidding at the 30 per cent level it would sneak up on the target firm's management and shareholders. It would form a '**concert party**' by persuading its friends, other firms and individuals, to buy stakes in the target. Each of these holdings would be below the threshold levels. When the acquirer was ready to pounce it would already have under its control a significant controlling interest, if not a majority. Today all concert party holdings are lumped together for the purposes of disclosure and trigger points.

A tactic that has become common recently is for a potential bidder to announce that they are thinking of making a bid rather than actually doing it – they make an '**indicative offer**' saying they might bid but not committing themselves to the expense and strict timetable of a formal offer. Shareholders in targets may gain from having potential bidders announce an interest in buying their shares and are in favour of allowing time for the bid to be put together. On the other hand, it is not in the shareholders' interest for the management to continually feel under siege. The Takeover Panel permits indicative offers, but after a few weeks (generally 6–8) without a genuine offer emerging it declares that the potential bidder has to 'put up or shut up' before a deadline date.

The bid

In both a friendly and a hostile bid the acquirer is required to give **notice** to the target's board and its advisers that a bid is to be made. The press and the Stock Exchange are

[4] Or if the purchases are immediately before the buyer announces a firm intention to make an offer if the offer is agreed by the target board.

usually also informed. The target management must immediately inform their shareholders (and the Takeover Panel). This is done through an announcement to the Stock Exchange and a press notice, which must be quickly followed by letter explaining the situation. In a hostile bid the target management tend to use phrases like 'derisory offer' or 'wholly unacceptable'.

Within 28 days of the initial notice the **offer document** has to be posted to each of the target's shareholders. Details of the offer, the acquirer and its plans will be given. If the acquisition would increase the total value of the acquirer's assets by more than 15 per cent, the acquirer's shareholders need to be informed about the bid. If the asset increase is more than 25 per cent then shareholders must vote in favour of the bid proceeding. They are also entitled to vote on any increase in the authorised share capital.

The target management have 14 days in which to **respond to the offer document**. Assuming that they recommend rejection, they will attack the rationale of the merger and the price being offered. They may also highlight the virtues of the present management and reinforce this with revised profit forecasts and asset revaluations. There follows a period of attack and counter-attack through press releases and other means of communication. **Public relations consultants** may be brought in to provide advice and plan tactics.

The offer remains open for target shareholders for at least **21 days** from the date of posting the offer document. If the offer is **revised** it must be kept open for a **further 14 days** from the posting date of the revision.[5] However, to prevent bids from dragging on endlessly the Panel insists that the **maximum period for a bid is 60 days** from the offer document date (posting day). The final offer date is day 46, which allows 14 days for acceptances. There are exceptions: if another bidder emerges, then it has 60 days, and its sixtieth day becomes the final date for both bidders; or if the Board of the target agrees to an extension. If the acquirer fails to gain control within 60 days then it is forbidden to make another offer for a year to prevent continual harassment.

Defence tactics

Here are a few of the tactics employed by target managers to prevent a successful bid or to reduce the chances of a bid occurring:

- **Attack the logic of the bid**. Also attack the quality of the bidder's management.
- **Improve the image of the firm**. Use revaluation, profit projections, dividend promises, public relations consultants.
- **Try to get a Competition Commission inquiry**.
- **Encourage unions, the local community, politicians, customers and suppliers to lobby on your behalf**.
- **White knight**. Invite a second bid from a friendly company.

[5] If an offer is revised all shareholders who accepted an earlier offer are entitled to the increased payment.

The following tactics are likely to be frowned upon by the Takeover Panel in the UK but are used in the USA and in a number of European countries:

- **Employee share ownership plans**. These can be used to buy a substantial stake in the firm which may make it more difficult for a bidder to take it over.
- **Share repurchase**. Reduces the number of shares available in the market for bidders.
- **Poison pills**. Make yourself unpalatable to the bidder by ensuring additional costs should it win, e.g. target shareholders are allowed to buy shares in target or acquirer at a large discount should a bid be successful.
- **Crown jewels defence**. Sell off the most attractive parts of the business.
- **Pac-Man defence**. Make a counter-bid for the bidder.
- **Asset lock-up**. A friendly buyer purchases those parts of the business most attractive to the bidder.
- **Golden parachutes**. Managers get massive pay-offs if the firm is taken over.
- **Give in to greenmail**. Key shareholders try to obtain a reward (e.g. the repurchase of their shares at premium) from the company for not selling to a hostile bidder or becoming a bidder themselves. (Green refers to the colour of US dollar bills.)

Post-bid

Usually an offer becomes **unconditional** when the acquirer has bought or has agreed to buy 50 per cent of the target's shares. Prior to the declaration of the offer as unconditional the bidding firm would have said in the offer documents that the offer is conditional on the acquirer gaining (usually) 50% of the voting shares. This allows the bidding firm to receive acceptances from the target shareholders without the obligation to buy.[6] Once it is declared unconditional the acquirer is making a firm offer for the shares which it does not already have, and that no better offer is to follow. Before the announcement of unconditionality those target shareholders who accepted the offer are entitled to withdraw their acceptance – after it, they are forbidden from doing so.

Usually in the days following unconditionality the target shareholders who have not already accepted quickly do so. The alternative is to remain a minority shareholder – still receiving dividends, but with power concentrated in the hands of a majority shareholder. There is a rule to avoid the frustration of having a small group of shareholders stubbornly refusing to sell. If the acquirer has bought nine-tenths of the shares it bid for, it can, within four months of the original offer, insist that the remaining shareholders sell at the final offer price.

[6] If 90 per cent of the target shares are offered to the bidder then it must proceed to unconditionality (unless there has been a material adverse change of circumstance). At lower levels of acceptance, it has a choice of whether to declare unconditionality.

Information

The *Financial Times* regularly reports the initiation and progress of merger bids. The Saturday edition summarises current bids, as does the weekly *Investors Chronicle*.

Who wins from mergers?

- **Do the shareholders of acquirers gain from mergers?** The evidence on the effects of acquisitions on the shareholders of the bidding firm is that they are at best neutral in their effect. Most of the evidence suggests that acquiring firms give their shareholders poorer returns on average than firms that are not acquirers. Even studies that show a gain to acquiring shareholders tend to produce very small average gains. This helps to explain why the share prices of acquirers generally fall when a merger intention is announced.
- **Do target shareholders gain from mergers?** Acquirers usually have to pay a substantial premium over the pre-bid share price to persuade target shareholders to sell. The evidence in this area is overwhelming – target shareholders gain from mergers.
- **Do the employees gain?** In the aftermath of a merger it sometimes happens that large areas of the target firm's operations are closed down, with a consequent loss of jobs. Often operating units of the two firms are fused and overlapping functions are eliminated, resulting in the shedding of staff. However, sometimes the increased competitive strength of the combined entity saves jobs and creates many more.
- **Do the directors of the acquirer gain?** Yes, they often gain increased status and power. They also, generally, receive increased remuneration packages.
- **Do the directors of the target gain?** We do not have a definitive answer as to whether the directors of the target gain. In the press they are often unfairly described as the failed managers and therefore out of a job. They are the losers in the 'market for managerial control'. In reality they often receive large pay-offs on their lengthy employment contacts and then take on another highly paid directorship.
- **Do the financial institutions gain?** This group benefits greatly from merger activity. They usually receive fees, regardless of whether they are on the winning side in a bid battle.

Final comment: why do mergers fail?

Mergers frequently fail to produce good returns for acquiring shareholders for a variety of reasons. This is an area where managers are very prone to tripping up. The most common stumbling blocks are: the strategy is misguided (the company should not be going into this area of business); the managers are over-optimistic about the future potential of their acquisition, while underestimating the costs associated with the resistance to change in the target and the counter-actions of competitors; there is a failure to prepare integration plans and implement an integration programme that engenders the commitment of the acquired workforce.[7]

Further reading

Sudi Sudarsanam's book (*Creating Value from Mergers and Acquisitions*, Financial Times Prentice Hall 2003) provides an excellent overview of the many aspects of merger and is easy to read and comprehensive. The rulebook (*The City Code on Takeovers and Mergers*) is available from the Panel on Takeovers and Mergers. Be warned though, it is written for lawyers who enjoy navigating their way through complicated mazes.

[7] There is more on the management of mergers in *Corporate Finance Management*, Glen Arnold, Financial Times Prentice Hall 2002.

19

Investor protection

Investing in shares and other financial instruments is, by nature, risky. If the business goes into liquidation your investment can become worthless. This is a risk all investors have to face. However, there are risks investors should not have to face: firstly, the risk of incompetence by advisers or financial service firms with control over investors' money; secondly, the risk of fraud. There is an extensive system of regulations designed to protect you from the unscrupulous, ignorant and incompetent. There are also systems to enable you to claim compensation should you suffer. This chapter describes both the protection systems and the fall-back compensation systems, as well as giving some advice on steps you can take to protect yourself against being taken for a ride.

There are four levels of protection for UK investors:

- protection from wayward financial services professionals;
- regulation of markets;
- regulation of companies;
- self-protection.

Protecting investors from wayward financial services professionals

At the centre of UK investor protection is the watchdog, **the Financial Services Authority**. The FSA is described as a 'super-regulator' because it regulates so many different aspects of the financial system from stockbrokers, banks and stock markets to independent financial advisers – see Exhibit 19.1. The FSA can be described as semi-detached from government: it is financed by the industries it regulates but its powers come from legislation; it often consults the financial services companies before deciding on rules but it has basic principles approved by the government and it is answerable to the Treasury which appoints its board.

The FSA has been given the objectives of maintaining confidence in the financial system, protecting consumers, reducing financial crime and helping people to gain the knowledge, aptitude and skills to manage their financial affairs effectively by promoting public understanding of the financial system.

Authorisation

All firms or individuals offering financial advice, products or services in the UK must be authorised by the FSA. Engaging in a regulated activity without authorisation can result in a two-year prison sentence. The FSA insists on high standards when assessing for authorisation. These require competence, financial soundness and fair treatment of customers. Firms are authorised to carry out specific activities (e.g. giving financial advice only, or managing a client's money in a fund, or stockbroking).

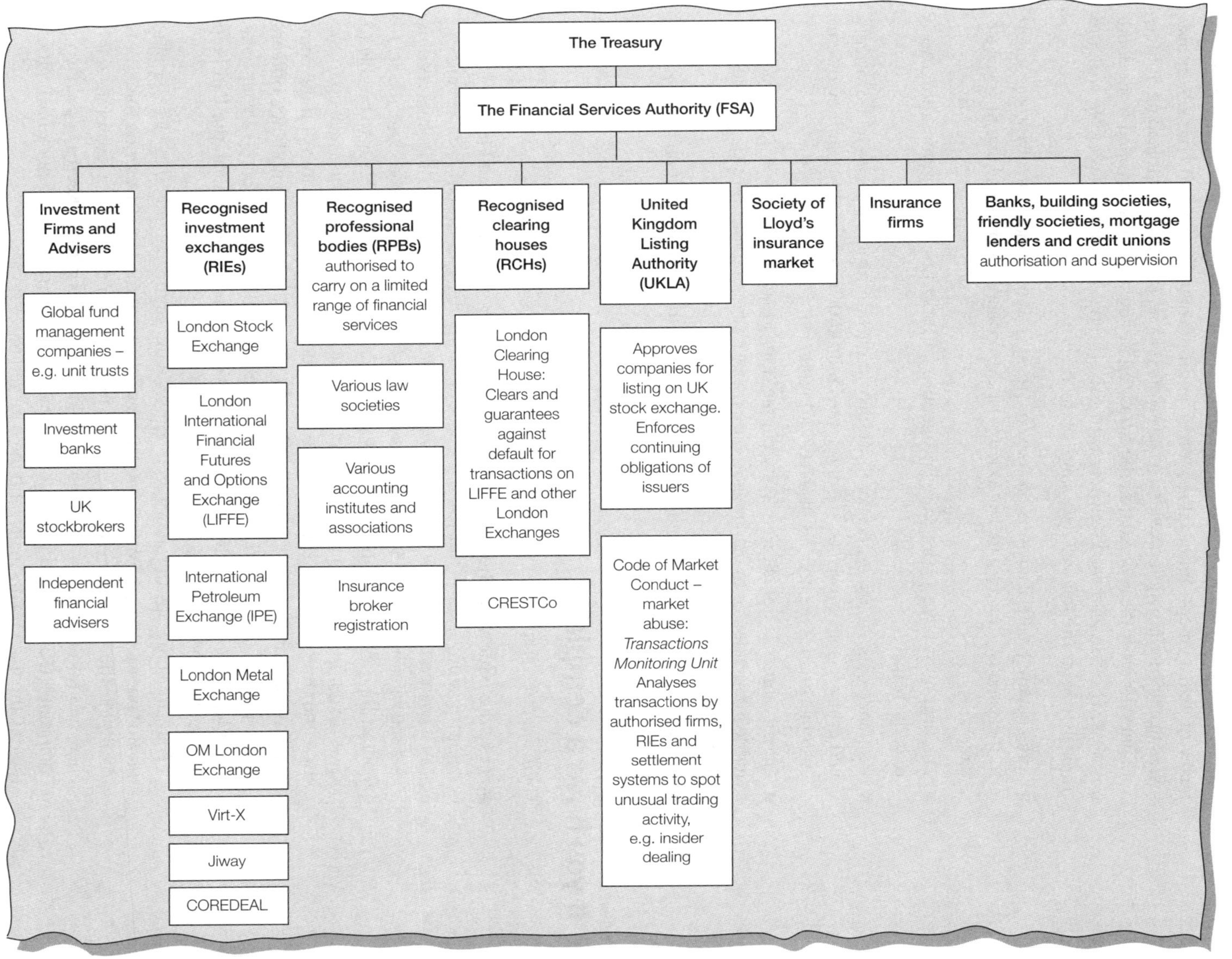

Exhibit 19.1 Financial services industry regulation

Even after initial approval, firms cannot relax as the FSA continues to monitor adequacy of management, financial resources and internal systems and controls. It also insists that any information provided to investors is clear, fair and not misleading. If there is a failure to meet these standards the firms can be fined or even stopped from doing business. The FSA also works closely with the criminal authorities and uses civil and criminal powers. The following are some of the rules it enforces:

- Independent financial advisers have to ensure the product sold to an investor is suited to their needs – this requires knowledge of the consumer's personal and financial situation.
- The firm must have a complaints procedure and a system for compensating those unfairly treated.
- Insurance companies, especially those providing with-profits policies, endowments and other savings products, should have significantly more assets than they owe to customers under the policies they have sold them.
- Market 'abuse' is not allowed. For example, individuals are not allowed to trade on inside information or to manipulate share prices by, for example, providing misleading information to the market.
- There must be a clear separation of clients' money from the firms' money ('ring fencing').

If you have a complaint

There are three steps you should take if you have a grievance.

- **Raise the issue with the financial service company.** All firms should have a formal complaints procedure, and you are encouraged by the FSA to start here, giving the firm a chance to right the wrong. After all, the firm is best placed to check its records and see what happened. So, ask for the details of the complaints procedure and try to contact the person you originally dealt with because they are most likely to be able to clear up the problem. If you do not get a satisfactory response at this level, go to the top – the chief executive (his/her name should be on company literature, on the company website or at a public library). Most regulated firms have **compliance officers** whose job it is to ensure the FSA rules are being followed. Send a copy of your complaint letter to him/her. (If the company has ceased to trade then call the FSA help line on 0845 606 1234 for advice.)

  Here are some tips to follow when complaining. Letters should be in black or blue ink (for photocopying). Write 'complaint' at the top of the letter. Describe the events clearly, in order, with relevant dates. Include reference numbers (e.g. customer reference) and photocopies of documents (hold on to the originals). Keep a copy of your complaint letter(s). If you phone to complain, note the name of the person who took the call, the main points made, and the date and time.

Roughly three out of four complainants dissatisfied with the response of the company choose not to pursue it further, believing it would be futile to do so. However, there are further positive steps you could take:

- **Independent complaints scheme.** Most financial services firms belong to an independent complaints scheme – the FSA insists in most cases.[1] There are two types: arbitration schemes and ombudsman schemes. Under both your complaint will be investigated and, if found to be justified, the firm will be ordered to put matters right. Many of the schemes provide for a financial award, up to a maximum of £100,000.

  You can only go the independent complaints scheme if you have exhausted the possibility of direct settlement with the firm. You know this has happened when you receive a letter from the firm saying it cannot reach agreement with you – a '**letter of deadlock**'. The FSA usually allows the firm up to 2 months to reach this point. If this letter (or agreement) is not forthcoming within this time, complain to the independent complaints scheme.

  Under **arbitration** both you and the firm agree in advance to accept the arbitrator's decision. Importantly, in accepting this you give up your right to take your case to court. The advantage is that it is much quicker and cheaper than going to court.

  Under the **Financial Ombudsman Scheme**[2] **(FOS)** the ombudsman collects together the facts of the case and arrives at what seems to him/her a reasonable and fair settlement. The firm is then under an obligation to accept the decision,[3] but you remain free to take your case to court. The service is free to consumers. The ombudsman's approach is less legalistic than arbitration and allows for more 'common-sense' factors of fairness. You have 6 months from the date of the company's final letter to take your complaint to the ombudsman. If the FOS finds in your favour it can order a firm to pay compensation up to a maximum of £100,000.

- **Go to court.** Litigation is often expensive, time-consuming and frustrating, and so should only be contemplated as a last resort. A relatively fast and informal service is provided by the **small claims court** (maximum claim in England £5,000, Northern Ireland £1,000 and Scotland £750). You do not need a solicitor, and court fees are low. You may not even have to attend the court as judges can make judgements on the paper evidence.

Compensation

The complaint steps are all well and good if the firm that has treated you badly is still in existence. But what if it is defunct? The **Financial Services Compensation Scheme (FSCS)**[4] can compensate consumers if an *authorised* company is unable to pay money it

[1] The firm's literature should set out its regulatory body and scheme.

[2] *www.financial-ombudsman.org.uk* or telephone 0845 080 1800.

[3] Although they can appeal through the courts.

[4] *www.fscs.org.uk* or telephone 020 7892 7300.

owes you (note that if you do business with an unauthorised firm, e.g. an offshore company, you are not covered by FSCS or the complaints procedure).

The FSCS covers your investments (e.g. bad advice, bad investment management), money deposited in accounts (at banks, building societies and credit unions) and insurance products (e.g. car insurance, life insurance).

The part of FSCS focused on investment products and services covers shares and bonds, unit trusts, futures and options, personal pension plans and long-term insurance policies such as endowments. It pays the first £30,000 of a valid claim in full and 90% of the next £20,000. Thus the maximum compensation is £48,000. For deposit claims the scheme pays the first £2,000 in full and 90% of the next £33,000 (maximum compensation £31,700). For non-compulsory insurance (e.g. home insurance) the scheme pays the first £2,000 and 90 per cent of the remainder of the loss. For long-term policies such as

How do I ... make a complaint stick?

by Isabel Berwick

■ **Make a nuisance of yourself.** The *Briefcase* postbag at the Financial Times is full of complaints about uncommunicative firms (the usual culprits are insurance companies) which fail to respond to repeated complaints.

Writing to the newspaper is one way to force a response. A quicker way is to ask the firm for the name of the person who deals with complaints (they may refuse to give you this, so just address your registered delivery letter to the relevant department). Or go straight for the chief executive's office.

Send copies of all the correspondence, and if this produces no response, bombard them with letters and call. No one likes a nuisance and you should eventually be put through to someone who can help. Resist the urge to lose your temper.

Outwit the call centres: we are all familiar with the problem of being trapped in an Orwellian automated call centre, staffed by people who are not allowed to make any decisions and simply read from a script. This can only get worse as companies increasingly rely on such centres.

If you need a decision or help with a problem do not be fobbed off or hang up. Ask to speak to a manager. There will be someone who is able to make decisions.

Remember to take copious notes about times, dates and names of people you speak to and the content of your conversations. This will help if you make a formal complaint.

■ **Ignore their jargon.** Complaints departments in big companies sometimes run off automated letters that contain gobbledegook designed to mollify customers without saying anything useful. Keep all letters, but do not be put off if you cannot understand them. You are not meant to.

■ **Decide what compensation you want.** An apology for some administrative mix-up, or cash compensation? Be realistic – you are not going to get a firm to return your £100,000 investment in a with-profits bond, plus damages, just because it is not doing very well. Poor investment performance is not a reason to receive compensation.

■ **Get a response.** After a formal complaint, the firm has to offer a solution (which you can accept or reject) or a 'deadlock letter' acknowledging that you cannot agree. You should also receive details of the 'next step' – the Financial Ombudsman Service, which mediates between customers and firms. A common ploy is for a firm to offer you, say, £100 'in full and final settlement' of your complaint. You have to decide whether it is worth rejecting the cash so you can pursue the matter with the ombudsman service, or whether £100 is enough.

If you worry that something more serious has happened – perhaps a firm is not following the complaints rules or has done something truly dodgy with your money – speak to the Financial Services Authority. The FSA 'polices' financial firms and has a helpline for the public: 0845 606 1234.

Exhibit 19.2 Making a complaint

Source: *Financial Times* 8/9 March 2003

pension plans and general insurance the scheme covers the first £2,000 and then 90 per cent of the value of the policy (in a liquidation) thereafter. Exhibit 19.2 gives some tips on complaining.

If your stockbroker holds your shares in a **CREST nominee account** (see Chapter 4) and then goes bust, don't panic. The nominee holdings should be ring-fenced and not combined with the broker's assets. You may still be frustrated by the length of time it takes to separate assets though.

Regulation of markets

Financial markets need high-quality regulation in order to induce investors to place their trust in them. There must be safeguards against unscrupulous and incompetent operators. There must be an orderly operation of the markets, fair dealing and integrity. However, the regulations should not be so restrictive as to stifle innovation and prevent the markets from being competitive internationally. London's financial markets have a unique blend of law, self-regulation and custom to regulate and supervise their members' activities.

The FSA supervises exchanges, clearing houses and settlement houses. It also conducts market surveillance and monitors transactions on eight **recognised investment exchanges (RIEs)** – see Exhibit 19.1. The RIEs work with the FSA to protect investors and maintain the integrity of markets. Much of the monitoring and enforcement is delegated to the RIEs. The London Stock Exchange, for example, vets new stockbrokers and tries to ensure compliance with LSE rules, aimed at making sure members (e.g. market makers and brokers) act with the highest standards of integrity, fairness, transparency and efficiency. It monitors market makers' quotations and the price of actual trades to ensure compliance with its dealing rules. It is constantly on the look-out for patterns of trading that deviate from the norm with the aim of catching those misusing information (e.g. insider dealing), creating a false or misleading impression to the disadvantage of other investors or some other market distorting action. The LSE, in partnership with the FSA, also requires companies to disseminate all information that could significantly affect their share prices.

Regulation of companies

If you invest in a company by buying its shares or bonds, you have a right to receive information about that company, and to expect that there are laws and other pressures to discourage the management from going astray and acting against your interests. There are various checks and balances in the corporate world, the most important being the requirements under the **Companies Acts**. **The Department of Trade and Industry** enforces the law and is able to intrude into a company's affairs. **Accountants** and **auditors** also function, to some extent, as regulators, helping to ensure companies do not misrepresent their position. Furthermore, any member of the public may access the accounts of any company easily and cheaply at **Companies House** (*www.companieshouse.gov.uk*). The **Serious Fraud Office** investigates cases of serious or complex fraud. The media keep a watchful stance – always ready to reveal stories of fraud, greed or incompetence. Finally, in the case of mergers of listed or other public limited companies, the **City Panel on Takeovers and Mergers** acts to ensure fairness for all shareholders – see Chapter 18.

Self-protection

Even with the complex and sophisticated structure of modern financial and corporate regulation, there is still a heavy responsibility on the ordinary investor to take precautions. It still boils down to 'buyer beware'. Here are some tips:

- If you want cover under the FSA rules and compensation scheme, make sure the financial service company is authorised.[5]
- If it sounds too good to be true, it probably is. Don't be taken in by promises of high returns way beyond the norm.
- Make sure you understand the risks of the underlying investments.
- Don't be afraid to ask questions if you don't understand.
- Make sure that your broker or independent financial adviser ring-fences your money – separates it from their own – so if they do go bust your money is safe.
- If you want your brokers to make investment decisions on your behalf make sure they are well informed about your investment aims, attitude to risk and tax position.
- Check what 'guaranteed' means for an investment product. Who is giving the guarantee, and are they sound? A common trick is that the income is guaranteed but your capital diminishes.
- When considering advice from independent financial advisers, brokers, or insurance product salesmen, ask how they are remunerated. If it is by receiving a commission on sales made you may view the advice differently. You might be even more sceptical if the level of commission varies depending on which product is sold. A product that might be ideal for you may not be mentioned if there is no commission to the sales person.
- Given the upper limits on compensation under the Financial Services Compensation Scheme, it might be wise to place a maximum of £50,000 of investments with any one provider, and a maximum of £35,000 on any one deposit account.

[5] See the FSA register at *www.fsa.gov.uk* or telephone 0845 606 1234.

- Ask your brokers what insurance they have against breach of professional duty (such as going outside your stated investment parameters or buying the wrong shares), insolvency and employee fraud, third-party fraud, and computer fraud.
- Avoid being classed as an **experienced investor**, as many of the safeguards outlined in the chapter will not apply.
- Don't be rushed into buying anything. There is generally a cooling-off period for pooled funds (e.g. with-profits policies).

20

Measuring performance: indices and risk

When judging the performance of your share portfolio, in addition to examining the absolute returns, you might like to observe how well you did against the market as a whole, or a particular sector of the market (e.g. technology shares). Furthermore, you may be interested in judging performance in relation to the risk of your portfolio. You may have outperformed the market, but did you take on a very high risk to do it? And, is that level of risk acceptable, given the extra return?

This chapter describes the main indices used to compare performance over time. It also explains the most commonly used measures for calculating share and portfolio risk.

Indices

Information on individual companies in isolation is less useful than information set in the context of the firm's peer group, or in comparison with quoted companies generally. For example, if Marks & Spencer's shares fall by 5 per cent on a particular day, an investor might be keen to learn whether the market as a whole rose or fell on that day, and by how much. The *Financial Times* (FT) joined forces with the Stock Exchange (SE) to create FTSE International in 1995, which has taken over the calculation (in conjunction with the Faculty and Institute of Actuaries) of a number of equity indices. These indicate the state of the market as a whole, or selected sectors of the market, and consist of 'baskets' of shares so that the value of the basket can be compared at different times.

To calculate the indices shown in Exhibit 20.1 the component shares each contribute to the index level. However, they do not have an equal weight in calculating the average. Rather, the average is derived by weighting each share by the size of the company (by its market capitalisation). Thus a 2 per cent movement in the share price of a large company has a greater effect on an index than a 2 per cent change in a small company's share price.[1] The characteristics of some of these indices are as follows.

- **FTSE 100.** The Footsie™ index is based on the 100 largest companies (generally with over £2 billion market capitalisation). Large and relatively safe companies are referred to as '**blue chips**'. This index has risen fourfold since it was introduced at the beginning of 1984 at a value of 1,000. This is the measure most watched by investors. It is calculated in real time (every 15 seconds) and so changes can observed throughout the day. The other international benchmarks are: for the USA, the **Dow Jones Industrial average** (30-share) index, the **Standard and Poor's 500 index** and the **NASDAQ 100**; for the Japanese market, the **Nikkei 225 index**; for France, the **CAC-40**; for Hong Kong, the **Hang Seng** index; and for Germany, the **DAX index**. For Europe as a whole there is **FTSE Eurotop 300**, and for the world the **FTSE All-World Index** (covering 49 countries).

[1] The weighting for some shares is reduced if a high proportion of the shares are held not in a free float but in the hands of people closely connected with the business (e.g. directors, major shareholders).

- **FTSE All-Share.** This index is the most representative in that it reflects the average movements of about 700 shares representing 98 per cent of the value of the London market. This index is broken down into a number of commercial and industrial sectors, so that investors and companies can use sector-specific yardsticks, such as those for mining or chemicals. Companies in the FTSE All-Share index have market capitalisation above £43 million. It is an aggregation of the FTSE 100, FTSE 250 and the FTSE SmallCap.
- **FTSE 250.** This index is based on the largest 250 firms which are in the next size range after the top 100. Capitalisations are generally between £200 million and £2 billion. (It is also calculated with investment trusts excluded.)
- **FTSE 350.** This index is based on the largest 350 quoted companies. It combines the FTSE 100 and the FTSE 250. This cohort of shares is also split into two to give high and low dividend yield groups. A second 350 index excludes investment trusts.
- **FTSE SmallCap.** This index covers companies included in the FTSE All-Share but excluded from the FTSE 350, with a market capitalisation of between about £43 million and £200 million.
- **FTSE Fledgling.** This includes over 700 companies too small to be in the FTSE All-Share index. This index is a mixture of Ordinary List and AIM shares.
- **FTSE AIM.** Index of all AIM companies.
- **FTSE techMARK 100.** Includes 100 techMARK companies with capitalisation less than £4 billion.
- **FTSE techMARK All share.** Includes all companies on the techMARK.
- **FTSE All-Small.** Combines companies in the FTSE SmallCap with those in the FTSE Fledgling.

The indices in the first column in Exhibit 20.1 are price indices only (share price movements only are reflected in the indices). The final column, 'Total return', shows the overall performance with both the combined share price rises and dividends reinvested in the portfolio. The Monday edition of the *Financial Times* also shows the highest and lowest levels of the indices during the current calendar year and the highest and lowest points reached since the FTSE started calculating it (for the All-Share this is 1962).

The Saturday edition of the *Financial Times* carries a table designed for investors to compare their portfolio's performance for various periods of time up to 5 years – see Exhibit 20.2. It shows the capital growth (or decline) only and therefore excludes dividend or interest income of three typical portfolios. The growth portfolio is more heavily weighted to equities than the income or balance portfolios, which have higher proportions of bonds and cash. To put more context on the comparison, the FTSE All-share index is also shown together with an index representing shares around the world, the UK gilt index, and the inflation index – Retail Price Index (RPI).

FTSE Actuaries Share Indices — **UK series**

Produced in conjunction with the Faculty and Institute of Actuaries

	£ Stlg Oct 9	Day's chge%	Euro Index	£ Stlg Oct 8	£ Stlg Oct 7	Year ago	Actual yield%	Cover	P/E ratio	Xd adj. ytd	Total Return
FTSE 100	4313.9	+1.1	4774.1	4268.6	4272.0	3777.3	3.30	1.74	17.44	125.29	2178.75
FTSE 250	5728.3	+0.9	6339.5	5679.4	5638.7	4089.3	2.72	1.66	22.15	135.41	2859.72
FTSE 250 ex Inv Co	5943.1	+0.8	6577.2	5894.7	5852.4	4202.3	2.77	1.72	21.08	141.93	2996.27
FTSE 350	2173.9	+1.0	2405.9	2151.7	2151.0	1855.3	3.22	1.73	17.97	61.51	2246.32
FTSE 350 ex Inv Co	2172.2	+1.0	2404.0	2149.9	2149.5	1857.5	3.24	1.74	17.80	61.81	1152.30
FTSE 350 Higher Yield	2688.3	+1.0	2975.1	2661.0	2664.7	2321.5	4.23	1.43	16.56	101.03	2498.10
FTSE 350 Lower Yield	1622.2	+1.0	1795.3	1605.5	1602.1	1369.4	2.16	2.34	19.73	30.89	1292.58
FTSE SmallCap	2431.67	+0.6	2691.10	2416.74	2405.14	1701.10	2.37	0.38	80.00†	44.97	2441.94
FTSE SmallCap ex Inv Co	2448.08	+0.5	2709.26	2436.38	2426.33	1712.07	2.54	0.24	80.00†	49.23	2503.20
FTSE All-Share	2135.21	+1.0	2363.02	2113.66	2112.68	1811.62	3.19	1.70	18.48	59.73	2239.26
FTSE All-Share ex Inv Co	2133.34	+1.0	2360.95	2111.76	2111.15	1815.68	3.22	1.71	18.22	60.23	1152.36
FTSE All-Share ex Multinational	754.04	+0.6	691.64	749.36	748.82	625.14	3.38	1.56	18.96	22.93	852.44
FTSE Fledgling	2435.14	+0.5	2694.95	2422.23	2410.54	1511.21	2.78	‡	‡	51.68	3172.64
FTSE Fledgling ex Inv Co	3133.56	+0.5	3467.88	3116.83	3099.02	1851.41	2.36	‡	‡	55.74	4066.92
FTSE All-Small	1579.86	+0.6	1748.42	1570.43	1562.88	1076.78	2.45	0.13	80.00†	30.13	2032.87
FTSE All-Small ex Inv Co	1685.79	+0.5	1865.64	1677.56	1670.16	1139.03	2.51	‡	‡	33.13	2192.76
FTSE AIM	768.2	+0.9	850.2	761.5	759.6	582.9	0.83	‡	‡	5.72	732.04
FTSE Actuaries Industry Sectors											
RESOURCES(23)	4907.44	+1.5	5431.02	4837.20	4838.08	4401.67	3.26	1.79	17.12	135.08	2623.88
Mining(9)	6533.64	+2.9	7230.71	6352.08	6277.37	4518.19	2.57	2.51	15.55	150.31	2475.53
Oil & Gas(14)	4983.09	+1.0	5514.74	4934.22	4954.46	4807.20	3.49	1.62	17.72	144.69	2728.63
BASIC INDUSTRIES(53)	2392.85	+1.3	2648.15	2363.23	2349.62	1854.81	3.42	2.25	13.01	70.50	1710.88
Chemicals(11)	1910.51	+1.8	2114.35	1877.04	1882.66	1786.83	3.85	1.60	16.25	53.46	1200.85
Construction & Bld Matls(40)	2602.51	+1.0	2880.18	2577.34	2559.62	1831.28	3.32	2.83	10.61	78.82	1734.52
Forestry & Paper(1)	8897.80	+1.2	9847.11	8795.53	8642.11	6724.49	5.06	2.01	9.83	450.00	5395.12
Steel & Other Metals(1)	577.73	+5.5	639.37	547.64	505.52	884.65	0.00	-	‡	0.00	407.97
GENERAL INDUSTRIALS(45)	1418.86	+1.6	1570.24	1395.96	1390.36	1136.65	3.84	1.73	15.04	37.33	1011.30
Aerospace & Defence(10)	1540.88	+1.2	1705.28	1523.04	1522.46	1311.93	4.10	1.92	12.69	36.13	1180.23
Electronic & Elect Equip(13)	1946.77	+2.8	2154.47	1893.57	1865.90	1696.64	3.17	1.22	25.90	35.38	1267.01
Engineering & Machinery(22)	1962.28	+2.0	2171.63	1923.77	1911.81	1345.91	3.64	1.54	17.79	67.17	1614.03
CYCLICAL CONSUMER GOODS(14)	5742.28	+0.7	6354.93	5700.39	5656.41	3739.53	3.37	2.25	13.15	180.13	2712.35
Automobiles & Parts(9)	3739.51	+0.9	4138.48	3705.28	3670.19	2563.23	3.63	2.39	11.53	133.42	2440.00
Household Goods & Texts(5)	3519.89	-0.1	3895.43	3522.28	3521.31	1940.94	2.29	1.33	32.94	66.97	2010.40
NON-CYCLICAL CONS GOODS(57)	5135.91	+1.2	5683.87	5073.83	5078.39	4908.30	2.95	1.93	17.57	133.93	2328.13
Beverages(5)	3533.52	+0.7	3910.51	3507.82	3535.96	4013.52	4.24	1.75	13.45	144.42	1680.87
Food Producers & Processors(14)	3138.18	+0.8	3472.99	3112.70	3153.42	3396.61	3.23	2.65	11.67	80.62	1766.12
Health(14)	2980.24	+1.4	3298.20	2939.97	2767.83	2503.49	1.62	2.64	23.32	45.09	2098.82
Personal Care & Hse Prods(3)	3540.63	+0.6	3918.38	3519.35	3569.15	3304.08	2.21	2.37	19.07	76.74	1765.22
Pharma'ls & Biotech(18)	8227.55	+1.6	9105.35	8097.10	8092.31	7302.61	2.44	1.86	22.04	166.13	3276.22
Tobacco(3)	9225.85	+0.4	10210.15	9192.94	9278.78	9174.11	4.84	1.48	14.01	446.49	3428.00
CYCLICAL SERVICES(208)	2658.50	+0.5	2942.14	2644.78	2634.78	2100.20	2.77	1.89	19.13	62.72	1669.57
General Retailers(45)	1955.46	-0.5	2164.09	1965.32	1960.70	1550.16	3.30	1.96	15.42	53.12	1416.26
Leisure & Hotels(32)	3008.82	+0.1	3329.83	3005.46	2996.92	2218.35	2.88	2.35	14.77	64.42	1989.93
Media & Entertainment(40)	3510.05	+2.0	3884.54	3440.58	3417.36	2715.80	1.91	1.56	33.75	62.32	1453.92
Support Services(64)	3101.42	-0.4	3432.31	3114.12	3104.56	2583.79	2.90	1.92	18.00	76.34	2273.03
Transport(27)	2073.89	+1.2	2295.15	2049.45	2044.86	1688.50	3.34	1.65	18.08	62.33	1104.54
NON-CYCLICAL SERVICES(19)	1829.11	+0.8	2024.26	1813.96	1808.27	1405.64	1.85	2.42	22.41	23.02	1089.28
Food & Drug Retailers(8)	3068.38	+0.2	3395.74	3062.97	3089.59	2485.05	2.92	2.16	15.85	79.48	2418.65
Telecommunication Services(11)	2489.46	+1.0	2755.06	2464.54	2449.03	1886.50	1.56	2.54	25.16	22.60	1292.60
UTILITIES(14)	3170.70	-0.5	3508.98	3185.97	3199.87	3225.16	5.20	1.29	14.97	121.40	1886.57
Electricity(5)	3133.31	-0.3	3467.61	3142.96	3137.00	3089.40	5.89	1.12	15.21	154.97	2343.80
Utilities Other(9)	3116.49	-0.6	3448.99	3134.15	3157.35	-	4.86	1.39	14.86	102.32	1843.82
INFORMATION TECHNOLOGY(44)	441.43	+1.3	488.52	435.77	426.94	201.15	1.05	‡	‡	4.45	463.60
Information Tech Hardware(13)	419.76	+1.9	464.55	411.80	406.04	153.27	0.41	‡	‡	0.57	437.68
Software & Computer Services(31)	536.62	+1.1	593.87	530.95	518.99	257.69	1.29	2.11	36.83	6.73	563.29
NON FINANCIALS(477)	2042.29	+1.0	2260.18	2022.16	2018.95	1753.47	2.94	1.85	18.37	49.58	1901.43
FINANCIALS(211)	5042.13	+1.1	5580.08	4988.31	4999.58	4154.99	3.82	1.40	18.77	188.14	2794.94
Banks(11)	8719.39	+1.2	9649.67	8617.42	8659.79	7308.59	4.09	1.55	15.79	360.92	3708.41
Insurance(16)	943.83	-0.8	1044.52	951.29	952.99	843.80	2.77	‡	‡	21.91	945.33
Life Assurance(7)	3760.17	+0.7	4161.34	3732.87	3725.35	3216.31	4.77	0.52	40.28	167.31	2060.06
Investment Companies(115)	3384.03	+0.9	3745.07	3352.98	3328.24	2514.86	2.14	1.09	43.03	59.86	1366.02
Real Estate(34)	2209.61	+0.9	2445.35	2190.57	2182.03	1855.65	2.84	1.41	24.96	53.22	1680.09
Speciality & Other Finance(28)	3827.90	+1.4	4236.29	3774.36	3764.24	2595.57	2.72	2.01	18.29	93.51	2663.38

■ Hourly movements	8.03	9.00	10.00	11.00	12.00	13.00	14.00	15.00	16.00	High/day	Low/day
FTSE 100	4273.6	4267.5	4284.0	4300.6	4295.2	4294.8	4313.4	4309.0	4305.9	4316.8	4259.2
FTSE 250	5680.7	5680.4	5679.9	5690.8	5694.5	5698.6	5710.2	5714.8	5720.4	5728.3	5679.5
FTSE SmallCap	2419.23	2420.05	2421.93	2423.88	2425.72	2424.65	2425.95	2428.03	2429.63	2431.67	2419.19
FTSE All-Share	2115.87	2113.35	2120.19	2127.62	2125.66	2125.64	2133.96	2132.43	2131.49	2135.59	2109.95

Time of FTSE 100 Day's high: 14:39:00 Day's low: 8:50:00. FTSE 100 2002/03 High: 4314.7 (18/09/2003) Low: 3287.0 (12/03/2003)
Time of FTSE All-Share Day's high: 14:39:00 Day's low: 8:50:00. FTSE All-Share 2002/03 High: 2135.04 (18/09/2003) Low: 1593.34 (12/03/2003)

Further information is available on http://www.ftse.com. © FTSE International Limited 2003. All Rights reserved. 'FTSE', 'FT-SE' and 'Footsie' are trade marks of the London Stock Exchange and The Financial Times and are used by FTSE International under license. † Sector P/E ratios greater than 80 are not shown. ‡ Values are negative.

Exhibit 20.1 The main UK share indices shown in the *Financial Times*

Source: *Financial Times* 10 October 2003

● **Private investors' indices**

Capital performance		% change			
	09/10/2003	1 month	3 months	One year	Five years
Growth	2442.04	0.06	5.21	17.98	3.33
Balanced	2212.65	0.10	4.36	15.13	1.34
Income	1845.13	0.33	2.77	9.01	-1.17
FTSE All-Share index	2135.21	0.96	7.21	18.61	-4.10
FTSE World Ex UK (Loc)	233.54	-2.09	4.49	28.99	12.35
FTSE UK Gilts (All Stocks)	151.62	-0.26	-2.68	-4.43	-6.10
RPI	181.5	0.00	0.00	2.89	10.87

Calculated by FTSE Intl. in association with APCIMS. © FTSE International Ltd 2003. All rights reserved. These private investor indices, produced by FTSE International, in conjunction with the Association of Private Client Investment Managers and Stockbrokers, are designed to give private investors a benchmark against which to measure the performance of their own portfolios. The income portfolio contains 50 per cent UK equities, 5 per cent international equities and 40 per cent bonds and 5 per cent cash. The Growth Portfolio contains 60 per cent UK equities, 25 per cent International equities, 10 per cent bonds and 5 per cent cash. The Balanced portfolio contains 55 per cent UK equities, 20 per cent International equities, 20 per cent bonds and 5 per cent cash. Their values are calculated using the FTSE All-Share index, the FTSE World Index (excluding the UK), the FTSE Gilts All Stocks Index and 7-day London Interbank Offer Rate (LIBOR) - 1%.
RPI shown above is for August 2003.

Exhibit 20.2 Private investors' indices shown in the *Financial Times*

Source: *Financial Times* 11/12 October 2003

Some monthly financial magazines (e.g. *Money Management* or *What Investment?*) carry performance tables showing how particular unit trusts, OEICs and investment trusts have performed over periods of 1, 3, 5 and 10 years. You can even compare your investments with leading market indices online (e.g. at *www.hemscot.net*).

When using indices make sure you are comparing like with like. For example, if you calculate your portfolio including dividends as well as capital value changes then the index you use should likewise include dividend income – that is, a total return index. Most of the indices used in the press reports are capital only, so when you see a graph of the FTSE 100 going back 5 years it will probably be one that excludes income.

Risk

The greatest risk of all comes about because share buyers do not understand what they are buying. Frequently, they don't have a clue as to what makes the business tick. We only need go back to the late 1990s to see this tendency in all its glory as thousands of investors piled into dot-coms despite not being able to assess whether the business model proposed had any hope of success. The great investors tell us that the best way to reduce risk is to investigate what you are buying into.[2] Don't flail around buying this, that or the other on a whim, a tip or even broker advice. Find out about the people you are

[2] See Glen Arnold, *Valuegrowth Investing* (Financial Times Prentice Hall, 2002).

handing your money over to (the directors of the company), about the state of the industry (see Chapter 14), whether the company has any extraordinary resources (see Chapter 15) and the financial standing of the firm (see Chapters 11, 12 and 13). *Risk is proportional to ignorance more than it is proportional to any other factor.*

Set against the issue of ignorance of what punters are buying, the measures described below are pretty unimportant. Nevertheless, they are referred to by many analysts and journalists, and so you need to know what they are talking about.

Volatility

One way of measuring risk is to observe the way in which the investment swings around over a period of time. If it is highly volatile then there is a greater chance of you losing your money. If its value has been fairly constant or rising in a steady fashion, then you may feel more reassured that there won't be a sudden plunge.

Exhibit 20.3 shows the share prices for two companies over a period of 8 weeks. It is obvious from the chart that shares in Hyperactive plc are much more volatile than shares in Steady plc. Volatility describes the way in which the share price wanders around its average (in this case the average price for both shares is £1).

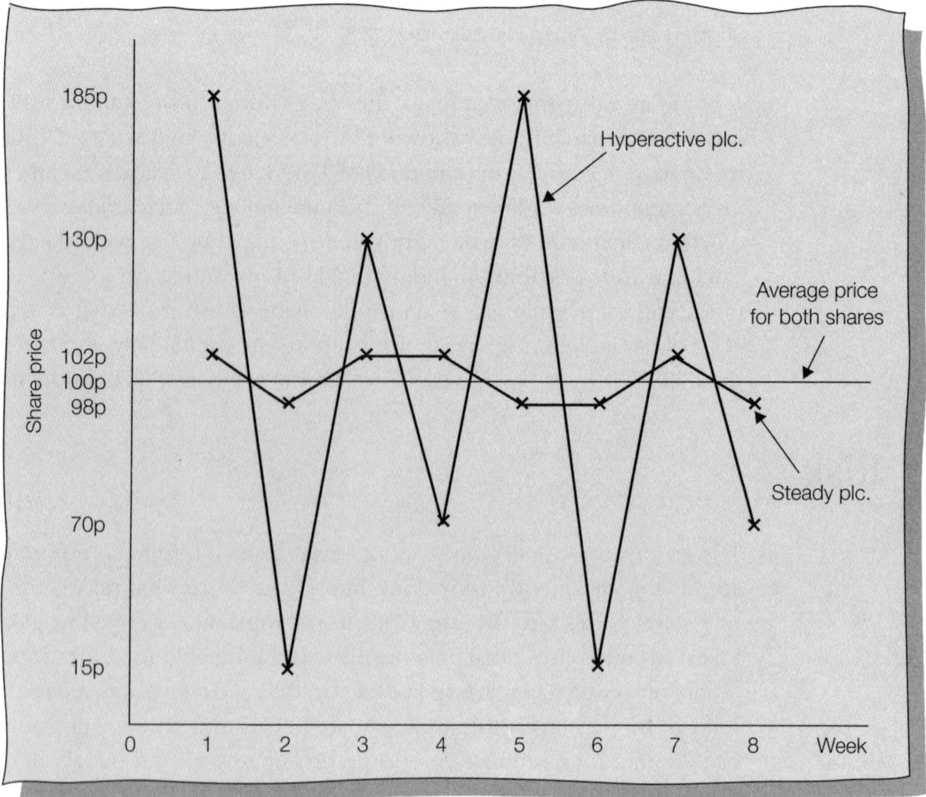

Exhibit 20.3 Volatility of share prices

Observing the higher degree of movement in Hyperactive's shares around its average share price is very easy in this case. However, it might be useful to summarise the degree of movement in a number (a statistic), particularly if we were looking at more subtle cases and could not gauge relative volatility by looking at a chart. The measure of this bobbing about the average that is most often used is called the **standard deviation**. The way in which it is calculated is by looking at the difference between the average share price over the entire study period (8 weeks in this case) and the actual share price in each week. In the case of Steady plc the difference is 2p in each week (102p–100p or 100p–98p). Each of these differences (deviations) is squared and then the squares are added together:

$$2 \times 2 + 2 \times 2 + 2 \times 2 + 2 \times 2 + 2 \times 2 + 2 \times 2 + 2 \times 2 + 2 \times 2 = 32.$$

The number 32 is the **variance** of the share price of Steady over the period of 8 weeks and is a measure of risk in its own right. This is a large number compared with the size of the weekly movements around the average – only 2 pence. This is because we squared the weekly deviations. So, what we do to bring us back to the same units as the original data is to take the square root of the variance. The square root of 32 is 5.65. This is called the standard deviation (in pence). If we follow the same procedure for Hyperactive, we get a variance of

$$85 \times 85 + 85 \times 85 + 30 \times 30 + 30 \times 30 + 85 \times 85 + 85 \times 85 + 30 \times 30 + 30 \times 30 = 32{,}500.$$

and, therefore, taking the square root, a standard deviation of 180p.

So now, instead of having a general impression of Hyperactive's higher volatility we have precise measures: Hyperactive's standard deviation, at 180 pence, has been many times greater than Steady's, at a mere 5.65 pence. In reality, when calculating standard deviation analysts will examine more than eight periods. So they might use 3 years of monthly data, 1 year of daily data or 2 years of weekly data, for example. Also total return (including dividends as well as price movement) rather than share price could be analysed.

Be aware that, as investors, we are interested in the likelihood of loss in the *future*. Variance and standard deviation tell you about *past* volatility. It is a leap of faith to then assume that the future will be like the past. You need to examine the circumstances to see if such faith can be justified. It is remarkable how measures of standard deviation change over time for the same company. Often a measure of volatility calculated 2 years ago puts the company into the low-risk category but one calculated last month puts it into the high-risk category (and vice versa). Standard deviation also changes depending on whether your data consists of daily, weekly, monthly, quarterly or yearly movements.

Diversifiable risk

We have all heard the adage 'don't put all your eggs in one basket'. Well, this applies to your portfolio as much as to other aspects of life. If you place all your money in one company you are vulnerable to adverse news (e.g. a product failure, chief executive's resignation, government rule change) causing a plummet in price. So holding one company's shares in your portfolio will typically result in a high standard deviation. However, if you split your fund between two companies, at any one time there is a fair chance that bad news affecting one is offset by good news affecting the other, so that overall portfolio returns do not oscillate as much. This principle works even better if you have three, four or five shares in your portfolio – standard deviation tends to decrease (see Exhibit 20.4). Diversification is a cheap and practical way of reducing your risk. You are highly recommended to do it.

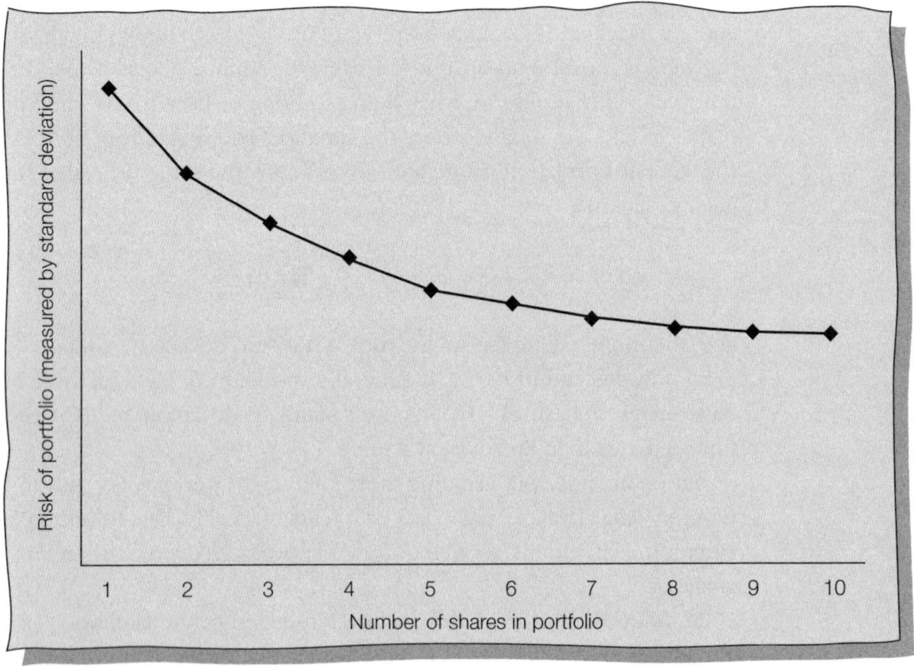

Exhibit 20.4 Decreasing risk by portfolio diversification

However, note that in Exhibit 20.4 the benefits of further diversification after a handful of different shares are held in the portfolio tail off – you can keep on reducing risk but the additional benefit starts to become very small. The great investors suggest that private investors should not over-diversify because the benefits of additional diversification become tiny and yet the disadvantage of not being able to understand all the companies you are buying a portion of starts to loom large. Not only do you sacrifice the ability to understand the companies at the time of share purchase, but also you are unable to follow the unfolding stories thereafter if you are trying to keep track of dozens of shares.

Note also that the benefits of diversification are very much reduced if you buy shares all in the same sector of the market (e.g. all telecommunications shares). These are likely to go up and down together.

Correlation

Correlation measures the degree to which the returns of two assets move together. Correlations are described on a scale that stretches from –1 to +1. A perfect positive correlation (+1) means that the two assets move in lock step with one another. So, if Tesco's share price went up or down by a certain percentage and Sainsbury always went up or down by the same percentage then Tesco and Sainsbury would have perfect positive correlation. A correlation of –1 is perfect negative correlation. This time the movements are exact opposites. If you had an umbrella company that did well in a wet year and its share price rose, you might also have an ice cream company that does badly in a wet year but well in a warm dry year. So the returns for these companies move in opposite directions, depending on the weather. If they moved exactly proportionately in the opposite directions the correlation coefficient would be –1. If they moved in opposite directions most of the time but not perfectly, then the correlation coefficient could be say –0.5. Assets that do not have any co-movement at all – if one goes up the other may either go up or down – show a correlation of 0.

Diversification is going to be most effective with shares that are negatively correlated. You may have noticed that when the London equity market is up the equity markets in the US and in Europe are also (generally) up. This impression is confirmed by the calculation of correlations which turn out to be around 0.6–0.9 (don't ask about the maths to figure this out).

Beta

Beta measures the extent to which a share has, historically, gone up when the market as a whole rose, and gone down when the market went down. It is a share's sensitivity to the market movements. A beta of 1 indicates that generally (on average) in the past when the market rose by 10 per cent this share rose by 10 per cent. A beta of, say, 2 indicates a high sensitivity to market movements in the past. If the market rose by 10 per cent this share tends to rise by 20 per cent. This is fine if things are going well – you outperform the market. On the other hand, if the market fell by 10 per cent your share showed a tendency to exaggerate the market movement by falling 20 per cent. Shares with betas less than 1 have historically been more stable than the market as a whole. So, a share with a beta of 0.5 generally responded to a 10 per cent fall in the market by only falling 5 per cent.

The danger of relying on beta for future-orientated investment decisions is that you have to assume that the relationship with market returns will continue. This is often not the case.

Sharpe's ratio

Investors cannot simply look at performance figures and judge whether one portfolio or one fund manager has done better than another. They need to take account of the level of risk each portfolio was subject to. For example imagine fund manager X achieved a return of 10 per cent over the same period that fund manager Y achieved a return of 11 per cent. We cannot automatically award manager Y the rosette for best performance. It could be that manager Y exposed the investor's money to much higher risk. It happened to pay off this year, but may not do so in future years. The Sharpe's ratio (also called the 'reward-to-variability ratio') judges performance in relation to risk. It is the extent to which the portfolio's return has been greater than that on a risk-free asset (e.g. lending to the UK government by buying its treasury bills) divided by its standard deviation. So if the risk-free return is currently 4 per cent and manager X's fund had a standard deviation of 5 per cent whereas manager Y's fund had a standard deviation of 9 per cent, we see that fund manager X outperformed on a 'risk-adjusted' basis:

$$\text{Manager X: } (10 - 4)/5 = 1.2$$
$$\text{Manager Y: } (11 - 4)/9 = 0.78$$

Treynor's ratio

Treynor's ratio (also called the 'reward-to-volatility ratio') adjusts performance by beta (rather than standard deviation as in Sharpe's ratio). Treynor's ratio is return minus the risk-free rate of return divided by beta. A higher Treynor ratio indicates that the portfolio or fund has managed a stronger performance relative to the risk it has taken.

Different types of risk

- **Liquidity risk**. Liquidity is the degree to which an asset can be sold quickly and easily without loss in value. Property investment assets are relatively illiquid investments because they may take weeks to sell. If a quick sale is needed, a reduction in price is usually required. Shares are generally more liquid than property, but it can still be hard to sell quickly and without moving the price against you. If other investors and market makers see you coming with a lot of shares that are infrequently traded they may well drop the price. Smaller company shares tend to be most illiquid. There are medium-sized firms where the majority of shares are held by a family or a few close associates. Trading here can be thin and illiquid. Many stock market listed companies see only one trade per month.
- **Event risk.** September 11 and the war in Iraq were events that had profound impacts on airline companies. Event risk is the risk of suffering a loss due to unforeseen events. It could be less dramatic than war, e.g. a merger, a loss of a major contract.
- **Political risk.** Changes in government or government policies may affect investors. This is more usually the case in developing countries where confiscation or forced

nationalisation could take away all value from an overseas share holding. Even limits on dividends can have an impact. Note that investors in UK listed companies conducting activities abroad can be affected by political events in other countries.

- **Exchange rate risk.** It is possible to lose money on investments abroad simply because the foreign exchange rate moves against you even if the value of the shares (when valued in the overseas currency) remains constant. However, if you are diversified internationally you may be able to take a swings-and-roundabout attitude to this risk.
- **Market risk.** Your investment could be affected by a general slide in the whole stock market.
- **Manager risk.** Most fund managers (of ISAs, unit trusts, OEICs, investment trusts, pensions, etc.) do not consistently manage to beat the market index average. Given this fact, you might like to save on the high fees of 'active' fund managers and either manage your own investments or go for low-fee 'tracker' funds or exchange traded funds.
- **Inflation risk.** If you select 'safe' investments such as building society accounts or government bonds you may suffer from inflation risk. That is, what seems like a reasonable return when inflation is 2 per cent loses purchasing power if inflation rises in the future to, say, 10 per cent. Investors in government securities were very badly hit in the 1970s as inflation rose to over 20 per cent: they had fixed their 'safe' returns at around 5–6 per cent. Index-linked gilts (Chapter 6) and variable-rate deposit accounts alleviate this problem.

Websites

Risk of shares and indices

- *www.riskgrades.com* provides ratings based on a share's volatility relative to the volatility of a basket of global equities.
- *www.onvista.co.uk* provides beta, correlation and volatility.

Risk of funds

- *www.onvista.co.uk* provides beta, correlation and volatility values.
- *www.ft.com/fundratings* provides a risk-level profile of each fund based on volatility. Total expense ratios are also given.
- *www.morningstar.co.uk* provides average return, standard deviation, Sharpe's ratio and beta for each fund.
- *www.wmcompany.com* provides performance and risk statistics on funds. It examines maximum and minimum monthly returns and standard deviation.

- *www.lipperleaders.com* provides a 'preservation score' based on the difference between the best and worst three-month periods over the past 36 months, relative to other funds of the same type (same 'asset class'). 'Consistent return' is based on excess return, or how much its return 'surpassed its peers' average performance for the previous 36 months.
- *www.funds-sp.com* Fund ratings (e.g. AA or AAA) are determined by various risk factors including portfolio concentration, the experience of the managers, culture and discipline of the team. They are based on 30 per cent quantitative factors (e.g. volatility) and 70 per cent qualitative. Standard measures of risk (e.g. beta), are also provided.

Further reading

Chapter 6 of R. Vaitilingam, *The Financial Times Guide to Using the Financial Pages*, 4th edition (Financial Times Prentice Hall, 2001) provides an excellent overview of indices. The website of the FTSE (*www.ftse.com*) has a lot of very useful descriptions and explanations to download, as do many of the websites listed above.

21

Investment clubs

Investing can be great fun. Looking for bargains unrecognised by the mass of investors, buying them and following their fortunes is exhilarating. Some people become so enthusiastic about investing that it becomes a hobby as well as a way of building up capital. It can be even more exciting if you can share the ups and downs, triumphs and disasters with fellow enthusiasts.

Investment clubs are groups of people who each contribute a few pounds per month (usually £25 to £40), which is then pooled to buy shares for the club. There are now over 12,000 investment clubs in the UK, with over 120,000 members.

The social aspect is very important – most members of a club are friends, or work colleagues, and about half of the clubs meet in a pub! There is generally a lot of lighthearted banter, and, frequently, social events beyond the regular meetings – annual dinners, even club trips abroad.

An investment club is a great place to start if you feel daunted by the prospect of investing as an individual. You can learn a lot from the others and you can enjoy the thrills and spills without betting your life savings. Even experienced investors value clubs for the ability to socialise with like-minded people and the chance to share tips and ideas. Many members, in addition to their monthly contribution to the club, set up their own personal portfolio to gain greater exposure to shares they feel are particularly undervalued.

Club members often have years of experience of particular industries from their working lives and so may have special insight to offer at club meetings. Some clubs encourage members to agree to look at different companies or sectors to enable them to gain a depth of knowledge rather than trying to be jacks-of-all-trades.

How to set up a club

Investment clubs are usually begun when two or three friends think it would be a good idea to meet regularly to discuss investments. Each of these people, in turn, probably know two or three others who would like to join, and soon you have a club of between 10 and 20 members. Most clubs do not go beyond 20 members (the average is 11). This is because firstly, the friendly atmosphere can be lost and meetings can become unwieldy, and secondly, clubs are usually set up under the law of partnership and this form of organisation was until 2002 limited to 20 members in the UK (you can now have as many partners as you like).

At the first meeting you need to agree how frequently you should meet and where (members' houses and pubs are the favourite options). You must also agree on the rules for recruiting additional members – there must be trust and a certain rapport within the club, so care is needed when extending the invitation to join. The monthly subscription also needs to be agreed – it can be as little as £10. Also, clubs often start with an initial lump-sum payment by members so that investments of hundreds or thousands of pounds can be made right away without having to wait until the monthly subscription builds up.

You will need to appoint three club officers: a chairman to chair meetings; an honorary secretary to record proceedings and produce minutes; and an honorary treasurer to receive monthly subscriptions (usually by standing order) and pay brokers. These officers should not have to put in more than two hours per month. They are elected by simple majority at the inaugural meeting or subsequently at a general meeting of the club. They are required to resign at the AGM but are entitled to stand again for re-election. The club is able to create other administrative posts as the need arises.

You need to decide on a name for the club and discuss the general investment philosophy and boundaries (e.g. long-term or short-term trading focus, whether to invest in overseas shares, or in traded options).

A rulebook or constitution needs to be drawn up to deal with practical issues. For example: What happens when a member leaves? How much notice should a member give before leaving? How do you calculate what is due to a member on departure? What are the rules for changing the constitution? What size majority is needed to agree investment decisions? How do you elect new members?

The *ProShare Investment Club Manual* contains a draft constitution, which you could adopt with or without modification.

The unit valuation system

It is important that every member is clear about how the value of their portion of the clubs' pot is calculated. ProShare, the leading support organisation for investment clubs in the UK, recommends the unit valuation system.[1] When the club is established each £1 contributed gives a member one unit. Thereafter, to calculate the value of units you divide the club's assets by the number of units. Each month the fund is revalued to create a new unit value. This is then used to work out the number of units to be purchased with each month's cash subscriptions. This system allows new members to join and existing members to buy extra units should they wish to do so. It is also possible for members to sell a portion of their holdings; after a few years a member may be holding £20,000 or so in the club and may wish to turn some of that into cash.

Bank account

High street banks offer special accounts for clubs (e.g. 'Clubs and Societies' or 'Treasurers') in which two signatories are usually required. Some accounts pay interest and some provide cheque facilities.

[1] In 2003 Digital Look bought ProShare's investment club division – see *www.proshareclubs.co.uk* and *www.digitallook.com*.

Brokers

Many stockbrokers are keen to help investment clubs. The charges are the same as for individuals. Clubs usually opt for nominee stockbroking accounts (see Chapter 4) because of the ease and efficiency of dealing. (Make sure you don't lose your shareholder rights, e.g. to receive company communications and reports, to vote and to attend shareholder meetings.) Clubs usually select an 'execution-only' service which is cheap and allows the club members to make investment decisions. Brokers usually ask to see a copy of the investment club constitution in case a disagreement arises within the club. The club appoints two members to act on behalf of the club, and both their signatures are required for all documents. The website *www.proshare.org* list stockbrokers offering services specifically for investment clubs accredited by ProShare.

Tax

There are no special tax advantages in investing through a club. Each member is taxed individually and everyone is liable to pay income tax on his or her share of dividends and capital gains tax on share price rises. The treasurer or secretary will provide to each member the details of his/her profits or losses made and dividends received for the year. It is up to the members to declare their club profits or losses on their individual tax returns. The local Inland Revenue office will expect you to notify them of the club's existence and to make returns for the club each year.

Further reading

The ProShare Investment Club Manual (*www.proshare.org*, tel. 020 7220 1730, ProShare, Centurion House, 24 Monument St., London EC3R 8AQ).

T. Bond, *The Company of Successful Investors* (Financial Times Prentice Hall, 2002).

Glossary

'A' shares Usually the ordinary shares that carry fewer or no votes are designated 'A' shares. However, in many cases 'A' shares carry more votes than the 'B' shares.

Abandon The choice made by a holder of a warrant or option to allow it to expire without exercise.

Abnormal return (residual return) A return greater than the market return after adjusting for differences in risk.

Accounting rate of return A measure of profitability; profit divided by assets devoted to the activity (e.g. project, entire business).

Accounting standards A set of formal rules and conventions set by the accounting profession to calculate accounting numbers.

Accumulation (Acc) units Unit trust units that reinvest income (e.g. dividends) earned from a portfolio, on behalf of unit holders, in more units.

Acid test *See* Quick ratio.

Actively managed fund The managers of the fund spend time and effort carefully selecting shares (the costs of this are passed on to investors).

Actuary A person who makes a judgement on whether a fund has enough assets to deliver on its promises (e.g. to pensioners). The actuary is then able to suggest appropriate premium levels to raise or lower total assets.

Adjusted earnings per share *See* Headline earnings per share.

Administered prices Prices controlled by some authority (e.g. government).

Administration An administrator takes over the running of a distressed company to help it survive and avoid liquidation.

Advisory service A type of service provided by a stockbroker in which the broker will offer advice prior to the investor's purchase or sale. The decision on whether to carry out a transaction still rests with the investor, unlike with a discretionary service.

Affirmative covenants Loan agreement conditions (e.g. a statement that a bond will pay regular dividends).

Agency Acting for or in the place of another with his/her/their authority.

Aggressive shares Shares having a beta value greater than 1.

AGM *See* Annual general meeting.

AITC The Association of Investment Trust Companies. Trade body for investment trusts.

Allocation of capital The mechanism for selecting competing investment projects leading to the production of a mixture of goods and services by a society. This can be influenced by the forces of supply and demand, and by central authority direction.

Allocational efficiency of markets Efficiency in the process of allocating society's scarce resources between competing real investments.

Allotment In a new issue of shares, if more shares are demanded at the price than are available, they may be apportioned (allotted) between the applicants.

Allowance *See* tax allowance.

All-paper deal When a bidder offers to buy shares in a target the payment is entirely in the form of shares in the bidder.

Alpha A measure of market outperformance (underperformance) after allowing for beta.

That portion of a share's return that cannot be explained by its responsiveness to moves in the market as a whole. Sometimes called stock-specific return.

Alternative investment Outside of the mainstream (e.g. art, stamps, coins, wine).

Alternative Investment Market (AIM) The lightly regulated share market operated by the London Stock Exchange, focused particularly on smaller, less well-established companies.

American Depositary Receipts Depositary receipts issued in the USA.

American-style option (American option) An option which can be exercised by the purchaser at any time up to the expiry date.

AMEX The American Stock Exchange. Trades equities, options and exchange traded funds.

Amortisation The repayment of a debt by a series of instalments.

Amortisation of assets The reduction in book value of an intangible asset such as goodwill.

Analyst A researcher of companies' prospects and predictor of their share price performance.

Angel *See* Business angel.

Annual Equivalent Rate (AER) – see definition for Annual Percentage Rate.

Annual general meeting (AGM) A limited company must hold in each calendar year an annual general meeting. This is an opportunity for shareholders to meet and talk with each other and with those who run the company on their behalf. The managers give an account of their stewardship. All shareholders are entitled to attend and vote.

Annual percentage rate (APR) The true annual interest rate charged by a lender, it taking full account of the timing of payments of interest and principal.

Annual results Annual company accounts. This term is often used for the preliminary results.

Annuity An even stream of payments (same amount each time) over a given period of time.

APCIMS Association of Private Client Investment Managers and Stockbrokers. A trade association for investment managers and stockbrokers.

Appropriable resource The resource which supplies value must be one that allows the company to capture the value rather than allow it to be captured by another organisation or individual(s).

Arbitrage The act of exploiting price differences on the same instrument or similar securities by simultaneously selling the overpriced security and buying the underpriced security.

Arbitration An arbitrator decides on a just settlement between a complainant and a financial services firm. The decision is binding on both parties.

Articles of association Internal rules governing a company. These can be unique to the company.

Asset In the financial market, anything that can be traded as a security (e.g. share, option, commodity, bond).

Asset allocation An investment methodology which specifies the proportion of funds to be invested in different asset classes (e.g. property, shares, bonds).

Asset-backed securities *See* Securitisation.

Asset backing The value of the assets held in the business – often measured on a per share basis.

Asset class Asset type (e.g. bonds, shares).

Asset liquidity The extent to which assets can be converted to cash quickly, at a low transaction cost and without lowering the price.

Asset lock-up In a hostile takeover situation, the target sells to a friendly firm those parts of the business most attractive to the bidder.

Asset transformers Intermediaries who, by creating a completely new security – the intermediate security – mobilise savings and encourage investment. The primary security is issued by the ultimate borrower to the intermediary, who offers intermediate securities to the primary investors.

Associated company A company in which an investor (usually a holding company) holds a participating interest and exercises significant influence. 'Interest' includes shares, options and convertible securities. 'Participating' means the interest is held on a long-term basis and there is significant influence. Usually a 20% or more holding of the shares is presumed to be participating.

Asymmetric information Situation where one party in a negotiation or relationship is not in the same position as other parties, being ignorant of, or unable to observe, some information which is essential to the contracting and decision-making process.

At best A type of buy or sell instruction given by an investor to a broker. The trade is to be completed immediately at the best price available.

At-the-money option The current underlying price is equal to the option exercise price.

Attribute markets Subsections of the Official List consisting of firms with common characteristics – for example, technologically led (techMARK) or belonging to a particular UK region (landMARK).

Audit committee A committee of company directors responsible for validating their company's financial figures (e.g. by appointing effective external auditors).

Auditor An auditor determines whether a company's financial statements are misleading and whether the accounts presents a true and fair picture.

Authorised share capital The maximum amount of share capital that a company can issue. The limit can be changed by a shareholder vote.

Autif The Association of Unit Trust and Investment Funds.

Back office That part of a financial institution which deals with the settlement of contracts, accounting and management information processes.

Bad debts Debts that are unlikely to be paid.

Balance sheet Summary of assets and liabilities, showing what a company owns and is owed on a particular day in the past.

Ballot In a new issue of shares when a company floats on a stock exchange, if the demand is greater than supply, the shares are allocated to some applicants but not others, selected at random.

Bancassurance Companies offering both banking and insurance.

Bank covenant *See* covenant.

Bank for International Settlements (BIS) Controlled by central banks, the BIS was established to assist international financial co-ordination. It promotes international monetary co-ordination, provides research and statistical data, co-ordination and trusteeship for intergovernmental loans, and acts as a central bank for national central banks, accepting deposits and making loans.

Bank of England The central bank of the United Kingdom, responsible for monetary policy. It oversees the affairs of other financial institutions, issues banknotes and coins, manages the national debt and exchange rate, and is lender of last resort.

Bank of England index Shows the extent to which a currency has strengthened or weakened against sterling since 1990.

Bargain A term used interchangeably with the term 'a contract to buy/sell shares'.

Barriers to entry The obstacles that a company entering a market for the first time has to overcome to do well in that market.

Base rate The reference rate of interest that forms the basis for interest rates on bank loans, overdrafts and deposit rates.

Basic (FRS 3) earnings per share Includes deductions from profit of one-off exceptional items and goodwill amortisation.

Basis point One-hundredth of 1 per cent, usually applied to interest rates.

Bear An investor who takes the view that prices are likely to fall.

Bear fund Designed to do well when shares are falling in price.

Bearer bond The ownership of a bond is not recorded on a register. Possession of the bond is sufficient to receive interest, etc.

Bed and breakfasting shares Selling shares to realise a gain below the annual threshold for capital gains tax. This is followed by a repurchase the next day.

Bed and spousing Selling shares to realise a gain below the annual threshold for capital gains tax. This is followed by a spouse repurchasing the shares in the market.

Bells and whistles Additional features placed on derivatives or securities (such as bonds) that are designed to attract investors.

Benchmark index An index of shares or other securities that sets a standard for fund manager performance; for example, a fund manager controlling a portfolio of pharmaceutical shares would measure performance against a pharmaceutical index. This is calculated by an independent person to be representative of the sector.

Best execution A broker must carry out a transaction on behalf of a client at the best possible price available at the time.

Beta This measures the systematic risk of a financial security. It is a measure of sensitivity of a financial security's return to market movements. In practice a proxy (e.g. the FT100 index) is used for the market portfolio.

Bid–offer spread The difference between the market maker's buy and sell prices.

Bid premium The additional amount an acquirer has to offer above the pre-bid share price in order to succeed in a takeover offer.

Bid price The price at which a market maker will buy shares or a dealer in other markets will buy a security or commodity.

Big Bang A term used for a collection of reforms to the running of share trading in the UK implemented in 1986.

Bill of exchange A document which sets out a commitment to pay a sum of money at a specified point in time (e.g. an importer commits itself to paying a supplier). Bills of exchange may be discounted – that is, sold before maturity for less than face value.

BIMBO Buy-in management buy-out: a combination of a management buy-out and a buy-in. Outside managers join forces with existing managers to take over a company, subsidiary or unit.

Black Monday 19 October 1987, the date of a large fall in stock market prices.

Black Wednesday 16 September 1992, a day of severe currency turbulence when sterling and the Italian lira devalued significantly and were forced to leave the exchange rate mechanism.

Blue chips The shares with the highest status as investments. Regarded (often mistakenly) as safest.

Board of directors People elected by shareholders to run a company.

Bond A debt obligation with a long-term maturity, usually issued by firms and governments.

Bond covenant *See* Covenant.

Bonus issue *See* Scrip issue.

Book-building A book runner invites major institutional investors to suggest how many shares, bonds, etc they would be interested in purchasing and at what price in a new issue or secondary issue of securities. This helps to establish the price and allocate the financial assets.

Book-to-market equity ratio The ratio of a firm's balance sheet value to the total market value of its shares.

Book value Balance sheet value. This can be expressed on a per share basis.

Bootstrapping game *See* Price–earnings ratio game.

Borrowing capacity Limits to total borrowing levels imposed by lenders, often determined by available collateral.

Bottom fishing Looking for value amongst shares that have fallen sharply.

Bottom line Profit attributable to the shareholders produced by a company over a period of time e.g. one year.

Bottom up Analysis of shares or markets where priority is given to individual firm prospects rather than macroeconomic prospects and asset allocation.

Bought deal An investment bank buys an entire security issue (e.g. shares) from a client corporation raising finance. The investment bank usually intends to sell it on to institutional clients within hours.

Bourse Alternative name for a stock exchange. Used particularly in continental Europe.

Break-even analysis Analysing the level of sales at which a project, division or business produce a zero profit (accounting emphasis).

Break-out In chartism the point where a share breaks out of an established pattern.

Break-up value The total value of separate parts of the company if the parts are sold off to the highest bidder.

Broker Assists in the buying and selling of financial securities by acting as a 'go-between', helping to reduce search, transaction and information costs.

Broking account An account with a stockbroker used by an investor to deposit and withdraw cash in the course of share transactions.

Bubble An explosive upward movement in financial security prices not based on fundamentally rational factors, followed by a crash.

Bubble stock Shares buoyed up by market optimism. Such optimism is not based on any rational standards of value.

Budget (national) Sets out government expenditure and revenue for the financial year. In the UK it is presented to Parliament by the Chancellor of the Exchequer.

Building society A UK financial institution, the primary role of which is the provision of mortgages. Building societies are non-profit-making mutual organisations. Funding is mostly through small deposits by individuals.

Bulge bracket A leading investment bank.

Bull An investor taking the view that prices will rise.

Bulldog A foreign bond issued in the UK.

Bullet bond A bond where all the principal on a loan is repaid at maturity.

Bulletin board A computer based site for infrequently traded shares on which investors (via brokers) can display their unfilled orders in the hope of finding a match.

Business angel Wealthy individual prepared to invest between £10,000 and £250,000 in a start-up, early-stage or developing firm. He/she will often have managerial and/or technical experience to offer the management team as well as equity and debt finance. This is medium- to long-term investment in high-risk situations.

Business risk The risk associated with the underlying operations of a business. The variability of the firm's operating income: this dispersion is caused purely by business-related factors and not by the debt burden.

Buy-and-hold investor Investor who tends to trade infrequently.

Buyers' strike When there are many sellers of a financial security and buyers are difficult or impossible to find.

Buy-side Fund managers use buy-side (internal) analysts to select shares.

BVCA British Venture Capital Association.

CAC 40 A stock market index of French shares quoted in Paris.

Cadbury report The Committee on the Financial Aspects of Corporate Governance, chaired by Sir Adrian Cadbury, made recommendations on the role of directors and auditors, published in 1992.

Call option This gives the purchaser the right, but not the obligation, to buy a fixed quantity of a commodity, financial instrument or some other underlying asset at a given price, at or before a specified date.

Called-up (issued) share capital The total value of shares sold by a company when expressed at par or nominal value.

Cap An interest rate cap is a contract that effectively gives the purchaser the right to set a maximum level for interest rates payable. Compensation is paid to the purchaser of a cap if interest rates rise above an agreed level.

Capital Stored wealth and resources.

Capital asset pricing model (CAPM) An asset (e.g. share) pricing theory which assumes that financial assets, in equilibrium, will be priced to produce rates of return which compensate investors for systematic risk, as measured by the covariance of the assets' return with the market portfolio return (i.e beta).

Capital budgeting The process by which a company selects long-term capital investments.

Capital expenditure The purchase of long-lived (more than one year) assets (i.e. fixed assets).

Capital gearing The extent to which a firm's total capital is in the form of debt.

Capital lease *See* Financial lease.

Capital market Where those raising finance can do so by selling financial investments to investors (e.g. bonds, shares).

Capital shares *See* Split-capital investment trusts.

Capital structure The proportion of the firm's capital which is equity or debt.

Capitalisation (1) An item of expenditure is taken on to the balance sheet and capitalised as an asset rather than written off against profits. (2) Short for market capitalisation.

Capitalisation factor A discount rate.

Capitalisation issue *See* Scrip issue.

Capitalisation rate Required rate of return for the class of risk.

Capped bonds The floating interest rate charged cannot rise above a specified level.

Carpetbagger A person who becomes a member of a mutually owned organisation (such as a building society) in the hope of cashing in should it demutualise, for example, by receiving shares in the organisation and then selling them.

Cartel A group of firms supplying the same market entering into an agreement to set mutually acceptable prices for their products.

Cash cow A company with low growth, stable market conditions and low investment needs. The company's competitive strength enables it to produce surplus cash.

Cash flow statement The formal statement of a company's cash movements.

Cash fund Funds that invest in money market investments.

Cash settlement In the derivative market some contracts are physically settled at expiry date (e.g. pork bellies are delivered in return for cash under the derivative contract). However, many derivatives are not physically delivered, rather a cash difference representing a gain or loss on the closed derivative position changes hands.

CAT standard CAT stands for 'Charges, Access, Terms'. The UK government accredits ISAs that have good characteristics under these headings. The award of the CAT standard does not guarantee a good return.

Causal ambiguity A potential imitator is unable to clearly see which resource is giving the sustainable competitive advantage to a firm, or it is difficult to identify the way in which the extraordinary resource was created in the first place.

Central bank A bankers' bank and lender of last resort which controls the credit system of an economy (e.g. controls note issue), acts as the government's bank, controls interest rates and regulates the country's banking system.

Certificate of deposit (CD) A deposit is made at a bank. A certificate confirming that a deposit has been made is given in return, to the lender. This certificate is normally a bearer security. The CD can then be sold in the secondary market whenever the depositor needs cash.

Chairman's statement A company's annual report and accounts usually has a chairman's statement commenting on the results and progress.

CHAPS (Clearing House Automated Payment System) The UK same-day interbank clearing system for sterling payments.

Chartism Investment analysis that relies on historic price charts (and/or trading volumes) to predict future movements.

Chasing the trend Buying financial securities after a recent upward trend in prices and selling after a recent downward trend.

Chicago Board of Trade The futures and options exchange in Chicago, USA – the world's oldest (established 1848).

Chicago Board Options Exchange The largest options exchange in the world, trading options on shares, indices and interest rates.

Chicago Mercantile Exchange (CME) An exchange which trades a wide range of currency futures and options, interest rate futures and options, commodity futures and options, and share index futures and options.

Chief executive's review (operational review) A comment, contained in a company's annual report and accounts, on performance, strategy and managerial intentions.

Chinese walls Barriers within a financial service company designed to prevent sensitive information being passed on to another branch of the organisation.

CHIPS (Clearing House Interbank Payment System) The US system for US dollar payment between banks.

Churn Buying and selling shares frequently. Fund managers are often accused of doing this to generate fees or just in the vain search for higher returns.

Circle of competence The business areas that an individual thoroughly understands and is equipped to analyse.

City Code on Takeovers and Mergers Provides the main governing rules for companies engaged in merger activity. Self-regulated and administered by the Takeover Panel.

City of London A collective term for the financial institutions located in the financial district to the east of St Paul's Cathedral in London (also called the Square Mile). However, the term is also used to refer to all UK financial institutions, wherever they are located.

Claw back Existing shareholders often have the right to reclaim shares sold under a placing as though they were entitled to them under a rights issue.

Clean price On a bond the prices are general quoted 'clean', that is, without taking account of the accrued interest since the last coupon payment.

Clearing a trade The stock exchange ensures that all reports of a trade are reconciled to make sure all parties are in agreement as to the number of shares traded and the price, and that the buyer and seller have the cash and securities to do the deal.

Clearing bank Member of the London Bankers' Clearing House, which clears cheques, settling indebtedness between two parties.

Clearing house An institution which settles mutual indebtedness between a number of individuals or organisations. The clearing house may also act as a counterparty.

Closed-end funds Collective investment vehicles (e.g. investment trusts) that do not create or redeem shares on a daily basis in response to increases and decreases in demand. They have a fixed number of shares for lengthy periods.

Closet indexing Fund managers declare themselves as active (i.e. searching out bargains) but really construct portfolios that are close to the market benchmark indices.

Closing out a futures position The act of taking a second action in the futures market (say, selling the future) which is exactly opposite to the first action (say, buying the future). Also called 'reversing the trade'.

Collateral Property pledged by a borrower to protect the interests of the lender.

Collective funds *See* Pooled funds.

Commercial banking Taking deposits and making loans.

Commercial bill (bank bill or **trade bill)** A document expressing the commitment of a borrowing firm to repay a short-term debt at a fixed date in the future.

Commercial paper (CP) An unsecured note promising the holder (lender) a sum of money to be paid in a few days – average maturity of 40 days. If they are denominated in foreign currency and placed outside the jurisdiction of the authorities of that currency, then the notes are euro-commercial paper.

Commission Fee charged by brokers, usually a percentage of the amount of the transaction.

Commitment fee A fee payable in return for a commitment by a bank to lend money payable even if no borrowing subsequently takes place.

Commodity product Undifferentiated compared with competitor offerings in any customer-important way by factors such as performance, appearance, service support, etc.

Common stock Term used in the USA to describe ordinary shares in a company.

Companies Acts The series of laws enacted by Parliament governing the establishment and conduct of incorporated business enterprises. The Companies Act 1985 consolidated the Acts that preceded it.

Companies House The place where records are kept of every UK company. These records are then made available to the general public.

Company registrar *See* Registrar.

Comparative advantage A firm or a country has a comparative advantage in the production of good X if the opportunity cost of producing a unit of X, in terms of other goods forgone, is lower in that country compared with another country, or in that firm compared with another firm.

Competition Commission The Commission may obtain any information needed to investigate possible monopoly anti-competitive situations referred to it. It may recommend competition-enhancing remedies such as blocking a merger.

Competitive advantage (edge) The possession of extraordinary resources that allow a firm to rise above the others in its industry to generate exceptional long-run rates of return on capital employed.

Competitive floor Where shareholders receive a rate of return that only just induces them to put money into the firm and hold it there.

Competitive position The competitive strength of the firm *vis-à-vis* rivals in a product market.

Complementary product One that is generally bought alongside the product in question.

Compliance officers Financial service firms regulated by the Financial Services Authority often have a designated compliance officer who ensures that FSA rules are followed.

Compound interest Interest is paid on the sum which accumulates, whether or not that sum comes from principal or from interest received.

Compound return The income received on an investment is reinvested in the investment and future returns are gained on both the original capital and the ploughed-back income.

Concentration When there are few investments in a portfolio, it is said to be concentrated.

Concert party A group of investors, acting together or under the control of one person, buys shares in a company.

Conglomerate bank A bank with a wide range of activities, products and markets.

Conglomerate merger The combining of two firms which operate in unrelated business areas.

Consideration The price paid for something.

Consolidated accounts All the income costs, assets and liabilities of all group companies, whether wholly or partially owned, are brought together in the consolidated accounts.

Consolidation of shares Reduction in the number of shares so that the nominal value of each remaining share rises.

Consumer price index (CPI) The main US measure of general inflation.

Continuing obligations Standards of behaviour and actions required of firm's listed on the London Stock Exchange, enforced by the United Kingdom Listing Authority.

Contract note A statement from a broker to an investor stating the price, the time of deal, the number of shares, the broker's commission and the stamp duty for a recent share transaction.

Contract for difference (CFD) The buyer and seller agree to pay, in cash, at the closing of the contract, the difference between the opening and closing price of the underlying shares, multiplied by the number of shares in the contract.

Contrarians Those taking the opposite position to the generality of investors.

Convergence The coming together of the futures price and the underlying share price in the final trading day of a futures contract.

Conversion premium The difference between the current share price and the conversion price, expressed as a percentage of the current share price for convertible bonds.

Conversion price The share price at which convertible bonds may be converted.

Conversion ratio (1) The nominal (par) value of a convertible bond divided by the conversion price. The number of shares available per bond. (2) The ratio of the number of warrants that must be held and exercised in order to buy or sell a single unit of the asset (e.g. one share).

Conversion value The value of a convertible bond if it were converted into ordinary shares at the current share price.

Convertible bonds Bonds which carry a rate of interest and give the owner the right to exchange the bonds at some stage in the future into ordinary shares according to a prearranged formula.

Convertible loan stock *See* Convertible bonds.

Convertible preference stock A preference share that can be changed into another type of security (e.g. an ordinary share).

Coredeal An international exchange for international debt-related securities, owned by the International Securities Markets Association (ISMA).

Corporate bond A bond issued by a company.

Corporate broker Stockbrokers who act on behalf of companies quoted on an exchange (e.g. providing advice on market conditions or representing the company to the market). Corporate brokers are knowledgeable about the share and other financial markets. They advise companies on fund raising (e.g. new issues). They try to generate interest amongst investors for the company's securities, and stand prepared to buy and sell companies' shares.

Corporate finance department of investment banks The department assisting firms in raising funds (e.g. rights issues, bond issues) and managing their finances.

Corporate governance The system of management and control of the corporation.

Corporate raider An organisation that makes hostile takeover approaches for quoted companies.

Corporate venturing Large companies fostering the development of smaller enterprises through, for example, joint capital development or equity capital provision.

Corporation tax A tax levied on the profits of companies.

Correction A minor fall during a market rise.

Correlation coefficient A measure of the extent to which two variables show a relationship, expressed on a scale of –1 to +1. A correlation of –1 implies that two share prices, two markets, etc., move in opposite directions by the same percentages.

Cost leadership strategy Emphasis on standard no-frills product, exploiting scale economies and other cost advantages.

Cost of capital The rates of return that a company has to offer finance providers to induce them to buy and hold a financial security.

Cost of sales The expense incurred for bought-in raw materials or components.

Counterparty The buyer for a seller, or the seller for a buyer.

Counterparty risk The risk that a counterparty to a contract defaults and does not fulfil obligations.

Coupon An attachment to a bond or loan note document which may be separated and serve as evidence of entitlement to interest. Nowadays it refers to the interest itself.

Covariance Measure of the extent to which two variables move together.

Covenant A solemn agreement.

Covered call option writing Writing a call option on an underlying when the writer owns at least the number of underlying securities included in the option.

Covered warrants The same as warrants, except that financial institutions issue them, selling the right to buy or sell shares in industrial and commercial companies.

Creative accounting The drawing up of accounts which obey the letter of the law and accounting body rules, but which involve the manipulation of accounts to show the most favourable profit and balance sheet.

Credit period The average length of time between the purchase of inputs and the payment for them. Equal to the average level of creditors divided by the purchases on credit per day.

Credit rating An estimate of the quality of a debt from the lender viewpoint in terms of the likelihood of interest and capital not being paid and of the extent to which the lender is protected in the event of default. Credit rating agencies are paid fees by companies, governments, etc., wishing to attract lenders.

Credit risk The risk that a counterparty to a financial transaction will fail to fulfil their obligation.

Credit union A non-profit organisation accepting deposits and making loans, operated as a co-operative.

Creditor One to whom a debt is owed.

CREST An electronic means of settlement and registration of shares following a sale on the London Stock Exchange, operated by CRESTCo.

CREST nominee account *See* Nominee company.

Crown jewels defence In a hostile merger situation, the target sells off the most attractive parts of the business.

Cum-dividend When an investor buys a government **bond** which it is still designated cum-dividend, he/she is entitled to the accrued interest since the last coupon was paid. A **share designated cum-dividend** indicates that the buyer will be entitled to a dividend recently announced by the company.

Cum-rights Shares bought on the stock market prior to the ex-rights day are designated cum-rights and carry to the new owner the right to subscribe for the new shares in the rights issue.

Cumulative If a payment (interest or dividend) on a bond or preference share is missed in one period those securities are given priority when the next payment is made. These arrears must be cleared up before shareholders receive dividends.

Currency swap *See* Swap.

Current assets Cash and other assets that can be rapidly turned into cash. Includes stocks of raw materials, partially finished goods and finished goods, debtors and investments expected to be sold within 1 year.

Current asset value (net) Current assets (cash, accounts receivable, inventory) minus current liabilities (also called working capital).

Current liabilities Amounts owed that the company expects to have to pay within the next year.

Current ratio The ratio of current liabilities to the current assets of a business.

Custodian An organisation that acts for investors in an administrative capacity, managing the holding of shares and other financial securities. The custodian may handle dividend payments and carry out various other administrative duties for the investor.

Cyclical companies (shares) Those companies in which profits are particularly sensitive to the growth level in the economy, which may be cyclical.

Cyclical industries Those industries in which profits are particularly sensitive to the growth level in the economy, which may be cyclical.

Daily Official List (DOL) The daily record setting out the prices of all trades in securities conducted on the London Stock Exchange.

Darling A stock market darling is one which receives a lot of attention and is regarded as very attractive.

Dawn raid Situation where an acquirer acts with such speed in buying the shares of the target company that the raider achieves the objective of accumulating a substantial stake in the target before its management has time to react.

DAX 30 A stock market index of German shares quoted on the Deutsche Börse.

Day trader Someone who trades in and out of a share in one day. He/she may have both buy and sell trades for many shares in the same day.

Dead cat bounce Even a dead cat thrown from a tall building will bounce. Likewise, a market may rally a little, but this is temporary. Also known as a sucker's rally.

Debentures Bonds issued with redemption dates a number of years into the future. Usually secured against specific assets (mortgage debentures) or through a floating charge on the firm's assets.

Debt capital Capital raised with (usually) a fixed obligation in terms of interest and principal payments.

Debt Management Office (DMO) Organises the sale of gilts. An Executive Agency of the UK Treasury.

Debt maturity The length of time left until the repayment on a debt becomes due.

Debt-to-equity ratio The ratio of a company's long-term debt to shareholders' funds.

Debtor conversion period The average number of days to convert customer debts into cash. Equal to the average value of debtors divided by the average value of sales per day.

Debtor One who owes a debt.

Declining (reducing) balance method of depreciation The amount an asset is depreciated declines from one year to the next as it is determined by a constant percentage of the asset's depreciated value at the start of each year.

Deep discounted bonds Bonds sold well below par value.

Deep discounted rights issue A rights issue priced much lower than the present market price of the old shares.

Default A failure to make agreed payments of interest or principal.

Defensive industries Those industries where profits are not particularly sensitive to the growth rate of the economy.

Defensive shares Having a beta value of less than 1.

Deferred ordinary shares These rank below preferred ordinary shares for dividends. So, if profits are low, holders of deferred ordinary shares may not receive a dividend.

Dematerialisation Traditionally the evidence of financial security ownership is by written statements on paper (e.g. share certificates). Increasingly such information is being placed in electronic records and paper evidence is being abandoned.

Demerger The separation of companies or business units that are currently under one corporate umbrella. It applies particularly to the unravelling of a merger.

Depositary receipts Tradable certificates representing evidence of ownership of a company's shares held by a depository.

Depreciation The reduction in the stated value of assets with a useful life of more than 1 year that are not bought and sold as part of normal trading.

Derivative A financial asset, the performance of which is based on (derived from) the behaviour of the value of an underlying asset.

Deutsche Börse The German Stock Exchange based in Frankfurt.

Differentiated product One that is slightly different in significant ways than those supplied by other companies.

Differentiation strategy The unique nature of the product/service offered allows for a premium price to be charged.

Diluted earnings per share This takes into account any additional shares that may be issued in the future under executive share option schemes and other commitments.

Diminishing marginal attractiveness If stocks are listed in order of attractiveness based on the difference between their value and current price, then the marginal (next stock) on the list would be less attractive.

Direct foreign investment The purchase of commercial assets such as factories and industrial plant for productive purposes by overseas organisations.

Directors' dealings Directors' purchase or sale of shares in their own company. This is legal (except at certain times of the company's year). Some investors examine directors' dealings to decide whether to buy or sell. Dealings are listed in Saturday's *Financial Times* and in the Investors Chronicle.

Directors' report Information and commentary on company performance and other matters contained in a company's annual report and accounts.

Dirty price On a bond a buyer pays a total of the clean price and the accrued interest since the last coupon payment.

Disclosure of shareholdings If a stake of 3 per cent or more is held by one shareholder in a UK public company, then this has to be declared to the company.

Discount (a) The amount below face value at which a financial claim sells (e.g. bill of exchange or zero coupon bond). (b) The extent to which an investment trust's shares sell below the net asset value. (c) The amount by which a future value of a currency is less than its spot value. (d) The action of purchasing financial instruments (e.g. bills) at a discount. (e) The degree to which a security sells below its issue price in the secondary market.

Discount to net asset value Shares (e.g. investment trust shares) sometimes sell at a value less than the per share net asset value of the companies.

Discount house An institution that purchases promissory notes (a form of debt) and resells them or holds them until maturity.

Discount market deposit Money deposited with a London discount house. Normally repayable at call or very short term. Clearing banks are the usual depositors.

Discount rate (1) The rate of return used to discount cash flows received in future years. This is the opportunity cost of capital given the risk class of the future cash flows. (2) The rate of interest at which some central banks lend money to the banking system.

Discounted cash flow Future cash flows are converted into the common denominator of time zero money by adjusting for the time value of money.

Discounting The process of reducing future cash flows to a present value using an appropriate discount rate.

Discretionary service. A type of service provided by a stockbroker in which the broker will manage the investor's portfolio at the broker's discretion – the investor is not consulted on every deal.

Disintermediation Borrowing firms bypassing financial institutions and obtaining debt finance directly from the market.

Disinvest To sell an investment.

Distribution bonds A type of insurance company bond which invests in a mixture of equity and fixed-income securities.

Diversifiable risk *See* Unsystematic risk.

Diversification Investing in varied projects, enterprises, financial securities, etc., in a portfolio.

Divestiture To remove assets from a company or individual.

Dividend The profit paid to ordinary shareholders, usually on a regular basis.

Dividend cover The number of times net profits available for distribution exceed the dividend actually paid or declared. Defined as earnings per share divided by gross dividend per share, or total post-tax profits divided by total dividend payout.

Dividend per share The total amount paid or due to be paid in dividends for the year (interim and final), divided by the number of shares in issue.

Dividend policy The determination of the proportion of profits paid out to shareholders, usually periodically.

Dividend reinvestment plan (DRIP) A shareholder receives shares in lieu of a cash dividend. This avoids the cost and trouble of receiving cash and then reinvesting.

Dividend valuation models These methods of share valuation are based on the premise that the market value of ordinary shares represents the sum of the expected future dividend flows, to infinity, discounted to present value.

Dividend yield The amount of dividend paid on each share as a percentage of the share price.

Divorce of ownership and control In large corporations shareholders own the firm but may not be able to exercise control. Managers often have control because of a diffuse and divided shareholder body, proxy votes and apathy.

Dow or Dow Jones Industrial Average The best known index of movements in the price of US stocks and shares. There are 30 shares in the index.

Dow theory A method of predicting share price trends by identifying primary trends from historic share price data.

Drawdown arrangement A loan facility is established and the borrower uses it (takes the money available) in stages as the funds are required.

Drawdown (pension) With a personal pension, instead of taking benefits in the form of an annuity, you can draw money from your pension pot. There are minimum and maximum limits on the income you must take each year.

Dual capital trusts *See* Split-capital investment trusts.

Durable good One with an expected life of more than 1 year.

Early-stage capital Funds for initial manufacturing and sales for a newly formed company. High-risk capital available from entrepreneurs, business angels and venture capital funds.

Earn-out The purchase price of a company is linked to the future profits performance. Future instalments of the purchase price may be adjusted if the company performs better or worse than expected.

Earning power The earning (profit) capacity of a business in a normal year, that is, what company might be expected to earn year after year if business conditions continue unchanged.

Earnings guidance A company guiding analysts to estimates of profits for the current period.

Earnings multiple *See* Price–earnings ratio.

Earnings per share (eps) Profit after tax and interest divided by number of shares in issue.

Earnings yield Earnings per share divided by current market price of share.

EBIT A company's earnings (profits) before interest and taxes are deducted.

EBITDA Earnings before interest, taxation, depreciation and amortisation.

Economic franchise Pricing power combined with strong barriers to entry. The strength and durability of an economic franchise is determined by (a) the structure of the industry, and (b) the ability of the firm to rise above its rivals in its industry and generate exceptional long run rates of return on capital employed.

Economic profit The amount earned by a business after deducting all operating expenses and a charge for the opportunity cost of the capital employed.

Economies of scale Producing a larger output results in lower unit cost.

Economies of scope The ability to reduce unit costs of an item by sharing some costs between a number of product lines (e.g. using the same truck to deliver both ketchup and beans to a store).

EDX London An equity derivative exchange based in London owned by the London Stock Exchange and OM AM of Sweden.

Efficient stock market Prices rationally reflect available information. The efficient market hypothesis implies that new information is incorporated into a share price (a) rapidly, and (b) rationally. In an efficient market no trader will be presented with an opportunity for making an abnormal return, except by chance.

EGM *See* Extraordinary general meeting.

Electronic settlement Transferring shares from sellers to buyers without certificates – computer entry only.

Emerging markets Security markets in newly industrialising countries and/or capital markets at an early stage of development.

Employee share ownership plans Schemes designed to encourage employees to build up a shareholding in their company.

Endowment saving schemes Life assurance schemes with the additional feature of a huge lump-sum payment at the end of a period, should the policyholder survive. One important use is for the repayment of house mortgages.

Enfranchisement Granting voting rights to holders of non-voting shares.

Enterprise Investment Scheme (EIS) Tax relief is available to investors in qualifying company shares (unquoted firms not focused on financial investment and property).

Enterprise value The sum of a company's total equity market capitalisation and borrowings minus the cash it holds. (Some analysts add pension provisions, minority interest and other claims on the business.)

Entrepreneur Defined by economists as the owner-manager of a firm. Usually supplies capital, organises production, decides on strategic direction and bears risk.

Equilibrium in markets When the forces of supply and demand are evenly balanced.

Equities An ownership share of a business; each equity share represents an equal stake in the business.

Equitisation An increasing emphasis placed on share (equity) finance and stock exchanges in economies around the world. A growing equity culture.

Equity kicker (sweetener) The attachment of some rights to participate in and benefit from a good performance (e.g. exercise option to purchase shares) to a bond or other debt finance. Used with mezzanine finance.

Equity-linked bonds *See* Convertible bonds.

Equity risk premium The additional average annual rate of return for an averagely risky share over the return on risk-free asset. It is the average extra return over many decades – a short period of observation will lead to a biased estimate.

Equity shareholders' funds *See* Shareholder's funds.

Ethical investment The avoidance of securities that benefit from unethical activities (e.g. tobacco shares, genetically modified agriculture, arms sales).

Euro The name of the new single European currency.

Eurobond Bond sold outside the jurisdiction of the country in whose currency the bond is denominated (e.g. a bond issued in Yen outside of Japan).

Euro-commercial paper *See* Commercial paper.

Eurocurrency Currency held outside its country of origin (e.g. Australian dollars held outside of Australia). Note: this market existed long before the creation of the euro, and has no connection with the euro.

Eurocurrency banking Transactions in a currency other than the host country's currency (e.g. transactions in Canadian dollars in London). No connection with the euro.

Eurodollar A deposit or credit of US dollars held outside of the regulation of the US authorities, say in Tokyo, London or Paris. No connection with the euro.

Euromarkets Markets outside of the jurisdictions of any country; often termed international securities markets. Euromarkets began in the late 1950s.

Euro medium-term notes (EMTN) *See* Medium-term note.

Euronext The combined financial stock market comprising the French, Dutch, Belgian and Portuguese bourses.

Euronext.liffe Euronext, the organisation combining the French, Dutch, Belgian and Portuguese stock markets, bought LIFFE and renamed it Euronext.liffe.

Euro-security markets Informal (unregulated) markets in money held outside the jurisdiction of the country of origin (e.g. Swiss franc lending outside of the control of the Swiss authorities – perhaps the francs are in London).

European exchange rate mechanism (ERM) A system set up by members of the European Union which restricts the movement of the currencies of those member states belonging to the system.

European Monetary Union (EMU) A single currency with a single central bank having control over interest rates being created for those EU member states which join.

European-style options (or European options) Options which can only be exercised by the purchaser on a predetermined future date.

Eurozone Those countries that joined together in adopting the euro as their currency.

Event risk The risk that some future event may increase the risk on a financial investment (e.g. an earthquake event affects returns on Japanese bonds).

Ex-ante Intended, desired or expected before the event.

Ex-coupon A bond sold without the right to the next interest payment.

Ex-dividend When a share or bond is designated ex-dividend a purchaser will not be entitled to a recently announced dividend or the accrued interest on the bond since the last coupon – the old owner will receive the dividend (coupon).

Ex-post The value of some variable after the event.

Ex-rights When a share goes 'ex-rights' any purchaser of a share after that date will not have a right to subscribe for new shares in the rights issue.

Ex-rights price of a share The theoretical market price following a rights issue.

Exceptional items Gains or costs which are part of the company's ordinary activities but are either unusual in themselves or have an exceptionally large impact on profits that year.

Exchange controls The state controls the purchase and sale of currencies by its residents.

Exchange rate The price of one currency expressed in terms of another.

Exchange traded funds (ETFs) Companies that issue shares using the proceeds to invest in the range of shares in a particular stock market index or sector, such as the FTSE 100 index.

Exchangeable bond A bond that entitles the owner to choose at a later date whether to exchange the bond for shares in a company. The shares are in a company other than the one that issued the bonds.

Exclusive franchise *See* economic franchise.

Execute and eliminate A type of buy or sell order instruction given by an investor to a broker. A price limit is set and the transaction is completed in part or in whole immediately and then expires on the spot. If only some of the order is fulfilled the remainder expires.

Execution-only broker A stockbroker who will buy or sell shares cheaply but will not give advice or other services.

Exercise price (strike price) The price at which an underlying will be bought (call) or sold (put) under an option contract.

Exit The term used to describe the point at which a venture capitalist can recoup some or all of the investment made.

Exit barrier A factor preventing firms from stopping production in a particular industry.

Exit charge Unit trusts may charge the investor when the units are sold.

Exotic A term used to describe an unusual financial transaction (e.g. exotic option, exotic currency, i.e. one with few trades).

Expansion capital Companies at a fast-development phase needing capital to increase production capacity, working capital and capital for the further development of the product or market. Venture capital is often used.

Expected return The mean or average outcome calculated by weighting each of the possible outcomes by the probability of occurrence and then summing the result.

Experience curve The cost of performing a task reduces as experience is gained through repetition.

Expert investor Legal term denoting an investor who may by his/her previous experience be taken to fully understand the nature of investment undertaken. An expert investor is given less protection under the financial regulatory regime.

Expiry date of an option The time when the rights to buy or sell the option cease.

Exposure The amount of a portfolio invested in a particular area (e.g. a £50,000 portfolio with £25,000 in overseas shares has 50 per cent overseas exposure).

External finance Outside finance raised by a firm (i.e. finance that it did not generate internally, for example through profit retention).

extraMARK An attribute market for investment companies and products on the Official List of the London Stock Exchange.

Extraordinary general meeting (EGM) A meeting of the company (shareholders and directors) other than the annual general meeting. It may be convened when the directors think fit. However, shareholders holding more than 10 per cent of the paid-up share capital carrying voting rights can insist on a meeting.

Extraordinary resources Those that give the firm a competitive edge. A resource, which when combined with other (ordinary) resources enables the firm to outperform competitors and create new value-generating opportunities. Critical extraordinary resources determine what a firm can do successfully.

Extrapolate To estimate values beyond the known values by the extension of a curve or line.

Face value *See* Par value.

Fair game In the context of a stock market, the situation where some investors and fundraisers are not able to benefit at the expense of other participants. The market is regulated to avoid abuse, negligence and fraud. It is cheap to carry out transactions and the market provides high liquidity.

Fair value The amount an asset could be exchanged for in an arm's-length transaction between informed and willing parties.

Fallen angel Debt which used to rate as investment grade but which is now regarded as junk, mezzanine finance, or high-yield finance.

Fill or kill A type of buy or sell instruction given by an investor to a broker. If the deal cannot, in its entirety, be executed at the maximum (minimum) price stated by the (investor or better) then the entire order expires.

Filter approach to investment A technique for examining shares using historic price trends. The trader focuses on the long-term trends by filtering out short-term movements.

Final dividend The dividend announced with the annual accounts. The final dividend plus the interim dividend make the total dividend for the year for a company that reports results every 6 months.

Finance house A financial institution offering to supply finance in the form of hire purchase, leasing and other forms of instalment credit.

Finance lease (also called '**capital lease**' or '**full payout lease**') The lessor expects to recover the full cost (or almost the full cost) of the asset plus interest, over the period of the lease.

Financial assets (securities) Contracts that state agreement about the exchange of money in the future.

Financial distress Obligations to creditors are not met or are met with difficulty.

Financial gearing (leverage) *See* Gearing.

Financial Ombudsman Scheme (FOS) The ombudsman tries to find a just settlement between a complainant and a financial service company. The company is bound by the Ombudsman's decision, whereas the complainant is able to reject it.

Financial review An explanation of financial performance and strategy contained in a company's annual report and account.

Financial risk The additional variability in a firm's returns to shareholders which arises because the financial structure contains debt.

Financial Services Authority (FSA) The chief financial services regulator in the UK, established in 1997.

Financial Services Compensation Scheme (FSCS) If an dishonest or incompetent financial services company is unable to pay money owed to a complainant (e.g. it has been liquidated) the FSCS will pay the customer (up to fixed limits) to compensate for loss if the financial services company was authorised by the Financial Services Authority.

Financial Services and Markets Act The 2000 Act (and orders made under it) form the bedrock of financial regulations in the UK.

Financial slack Having cash (or near-cash) and/or spare debt capacity available to take up opportunities as they appear.

Financing gap The gap in the provision of finance for medium-sized, fast-growing firms. Often these firms are too large or growing too fast to ask the individual shareholders for more funds or to obtain sufficient bank finance. Also they are not ready or not willing to launch on the stock market.

Firm prices Market makers are required to trade at the prices posted on the SEAQ system unless the transaction is above the normal market size.

Fixed assets Those not held for resale, but for use in the business.

Fixed charge (e.g. **fixed charge debenture or loan)** A specific asset(s) is assigned as collateral security for a debt.

Fixed cost A cost that does not vary according to the amount of goods or services that are produced, and has to be paid regardless of the firm's turnover and activity.

Fixed exchange rate The national authorities act to ensure that the rate of exchange between two currencies is constant.

Fixed-interest securities Securities such as bonds on which the holder receives a predetermined interest pattern on the par value (e.g. gilts, corporate bonds, eurobonds).

Fixed-rate borrowing (fixed interest) The interest rate charge is constant throughout the period of the loan.

Flat yield *See* Yield.

Float (for insurance companies) A pool of money held in the firm in readiness to pay claims.

Floating charge The total assets of the company or an individual are used as collateral security for a debt.

Floating exchange rate A rate of exchange which is not fixed by national authorities but fluctuates depending on demand and supply for the currency.

Floating rate borrowing (floating interest) The rate of interest on a loan varies with a standard reference rate (e.g. LIBOR).

Floating rate notes Notes (legal contracts for borrowing) in which the coupon fluctuates according to a benchmark interest rate charge (e.g. LIBOR), issued in the Euromarkets generally with maturities of 7–15 years. With reverse floaters the interest rate declines as LIBOR rises.

Floor An agreement whereby, if interest rates fall below an agreed level, the seller (floor writer) makes compensatory payments to the floor buyer.

Flotation The issue of shares in a company for the first time on a stock exchange.

Focus strategy The selection of a segment in the industry to serve to the exclusion of others.

'Footsie' Nickname for FTSE 100 index. Trade marked.

Foreign banking Transactions in the home currency with non-residents.

Foreign bond A bond denominated in the currency of the country where it is issued when the issuer is a non-resident.

Foreign exchange control Limits are placed by a government on the purchase and sale of foreign currency.

Foreign exchange (forex or **FX) markets** Markets that facilitate the exchange of one currency into another.

Forex A contraction of 'foreign exchange'.

Forfeiting A bank purchases a number of sales invoices or promissory notes from an exporting company; usually the importer's bank guarantees the invoices.

Forward A contract between two parties to undertake an exchange at an agreed future date at a price agreed now.

Forward basis The price investors pay for unit trust units will be fixed at a particular time of day (usually 12 noon) that is yet to come.

Forward PER Current share price divided by the anticipated earnings for the current year.

Forward-rate agreement An agreement about the future level of interest rates. Compensation is paid by one party to the other to the extent that market interest rates deviate from the 'agreed' rate.

Founders' shares Dividends are paid on these shares only after all other categories of equity shares have received fixed rates of dividend. They usually carry a number of special voting rights over certain company matters.

Free cash flow Cash generated by a business not required for operations or for reinvestment. Profit before depreciation, amortisation and provisions, but after interest, tax, capital expenditure on long-lived items and increases in working capital.

Free float The proportion of a quoted company's shares not held by those closest (e.g. founding directors' families) to the company who may be unlikely to sell their shares.

Free plus A return an investor enjoys over and above initial expectations.

Friendly merger Merger to which the two companies agree.

Friendly Society A mutual (co-operative) organisation involved in saving and lending.

Front-end charge A charge made when an investment is first made (e.g. by a unit trust manager when an investor first buys the units).

FRS 3 earnings *See* Basic earnings per share.

FTSE 100 share index An index representing the UK's 100 largest listed shares.

FTSE Actuaries All-Share Index (the 'All-Share') The most representative index of UK shares, reflecting around 700 companies' shares.

FTSE International (Financial Times and the London Stock Exchange) This organisation calculates a range of share indices published on a regular (usually daily) basis.

Full-payout lease *See* Leasing.

Fully automated trading *See* Real-time dealing.

Fully paid The holder of shares has paid the full price and does not owe an instalment(s).

Fund management Investment and administration of a quantity of money (e.g. pension fund, insurance fund) on behalf of the fund's owners.

Fund of funds Funds that then invest the money that they raise from investors in a range of funds (e.g. hedge funds).

Fund supermarkets Online or offline organisations that allow investors to invest in a range of unit trusts, investment trusts and OEICs. Investors can select one, two or a dozen funds from different management companies. They usually offer discounts on the initial charge imposed when investing in a fund.

Fundamental analysts Individuals who try to estimate a share's true value, based on future returns to the company.

Fundraising Companies can raise money through rights issues, etc.

Fungible Interchangeable securities; can be exchanged for each other on identical terms.

Future A contract between two parties to undertake a transaction at an agreed price on a specified future date.

Futures-based bet A bet with a spread betting company placed on the price of shares or the level of an index on the next quarter day or the one after that.

GAAP Generally accepted accounting principles. United States accounting rules for reporting results. The term is increasingly used in reference to accounting rules in other countries.

GDP (nominal, real) Gross domestic product, the sum of all output of goods and services produced by a nation. Nominal GDP includes inflation, and real excludes it.

Gearing (financial gearing) The proportion of debt capital in the overall capital structure. Also called 'leverage'. High gearing can lead to exaggeratedly high returns if things go well or exaggerated losses if they do not go well.

Gearing (operating) The extent to which the firm's total costs are fixed. This influences the break-even point and the sensitivity of profits to changes in sales level.

General inflation The process of steadily rising prices resulting in the diminishing purchasing power of a given nominal sum of money. Measured by an overall price index which follows the price changes of a 'basket' of goods and services through time.

General insurance Insurance against specific contingencies (e.g. fire, theft and accident). The term excludes life insurance.

Gilt-edged market makers (GEMMs) These organisations are at the centre of trading in UK government bonds. They stand ready to buy from or sell to investors at all times (when markets are open) quoting bid and offer prices.

Gilts (gilt-edged securities) Fixed-interest UK government securities (bonds) traded on the London Stock Exchange – a means for the UK government to raise finance from savers. They usually offer regular interest and a redemption amount paid years in the future.

Global depositary receipts (GDR) Certificates which represent ownership of a given number of a company's shares and which are traded independently of the underlying shares.

Globalisation The increasing internationalisation of trade, particularly financial product transactions. The integration of economic and capital markets throughout the world.

Goal congruence The aligning of the actions of senior management with the interests of shareholders.

Going concern A judgement as to whether a company has sufficient financial strength to continue for at least one year. Accounts are usually drawn up on the assumption that the business is a going concern.

Going long Buying a financial security (e.g. share) in the hope that its price will rise.

Going public A phrase used when a company becomes quoted on a stock exchange (the company may have been a public limited company for years before this).

Going short *See* Short selling.

Golden handcuffs Financial inducements for managers to remain working for a firm.

Golden parachutes In a hostile merger situation, managers will receive large pay-offs if the firm is acquired.

Golden shares Shares with extraordinary special powers over the company (e.g. power of veto over a merger).

Good for the day A buy or sell order for a financial security has a limit above/below which the investor does not want the broker to go. If the order is not completed that day it is cancelled.

Good till cancelled A buy or sell order for a financial security has a price limit. The order stays in place until the investor tells his/her broker that it is cancelled it or it has been satisfied by a trade.

Goodwill An accounting term for the difference between the amount that a company pays for another company and the market value of the other company's assets. Goodwill is thus an intangible asset representing such things as the value of the company's brand names and the skills of its employees.

Grace period A lender grants the borrower a delay in the repayment of interest and/or principal at the outset of a lending agreement.

Grey market A market in shares which have not yet come into existence (e.g. in the period between investors being told they will receive shares in a new issue and the actual receipt they may sell on the expectation of obtaining them later).

Greater fool investing The object is to pass on a share which is currently of great interest to the market speculators and traders after making a return on the 'investment' without really bothering to understand the fundamentals of the business.

Greenbury report Recommendations on corporate governance.

Greenmail Key shareholders try to obtain a reward (e.g. the repurchase of their shares at a premium) from the company for not selling to a hostile bidder or becoming a bidder themselves.

Greenshoe An option that permits an issuing house, when assisting a corporation in a new issue, to sell more shares than originally planned. They may do this if demand is particularly strong.

Gross dividend yield The gross (before tax) dividend per share as a percentage of share price.

Gross domestic product *See* GDP.

Gross margin *See* Gross profit margin.

Gross profit Turnover less cost of sales.

Gross profit margin (gross margin) Profit defined as sales minus cost of sales, expressed as a percentage of sales.

Growth industries Those industries which grow almost regardless of the state of the economy.

Growth stock Where the company has performed better than average (in growth in earnings per share) for a period of years and is expected to do so in the future. Second-rate investors call some companies growth stocks even if there is no history of good performance growth.

Guaranteed equity bonds Offered by insurance companies, banks, building societies and other investment firms, they provide a return linked to stock market indices. The investor commits to holding the bond for, say, 5 years and is guaranteed a minimum amount back and may also benefit from a rise in the stock market.

Guaranteed income bonds (GIBs) *See* Insurance company bonds.

Guaranteed loan stock An organisation other than the borrower guarantees to the lender the repayment of the principal plus the interest payment.

Hampel report A follow-up to the Cadbury and Greenbury reports on corporate governance. Chaired by Sir Ronald Hampel and published in 1998.

Hang Seng index Main index for Hong Kong shares.

Hard currency A currency traded in a foreign exchange market for which demand is persistently high.

Head and shoulders formation A chartists' (technical analyst's) share price pattern in which the chart line resembles a shoulder followed by a head (a rise in price to a peak, followed by a fall) and then another shoulder.

Headline (underlying, adjusted or normalised) earnings per share Directors produce these profit per share numbers by excluding one-off costs, exceptional items and goodwill amortisation to show underlying profit-per-share trend (or just to make the managerial performance look better).

Hedge fund A collective investment vehicle that operates free from regulation, allowing it to take steps in managing a portfolio that other fund managers are unable to take (e.g. borrowing to invest, shorting the market).

Hedging Reducing or eliminating risk by undertaking a countervailing transaction.

Herstatt risk In 1974 the German bank Herstatt was closed by the Bundesbank. It had entered into forex transactions and received Deutschmarks from counterparties in European time, but had not made the corresponding transfer of US dollars to its counterparties in New York time. It is the risk that arises when forex transactions are settled in different time zones.

High-yield debt *See* Mezzanine finance; Junk bonds.

High-yield shares (yield stocks) Shares offering a high current dividend yield because the share price is low due to the expectation of low growth in profits and dividends. Sometimes labelled 'value shares'.

Historic basis The price that an investor in unit trusts pays is determined by the price calculated at a specific time that has already past – usually 12 noon today or the previous day.

Holding company *See* Parent company.

Holding period returns Total holding period returns on a financial asset consist of (a) income (e.g. dividend paid), and (b) capital gain – a rise in the value of the asset.

Horizontal merger The two companies merging are engaged in similar lines of activity.

Hostile merger The target (acquired) firm's management is opposed to the merger.

Hot shares/sectors Those currently receiving a lot of attention from the press and investors.

Hubris Overweaning self-confidence.

Hurdle rate The required rate of return. The opportunity cost of the finance provider's money.

Impact day The day during the launch of a new issue of shares when the price is announced, the prospectus published and offers to purchase solicited.

In-house share trading A broker is allowed to complete a share transaction without going to the stock exchange by taking on the deal himself if he can match the best prices offered by the market makers.

In-the-money option An option with intrinsic value. For a call option the current underlying price is more than the option exercise price. For a put option the current price of the underlying is below the exercise price.

Income drawdown *See* Drawdown (pension).

Income gearing The proportion of the annual income streams (i.e. pre-interest profits) devoted to the prior claims of debt holders. The reciprocal of income gearing is the interest cover.

Income ('Inc') units Unit trust units that pay out all income after deducting charges on set dates.

Income reinvested The performance of shares, other securities or portfolios is usually expressed as 'total return' including both capital gains or losses and the benefits of periodic reinvestment of income distributions in further shares or units.

Income shares *See* Split-capital investment trusts.

Income statement *See* profit and loss account.

Income yield *See* Yield.

Incorporation The forming of a company, including the necessary legal formalities.

Independent complaints scheme Financial service companies generally belong to an independent complaints scheme, either an arbitration scheme or Ombudsman scheme. This permits customers to have their complaints looked into by an independent body.

Independent director One who is not beholden to the dominant executive directors. Customers, suppliers or friends of the founding family are not independent, for example.

Independent financial advisers (IFAs) Individuals authorised by the Financial Services Authority to provide financial advice.

Independent variables Two variables which are completely unrelated and show no co-movement.

Index *See* Market index.

Index-linked gilts (stocks) The redemption value and the coupons rise with inflation over the life of the UK government bond.

Index option An option on a share index (e.g. FTSE 100 or Standard and Poor's 500).

Index trackers (indexed funds) Collective investment funds (e.g. unit trusts) which try to replicate a stock market index rather than to pick winners in an actively managed fund.

Individual savings account (ISA) A savings account with special tax privileges. The saver can invest savings in cash deposits, shares, insurance products and/or other securities.

Industry attractiveness The economics of the market for the product(s), part of which is determined by industry structure.

Industry structure The combination of the degree of rivalry within the industry among existing firms; the bargaining strength of industry firms with suppliers and customers; and the potential for new firms to enter and for substitute products to take customers. The industry structure determines the long-run rate of return on capital employed within the industry.

Inevitable A company likely to dominate its field for an investment lifetime due to its competitive strength. A term used (invented?) by Warren Buffett.

Inflation The process of prices rising.

Inflation risk The risk that your fund loses purchasing power by providing returns less than the rate of inflation.

Informal venture capitalist *See* Business angel.

Informed investors Those who are highly knowledgeable about financial securities and the fundamental evaluation of their worth.

Inheritance tax A tax payable on transfers made on an individual's estate at the time of death (it also covers some gifts made during the individual's lifetime).

Initial margin An amount that a derivative contractor has to provide to the clearing house when first entering upon a derivative contract.

Initial public offering (new issue) The offering of shares in the equity of a company to the public for the first time.

Inland Revenue The principal tax-collecting authority in the UK.

Insider trading (dealing) Trading shares, etc., on the basis of information not in the public domain.

Institutional imperative An insidious and dangerous unseen force at work in companies. It is the tendency of organisations to stray from the path of rationality, decency and intelligence.

Institutional neglect Share analysts, particularly at the major institutions, may fail to spend enough time studying small firms, preferring to concentrate on the larger 100 or so.

Institutionalisation The increasing tendency towards investment through organisations, as opposed to individuals investing money in securities (e.g. pension funds and investment trusts collect the savings of individuals to invest in shares).

Insurance company bonds A lump-sum investment is made with an insurance company for a fixed period, say 5 years. Guaranteed income bonds (GIBs) pay regular income. With growth bonds the interest accumulates until the maturity date.

Intangible assets Those that you cannot touch (e.g. goodwill).

Intelligent speculation A focus on information that is quantifiable. Based on a calculation of probabilities. Keeping the speculative element within minor limits. The odds are strongly in favour of success. (A term used by Benjamin Graham.)

Interbank brokers Brokers in the forex markets who act as intermediaries between buyers and sellers. They provide anonymity to each side.

Interbank sterling The money market in which banks borrow and lend sterling among themselves.

Interest cover The number of times the income of a business exceeds the interest payments made to service its loan capital.

Interest rate risk The risk that changes in interest rates will have an adverse impact.

Interest rate swap *See* Swap.

Interest yield *See* Yield.

Interim dividend Dividend announced at the time of the interim profit statement.

Interim profit statement Describes the company's activities and profit and loss for the first 6 months of the financial year.

Interim report *See* Interim profit statement.

Intermediaries offer A method of selling shares in the new issue market. Shares are offered to financial institutions such as stockbrokers. Clients of these intermediaries can then apply to buy shares from them.

Intermediate debt *See* Mezzanine finance; Junk bonds.

International Petroleum Exchange The energy futures and options exchange in London.

International Retail Service (IRS) A system run by the London Stock Exchange allowing UK private investors to trade in over 380 major European and US companies. Trades are in sterling.

International Securities Market Association (ISMA) A self-regulatory organisation designed to promote orderly trading and the general development of the euromarkets.

Intraday (cash or spot) bet A bet with a spread betting company that starts and is closed in the same trading day.

Intrinsic value (company) The discounted value of the cash that can be taken out of a business during its remaining life.

Intrinsic value (options) The payoff that would be received if the underlying is at its current level when the option expires.

Introduction A company with shares already quoted on another stock exchange, or where there is already a wide spread of shareholders, may be introduced to the market. This allows a secondary market in the shares.

Inventory *See* Stock.

Investment bank Banks that carry out a variety of financial services, usually excluding high street banking. Their services are usually fee-based (e.g. fees for merger advice to companies).

Investment club A group of people who each contribute a few pounds per month which is then pooled to buy shares (or other financial securities) for the club.

Investment-grade debt Debt with a sufficiently high credit rating to be regarded as safe enough for institutional investors who are restricted to buying safe debt only.

Investment operation One that, upon thorough analysis, promises safety of principal and a satisfactory return.

Investment trusts (investment companies) Collective investment vehicles set up as companies selling shares. The money raised is invested in assets such as shares, gilts, corporate bonds and property.

Invoice An itemised list of goods shipped, usually specifying the terms of sale and price.

IOU A colloquialism intended to mean 'I owe you'. The acknowledgement of a debt.

Irredeemable Financial securities with no fixed maturity date at which the principal is repaid.

ISA *See* Individual Savings Account.

iShares A type of exchange traded fund (ETF) created by Barclays Global Investors.

Issued share capital That part of a company's share capital that has been subscribed by shareholders, either paid up or partially paid up. *See also* Called-up share capital.

Issuing house *See* Sponsor.

Jiway A recognised investment exchange trading shares for private investors across borders electronically. Owned by Sweden's OM group, it is very small, with very few traders.

Joint stock enterprise The capital is divided into small units, permitting a number of investors to contribute varying amounts to the total. Profits are divided between stockholders in proportion to the number of shares they own.

Junior debt *See* Subordinated debt.

Junk bonds Low-quality company bonds rated below investment-grade. Risky and with a high yield.

landMARK Groups of London Stock Exchange Official List companies from particular UK regions.

Lead manager In a new issue of securities (e.g. shares, bonds, syndicated loans) the lead manager controls and organises the issue. There may be joint lead managers, co-managers and regional lead managers.

Lead steer A term used to describe a dominant person with the power to induce others to follow.

Leasing The owner of an asset (lessor) grants the use of the asset to another party (lessee) for a specified period in return for regular rental payments. The asset does not become the property of the lessee at the end of the specified period. *See also* Finance lease; Operating lease.

Level II data Online brokers provide streaming data on share prices. Level II data allow the investor to observe a lot of detail about trades (e.g. market makers' transactions as they take place), allowing the investor a better feel for the supply and demand balance in the market.

Leverage *See* Gearing.

Leveraged buyout (LBO) The acquisition of a company, subsidiary or unit by another, financed mainly by borrowings.

Leveraged recapitalisation The financial structure (debt–equity ratio) of the firm is altered in such a way that it becomes highly geared.

LIBOR (London Inter-Bank Offered Rate) The rate of interest offered on loans to highly rated (low-risk) banks in the London interbank market for a specific period (e.g. 3 months). Used as a reference rate for other loans.

Life insurance Insurance against death. Beneficiaries receive payment upon death of the policyholder or other person named in the policy. Endowment policies offer a savings vehicle as well as cover against death.

Lifestyle pension fund Invests mostly in equities when the investor is decades away from retirement and then gradually switches to cash and bonds as retirement approaches.

LIFFE (London International Financial Futures and Options Exchange) The main derivatives exchange in London.

LIFFE CONNECT™ The computer system used by LIFFE for trading derivatives.

Limit order A type of buy or sell order instruction given by an investor to a broker. A maximum purchase price or minimum sale price is stated.

Limited company (Ltd) 'Private' company with no minimum amount of share capital, but with restrictions on the range of investors who can be offered shares. It cannot be quoted on the London Stock Exchange.

Limited liability The owners of shares in a business have a limit on their loss, set as the amount they have committed to invest in shares.

Liquidation The winding up of the affairs of a company when it ceases business. This could be forced by an inability to make payment when due or it could be voluntary when shareholders choose to end the company. Assets are sold, liabilities paid (if sufficient funds) and the surplus (if any) is distributed to shareholders.

Liquidity The degree to which an asset can be sold quickly and easily without loss in value.

Liquidity risk The risk that an organisation or individual may not have, or may not be able to raise, cash funds when needed.

Listed companies Those on the Official List of the London Stock Exchange.

Listing agreement The UK Listing Authority insists that a company signs a listing agreement committing the directors to certain standards of behaviour and levels of reporting to shareholders.

Listing particulars *See* Prospectus.

Lloyd's Insurance Market A medium-sized insurance business in London founded over two centuries ago. 'Names' supply the capital to back insurance policies. Names can now be limited liability companies rather than individuals with unlimited liability to pay up on an insurance policy.

LME London Metal Exchange.

Loan stock A fixed-interest debt financial security. May be unsecured.

Local authority deposits Lending money to a UK local government authority.

London Clearing House (LCH) Settles mutual indebtedness between a number of organisations. It settles ('clears') trades for LIFFE traders, for example, and guarantees all contracts. It often acts as counterparty to all trades on an exchange.

London Metal Exchange (LME) Trades metals (e.g. lead, zinc, tin, aluminium and nickel) in forward and option markets.

London Stock Exchange (LSE) The London market in which securities are bought and sold.

Long bond UK government bond (gilt) with more than 15 years to maturity.

Long-form report A report produced by accountants for the sponsor of a company being prepared for flotation. The report is detailed and confidential. It helps to reassure the sponsors when putting their name to the issue and provides the basis for the short-form report included in the prospectus.

Long position A positive exposure to a quantity. Owning a security or commodity; the opposite of a short position (selling).

Long-range structural analysis A process used to forecast the long-term rates of return of an industry.

Lot A standard unit of trading (e.g. 1,000 shares for universal stock futures).

Low-grade debt *See* Mezzanine finance; Junk bonds.

Low-yield shares (stocks) Shares offering a relatively low dividend yield expected to grow rapidly. Often labelled 'growth stocks'.

Ltd Private limited company.

Macroeconomics The study of the relationships between broad economic aggregates: national income, saving, investment, balance of payments, inflation, taxation, etc.

Maintenance margin (futures) The level of margin that must be maintained on a futures account (usually at a clearing house). Daily marking to market of the position may reveal the necessity to put more money into the account to top up to the maintenance margin.

Making a book Market makers offering two prices: the price at which they are willing to buy (bid price) and the price they are willing to sell (offer price).

Management buy-in (MBI) A new team of managers makes an offer to a company to buy the whole company, a subsidiary or a section of the company, with the intention of taking over the running of it themselves. Venture capital often provides the major part of the finance.

Management buy-out (MBO) A team of managers makes an offer to its employers to buy a whole business, a subsidiary or a section so that the managers own and run it themselves. Venture capital is often used to finance the majority of the purchase price.

Managementism/managerialism Management not acting in shareholders' best interests by pursuing objectives attractive to the management team. Three levels can be distinguished: dishonest managers; honest but incompetent managers; honest and competent managers, but subject to the influence of conflicts of interest.

Manager risk The risk that you may choose a poor manager (e.g. of ISAs, OEICs) to invest your money.

Mandatory bid If 30 per cent or more of the shares of a company are acquired, the holder is required under Takeover Panel rules to bid for all the company's shares.

Margin (futures) Money placed aside to back a futures purchase or sale. This is used to reassure the counterparty to the future that money will be available should the purchaser/seller renege on the deal.

Margin of safety A share should only be purchased when the value of a share is well in excess of the price paid. A probability of protection against loss under all normal or reasonably likely conditions or variations.

Market capitalisation The total value at market prices of the shares in issue for a company (or a stock market, or a sector of the stock market).

Market index A sample of shares is used to represent a share market's level and movements as a benchmark against which individual shares are judged.

Market in managerial control Teams of managers compete for control of corporate assets (e.g. through merger activity).

Market makers Organisations that stand ready to buy and sell shares from investors on their own behalf at the centre of the London Stock Exchange's quoted-driven system of share trading.

Market order An investor instructs a broker to buy/sell at whatever is the current market price.

Market portfolio A portfolio that contains all assets. Each asset is held in proportion to the asset's share of the total market value of all the assets. A proxy for this is often employed (e.g. the FTSE 100 index).

Market power The ability to exercise some control over the price of the product.

Market risk *See* Systematic risk.

Market to book ratio Share price divided by net assets per share (book value per share).

Market weightings The capitalisation of all the firms in an industry as a proportion of the total capitalisation of all the shares on the stock market.

Market value adjuster (MVA) An exit penalty that may be imposed on a with-profits policyholder should he/she withdraw money from the fund.

Marking down Market makers adjust down bid and offer prices in response to news in anticipation of a high volume of sell orders at the previous price.

Marking to market The losses or gains on a derivative contract are assessed daily in reference to the value of the underlying price.

Matador A foreign bond issued in Spain.

Matched-bargain systems *See* Order-driven trading system.

Maturity date The time when a financial security (e.g. a bond) is redeemed and the par value is paid to the lender.

Maturity structure The profile of the length of time to the redemption and repayment of a company's various debts.

Maturity transformation Intermediaries offer securities with liquid and low risk characteristics to induce primary investors to purchase or deposit funds. The money raised is made available to the ultimate borrowers on a long-term, illiquid basis.

Maximisation of long-term shareholder wealth The assumed objective of the firm in finance theory and the objective generally mouthed by executives.

Medium-term note (MTN) A document setting out a promise from a borrower to pay the holders a specified sum on the maturity date and, in many cases, a coupon interest in the meantime. Maturity can range from 9 months to 30 years. If denominated in a foreign currency, they are called euro medium-term notes.

Memorandum of Association Lays down the rules which govern a company and its relations with the outside world (e.g. states the objective of the company).

Merchant bank *See* Investment bank.

Merger The combining of two business entities under common ownership.

Mezzanine finance Unsecured debt or preference shares offering a high return with a high risk. Ranked behind secured debt but ahead of equity. It may carry an equity kicker.

Mid-market price A price between the offer and bid prices of a market maker at which shares are bought and sold.

Minority shareholder A shareholder who owns less than 50 per cent of a company.

Mobilisation of savings The flow of savings primarily from the household sector to the ultimate borrowers to invest in real assets. This process is encouraged by financial intermediaries.

Model Code for Directors' Dealings London Stock Exchange rules for directors dealing in shares of their own company.

Momentum investing Buying shares that have recently risen and selling shares that have recently fallen.

Monetary policy The deliberate control of the money supply and/or rates of interest by the central bank.

Money market Wholesale (large-volume) financial markets in which lending and borrowing take place on a short-term basis (less than 1 year).

Money rate of return The rate of return which includes a return to compensate for inflation.

Monopoly One producer in an industry. However, for Competition Commission purposes a monopoly is defined as a market share of 25 per cent.

Moral hazard The presence of a safety net (e.g. insurance policy) encourages adverse behaviour (e.g. carelessness).

Mortgage debentures Bonds secured using property as collateral.

Multi-bagger A share that rises to a multiple of the buying price.

Mutual fund A collective investment vehicle for shares or other financial securities. Many investors own stakes in the mutual fund which then invests in securities.

Mutually owned organisations Organisations run for the benefit of the members (usually the same as the consumers of the organisation's output) and not for shareholders. Examples include some insurance organisations, building societies and the co-operative societies.

Naked call option writing *See* Uncovered call option writing.

NASDAQ (National Association of Securities Dealers Automated Quotation System) A series of computer-based information services and an order execution system for the US over-the-counter securities (e.g. share) market.

National Savings Lending to the UK government through the purchase of bonds, and placing money into savings accounts.

NAV Net Asset Value.

Near-cash (near-money) Highly liquid financial assets but which are generally not usable for transactions such as buying an ice cream and therefore cannot be fully regarded as cash, e.g. Treasury bills.

Negative covenants Loan agreements conditions that restrict the actions and rights of the borrower until the debt has been repaid in full.

Negotiable (1) Transferable to another – free to be traded in financial markets. (2) Capable of being settled by agreements between the parties involved in a transaction.

Net assets Total assets minus all the liabilities. Fixed assets, plus stocks, debtors, cash and other liquid assets, minus long- and short-term creditors.

Net current assets The difference between current assets and current liabilities.

Net operating cash flow Profit before depreciation, less periodic investment in net working capital.

Net present value (NPV) The present value of the expected cash flows associated with a project after discounting at a rate which reflects the value of the alternative use of the funds.

Net profit Profit after tax.

Net realisable value What someone might reasonably be expected to pay less the costs of the sale.

New entrant A company entering a market area to compete with existing players.

New issue The sale of securities (e.g. debentures or shares), to raise additional finance or to float existing securities of a company on a stock exchange for the first time.

Newstrack A small company news service and a place where share prices for companies trading on OFEX are posted.

Niche company A fast growing small to medium-sized firm operating in a niche business with high potential.

Nifty fifty Fifty stocks declared in the late 1960s and early 1970s to have such a marvellous future that supposedly almost any multiple of current income could be justified as a share price.

Nikkei 225 Stock Average A share index based on the prices of 225 shares quoted on the Tokyo Stock Exchange.

Nil paid rights Shareholders may sell the rights to purchase shares in a rights issue without having paid anything for these rights.

Noise trading Uninformed investors buying and selling financial securities at irrational prices, thus creating noise (strange movements) in the price of securities.

Nominal return The return on an investment including inflation. If the return necessary to compensate for the decline in purchasing power of money (inflation) is deducted from the nominal return we have the real rate of return.

Nominal value *See* Par value.

Nominated adviser (nomad) Each company on the AIM has to retain a nomad. They act as quality controllers, confirming to the London Stock Exchange that the company has complied with the rules.

Nominated brokers Each company on the AIM has to retain a nominated broker, who helps to bring buyers and sellers together and comments on the firm's prospects.

Nominee company Brokers and investment managers hold investors' shares electronically in a nominee company which appears as the registered owner. *See also* Dematerialisation.

Non-executive director A director without day-to-day operational responsibility for the firm.

Non-voting shares A company may issue two or more classes of ordinary shares, one of which may not carry any votes.

Normal market size (NMS) The threshold below which the market makers have to sell/buy shares at the prices they posted on the SEAQ system without modification. It is normally set at 2.5 per cent of the average daily customer turnover of a share on the LSE in the previous year.

Normal rate of return A rate of return that is just sufficient to induce shareholders to put money into the firm and hold it there.

Normalised earnings per share *See* Headline earnings per share.

Note (promissory note) A financial security with the promise to pay a specific sum of money by a given date (e.g. commercial paper, floating rate notes). Usually unsecured.

Notional trading requirement A sum of money that has to be deposited by an investor with a spread betting company to reassure the company that the investor will not renege on the deal should the bet start to go against him/her.

NYSE The New York Stock Exchange.

OFEX An unregulated share market offering a secondary market trading facility.

Off-balance-sheet finance Assets are acquired in such a way that liabilities do not appear on the balance sheet (e.g. some lease agreements permit the exclusion of the liability in the accounts).

Off-market transfer The transfer of ownership of shares and other securities without the use of a broker or the stock market. A stock transfer form can be used.

Offer document A formal document sent by a company attempting to buy all the shares in a target firm to all the shareholders of the target, setting out the offer.

Offer for sale A method of selling shares in a new issue. The company sponsor offers shares to the public by inviting subscriptions from investors. In an offer for sale by fixed price, the sponsor fixes the price prior to the offer. In an offer for sale by tender, investors state the price they are willing to pay. A strike price is established by the sponsors after receiving all the bids. All investors pay the strike price.

Offer for subscription A method of selling shares in a new issue. The issue is aborted if the offer does not raise sufficient interest from investors.

Offer price The price at which a market maker in shares will sell a share, or a dealer in other markets will sell a security or asset.

Office of Fair Trading (OFT) The Director-General of Fair Trading has wide powers to monitor, investigate and correct trading activities and to refer monopoly or anti-competitive situations to the Competition Commission.

Official List (OL) The daily list of securities admitted for trading on the London Stock Exchange. It does not include securities traded on the Alternative Investment Market (AIM).

Offshore investment Outside UK jurisdiction and financial regulation, usually in tax havens.

Oligopoly A small number of producers in an industry.

Onshore fund A fund authorised and regulated by the regulator in the investor's home country.

Open-ended fund The size of the fund and the number of units depends on the amount investors wish to put into the fund.

Open-ended investment companies (OEIC) Collective investment vehicles with one price for investors. OEICs are able to issue more shares if demand increases from investors, unlike investment trusts. OEICs invest the finance raised in securities, primarily shares.

Open interest The sum of outstanding long and short positions in a given futures or option contract.

Open offer New shares created by a company are offered to a wide range of external investors. However, under claw-back provisions, existing shareholders can buy the shares at the offer price if they wish.

Open outcry Where trading is through oral calling of buy and sell offers by market members.

Operating gearing *See* Gearing.

Operating lease The lease period is significantly less than the expected useful life of the asset.

Operating margin *See* Operating profit margin.

Operating profit (operating income) The income remaining after paying all costs other than interest.

Operating profit margin (operating margin, trading margin) Operating profit as a percentage of sales.

Operational efficiency of a market The cost to buyers and sellers of transactions in securities on the exchange.

Opportunity cost The value forgone by opting for one course of action; the next best use of, say, financial resources.

Option A contract giving one party the right, but not the obligation, to buy or sell a financial instrument, commodity or some other underlying asset at a given price, at or before a specified date.

Option premium The amount paid by an option purchaser (holder) to obtain the rights under an option contract.

Order book system *See* Order-driven trading system.

Order-driven trading system (matched bargain in order book systems) Buy and sell orders for securities are entered on a central computer system, and investors are automatically matched according to the price and volume they entered. SETS is an example.

Order placing service An online brokerage service. The investor emails the broker with an order who then trades with market makers.

Ordinary resources Those that give the firm competitive parity. They provide a threshold competence.

Ordinary shares The equity capital of the firm. The holders of ordinary shares are the owners and are therefore entitled to all distributed profits after the holders of debentures and preference shares have had their claims met.

Organic growth Growth from within the firm rather than through mergers.

Orphan assets Reserves that an insurance company has held back from with-profits policyholders to act as a buffer should the market decline. Critics claim that the insurance companies have been too cautious and should give the majority of these assets back to policyholders.

Out-of-the-money option An option without intrinsic value. For a call option the current price of the underlying is less than the exercise price. For a put option the current price of the underlying is more than the exercise price.

Over-allotment issue *See* Greenshoe.

Over-capacity An industry or company has significantly more capacity to supply product than is being demanded.

Over-the-counter (OTC) trade Security trading carried on outside regulated exchanges. Allows tailor-made transactions.

Overdraft A permit to overdraw on an account (e.g. a bank account) up to a stated limit; to take more out of a bank account than it contains.

Overhang Situation where a share price is depressed because of an anticipated sale of a large block of shares.

Overhead The business expenses not chargeable to a particular part of the work or product.

Over-subscription In a new issue of securities investors offer to buy more securities (e.g. shares) than are made available.

Overtrading When a business has insufficient finance to sustain its level of trading. A business is said to be overtrading when it tries to engage in more business than the investment in working capital will allow. This can happen even in profitable circumstances.

Overweighting When a fund invests in an individual asset, industrial sector or country more than in proportion to the asset's, sector's or country's weighting in the relevant benchmark index.

Owner earnings Reported earnings plus depreciation, depletion, amortisation and certain other non-cash charges less the amount of expenditure for plant and machinery and working capital etc. that a business requires to fully maintain its long-term competitive position, its unit volume and its investment in value-generating opportunities.

Pac-Man defence In a hostile merger situation the target makes a counter-bid for the bidder.

Par value (nominal or **face value)** A stated nominal value of a share or bond. Not related to market value.

Parent company (holding company) The one that partially or wholly owns other companies.

Partnership An unincorporated business formed by the association of two or more persons who share the risk and profits.

Passive fund *See* Tracker.

Path-dependent resources Firm resources that have been created because of the route that the firm took to get to where it is today.

Pathfinder prospectus In a new issue of shares a detailed report on the company is prepared and made available to potential investors a few days before the issue price is announced.

Payout ratio The percentage of after-tax profit paid to shareholders in dividends.

Penny shares Shares priced at only a few pence. Some investors like these, despite the risk of liquidation, because of their large potential if management turns the company around.

Pension funds These manage money on behalf of members to provide a pension upon the members' retirement. Most funds invest heavily in shares.

Pension holiday When a pension fund does not need additional contributions for a time, it may grant the contributors (e.g. companies and/or members) a break from making payments.

Perfect competition (perfect market) Entry to the industry is free and the existing firms have no bargaining power over suppliers or customers. Rivalry between existing firms is fierce because products are identical. The following assumptions hold: There are a large number of buyers. There are a large number of sellers. The quantity of goods bought by any individual transaction is so small relative to the total quantity traded that individual trades leave the market price unaffected. The units of goods sold by different sellers are the same – the product is homogeneous. There is perfect information – all buyers and all sellers have complete information on the prices being asked and offered in other parts of the market. There is perfect freedom of exit from the market.

Perfect hedge Eliminates risk.

Perfect market *See* Perfect competition.

Performance attribution Identifying the factors that led to a fund's performance (e.g. share selection, asset allocation).

Permanent interest-bearing shares (PIBS) Loan stock issued by building societies. The 'shares' pay interest and are irredeemable.

Perpetuity A regular sum of money received at intervals for ever.

Perks In addition to paying dividends to investors, some companies provide perks such as a reduced rate in hotels or on ferries owned by the company.

Personal equity plan (PEP) Personal investment vehicle with tax advantages. Directed mostly to encourage investment in quoted shares.

Personal membership of CREST Investors hold shares in their own accounts with CREST rather than in a broker's nominee company or in certificated form.

Personal pension A pension scheme set up for an individual by that individual. Contributions to the fund are subject to tax relief.

Physical delivery Settlement of a futures contract by delivery of the underlying.

Placing A method of selling shares and other financial securities in the primary market. Securities are offered to the sponsors' or brokers' private clients and/or a narrow group of institutions.

Plc Public limited company.

Poison pills Actions taken, or which will be taken, which make a firm unpalatable to a hostile acquirer.

Political risk Changes in government or government policies impacting on returns and volatility of returns.

Pooled funds Organisations (e.g. unit trusts) that gather together numerous small quantities of money from investors and then invest in a wide range of financial securities.

Portfolio A collection of investments.

Portfolio theory Formal mathematical model for calculating risk–returns trade-offs as securities are combined in a portfolio.

Pound-cost averaging An investment strategy whereby sums are invested evenly over time without regard to price levels at any one time.

Precipice bonds Bonds sold by insurance companies to investors offering high income based on stock market returns. The initial capital is guaranteed up to a point, but if the stock market declines by more than a set percentage (say, 20 per cent) investors lose capital. This loss can be highly geared (e.g. for every 1 per cent drop in the FT100 index the capital value falls by 2 per cent).

Pre-emption rights The strong right of shareholders of UK companies to subscribe for further issues of shares. *See* Rights issue.

Preference shares These normally entitle the holder to a fixed rate of dividend, but this is not guaranteed. Holders of preference shares precede the holders of ordinary shares, but follow bondholders and other lenders in payment of dividends and return of principal. A **participating preference share** is a share in residual profits. A **cumulative preference share** carries forward the right to preferential dividends. A **redeemable preference share** is a preference share with a finite life. A **convertible preference share** may be converted into ordinary shares.

Preferred ordinary shares Rank higher than deferred ordinary shares for an agreed rate of dividend.

Preliminary annual results (prelims) After the year-end and before the full reports and accounts are published, a statement on the profit for the year and other information is provided by companies quoted on the London Stock Exchange.

Premium (investment trusts) The amount by which the share price exceeds the net asset value per share.

Premium (on an option) The amount paid to an option writer to obtain the right to buy or sell the underlying.

Present value Future cash flow is discounted to time zero.

Pre-tax margin *See* Pre-tax profit margin.

Pre-tax profit Profit on ordinary activities before deducting taxation.

Pre-tax profit margin (pre-tax margin) Profit after all expenses, including interest, expressed as a percentage of sales.

Price discovery The process of forming prices through the interaction of numerous buy and sell orders in an exchange.

Price–earnings ratio (PER) Share price divided by earnings per share.

Historic PER is share price divided by most recently reported annual earnings per share.

Forward (prospective) PER is share price divided by anticipated annual earnings per share.

Price–earnings ratio game (bootstrapping) Companies increase earnings per share by acquiring other companies with lower price-earnings ratios than themselves. Share price can rise despite the absence of economic value gain.

Price-sensitive information That which may influence the share price or trading in the shares.

Price-to-book ratio (market-to-book) The price of a share as a multiple of per share book (balance sheet) value.

Pricing power An ability to raise prices even when product demand is flat without the danger of losing significant volume or market share.

Primary equity market (new issue market) Where companies first sell shares to investors through a regulated exchange.

Primary investors The household sector contains the savers in society who are the main providers of funds used for investment in the business sector.

Primary market A market in which securities are initially issued.

Principal (a) The capital amount of a debt, excluding any interest. (b) A person acting on their own account accepting risk in financial transactions, rather than someone acting as an agent for another.

Principal–agent problem In which an agent, (e.g. a manager), does not act in the best interests of the principal (e.g. the shareholder).

Private client brokers Stockbrokers acting for investors in the buying and selling of financial instruments and providing other investment-related services for investors.

Private equity Share capital invested in companies not quoted on an exchange.

Private investors (private clients) Investors buying and selling small quantities of shares on their own account rather than institutions buying and selling for funds.

Private limited company (Ltd) A company which is unable to offer its shares to the wider public.

Privatisation The sale to private investors of government-owned equity (shares) in nationalised industries or other commercial enterprises.

Profit and loss account Records whether a company's sales revenue was greater than its costs.

Profit margin Profits as a percentage of sales.

Project finance Finance assembled for a specific project. The loan and equity returns are tied to the cash flows and fortunes of the project rather than being dependent on the parent company/companies.

Pro-forma earnings Projected or forecast earnings. These are not audited and may be unreliable.

Promising company Company with an mediocre/ordinary earnings record which the investor *expects* it to do better than the average in the future.

Proprietary transactions A financial institution, as well as acting as an agent for a client, may trade on the financial markets with a view to generating profits for itself (e.g. speculate in foreign exchange).

ProShare An independent not-for-profit company set up to help private investors, promote knowledge about investment and assist investment clubs.

Prospectus A document containing information about a company (unit trust or OEIC), to assist with a new issue (initial public offering) by supplying detail about the company and how it operates.

Provision An allowance for a liability that you are unable to be precise about concerning either the amount or when it will be paid (anticipated loss or expenditure).

Proxy votes Shareholders unable to attend a shareholders' meeting may authorise another person (e.g. a director or the chairman) to vote on their behalf, either as instructed or as that person sees fit.

Public limited company (plc) A company which may have an unlimited number of shareholders and offer its shares to the wider public (unlike a limited company). Must have a minimum share value of £50,000. Some plcs are listed on the London Stock Exchange.

Public-to-private The management of a company currently quoted on a stock exchange return it to unquoted status. The finance to buy the shares often comes from venture capital firms.

Put option This gives the purchaser the right, but not the obligation, to sell a financial instrument, commodity or some other underlying asset at a given price, at or before a specified date.

Qualitative analysis Relying on subjective elements to take a view (e.g. valuing shares by judging the quality of management and strategic position).

Quant (Quantum) analysis Quantitative analysis using complex mathematical models.

Quick asset value (net) Current assets minus inventory minus current liabilities.

Quick ratio (acid test) The ratio of current assets, less stock, to total current liabilities.

Quoted Those shares with a price quoted on a recognised investment exchange (RIE) or AIM (e.g. the Official List of the London Stock Exchange).

Quote-driven trading system Market makers post bid and offer prices on a computerised system.

R&D Research and development.

Rally A small rise in a market that is generally falling.

Random walk theory The movements in (share) prices are independent of one another; one day's price change cannot be predicted by looking at the previous day's price change.

Ranking (debt) Order of precedence for payment of obligations. Senior debt receives annual interest and redemption payments ahead of junior (or subordinated) debt. So, if the company has insufficient resources to pay its obligation the junior debt holders may receive little or nothing.

Real assets Assets used to carry on a business. These assets can be tangible or intangible.

Real cash flows Future cash flows are expressed in terms of constant purchasing power.

Real rate of return The rate that would be required in the absence of inflation.

Real-time dealing An online brokerage service. The investor is directly connected to the market maker system. Retail service providers (RSPs) offer competing price quotes and the investor trades directly with one RSP online.

Recapitalisation A change in the financial structure (e.g. in debt–equity ratio).

Receiver A receiver takes control of a business if a debtor successfully files a bankruptcy petition. The receiver may then sell the company's assets and distribute the proceeds among the creditors.

Recognised investment exchange (RIE) A body authorised to regulate securities trading in the UK (e.g. the London Stock Exchange).

Recovery stock A share that has performed poorly but is expected to pick up.

Redemption The repayment of the principal amount, or par value, of a security (e.g. bond) at the maturity date.

Redemption yield *See* Yield.

Registrar An organisation that maintains a record of share ownership for a company. It also communicates with shareholders on behalf of the company.

Regular bonus *See* Reversionary bonus.

Regulatory News Service (RNS) A system for distributing important company announcements and other price-sensitive financial news run by the London Stock Exchange.

Relationship banking A long-term, intimate and relatively open relationship is established between a corporation and its banks. Banks often supply a range of tailor-made services rather than one-off services.

Rembrandt A foreign bond issued in The Netherlands.

Repayment holiday *See* Grace period.

Rescheduling Rearranging the payments made by a borrower to a lender – usually over a long period.

Resistance line A line drawn on a price (e.g. share) chart showing the market participants' reluctance to push the price below (or above) the line over a period of time.

Resolution A proposal put to the vote at a shareholders meeting.

Restructuring costs The costs associated with a reorganisation of the business (e.g. closing factories, redundancies).

Retail banking Banking for individual customers or small firms, normally for small amounts.

Retail Price Index (RPI) A measure of general inflation for the economy as a whole.

Retail service providers (RSPs) Some market makers also offer automated computer dealing service to investors as RSPs. *See also* Real-time dealing.

Retention ratio Retained profits for the year as a proportion of profits after tax attributable to ordinary shareholders for the year.

Return on capital employed (ROCE); return on investment (ROI) Traditional measures of profitability. Profit return divided by the volume of resources devoted to the activity. 'Resources' usually includes shareholders, funds, net debt and provisions. Cumulative goodwill, previously written off, may be added back to the resources total. *See also* Accounting rate of return.

Return on equity (ROE) Profit attributable to shareholders as a percentage of equity shareholders' funds.

Revaluation reserve A balance sheet entry that records accumulated revaluations of fixed assets.

Reverse floating rate notes *See* Floating rate notes.

Reversing the trade *See* Closing out a futures position.

Reversionary bonus The annual bonus given by an insurance company to with-profits policyholders.

Revolving credit An arrangement whereby a borrower can draw down short-term loans as the need arises, to a maximum over a period of years.

Revolving underwriting facility (RUF) A bank underwrites a corporate borrower's access to funds at a specified rate in the short-term financial markets throughout an agreed period.

Reward-to-variability ratio *See* Sharpe's ratio.

Reward-to-volatility ratio *See* Treynor's ratio.

Rights issue An invitation to existing shareholders to purchase additional shares in the company in proportion to their existing holdings.

Ring-fencing The separation of assets so that, for example, a customer's cash and investments are not combined with his/her broker's assets.

Risk A future return has a variety of possible values. Sometimes measured by standard deviation.

Risk arbitrage Taking a position (purchase or sale) in a security, commodity, etc., because it is mispriced relative to other securities with similar characteristics. The comparator securities are not identical (e.g. shares in Royal Dutch and shares in Shell) and therefore there is an element of risk that the valuation gap will widen rather than reduce. An extreme form of risk arbitrage is to take a position hoping to make a profit if an event occurs (e.g. a takeover). If the event does not occur there may be a loss. The word 'arbitrage' has been stretched beyond breaking point, as true arbitrage should be risk-free.

Risk averter Someone who prefers a more certain return to an alternative with an equal return but which is more risky.

Risk-free rate of return (RFR) The rate earned on riskless investment. A reasonable proxy is short-term lending to a reputable government.

Risk transformation Intermediaries offer low-risk securities to primary investors to attract funds, which are then used to purchase higher-risk securities issued by the ultimate borrowers.

Roadshow Companies and their advisers make a series of presentations to potential investors, usually to entice them into buying a new issue of securities.

Rolled-over overdraft Short-term loan facilities are perpetuated into the medium term and long term by the regular renewal of the facility.

Rolling cash spread betting A bet with a spread betting company on the cash price of the share. The investor 'rolls' his/her position overnight to the next day.

Rolling settlement Shares and cash are exchanged after a deal had been struck a fixed number of days later (usually 3 days) rather than on a specific account day.

RPI (Retail Price Index) A UK measure of general inflation.

Running yield *See* Yield.

S&P 500 Standard and Poor's index of 500 leading US shares.

Safe haven A secure investment in time of trouble, such as major financial turmoil. UK or US government bonds and Treasury bills are usually regarded as safe havens.

Sale and leaseback Assets (e.g. land and buildings) are sold to another firm (e.g. bank, insurance company) with a simultaneous agreement for the vendor to lease the asset back for a stated period under specific terms.

Samurai bonds A foreign bond issued in Japan.

Scaledown In a new issue, when a company floats on a stock exchange, if demand is greater than supply at the offer price the applicants receive fewer shares than they applied for.

Scrip dividends Shareholders are offered the alternative of additional shares rather than a cash dividend.

Scrip issue The issue of more shares to existing shareholders according to their current holdings. Shareholders do not pay for these shares.

Scuttlebutt Obtaining knowledge about a company by talking to a wide range of people who have had dealings with the corporation: customers, suppliers, employees, ex-employees etc.

SEAQ (Stock Exchange Automated Quotation System) A computer screen-based quotation system for securities where market makers on the London Stock Exchange report bid–offer prices and trading volumes, and brokers can observe prices and trades.

SEAQI (Stock Exchange Automated Quotation International) A computer screen-based quotation system for securities that allows market makers in international shares based on the London Stock Exchange to report prices, quotes and trading volumes.

Seasoned equity offerings Companies that have been on a stock exchange for some time selling new shares (e.g. via a rights issue).

SEATS plus (Stock Exchange Alternative Trading Service) A London Stock Exchange system for trading less liquid securities where there is either a single, or no, market maker. Displays market maker prices and/or current public orders.

Secondary market Securities already issued are traded between investors.

Securities and Exchange Commission (SEC) The US federal body responsible for the regulation of securities markets (exchanges, brokers, investment advisers, etc.).

Securities house This may mean simply an issuing house. However, the term is sometimes used more broadly for an institute concerned with buying and selling securities or acting as agent in the buying and selling of securities.

Securitisation Financial payments (e.g. a claim to a number of mortgage payments) which are not tradable can be repackaged into other securities (e.g. a bond) and then sold. These are called asset-backed securities.

Security (1) A financial asset, e.g. a share or bond. (2) Asset pledged to be surrendered in the event of a loan default.

SEDOL *Stock Exchange Daily Official List*. A journal published daily giving prices and deals for shares on London's Official List.

Seedcorn capital The financing of the development of a business concept. High risk; usually provided by venture capitalists, entrepreneurs or business angels.

Self-Invested Personal Pension (SIPP) Similar to a standard personal pension scheme except that the investor can select the shares, etc., that the fund is invested into.

Self-regulation Much of the regulation of financial services in the UK is carried out by self-regulatory organisations (i.e. industry participants regulate themselves within a light-touch legislated framework).

Self-select ISA The investor can decide which shares, gilts, etc., should be bought for an individual savings account.

Sell-side Organisations in the securities business that sell their services to institutions (e.g. analysts, brokers and securities firms selling services to institutional fund managers).

Semi-strong efficiency Share prices fully reflect all the relevant, publicly available information.

Senior debt *See* Subordinated debt.

Sequence A computerised share trading platform introduced by the London Stock Exchange in 1996.

Serious Fraud Office Investigates and prosecutes crimes of serious fraud in the UK.

SETS (Stock Exchange Electronic Trading Service) An electronic order book-based trading system for the London Stock Exchange. Brokers input buy and sell orders directly into the system. Buyers and sellers are matched and the trade executed automatically. The system was used for the largest UK shares and the Stock Exchange plans to increase the number of shares on SETS – eventually SEAQ might be completely replaced.

Settlement The completion of a transaction, e.g. there is a transfer of ownership of a share from seller to buyer in return for a cash payment.

Settlement price The price calculated by a derivatives exchange at the end of each trading session as the closing price that will be used in determining profits and losses for the marking-to-market process for margin accounts.

Share Companies divide the ownership of the company into ordinary shares. An owner of a share usually has the same rights to vote and receive dividends as another owner of a share.

Share buy-back The company buys back a proportion of its shares from shareholders.

Share certificate A document showing ownership of part of the share capital of a company.

Share exchange scheme Some unit trusts permit investors to purchase units with shares rather than cash.

Share market Institutions which facilitate the regulated sale and purchase of shares; includes the primary and secondary markets.

Share option scheme Employees are offered the right to buy shares in their company at a modest price some time in the future.

Share perks *See* Perks.

Share premium account A balance sheet entry representing the difference between the price received by a company when it sells shares and the par value of those shares.

Share repurchase The company buys back its own shares.

Share split (stock split) Shareholders receive additional shares from the company. The nominal value of each share is reduced in proportion to the increase in the number of shares, so the total book value of shares remains the same.

Shareholders' funds The net assets of the business (after deduction of all short- and long-term liabilities and minority interests) shown in the balance sheet.

Sharpe's ratio A measure relating risk and return. The extent to which a portfolio's (or share's) return has been greater than a risk-free asset, divided by its standard deviation.

Shell company A company with a stock market quotation but with very little in the way of real economic activity. It may have cash but no production.

Short position In a derivative contract, the counterparty in a short position is the one that has agreed to deliver the underlying.

Short selling The selling of financial securities (e.g. shares) not yet owned, in the anticipation of being able to buy at a later date at a lower price.

Short-term selectivity The buying or selling of a financial security based on the analysis of a corporation's or an industry's near-term business prospects.

Short-termism A charge levelled at the financial institutions in their expectations of the companies to which they provide finance. It is argued that long-term benefits are lost because of pressure for short-term performance.

Shorting *See* Short selling.

Shorts UK government bonds (gilts) with less than 5 years to maturity.

Sight bank account (current account) One where deposits can be withdrawn without notice.

Sigma A measure of dispersion of returns; some as standard deviation.

Signalling Some financial decisions are taken as signals from the managers to the financial markets (e.g. an increase in gearing, or a change in dividend policy).

Simple interest Interest is paid on the original principal: no interest is paid on the accumulated interest payments.

Single stock futures *See* Universal stock futures.

Social technology Tools of social organisation that allow for the better working of society. Examples include: laws on limited liability, corporate entities and financial market regulations; accepted norms of behaviour; widespread knowledge of the way in which processes work, such as stock market buying and selling.

Solvency The ability to pay debts as and when they become due.

South Sea Bubble A financial bubble in which the price of shares in the South Sea Company were pushed to ridiculously high levels on a surge of over-optimism in the early eighteenth century. *See* Bubble.

Special dividend An exceptionally large dividend paid on a one-off basis.

Special-purpose entity Companies set these up as separate organisations for a particular purpose. They are designed so that their accounts are not consolidated with the rest of the group.

Special resolution A company's shareholders' vote at a AGM or EGM with a majority of 75 per cent of those voting. Normally special resolutions are reserved for important changes in the constitution of the company. Other matters are dealt with by way of ordinary resolution (50 per cent or more of the votes required).

Specific inflation The price changes in an individual good or service.

Speculators Those who take a position in financial instruments and other assets with a view to obtaining a profit on changes in price.

Split-capital investment trusts These investment trusts simultaneously issue different types of shares. Income shares entitle the holder to receive all (or most) of the income from the portfolio. Capital shares entitle the owner to receive all (or most) the rise in the capital value of the portfolio. Zero divided preference shares (Zeros) pay no income but do offer a predetermined return at the end of the trust's life.

Sponsor An organisation (usually an investment bank or stockbroker) that lends its reputation to a new issue of securities, advises the client company (along with the issuing broker) and co-ordinates the new issue process. Also called an issuing house.

Sponsored membership of CREST *See* Personal membership of CREST.

Spot market A market for immediate transactions (e.g. spot forex market, spot interest market), as opposed to an agreement to make a transaction some time in the future (e.g. forward, option, future).

Spread The difference between the price to buy and the price to sell a financial security. Market makers quote a bid–offer spread for shares. The lower price (bid) is the price an investor receives if selling to the market maker. The higher (offer) price is the price if the investor wishes to buy from the market maker.

Spread betting Laying a bet with a spread betting company that a particular outcome will occur in the future (e.g. that a share price will rise). You bet, say, £10 for every 1p rise.

Stagging Buying shares in a new issue and then selling immediately the shares begin trading on the market.

Stakeholder A party with an interest in an organisation (e.g. employees, customers, suppliers, the local community).

Stakeholder pension Similar to a standard personal pension except that there are low management charges, contributions can be small and the investor can move to another provider easily. Even non-taxpayers can claim back assumed tax paid on income

Stamp duty A tax levied on share purchase (0.5 per cent of the new purchase value).

Standard and Poor's 500 (S&P 500) An index of US shares.

Standard deviation A statistical measure of the dispersion around an average. A measure of volatility. The standard deviation is the square root of the variance. A fund or a share can be expected to fall within one standard deviation of its average two-thirds of the time if the future is like the past.

Start-up capital Finance for young companies which have not yet sold their product commercially. High risk; usually provided by venture capitalists, entrepreneurs or business angels.

Start-up companies Companies with a limited or non-existent trading history.

Statutory Established, regulated or imposed by or in conformity with laws passed by a legislative body (e.g. Parliament).

Sterling bonds Corporate bonds which pay interest and principal in sterling.

Stock Inventory of raw materials, work-in-progress and finished items.

Stocks and shares There is some lack of clarity as to the distinction between stocks and shares. Shares are equities in companies. Stocks are financial instruments that pay interest (e.g. bonds). However, in the USA shares are also called 'common stocks' and the shareholders are sometimes referred to as the stockholders. So when some people use the term 'stocks' they could be referring to either bonds or shares.

Stock exchange A market in which securities are bought and sold. In continental Europe the term *bourse* may be used.

Stock Exchange Automated Quotations *See* SEAQ.

Stock market *See* Stock exchange.

Stock market-linked bond *See* Guaranteed equity bond.

Stock transfer form A form used to transfer ownership of shares without the use of a broker or a stock exchange.

Stop-loss orders An order from an investor to a broker to sell if the share price breaches a lower threshold – used to limit possible losses. Stop-loss orders may also be used in derivative markets to prevent losses exceeding set limits with either a long or a short position.

Straight bond One with a regular fixed rate of interest and without the right of conversion (to, say, shares).

Straight-line depreciation A fixed asset is depreciated by the same amount each year over its useful life.

Strategic analysis The analysis of industries served by the firm and the company's competitive position within the industry.

Strategy Selecting which product or market areas to enter/exit and how to ensure a good competitive position in those markets/products.

Strike price (1) In the offer for sale by a tender it is the price which is chosen to sell the required quantity of shares given the offers made. (2) The price paid by the holder of an option when/if the option is exercised.

Strips Interest coupons in a bond are detached and sold separately.

Structured product Offered by insurance companies and other financial service companies, these collective investment vehicles invest most of the investor's cash in bonds. Some is used to buy derivatives to allow the provider to offer the investor a stock market-linked return (eg., 100 per cent return of capital plus 55 per cent of the rise in the FTSE 100 index over 5 years). Examples include guaranteed equity bonds and precipice bonds.

Style An investment style is an approach or strategy to selecting shares for purchase (e.g. high-dividend yields, small companies).

Subordinated debt A debt which ranks below another liability in order of priority for payment of interest or principal. Senior debt ranks above junior debt for payment.

Subscription rights A right to subscribe for some shares.

Subsidiary A company is a subsidiary of another company if the parent company holds the majority of the voting rights, or has a minority of the shares but has the right to appoint or remove directors holding a majority of the voting rights at meetings of the board on all, or substantially all, matters or it has the right to exercise a dominant influence.

Substitute Products or services that perform the same function (at least in approximate terms).

Sucker's rally A rise in prices during a period of overall market decline. The temporary rise draws in investors fooled into believing that the downward drift has ended.

Summary financial statement Companies often send small investors a summary of the financial statements rather than the full report and accounts. This suits many investors and saves the company some money. However, an investor is entitled to receive a full annual report and accounts. It may be necessary to make a request for this.

Supernormal returns A rate of return above the normal rate.

Surrender value The amount payable to an insurance policyholder (e.g. with-profits policy) when it is cancelled.

Swap An exchange of cash payment obligations. An interest rate swap is where one company arranges with a counterparty to exchange interest rate payments. In a currency swap the two parties exchange interest obligations (receipts) for an agreed period between two different currencies.

Swaption An option to have a swap at a later date.

Switching cost The cost of changing supplier.

Syndicated loan A loan made by more than one bank to one borrower.

Synergy A combined entity (e.g. two companies merging) will have a value greater than the sum of the parts.

Systematic (undiversifiable or **market) risk** That element of return variability from an asset which cannot be eliminated through diversification. Measured by beta. It comprises the risk factors common to all firms.

Takeover (acquisition) Many people use these terms interchangeably with 'merger'. However, some differentiate 'takeover' as meaning a purchase of one firm by another with the concomitant implication of financial and managerial domination.

Takeover Panel The committee responsible for supervising compliance with the City Code on Takeovers and Mergers.

Tangible assets Those that have a physical presence.

Taper relief The amount an investor pays in capital gains tax reduces the longer the investment that has been held.

Tariff Taxes imposed on imports.

Tax allowance An amount of income or capital gain that is not taxed.

Tax avoidance Steps taken to reduce tax that are permitted under the law.

Tax evasion Deliberately giving a false statement or omitting a relevant fact.

Tax haven A country or place with low rates of tax.

Taxable profit That element of profit subject to taxation. This frequently differs from reported profit.

techMARK The London Stock Exchange launched techMARK in 1999 as a subsection of the shares within the Official List. It is a grouping of technology companies for which there are different rules on seeking a flotation from those which apply to the other companies on the Official List (e.g. only one year's accounts is required).

techMARK mediscience A group of London Stock Exchange Official List companies focused on healthcare.

Technical analysis See Chartism.

Tender offer A public offer to purchase securities.

TER *See* Total expense ratio.

Term loan A loan of a fixed amount for an agreed time and on specified terms, usually with regular periodic payments. Most frequently provided by banks.

Term structure of interest rates The pattern of interest rates on bonds with differing lengths of time to maturity but with the same risk. Strictly it is the zero-coupon implied interest rate for different lengths of time. *See also* Yield curve.

Terminal bonus A bonus paid on a with-profits policy at the end of the policy's life.

Terminal value The forecast future value of sums of money compounded to the end of a common time horizon.

Three-day rolling settlement (T+3) After a share transaction in the stock exchange investors pay for shares three working days later.

Tick The minimum price movement of a future or option contract.

Time-loans Loan with a specific maturity (US usage).

Time value That part of an option's value that represents the value of the option expiring in the future rather than now. The longer the period to expiry, the greater the chance that the option will become in-the-money before the expiry date. The amount by which the option premium exceeds the intrinsic value.

Time value of money A pound received in the future is worth less than a pound received today – the value of a sum of money depends on the date of its receipt.

Tipsters People who put forward a view on the wisdom of buying or selling a share – usually based on superficial knowledge.

Top-down Analysis of shares or other securities or the market as a whole, where the first step is to consider macroeconomic influences, leading to sector allocations (e.g. shares rather than bonds, then mining company shares) and finally individual security analysis.

Total expense ratios (TERs) The annual costs imposed on investors for the running of collective investment funds (e.g. unit trusts) expressed as a percentage of the value of the fund. It incorporates all annual costs, including administration, custody, legal and audit, as well as the management charges for selecting shares and running the fund.

Total shareholder return (TSR) The total return earned on a share over a period of time: dividend per share plus capital gain, divided by initial share price.

Touch *See* Yellow strip.

Tracker An investment fund which is intended to replicate the return of a market index. Also called an index fund or passive fund.

Tracking error The extent to which the return on an (index tracking) fund differs from its benchmark over a period of time.

Trade credit Where goods and services are delivered to a firm for use in its production and are not paid for immediately.

Trade debtor A customer of a firm who has not yet paid for goods and services delivered.

Traded endowment policy market A market in the buying and selling of with-profits endowment policies between policyholders.

Trading floor A place where traders in a market (or their representatives) can meet to agree transactions face to face. However, the term has been stretched so that investment banks own 'trading floors', which means merely that they have a big office with lots of desks and employees transacting with investors and other financial institutions. They communicate with these other parties through telephones and computers over great distances. There is no face-to-face dealing.

Trading margin *See* Operating profit margin.

Traditional option An option available on any security but with an exercise price fixed as the market price on the day the option is bought. All such options expire after 3 months and cannot be sold to a secondary investor.

Trail commission A commission paid to fund (e.g. unit trusts) sales organisations such as fund supermarkets. This is derived as a share of the annual management charge on the fund.

Treasury UK government department responsible for financial and economic policy.

Treasury bill A short-term money market instrument issued (sold) by the central bank, mainly in the UK and USA, usually to supply the government's short-term financing needs.

Treynor's ratio A measure relating return to risk. It is the return on a portfolio (or share) minus the risk-free rate of rate of return, divided by beta.

TRRACK system A system to assist the analysis of a company's extraordinary resources under the headings: tangible; relationships; reputation; attitude; capabilities; and knowledge.

Trust deed A document specifying the regulation of the management of assets on behalf of beneficiaries of the trust.

Trustees Those that are charged with the responsibility for ensuring compliance with the trust deed.

Tulipmania A seventeenth-century Dutch bubble in which the price of tulip bulbs was bid up because people expected to be able to sell to someone else at a higher price. *See* Bubble.

Turnarounds Companies that have been going through a bad time and (it is hoped) will soon revive.

Turnover (revenue or sales) Money received or to be received by the company from goods and services sold during the year.

UK Shareholders' Association (*www.uksa.org.uk*) represents small shareholders and lobbies companies, regulators and government on their behalf.

Ultimate borrowers Firms investing in real assets need finance, which ultimately comes from the primary investors.

Umbrella structure for OEICs Open-ended investment companies may be created as a group of sub-funds each with a different investment objective.

Uncertainty Strictly (in economists' terms), uncertainty is when there is more than one possible outcome to a course of action; the form of each possible outcome is known, but the probability of any one outcome is not known. However, the distinction between risk (the ability to assign probabilities) and uncertainty has largely been ignored for the purposes of this text.

Unconditionality In a merger, once unconditionality is declared, the acquirer becomes obliged to buy. Target shareholders who accepted the offer are no longer able to withdraw their acceptance.

Uncovered (naked) call option writing Writing a call option on an underlying when the writer does not own the underlying securities included in the option.

Underlying The subject of a derivative contract.

Underlying earnings per share *See* Headline earnings per share.

Underweighting Allocating the money in a fund to particular securities, sectors or countries less than in proportion to their representation in the relevant benchmark index.

Underwriters These (usually large financial institutions) guarantee to buy the proportion of a new issue of securities (e.g. shares) not taken up by the market, in return for a fee paid at the time of the underwriting.

Undifferentiated product One that is much the same as that supplied by other companies.

Undiversifiable risk *See* Systematic risk.

Uninformed investors Those who have no knowledge about financial securities or the fundamental evaluation of their worth.

Unintelligent speculation Buying and selling shares and other financial securities with a lack of proper knowledge and skill; risking more money than the stock picker can afford to lose; ignoring quantitative material; placing the emphasis on the rewards of speculation rather than on the individual's capacity to speculate successfully.

Unit-linked policies These insurance policies incorporate both life insurance and investment on behalf of the policyholder. The investor (policyholder) buys units in a similar way to the purchase of units in a unit trust.

Unit trust An investment organisation that attracts funds from individual investors by issuing units to invest in a range of securities (e.g. shares or bonds). It is open-ended, the number of units expanding to meet demand.

Unitised with-profits policy Similar to a standard with-profits policy, except that premiums paid by investors buy units of a fund and there is no basic sum assured. Bonuses are smoothed.

United Kingdom Listing Authority (UKLA) This organisation is part of the Financial Services Authority and rigorously enforces a set of demanding rules on companies joining the stock market and in subsequent years.

Universal banks Financial institutions involved in many different aspects of finance, including retail banking and wholesale banking.

Universal stock futures (USF) Futures in a particular company's shares. Also called single stock futures.

Unlisted Shares and other securities not on the Official List of the London Stock Exchange are described as unlisted.

Unlisted Securities Market (USM) A lower-tier (less stringently regulated) market for shares in London, which ceased in 1996.

Unquoted Those shares with a price not quoted on a recognised investment exchange (e.g. the Official List or AIM of the London Stock Exchange).

Unsecured A financial claim with no collateral or any charge over the assets of the borrower.

Unsystematic (unique or diversifiable) risk That element of an asset's variability in returns that can be eliminated by holding a well-diversified portfolio.

Valuation risk (price risk) The possibility that, when a financial instrument matures or is sold in the market, the amount received is less than anticipated by the lender.

Value-based management A managerial approach in which the primary purpose is long-term shareholder wealth maximisation. The objective of the firm, its systems, strategy, processes, analytical techniques, performance measurements and culture have as their guiding objective long-term shareholder wealth maximisation.

Value chain The interlinking activities that take place within an organisation or between organisations in the process of converting inputs into its outputs. Identifying these activities and finding ways to perform them more efficiently is a way for companies to gain competitive advantage over their rivals.

Value drivers Crucial organisational capabilities, giving the firm competitive advantage.

Value investing The identification and holding of shares which are fundamentally undervalued by the market, given the prospects of the firm.

Vanilla bond *See* Straight bond.

Variable costs Costs that rise or fall with company output and sales.

Variable-rate bond (loan) The interest rate payable varies with short-term rates (e.g. six-month LIBOR).

Variance A measure of volatility around an average value: the square of the standard deviation.

Variation margin The amount of money paid after the payment of the initial margin required to secure an option or futures position, after it has been revalued by the exchange or clearing house on a daily basis by marking to market.

Vendor placing Shares issued to a company to pay for assets, or issued to shareholders to pay for an entire company in a takeover are placed with investors keen on holding the shares in return for cash. The vendors can then receive the cash.

Venture and development capital investment trusts (VDCITs) Standard investment trusts (without tax breaks) with a focus on more risky developing companies.

Venture capital (VC) Finance provided to unquoted firms by specialised financial institutions. This may be backing for an entrepreneur, financing a start-up or developing business, or assisting a management buyout or buy-in. Usually it is provided by a mixture of equity, loans and mezzanine finance. It is used for medium-term to long-term investment in high-risk situations.

Venture capital trusts (VCTs) An investment vehicle introduced to the UK in 1995 to encourage investment in small and fast-growing companies. The VCT invests in a range of small businesses. The providers of finance to the VCT are given important tax breaks.

Vertical merger Where the two merging firms are from different stages of the production chain.

Virtual portfolio Investors can create an imaginary portfolio on some websites and follow its progress.

Virt-x A share market operating electronically across borders. It mostly trades large Swiss company shares (it is part-owned by SWX Swiss Exchange). It is a recognised investment exchange supervised by the FSA in the UK.

Volatility The speed and magnitude of price change over time, measured by standard deviation or variance.

Volume transformation Intermediaries gather small quantities of money from numerous savers and repackage these sums into larger bundles for investment in the business sector or elsewhere.

Warrant A financial instrument which gives the holder the right to subscribe for a specified number of shares or bonds at a fixed price at some time in the future.

White knight A friendly company that makes a bid for a company which is welcomed by the directors of that target company. This is usually because the target is the subject of a hostile takeover bid from another company.

Wholesale bank *See* Investment bank.

Wholesale financial markets Markets available only to those dealing in large quantities. Dominated by interbank transactions.

Winding up The process of ending a company, selling its assets, paying its creditors and distributing the remaining cash among shareholders.

Winner's curse In winning a merger battle, the acquirer suffers a loss in value because it overpays.

With-profits bonds A long-term investment via a with-profits fund. *See also* With-profits policy.

With-profits policy A form of life insurance with a large element of saving so that if you survive a payout from the fund is received. The insurance companies use investors' payments to invest in financial securities and guarantee investors a minimum return. They then add bonuses as the fund makes profits.

Withholding tax Taxation deducted from payments to non-residents of the country.

Working capital The difference between current assets and current liabilities – net current assets or net current liabilities.

Write down (Write off) Companies change the recorded value of assets when they are no longer worth the previously stated value.

Writer of an option The seller of an option contract, granting the right but not the obligation to the purchaser.

Yankee A foreign bond issued in the USA.

Yellow strip The yellow strip is displayed on the London Stock Exchanges SEAQ share trading system. It shows the best market makers bid and offer prices for a share – these are collectively called the touch.

Yield The income from a security as a proportion of its market price. The flat yield (interest yield, running yield and income yield) on a fixed-interest security is the gross interest amount, divided by the current market price, expressed as a percentage. The redemption yield or yield to maturity of a bond is the discount rate such that the present value of all cash inflows from the bond (interest plus principal) is equal to the bond's current market price.

Yield curve A graph showing the relationship between the length of time to the maturity of bonds of the same risk class and the interest rate. *See also* Term structure of interest rates.

Yield stock *See* High-yield shares.

Zero coupon bond (or zero coupon preference share) A bond that does not pay regular interest (dividend) but instead is issued at a discount (i.e. below par value) and is redeemable at par, thus offering a capital gain.

Zero dividend preference shares *See* Split-capital investment trusts.

Zeros *See* Split-capital investment trusts.

List of useful Internet addresses

Accounting Standards Board UK	*www.asb.org.uk*
ADRs.com (J.P. Morgan and Thompson Financial site for ADRs and international equities)	*www.adr.com*
ADVFN	*www.advfn.com*
Allenbridge Hedge Fund Research	*www.hedgeinfo.com*
Ample	*www.iii.co.uk*
Ample (new issues)	*www.iii.co.uk/newissues*
Angel Bourse	*www.angelbourse.com*
Association of Investment Trust Companies	*www.aitc.co.uk* and *www.itsonline.co.uk*
Association of Private Client Investment Managers and Stockbrokers	*www.apcims.co.uk*
Bank of England	*www.bankofengland.co.uk*
Beer & Partners	*www.beerandpartners.com*
Bestinvest	*www.bestinvest.co.uk*
Bloomberg	*www.bloomberg.co.uk*
BlueSky Ratings	*www.blueskyratings.com*
Bondscape	*www.bondscape.net*
British Venture Capital Association	*www.bvca.co.uk*
Carol	*www.carol.co.uk*
City Comment	*www.citycomment.co.uk*
CityLine	*www.ftcityline.com*
Citywire	*www.citywire.com*
CNN Money	*www.money.cnn.com*
Cofunds	*www.cofunds.com*
Comdirect	*www.comdirect.co.uk*
Companies House	*www.companieshouse.gov.uk*
Corporate Information provided by Wright Investors' Services	*www.corporateinformation.com*
Crest	*www.crestco.co.uk*
Datastream	*www.datastream.com*
Debt Management Office (DMO)	*www.dmo.gov.uk*
Department of Trade and Industry	*www.dti.gov.uk*
Digital Look	*www.digitallook.com*
Dun and Bradstreet	*www.dnb.com*
EDGAR Online	*www.edgar-online.com*
Egg	*www.egg.com*
Entrust	*www.entrust.co.uk*
Euroland	*www.euroland.com*
Fame	*www.fame.bvdep.com*
Financial Ombudsman Scheme	*www.financial-ombudsman.org.uk*
Financial Services Authority	*www.fsa.gov.uk*

Financial Services Compensation Scheme (FSCS)	*www.fscs.org.uk*
Financial Times	*www.ft.com*
Fitch	*www.fitch.com*
FTSE Group	*www.ftse.com*
FundsNetwork – Fidelity Investments	*www.fidelity.co.uk/fundsnetwork* or *www.fundsnetwork.co.uk*
Futures and Options World	*www.fow.com*
Gomez	*www.gomezadvisors.com*
Hargreaves Landown	*www.h-l.co.uk*
Hedge Funds Review	*www.hedgefundsreview.com*
HedgeFund	*www.hedgefund.net*
Hemscott	*www.hemscot.net*
HFR Asset Management and Hedge Fund Research Inc.	*www.hfr.com*
Hoovers Online	*www.hoovers.com*
Hotbed	*www.hotbed.uk.com*
ICC	*www.icc.co.uk*
Inland Revenue	*www.inlandrevenue.gov.uk*
Inter-Alliance Group	*www.inter-alliance.com*
Investment Management Association, IMA	*www.investmentfunds.org.uk*
Investors Chronicle	*www.investorschronicle.co.uk*
Investors Chronicle (bonds)	*www.ic-community.co.uk/bonds*
ishares	*www.ishares.net*
Issues Direct	*www.issuesdirect.com*
K@talyst Ventures	*www.katalystventures.com*
Kauders Portfolio Management	*www.gilt.co.uk*
London International Financial Futures and Options Exchange	*www.liffe.com*
LIFFE (Information and learning tools)	*www.liffeinvestor.com*
LIFFE (Prices)	*www.liffe-style.com*
Lipper (Reuters)	*www.lipperweb.com*
Lipper Leader	*www.lipperleaders.com*
London Money Market	*www.londonmoneymarket.com*
London Stock Exchange	*www.londonstockexchange.com*
London Stock Exchange (new issues)	*www.londonstockexchange.com/newissues/*
Moneyweb	*www.moneyweb.co.uk*
Moody's	*www.moody.com*
J.P. Morgan	*www.jpmorgan.com*
Morningstar UK	*www.morningstar.co.uk*
MultexInvestor	*www.multexinvestor.com*
MyTrack	*www.mytrack.co.uk*
MX Money extra	*www.moneyextra.com*

National Business Angels Network (NBAN)	*www.bestmatch.co.uk* or *www.nban.com*
New York Stock Exchange	*www.nyse.com*
OFEX	*www.ofex.com*
OnVista	*www.onvista.co.uk*
ProShare	*www.proshare.org*
ProQuote	*www.proquote.net*
Quicken	*www.quicken.com*
Reuters	*www.bridge.com* or *www.reuters.com*
RiskGrades	*www.riskgrades.com*
Self Trade Mutual Funds	*www.selftrade.co.uk*
Smartmoney.com	*www.smartmoney.com*
Splits On Line (split capital trusts)	*www.splitsonline.co.uk*
Standard and Poor's	*www.standardpoor.com*
Standard and Poor's funds	*www.funds-sp.com*
Teletext	*www.teletext.co.uk*
Torquil Clark	*www.tqonline.co.uk*
TRADING Central	*www.tradingcentral.com*
Trustnet	*www.trustnet.com*
UKCityMedia	*www.ukcitymedia.co.uk/tradedoptions.html*
UK Government Treasury	*www.hm-treasury.gov.uk*
United Kingdom Listing Authority	*www.fsa.gov.uk/ukla*
UK-Wire Financial News, Regulatory News Services Stock Exchange announcements	*www.uk-wire.co.uk*
Venture Capital Report	*www.vcr1978.com*
Wall Street Research Net	*www.wsrn.com*
Wall Street Journal	*www.wsj.com*
Wave2	*www.wave2.org*
World Federation of Exchanges	*www.fibv.com*
WM Company	*www.wmcompany.com*

Index

Note: Emboldened items appear in the Glossary